Torah in a Connected World

A Halakhic Perspective on Communication Technology and Social Media

מגיד
MAGGID

Rabbi Jonathan Ziring

TORAH IN A CONNECTED WORLD

A HALAKHIC PERSPECTIVE ON COMMUNICATION TECHNOLOGY AND SOCIAL MEDIA

The Lax Family Edition

Maggid Books

Torah in a Connected World
A Halakhic Perspective on Communication Technology and Social Media

First Edition, 2024

Maggid Books
An imprint of Koren Publishers Jerusalem Ltd.

POB 8531, New Milford, CT 06776-8531, USA
& POB 4044, Jerusalem 9104001, Israel
www.korenpub.com

The publication of this book was made possible through the generous support of *The Jewish Book Trust.*

ISBN 978-1-59264-624-1, *hardcover*

Printed and bound in the United States

Dedicated in loving memory
of our dear sons and brothers

Jonathan Theodore Lax, ז״ל
Ethan James Lax, ז״ל

לעילוי נשמת

יונתן טוביה בן מרדכי ז״ל
איתן אליעזר בן מרדכי ז״ל

ת.נ.צ.ב.ה

Marsha and Michael Lax
Amanda and Akiva Blumenthal
Rebecca and Rami Laifer

This book is dedicated to my beloved father, the late

Lloyd Zerker

Though your physical presence may be absent,
your spirit continues to guide and inspire me.
I carry your values and teachings within me, and they serve
as a constant reminder of the incredible man you were.

Howard Zerker

Dedicated in memory of

Moe and Rose Litwack

&

Meyer and Masha Simon

Alan & Resa Litwack

Dedicated by Marvin and Roberta Newman
in loving memory of our dear parents:

Samuel Newman – שלמה מאיר בן משה ז"ל
Piri Newman – חנה פרל בת יצחק דוד ז"ל
Harry Lensky – יהודה צבי בן משה ז"ל
Phyllis Lensky – פרומה בת לוי משה ז"ל

In loving memory of our parents

Naftali Ben Mendel
&
Chaya Dabrusa bat Sarah

And in honour of our dear children and grandchildren
וראה בנים לבנך

Mimi & Byron Shore

To Rabbi Jonathan Ziring.

In appreciation and friendship.

Wishing you continued success in Torah scholarship.

Gershon Green and Marjorie

Dedicated in loving memory of our dear parents

David and Edith (Waldman) Klein

&

Vivian and Sela (Schlussel) Oster

who rebuilt their families with wisdom, compassion and enduring love.

They continue to inspire us.

Ruth and Gerard Klein

In loving memory and לעלוי נשמות

רות בת צבי

רייכל בת מנחם מנדל

אסתר בת נתן הלוי

Dedicated by Allan and Malka Rutman

in memory of their parents

גדליה בן יצחק ז״ל, לאה בת חיים דוד ז״ל

יוסף מתתיהו בן אברהם יצחק ז״ל, חיה שרה בת שמחה בונם ז״ל

In memory of my mother

Evelyn Silverberg ז״ל

הלכה לעולמה כ״ו אדר תשפ״ג

Samuel Silverberg

Dedicated in appreciation and gratitude of Rabbi Ziring

and in honor of my wife Shari on our 35th wedding anniversary

David Vodianoi

ישיבת הר עציון
FAX. 02-9931298 .פקס TEL. 02-9937300 .טל Alon Shevut Gush Etzion, ISRAEL, 9043300 אלון שבות גוש עציון
office@etzion.org.il

Halakhah, a system designed to guide us throughout our lives, must constantly address changing reality. This is both a spiritual need to instill sanctity into modern life and a practical necessity to enable us to properly fulfill our religious obligations. Throughout the ages, it has constantly evolved and developed as it responded to the challenges posed by economical and technological innovation as well as societal and historical forces. Anyone familiar with the Halakhic literature of the 20th century is well aware of this dynamic, as its discussions, dilemmas and decisions regarding the issues that arose in consequence of our return to *Eretz Yisrael*, the establishment of a state, the introduction of electricity into our lifestyles and medical breakthroughs not only provided practical advice but also enriched the halakhic literature and enhanced our religious sensibilities.

The time has now come to address the issues of the 21st century. Technological innovation is a constant of human life and, therefore, halakhic analysis of the changing circumstances must follow in its footsteps. This is not the place to discuss the crucial question of whether the shift to a digital society will bring about a fundamental change in our lives or will simply facilitate communication and the sharing of information while the basic human condition is not altered. Regardless of one's position on this issue, we must recognize that halakhic guidance relating to the digital age is necessary and that the formulation of clear guidelines to fulfill this need is imperative.

Torah in a Connected World sets out to fulfill this need. R. Jonathan Ziring, a dear *talmid* and an accomplished *talmid ḥakham,* who is well aware of the digital landscape and highly knowledgeable of the halakhic material, provides us with a comprehensive work that addresses the halakhic issues of contemporary technology. It is important to realize that such a work is, by definition, the first word but not the last word on its subject matter. The reader should be aware that due to its role as a book addressing cutting-edge technology and evolving social reality, and the nature of the halakhic process as taking into account different perspectives and many opinions, that much halakhic material relating to these topics will be added, debated and deliberated in coming years as the implications of the new reality become clearer and the halakhic perspective comes into sharper focus. It is safe to assume that R. Ziring will have to update the work in the future and that others will also add their say. I state this not to diminish the accomplishment, but rather to emphasize its pioneering nature, to recognize the great service of establishing the need for such a halakhic work and to applaud the achievement of embarking upon this important halakhic discussion. The best wish and the truest *berakha* that I can give R. Ziring is that he will have the need and the privilege to issue an updated version in due time.

May the KBH grant R. Ziring health and happiness to continue his halakhic work and may He grant him the privilege to enlighten us on this and many other issues.

יהי רצון שהרב המחבר יזכה להפיץ את מעיינותיו החוצה בכתב ובעל פה ויזכהו הקב״ה ללמוד וללמד מתוך בריאות גופא ונהורא מעליא, לאוי״ט.

Mosheh Lichtenstein
Alon Shevut
ערב זמן מתן תורתנו, תשפ״ג

Contents

Introduction: Motivation for This Book .... *xiii*

SECTION 1: RELATIONSHIPS AND COMMUNITY

1. By Way of Introduction, the Case of *Berakhot* 3
2. Social Media, Communication, and the "Classic" *Aguna* 16
3. The Videoteleconference *Get* 30
4. "Visiting" the Sick and Comforting the Mourner............. 41
5. *Teshuva* and Social Media 53
6. Prayer for the Sick: Connected Only by a Facebook Post 65
7. *Mara De'atra* in the Globalized World 74
8. Social Media-Driven Fundraisers in Halakha................. 92

SECTION 2: RESPONSIBILITY FOR WHAT IS POSTED ONLINE

9. Responsibility for Facilitating Sin or Harm on the Internet: General Introduction 113
10. The Parameters of *Lifnei Iver*................................ 123
11. Expanding the Discussion: Showing Support for Sin 150

12. Applying the Principles 164

13. The Potential Problems for Users, Rather than Platforms of Social Media 174

14. Another Angle for Responsibility: Protecting Victims 180

SECTION 3: ISSUES OF PERCEPTION IN THE DIGITAL AGE

15. Judging (Strangers) Favorably 193

16. *Marit Ayin, Ḥashad,* and Social Media 202

17. The Hashkafic and Psychological Downsides of Curiosity in the Age of Social Media 212

SECTION 4: PRIVACY, CONFIDENTIALITY, GOSSIP: THE DANGERS AND BENEFITS OF SPREADING INFORMATION

18. Privacy: The Halakhic Background 225

19. Modern Applications 243

20. Confidentiality in the Digital Age 252

21. *Lashon HaRa* on the Internet: A Fundamental Change? 276

22. When It Is Permitted to Share *Lashon HaRa* or Secrets 298

23. The Unique Challenges of the Digital Age: Transfer of Information, but No Audience 320

24. Shaming in Halakha: A General Overview 341

25. The Dangers of the Shame Storm: Public Humiliation in Halakha 361

26. Fake News 382

SECTION 5: MEDIATED EXPERIENCE, *MINYAN*, AND MITZVOT

27. The Virtual *Minyan* 411

28. The Webcam in Halakha: Mitzvot 422

Introduction: Motivation for This Book

> For almost two decades, the web has changed the world and revolutionized how information is stored, published, searched and consumed. The ripple effect has spread so wide that it impacts not just businesses and industries but crosses over into politics, medicine, media and breaches geographical locations, cultural boundaries and ultimately, affects people's day to day lives.[1]

The drastic improvements in communication technology – and more recently, the explosion of social media – have radically changed how people live their lives. However, while much academic and popular writing has been devoted to analyzing these effects, little has been written about how it affects halakha or the ways in which halakha can address the fundamental questions raised by these technological advances.

Several years ago, I began to think deeply about these issues, first by analyzing and teaching about some of these issues in the Toronto Jewish community when I served as the *sgan rosh beit midrash* of the Yeshiva University Torah MiTzion Beit Midrash Zichron Dov (now the Beit Midrash Zichron Dov of Toronto), and later by writing a series on halakha in the age of social media for Yeshivat Har Etzion's Virtual Beit Midrash (VBM). (I began to focus on issues of *lashon hara* as a fellow at the Summer Beit Midrash of the Center for Modern Torah Leadership

1. Jennifer Alejandro, "Journalism in the Age of Social Media," Reuters Institute fellowship paper (University of Oxford, 2010), available at: https://bit.ly/2IRuiPR.

and later as a fellow at the Tikvah Fund.) The focus of the VBM series was social media, though in truth, the series was more an exploration of halakha in the digital age. In my concluding comments for that series, I explained why I felt that I needed to explore this issue:

> Recent studies have found that on average, social media users spend two hours and twenty-two minutes a day on social media.[2] The average American adult spends over eleven hours on screens daily.[3] That is more time than is devoted to most other pursuits. According to those numbers, it is common for people to spend more time on screens than praying, eating, sleeping and learning Torah; social media usage alone takes up more time than the combined three daily prayers for most people. Nevertheless, while books have been and continue to be written (and for good reason) on the *halakhot* of prayer and *kashrut*, much less has been presented to provide halakhic guidelines and Torah perspectives on how we utilize the powerful and easily misused tools that the internet and social media offer us. It was to remedy that, to some extent, that I wrote this series.
>
> One of my teachers, R. Aryeh Klapper, writes as follows: "There is more and more Halakha, and ever more punctilious observance, and yet less and less of Halakha is relevant to the real moral and ethical issues facing individuals and communities."[4] Much of the community has begun "seeing Halakha more as an obstacle course rather than a moral highway." In discussions I've had over the year with people who wondered what I could possibly write about in a series on halakha in the age of social media, I've seen these sentiments to be true. Either people thought there was nothing to write, or they thought the sum total of the series should be a few *shiurim* spelling out how the laws of *lashon hara*

2. Available at: https://www.digitalinformationworld.com/2019/01/how-much-time-do-people-spend-social-media-infographic.html.
3. Available at: https://www.marketwatch.com/story/people-are-spending-most-of-their-waking-hours-staring-at-screens-2018-08-01.
4. *Acharayut Ketuvah: Responsibility Inscribed*, vol. 1, ed. Rachel Gelfman Schultz (The Center for Modern Torah Leadership).

apply in the modern world. The notion that communication technology in general and social media in particular have shaped the way we experience life and therefore the Torah, and that the Torah can in turn orient the way we utilize those tools, was surprising to them. But it should not be.

R. Haim David HaLevi argues in several places for the critical need to have halakhists approach the issues that challenge each generation, arguing that to fail to do so borders on heresy. As he writes: "Some argue that God's Torah is incapable, as it were, of answering new questions that arise in modern society, as if the Torah of God does not have a solution to social, economic, political and other problems. In this claim there is half truth; nevertheless, a person is not entitled to make this claim unless he has filled his belly with *Shas* and *Posekim*. This is because the simple truth is that for many of the problems that plague modern society, a reasonable halakhic solution can be found in every generation. A person who thinks otherwise is nothing but a heretic in the fundamentals, for one of the foundations of faith is that the Torah is from heaven, and God announced the generations in advance, foresees and looks until the end of all generations. Is it possible that His Torah should be ineffective in any time period?! There is no greater heresy than that!"[5]

Then, in 2019, the world was hit by the global pandemic of Covid-19. Suddenly, the world was turned upside down. Digital communication no longer supplemented our socializing, but in many cases, it replaced it. In Israel, there were weeks when, barring permitted outings to purchase food or medicine, all people were mandated to remain within a hundred meters of their home – even if they were not in quarantine. We barely saw our next-door neighbors. Zoom went from being a platform used by some for meetings to the main way in which many of us worked, went to school, and communicated with our family and friends. Zoom became the "scotch tape" of videoconferencing, the household name for

5. See *Responsa Aseh Lekha Rav* 3:56 and *Daat Torah BeInyanim Mediniyim, Techumin* 8: 365–367.

all similar communication. As I ready this book for publication, the world is still facing new waves of this virus, bringing into question whether the efforts to reopen will be slowed or reversed. With the encouragement of some friends, I decided that it was time to revisit the material in light of what I had learned and help myself grapple with these new realities.

The Rapid Development of Communication Technology

To understand why so little has been written about these issues, especially in the halakhic sphere, one must remember how quickly, in historical terms, these technologies have developed. In 1989, Ursula Franklin delivered the University of Toronto Massey Lectures and later collected and expanded those talks in a book, *The Real World of Technology*.[6] Though this was written several decades ago, and the developments in the relevant technologies have advanced rapidly since then, many of her comments capture the issues perfectly. She writes:

> We ought to keep in mind that the effects we perceive as so large come from technologies that are very recent in historical terms. For example, practical applications of electromagnetic and electronic technologies that have so profoundly changed the realities of the world are not more than one hundred and fifty years old. Think for a moment of the speed of transmission of messages; this really didn't change between the time of antiquity and about 1800. Whether Napoleon or Alexander the Great, even emperors had to rely on teams of horses and riders to send their messages and receive their responses. Then suddenly, around 1800, the speed of transmission of messages changed from the speed of galloping horses to the speed of the transmission of electricity – the speed of light…
>
> In 1833, Gauss and Weber, two German professors, strung a mile and a half of copper wire over the roofs of Göttingen and sent electrical impulses along it. And at that time in the United States, Samuel Morse (of the Morse Code) experimented with signal transmission. It was 1844 before he was able to string a line

6. U. M. Franklin & CBC Enterprises, *The Real World of Technology* (Montreal: CBC Enterprises, 1990).

> over sixty kilometers and transmit a message in Morse Code. He transmitted the sentence, "What hath God wrought?" and thus began the first usable method for the quick transmission of messages. In 1876, Alexander Graham Bell received his patent.... So it was essentially during the last 150 years that the speed of transmission of messages truly changed. This, in turn, so completely changed the real world of technology that we now live in a world that is *fundamentally* different.[7]

In historical terms, the pace of these advancements was quicker than at any other point in history. And humanity has not fully digested the full implications for our lives. It has changed the realities we live in, creating a world, as Franklin claims, that is "fundamentally different." We have also not sufficiently processed the nuances of how varying kinds of technology have shaped our lives, each in its own distinct way, with each advance in communication technology altering how we relate to others.

Synchronous and Asynchronous Communication Technology

Recently, researchers, primarily in the fields of psychology and education, have attempted to distinguish between the effects of synchronous and asynchronous communication technology.[8] Synchronous technologies are those in which people communicate directly and simultaneously, though without being in each other's presence, such as phone calls and videoconferences. Technologies such as email and social media are referred to as asynchronous, as one can respond to the communication at a later point. However, it seems that this very distinction elides critical insights into the way these technologies have changed our experiences.

Glen Cochrane, an instructional designer at Bow Valley College, noted that Franklin highlights a critical nuance often overlooked:

---

7. Franklin, 83–87, emphasis in original.
8. See, for example, D. Graham, T. Anderson, and D. Hassell, "The Viability of Skype to Reduce Learner Perceived Sense of Isolation," *Journal of Online Higher Education*, vol. 4, issue 12 (2013): 1–32.

> Society has come to a point, thinks Franklin, where the prevalence of asynchronous activity is so dominant over synchronous activity that there is little reciprocity left between the two. *Her observations are based on a definition of the word "synchronous" that has perhaps changed under our noses over the few decades since she recorded her ideas.* Drawing on the aspects of synchronous that are communal and undetachable from context, her concept is distinct from digitally situated, real-time activity. *Asynchronous enhanced synchronous communication tools (like Hangouts and Skype) are commonly referred to as "synchronous," and have afforded instructional designers with powerful educational options, distinct from asynchronous communication in their own right. Yet, the synchronous activity of digital environments is also distinct from off-line synchronous activity which cannot be overridden by a slew of asynchronous features, in the way that a Skype call bridges geographic distance digitally, and can be augmented with text, video, or countless other types of human controlled digital manipulation. It is the unmediated concept of "synchronous" that Franklin draws our attention to,* where we are forced to delegate control and choice to a greater context.[9]

Franklin herself captured this with the following illustration:

> Have you ever been in an overflow audience where they had to listen to a lecture on closed circuit television in an adjacent room because the main auditorium was full? Most people in this situation are quite disgruntled and feel cheated, although they see and hear exactly the same thing as people in the main auditorium. Still, they say, it doesn't feel real, it doesn't feel right. By the same token, the great hope of using TV or film to let many students benefit from exceptional interpreters, letting them be a part of an outstanding lecture, has not been realized. Students just do not like to be taught by a television screen. This does not mean that one can never make good use of a new technology, but here it

9. The emphasis is my own. Article available at: https://hybridpedagogy.org/synchronous-asynchronous-technologies-real-worlds-collide/.

> seems to work only in a supplementary mode, in terms of illustration and extension. Teaching on television is rarely engaging in the way news reports of floods and famine are.[10]

Yet, Franklin noted that there are other circumstances in which people find it adequate to interact virtually, even without any reciprocity. She notes:

> [V]iewers are riveted to television proceedings of judicial inquiries or public hearings. It seems that in situations where reciprocity is neither permissible nor desired – such as when observing an actual inquiry – images are acceptable substitutes for reality. However, whenever the potential for reciprocity exists and is valued – as in the lecture or teaching situation – images won't do.

It seems that synchronous digital communication can *almost* completely replace in-person experience in cases where people feel no need to interact directly. To be a spectator in such a situation by live feed is often good enough. The more involvement that is expected on behalf of the spectator, though, the less digital communication can compensate. This could be direct involvement, or even the participation of fans at sporting events, which adds significantly to the atmosphere, even if they are not truly part of the game.

As many universities have moved their courses online, and "Zoom-fatigue" has become an all-too-common phenomenon, some have begun to articulate why videoconferencing is not the same as in-person communication, forcing us to more carefully distinguish between "real" communication and synchronous communication.

Susan D. Blum, a professor of anthropology at the University of Notre Dame, recently wrote a reflection about her experience teaching on Zoom and how anthropology can help explain why even synchronous digital communication is not the same as in-person communication, "ordinary conversations," even while admitting its advantages over

10. Franklin, 103–105.

asynchronous technologies in creating holistic communication.[11] While noting the benefits that all videoconferencing platforms have over other forms of communication, and their contribution to allowing people to remain connected even while physically apart, she outlines where they fall short. Explaining why Zoom classes have left her drained in a way that regular classes do not, she comments:

> [It] is because videoconferencing is *nearly* a replication of face-to-face interaction but not quite, and it depletes our energy. And anthropology can help explain what's different....
>
> In a Zoom classroom with 30 students, we see faces – just like in a classroom. We see eye movement. We can hear voices. It can even be enhanced by chat – almost like hearing people thinking out loud. It is multimodal, to some extent. We see gestures, at least some big ones. All this is information used by our human capacity for understanding interaction. So far, so good.
>
> Zoom works well for faculty members who lecture, or for groups that have formal meetings, with rules for who speaks and how to signal an interest in speaking. As long as the symphony is directed by an authority figure, order can be kept. The trumpets come in on cue. It is calm. Information and views can be exchanged. It beats a long email exchange any day!
>
> But in the more interactive, active classrooms that I aim to create, this is terrible. When a classroom aims for (doesn't always achieve) democratic nonauthoritarian conversation, rather than orchestrated teacher-centered pedagogy, all the tools of human interaction are recruited.
>
> Anthropologists, linguists and sociologists who analyze conversation, which surely varies around the world, have shown some common traits. N. J. Enfield's recent book *How We Talk* and the work of conversation analysts such as the late Charles Goodwin points to multimodality, rules about eye gaze, patterns for rapid turn taking, and near-universal reliance on microsecond

11. https://www.insidehighered.com/advice/2020/04/22/professor-explores-why-zoom-classes-deplete-her-energy-opinion.

> timing. Goodwin reminds us that "co-operative action sits at the center of human language, and symbols are essentially co-operative structures in which one party is operating on another."
>
> This is not what my Zoom classrooms are like.

Her concluding comments perfectly capture the difference between "ordinary" conversations and those carried out over videoconference:

> When I see that technological platforms such as Zoom provide some imitations of face-to-face interaction, what I notice the most is that I miss the three-dimensional faces and the bodies and the eyes and the breaths.
>
> Humans are delicately attuned to each other's complete presence. If a perfectly tuned conversation provides a "vision of sanity," then it is no wonder that an awkward, clunky, interrupted conversation provides the opposite. We are constantly interpreting others' movements, timing, breaths, gazes, encouragement. It is our beautiful endowment. So we're interpreting the misaligned gazes, the interrupted conversation, as stemming from the technology, not from the interlocutor. And that, my human friends, is a tale of human-technology-semiotic mismatch.

When I first wrote about these issues, I implicitly related to these categories, but my experiences teaching and socializing over Zoom have forced me to re-examine my treatment of many of the halakhic issues and more carefully distinguish between the various modes of communication – both paying attention to synchronous and asynchronous digital communication, and how they are in turn distinct from in-person interactions.

Carefully considering these distinctions is particularly important in this work because of the nature of the project. One of my *ḥavrutot*, R. Dr. Shlomo Zuckier, noted that my methodology in treating these issues has, in many ways, been the reverse of that of much of modern halakhic literature. Many incredible books have been published to help guide people *min hamekorot ad lamaaseh*, from the sources to the practical implications. As we have seen, without a *siman* in *Shulḥan Arukh* on the laws of social media, we have had to invert this process. I start by asking about the ways in which our lives have been affected by communication technology and social media, and then turn back to potentially relevant issues in the Torah to gain insight. With that framing, it is even more important for me to understand the precise ways in which we are affected by and experience these various kinds of technology.

This book is divided into five sections, each assessing different realms of the human experience.

1. The first focuses on how definitions of relationships and community have changed. This is explored through topics as varied as the blessing recited upon seeing friends, to the parameters of rabbinic power and halakhic custom in a globalized community.
2. The second section focuses on our responsibility for what is posted online. As everything we write can become global (and permanent) in an instant, both users and platforms must consider their responsibility for what they post and what they facilitate.
3. The third section focuses on issues of perception. Halakha dictates how we view others and how we present to the world. When we are often connected to many without knowing who they are or how they will perceive what they see about us, we must explore the way in which these laws must adapt to the modern world.
4. The fourth section explores those topics most commonly identified with halakhic issues and social media. These include gossip and shaming – both their negative aspects as well as the opportunities they create for constructive communal criticism.
5. The final section is relatively short and addresses the performance of mitzvot through mediated experience. While this topic is extremely rich, the conceptual issues are distinct from those presented in the rest of the book. However, a basic overview of the issues, especially as they were implemented during the Covid-19 pandemic, is necessary.

In the coming years, our technologies will continue to change. As I write, the world has begun discussing our move into the metaverse. As new tools are created, these issues will have to be updated. In the meantime, I hope that this work begins the conversation, showing the world that the Torah has insights that can help us navigate this ever-changing world.

Acknowledgments

There are many people that must be acknowledged for their contributions to this book. First, while I love teaching, writing has always been harder for me. Had I not had the opportunity to write a series for the Israel Koschitzky Virtual Beit Midrash, the body of this book would never have come into being. Thank you to everyone involved at the VBM, especially R. Ezra Bick, R. Reuven Ziegler, and Debra Berkowitz. Furthermore, the feedback I received throughout the writing of that series helped improved the final version of this book.

For helping me turning this material into a book, thank you the wonderful staff at Koren and Maggid Books, specifically publisher Matthew Miller, R. Reuven Ziegler, Aryeh Grossman, David Silverstein, Tani Bayer, Ita Olesker, Yehoshua Duker, Nechama Unterman, and Tali Simon.

The issues of *lashon hara* in the modern world have been an interest of mine for many years. I first studied them with Rabbi Aryeh Klapper in his Summer Beit Midrash many years ago, where my interest the topic began. That summer was my first engagement in studying and writing about contemporary halakhic topics, and there I began my lifelong interest in deeply asking what halakha has to say our modern world. My thanks to Rabbi Klapper for his inspiration, as well as taking the time to review many of these chapters.

I returned to the topic of this book as a fellow at the Tikvah Fund, as a *semikha* student. My thanks to Rabbi Mark Gottlieb and Neal Kozodoy for their insights as some of the early sections of the book took form.

Thanks also to Rabbi Dr. Shlomo Zuckier, my long-time *ḥavruta* and friend, who also reviewed several of the chapters. Thank you to Galina Dostevsky Moerdler for her professional advice on the chapters about data privacy. Thank you for my friends who work in tech and provided feedback when I first published the series for the VBM, including Meir Hirsch, Daniel Reidler, and Yoni Halpern.

As mentioned above, my passion has always been for learning and teaching Torah. I would not have had the motivation to study these topics if it were not for the wonderful Toronto community where I began teaching these subjects. My profound thanks to Rabbi Mordechai Torczyner for his visionary leadership of the Beit Midrash Zichron Dov of Toronto, where I was privileged to serve as *sgan rosh kollel* for three years, and where I was able to expand what, how, and to whom I could teach. Thank you to Mr. Eli Rubenstein for founding the institution and bringing that jewel to the Toronto community. Thank you to all my students of all ages over the years, including those who learned with me in Toronto, who inspired me to probe these issues deeply. Thank you also to all my current students and colleagues who continue to challenge me at Yeshivat Migdal HaTorah.

It is particularly meaningful to me that this book is dedicated by the Lax family in memory of their sons Jonathan and Ethan. I was privileged to learn with both of them, as well as with Michael, and like the rest of the Toronto community, I was deeply shaken by their untimely deaths. I hope that this book and the conversations it inspires will be a merit for them. Thank you to Michael and Marsha Lax for their generosity and friendship.

Thank you to the other Toronto families who learned and continue to learn with me, and have extended friendship to my entire family. I would especially like to thank those families who partnered together to support the publication of this book – to the Green, Klein, Koschitzky, Litwack, Newman, Piwko, Rutman, Shore, Silverberg, Vodianoi, Wagner, and Zerker families, thank you for your friendship and support. A special thanks to Charles Wagner and Rabbi Seth Grauer for their help in organizing this partnership. It was amazing learning with all of you during my years in Toronto, and I am glad that we can continue to learn and spread Torah together.

On a personal level, thank you to my family who continue to support me in all my efforts. To my parents, Mark and Beth Ziring, for all their help over the years, their love of Torah learning, and their belief that Torah can and must always be relevant. Thank you to my in-laws, Mimi and Byron Shore, for always being there for our family, especially during the three years in Toronto when I was devoted to teaching throughout the entire community all day, every day. To my children, Meir, Aharon, Ezra, Temima, and Ayala, who keep me on my toes and make sure that I take nothing for granted. They make everything worthwhile.

Aḥarona aḥarona ḥaviva – every stage of life has been crazy, and only getting more so. I could not do anything without my wife and best friend, Ora. When I'm stretched thin, need perspective, support, or anything else, she is always there. For the Torah I teach and write, and for hopefully all that you, my readers, shall learn from this book – *sheli veshelakhem, shelah hi.*

And beyond that, thank you to God for ensuring I have been *zoche to* learn and teach Torah for so many years. I always hope I am living up to His expectations for me.

Jonathan Ziring
Efrat, Av 5783

Section 1

Relationships and Community

Chapter 1

By Way of Introduction, the Case of *Berakhot*

How Do We Experience Relationships?

The laws of *berakhot* are especially well suited for analyzing the way in which communication technology has impacted our lives, as well as the insights halakha can shed on those changes, as blessings capture the religious sentiments we do, or should, have. Thus, to begin our analysis, let us use two *berakhot*, *Meḥayeh HaMeitim* ("Who resurrects the dead") and *Sheheḥeyanu* ("Who has kept us alive"), to assess the different ways we deal with these new realities.

Information vs. Relationship

Increased communication has undeniably increased our *access to information.* In the past, it often took months or years to hear about world events or family celebrations/tragedies; in the modern world, we are instantly apprised of all that is happening. However, while we may know what is going on with all our Facebook "friends," the *relationships* we have on social media are usually shallower than those in real life. It is on these two axes, that of information and that of intimacy, that these two *berakhot* may function.

The Gemara in Berakhot (58b) records the following:

> **Rabbi Yehoshua ben Levi said: One who sees his friend after thirty days** have passed since last seeing him **recites: "Blessed... Who has kept us alive (*Sheheḥeyanu*), sustained us and brought us to this time."**
>
> One who sees his friend **after twelve months recites: "Blessed...Who resurrects the dead (*Meḥayeh HaMeitim*)."** As **Rav said: A dead person is only forgotten from the heart after twelve months** have elapsed, **as it is stated: "I am forgotten as a dead man out of mind; I am like a lost vessel"** (Ps. 31:13), and with regard to the laws of lost objects, it is human nature to despair of recovering a lost object after twelve months.[1]

Thus, there are two blessings to be said when seeing a friend after a time apart: after thirty days, *Sheheḥeyanu*; after a year, *Meḥayeh HaMeitim*. What is the nature of these *berakhot*?

Let us begin with *Meḥayeh HaMeitim*. At first glance, this blessing seems to be about *information*. In a world without advanced communication, if Reuven has not seen Shimon for a year, there is a chance that his friend Shimon has passed away. When Reuven then sees Shimon, he blesses God that his friend is alive. Maharsha (Berakhot 58b, cited in *Mishna Berura* 225:4) suggests that as all human beings are judged for life or death on Rosh HaShana, seeing someone alive after a year indicates that the friend had been judged for life.

However, there is a relationship component to this blessing. As Rashba notes (*Responsa* 4:76), even if the proximate cause for making this blessing is confirmation that one's friend is alive, it is only said *for friends*. One does not, for example, make this blessing when meeting a stranger

1. All Talmud quotations are from the *Noé Edition Koren Talmud Bavli*, with minor alterations, unless otherwise noted.

for the first time.[2] While meeting someone may "bring them to life," the blessing is warranted only when one wants to thank God for the relief of finding out that a friend is alive and well. (As we will see below, this Rashba becomes the basis for an alternative framing for this blessing.)

Implications of Communication Technology for Information-Based Laws

What implications does the increased flow of information have on a law predicated on lacking knowledge for long periods of time? Let us consider the question of whether the flow of information will affect saying the blessing when seeing a friend in person; then we will return to the question of whether "meeting someone" through phone calls, video calls, or any other mode of communication is sufficient to warrant a blessing.

The first authority to deal with this is R. Yaakov Hagiz, writing in the seventeenth century. In *Responsa Halakhot Ketanot* (1:220) he is asked whether one is required to recite *Meḥayeh HaMeitim* after not seeing a friend for a year, if during that time they were in contact through letters or kept updated through mutual acquaintances.

He answers, "It appears that one should not say the blessing of *Meḥayeh HaMeitim*... as there is no 'I am forgotten as a dead man out of mind' in this case." In other words, the communication is sufficient to negate the novelty of seeing his friend anew. It is not clear whether for R. Hagiz the central point is simply that *Meḥayeh HaMeitim* is said upon learning that a friend is alive or upon forgetting someone "as a dead man out of mind" and then having the friend "resurrected." Either way, this blessing is not said unless someone has been in the dark concerning a friend's well-being for a year, which is not the case when they have been in contact directly or indirectly. The suggestion is accepted as authoritative by most latter authorities.[3]

---

2. However, upon the birth of one's daughter, *Mishna Berura, OḤ* 223:2, rules that one does recite the blessing. R. Yosef Tzvi Rimon (Facebook post, May 9, 2020) derives from here that the Rashba's limitation is not fundamental, but rather an indication about the level of joy normally experienced in the various situations.
3. *Arukh HaShulḥan, OḤ* 225:3; *Ba'er Heitev, Shaarei Teshuva,* and *Mishna Berura, OḤ* 225:1. For a summary, see *Responsa Yeḥaveh Daat* 4:17; see, however, *Responsa Mishpetei Tzedek* 29 and discussion below.

In modern times, a Facebook post, a tweet, a message on WhatsApp, an email, or a phone call would all accomplish the same, thus making this *berakha* irrelevant in most modern circumstances. For these purposes, there should be no distinction between synchronous or asynchronous communication technology. R. Yisrael Kanievsky (*Orḥot Rabbenu,* vol. 1, Berakhot 15), writing in the twentieth century, takes this further (in the context of *Sheheḥeyanu*; see below): In the modern era, *lack of news is itself evidence that someone is alive.* When someone in a given social circle passes away, the information travels. Thus, if one hears nothing, this is de facto evidence that the person is alive, thus obviating the need to make a blessing upon seeing the person. This is even truer when Facebook accounts of those who pass away are often taken over by their loved ones to spread the word of their deaths and details of their funerals.

Limitations

Admittedly, there are limits to this. For example, R. Shmuel Wosner (*Responsa Shevet HaLevi* 5:24) notes that if one has heard from a friend but been told that the latter would be in a life-threatening situation (such as a soldier who has entered enemy territory), one *would* make a blessing upon seeing the friend after a twelve-month period. In this case, the requisite time has passed, and during that time the friend's survival was actually in question. In *Shaar HaTzeiyun* (225:3), the *Ḥafetz Ḥayim* makes this argument regarding a case in which the friend was known to have been sick.

These positions reflect two things:

1. In most cases, authorities have accepted that an information-based law such as *Meḥayeh HaMeitim* must change to capture the modern realities.
2. Sometimes it is specifically our access to information that creates our concern that a friend's well-being has been compromised.

Is *Sheheḥeyanu* the Same as *Meḥayeh HaMeitim*?

What about the other blessing, *Sheheḥeyanu*? Many authorities do indeed equate these two, arguing that they lie on the same continuum. From their perspective, one recites *Sheheḥeyanu* when seeing that a friend is well after a month's absence, and *Meḥayeh HaMeitim* after a year. Thus, they apply the same limitations to *Sheheḥeyanu* as we saw above. This is the position taken, for example, in *Mishna Berura* (225:5) and by R. Yisrael Kanievsky (above).

Sheheḥeyanu: It's About the Relationship

However, many authorities disagree. *Sheheḥeyanu* is said in many contexts: upon buying new clothes, eating a "new" seasonal fruit, etc. In each of these cases, one makes a blessing on the joy of experiencing newness. (The exact parameters are beyond the scope of our discussion.) In our context, therefore, this blessing should be understood as thanking God for the joy of *renewing a friendship or relationship*. Indeed, Tosafot (Berakhot 58b, s.v. *haro'eh*) cite R. Yitzchak of Dampierre (Ri) as saying that this blessing is only made upon seeing a "friend whom one loves," excluding acquaintances and (seemingly) friends who are not close from this category, a limitation accepted in *Shulḥan Arukh* (*OḤ* 225:2).

In the responsum of R. Yaakov Hagiz (as noted in *Arukh HaShulḥan, OḤ* 225:5) discussed above, he seems to accept this distinction. Thus, even if Reuven has been in communication with Shimon, Reuven says *Sheheḥeyanu* when seeing Shimon for the first time in a month. R. Ovadia Yosef (*Responsa Yeḥaveh Daat* 4:17) explains the logic: though it is true that one receives some level of emotional satisfaction by being in touch with friends through all kinds of media, "the excitement and emotional animation that one gets when he sees his friend face to face is with much greater power and strength." More simply, nothing replaces meeting up with friends in person. Here we have halakhic language to capture the sentiment that many people articulate about the modern world.

It is worth noting that R. Shmuel Ghermezian (*Responsa Mishpetei Tzedek* 29) contends that *Meḥayeh HaMeitim* is identical to *Sheheḥeyanu* and thus does apply in the modern world. Though his application is different than ours, the general contours of his assessment of the effects of communication on information flow versus relationships is similar to ours. However, based on the Rashba's comment above, that even *Meḥayeh HaMeitim* is limited to meeting friends, as well as the emphasis of the Talmud on twelve months being the time in which it takes for something to be forgotten from the heart, he rules that both blessings depend on joy rather than information.

Template for Other Laws

Following the analysis of this latter group of authorities, we have a distinction that can help assess other areas of law and the effect of communication technology on their application. Laws that are based purely or primarily on an assumption of limited information will have to change radically when applied to the modern world of social media. However, laws that are predicated on relationships and physical presence may be more resistant to change.

Are These Blessings Optional or Obligatory?

The Talmud (Eiruvin 40b) refers to the blessing of *Sheheḥeyanu* said on fruit as *reshut,* optional. R. Avraham ben Yitzchak of Narbonne (*Sefer HaEshkol* [Albeck], *Hilkhot Birkhot Hodaah* 23), interprets this line as meaning that *eating* a new fruit is optional, implying that it is obligatory to say the blessing if one chooses to eat the fruit. Rashba (*Responsa* 1:250) seems to understand that the blessing itself is optional, and this is how he is understood by R. Yosef Karo in *Beit Yosef, Or HaḤayim* 225:7. This is the position taken by *Mishna Berura* (ad loc. n. 9).

R. Moshe Sofer (*Responsa Ḥatam Sofer, OḤ* 55) takes a third approach. He argues that if one indeed feels the joy from the new fruit, one is obligated to capture that feeling with a blessing. However, it is optional in the sense that one can, with integrity, have the experience without the emotional charge that often accompanies it, and thus not be obligated in the blessing. This position is expanded upon by R. Wosner (*Responsa Shevet HaLevi* 4:25), who connects this conceptually to the position of R. Yoel Sirkes, *Baḥ* (*Bayit Ḥadash, OḤ* 29), that because this blessing is on the joy of the heart, and inherently subjective, one can recite it even in cases of doubt, in contradistinction to the normal rule of blessings that *safek berakhot lehakel,* when there is a doubt regarding blessings, one is lenient.[4]

4. Others argue that normal limitations on doubtful blessings refer only to cases where one says "who has commanded." For a summary of the issues, see R. Ovadia Yosef in *Responsa Yabia Omer, OḤ* 1:40 and 3:16.

For some, one can argue that the fact that this blessing is optional would push one to be reluctant to recite it unless one was convinced that it perfectly fit the template of *Ḥazal.* However, following the conceptual model of *Ḥatam Sofer* as expanded upon by R. Wosner, one could contend that even if the blessing is not obligatory, one who experienced deep joy upon seeing his friend would be allowed or obligated to recite the blessing, doubts notwithstanding, a position endorsed by R. Yosef Tzvi Rimon.[5] Thus, it will be even more critical to asses the emotional state of people in general and this person in particular.

Pragmatic Concerns

Some authorities argue that there is a pragmatic reason not to say this blessing. As we have seen, one recites *Sheheḥeyanu* only upon seeing a close friend, as reconnecting with such a person causes much joy. This limitation, however, can lead to several uncomfortable situations. One might refrain from saying the *berakha,* thus indicating to the other person that this friendship does not bring great joy. Alternatively, to avoid this, one might end up saying the *berakha* even when it is not warranted. R. Shlomo Zalman Auerbach (*Halikhot Shlomo,* vol. 3, ch. 23, 12) argues that these concerns lead to a general custom to avoid saying this blessing. (See also *Vezot Haberakha,* 170–171.)

R. Auerbach (ibid., *Devar Halakha* 17), however, does note that in extreme situations where the joy is particularly great, such as upon seeing a very close friend whose life has been in danger, one may say the blessing, as in this exceptional case, one avoids the pitfalls mentioned above. If one would want to say the blessing in a regular situation, he suggests creating a situation where one may say *Sheheḥeyanu* for other reasons, such as eating a new fruit. It is recorded (ibid., n. 53) that this was R. Auerbach's practice when his daughter and son-in-law would visit on rare occasions from outside Israel. His students further record that while R. Auerbach justified this custom and concurred with it, he felt that fundamentally one should be allowed to say this blessing and wanted to recite it upon seeing R. Yaakov Kamenetsky. R. Yechiel Michel

5. Facebook post, May 9, 2020, and audio lecture entitled *birkat she-hecheyanu be'reyiat chaver,* https://tinyurl.com/bddskhk5.

Charlap (cited in *Vezot Haberakha*) felt that one could recite the blessing in cases where the joy is apparent, e.g., for close relatives or after not seeing intimate friends for extended periods of time. R. Mordechai Eliyahu (cited in *Vezot Haberakha,* 171) suggests saying neither *Sheheḥeyanu* nor *Meḥayeh HaMeitim* out loud, but rather thinking them in one's mind.

R. Auerbach (ibid., *Devar Halakha* 15) further argues that if one had the ability to see a friend but simply did not, the joy of seeing the friend again is not great enough to warrant a *berakha.* Thus, two friends in one city who just don't get together for a while do not say a *berakha* when they finally find time to meet.

On the other hand, authorities such as R. Ovadia Yosef (above) rule that one should indeed make these blessings, subject to the parameters set forth above.

"Seeing Someone" Not in Person

So far, we have dealt with seeing friends in person after periods of absence, while still in communication. Now we move to the opposite question: If one has had no contact with a friend for an extended period of time, should one say *Sheheḥeyanu* or *Meḥayeh HaMeitim* upon talking to them via synchronous communication technology such as the phone? Does it matter if one adds the visual component through videoconferencing platforms such as Zoom or FaceTime? Can this not-in-person experience generate the requisite joy to require a blessing (or information for *Meḥayeh HaMeitim*)?

R. Yaakov Toledano (*Responsa Yam HaGadol* 24) argues that it does provide enough for both. For *Meḥayeh HaMeitim,* if one has had no contact with someone for a year and has concerns about the friend's well-being, then receiving a phone call which dispels these doubts is enough to obligate one to make a *berakha.* As for *Sheheḥeyanu,* he argues that even hearing someone's voice can create the same sense of joy as seeing someone. He proves this from the experience of the Revelation at Sinai, in which the Jews "saw the voices" (Ex. 20:14), thus indicating that the line between these two senses is often blurry. Furthermore, we rely on voice recognition for many areas of halakha, such as allowing a blind man to be intimate with his wife, relying on his ability to discern her voice from that of a possible imposter. R. Toledano notes that if this is true of phone calls, it is definitely true of live television – or, we might add, Zoom, Skype, or FaceTime.

However, most authorities rule that a phone call is not enough to enable one to make these blessings. R. Shlomo Zalman Auerbach (above, ch. 23, 11) seems to take a formal approach to this question, arguing that even if the joy might be similar, *Ḥazal* never instituted the *berakha* under these circumstances. R. Ovadia Yosef (above) concurs.

A more substantive argument can be marshaled as well, especially for the "relationship-oriented" understanding of *Sheheḥeyanu*. If, as we have seen, R. Ovadia argues that the joy of seeing someone in person is not diminished by having been in contact with him or her, such that one can make a *berakha* upon seeing the friend again, the enjoyment of speaking to someone not in person is not great enough to require a blessing. Halakha considers the in-person experience to be fundamentally unique and superior to other kinds of interaction. One could have distinguished between phone calls and communication technology with a visual component, arguing that the latter does diminish the joy of seeing one's friend later in person. R. Yosef Tzvi Rimon understood this to be the most likely understanding of R. Ovadia (though this is not R. Rimon's personal ruling).[6] However, it seems to me that the thrust of R. Ovadia's argument points to the central factor being physical presence rather than sight that generates/diminishes the joy felt.

An indication for this may emerge from a discussion R. Ovadia hints to at the end of his responsum. One of many "experience-based" *berakhot* is the blessing on seeing kings. The Talmud (Berakhot 58a) states that R. Sheshet would make the blessing even though he was blind. The Gemara tells an elaborate story of how a heretic mocked R. Sheshet for running to the king's procession even though he could not see him. R. Sheshet, however, proved that he was more in tune with the experience despite his lack of sight, intuiting when the king was passing based on the changing sounds of the procession. The heretic challenged R. Sheshet's blessing of the king without seeing him, for which this heretic was punished by Heaven. From this, the law emerges that

6. See the Facebook post and audio lecture cited in note 5.

though the Gemara says that one makes the blessing upon "seeing the king," what is most critical is feeling the royal presence.

R. Ovadia notes that some authorities, such as R. Yaakov Reischer (*Responsa Shevut Yaakov* 2:38), argue that other "sight" blessings are really "experience" blessings, thus allowing a blind person to say *Sheheḥeyanu* on new fruit. While most authorities reject this for formal reasons, arguing that in most cases *Ḥazal* only instituted these as visual blessings, R. Reischer's position, coupled with the generally accepted opinion concerning the blessing on kings, suggests the following. As R. Ovadia notes, the joy of seeing someone in person is unique. Thus, mere contact does not significantly diminish the joy of seeing a good friend. Sometimes, presence alone creates so much happiness that it can justify making a blessing even though one cannot see the object of joy. If this is true, the majority view would argue that halakha prioritizes the *sui generis* feeling of in-person contact, differing from R. Toledano who argues that one can be just as happy talking to someone on the phone as hanging out with a friend.

However, as noted, while R. Toledano rules that a letter informing one of a friend's well-being is enough to justify *Meḥayeh HaMeitim,* as the consensus would be that the doubts about the friend being alive have been dispelled, most *posekim* reject this reason to make a blessing, for the formal reasons mentioned above. Even R. Ghermezian, who was more expansive in his understanding of *Meḥayeh HaMeitim,* may require synchronous communication to recite the blessing.

R. Avraham Stav[7] has noted that in theory, one could entertain a model in which videoconferencing would be considered sight and enable the recitation of *Sheheḥeyanu,* but one would still be allowed/obligated to recite the blessing when seeing the friend in person. R. Stav explains this by assuming that one can say the blessing both for formal reasons ("seeing a friend") and substantive ones (the joy of renewing the in-person contact). One could offer a similar model, arguing that both the joy of seeing someone via synchronous communication technology and that of in-person meetings each generates enough joy to warrant a blessing. However, both models seem novel.

---

7. *Ha'Im Levarech Sheheḥeyanu al Mifgash Aḥarei HaKorona,* https://tinyurl.com/bdecx76z.

Hearing a Friend

During the Covid-19 shutdowns, I was asked whether one would say *Sheheḥeyanu* upon seeing a friend whom he heard in person, but did not see. For example, in a case where one participated in a "porch *minyan*" with a neighbor who could be seen by the *ḥazan* but not by all. Similarly, would one recite the blessing upon hearing a friend in person, as in the above case, for the first time in thirty days?

Based on the case of the blind person and the king, one could argue that merely being in the presence of a friend might generate enough joy to warrant a blessing. Alternatively, one could conclude that hearing does not provide nearly enough joy and thus seeing the friend anew would require a blessing. However, I would propound that hearing a friend generated enough joy to dampen the newness of seeing him again but was not sufficient to generate enough joy to require a blessing. I have seen no authorities weigh in on this issue directly.

Have Things Changed? Lessons from Covid-19

Has our analysis missed a key demographic? While for some people, social media may encourage superficial friendships, rather than intimate in-person relationships, there are those for whom genuine bonds of affection are not easily formed. Some painfully shy individuals have difficulty or discomfort forming relationships, and social media allows them to create a sense of comradery and community while avoiding aspects of social interactions that make them most uncomfortable. For such people, it could be that friendships forged with the distance allowed by social media bring them more joy and meaning than real-world relationships. Perhaps, for them, it would be justifiable to treat these virtual connections like in-person meetings.

A second point was suggested to me by R. Aryeh Klapper. I assume that it is possible to tease out implications for contemporary reality from the earlier sources presented above. However, it is possible that the way in which we interact has been so radically altered by communication technology that we do not relate to others in ways analogous to those experienced by halakhic authorities of even twenty years ago, to say nothing of a few centuries ago. Our assumptions about when we will interact, how, and with whom, are so different that the laws on the books may in no way reflect our current realities. Considering that these *berakhot* are built on assumptions about human emotions, such a paradigm shift may require more than tweaking the existing laws.

When I first taught and wrote about these issues, I thought it possible that our world has indeed changed, and that we no longer need face-to-face connections. However, the outbreak of Covid-19 and the imposition of social distancing and quarantine clarified these issues. For months, we were all in virtual contact with family and friends constantly, perhaps more than usual. Yet, in many ways, people had never felt so lonely.

Israeli musician Hanan Ben-Ari captured these sentiments in a song that reflected what he learned from Covid-19.[8] "We thought ... what person needs another person? ... How you [Covid-19] have returned sanity, longings for people?! Suddenly, loneliness burns, we no longer fly from here to there. The parks are closed. Weddings are almost without people. We have almost lost ourselves; we have almost stopped feeling." Indeed – we thought we forgot that we need each other, in person. People in the overflow livestream room feel left out of the main event and Zoom classes cannot recreate the dynamic of a real one. As Susan Blum put it, "When I see that technological platforms such as Zoom provide some imitations of face-to-face interaction, what I notice the most is that I miss the three-dimensional faces and the bodies and the eyes and the breaths. Humans are delicately attuned to each other's complete presence."[9]

To put it differently: When I visit a city for a few days, I am most likely to meet up with the friends I regularly talk to, rather than those I don't feel the need to communicate with regularly. Synchronous and asynchronous communication technology supplement our relationship so that I am *more* invested in enjoying their actual presence, but no amount of Zoom and FaceTime will replace it.[10]

---

8. https://www.youtube.com/watch?v=G9m54DdWgoo&feature=emb_title.
9. https://www.insidehighered.com/advice/2020/04/22/professor-explores-why-zoom-classes-deplete-her-energy-opinion.
10. R. Stav makes a similar suggestion.

Some halakhic decisors, even in light of Covid-19, followed the position of the *Mishna Berura* and ruled that these blessings should be said for friends with whom one has been in contact. This, for example, was the position of R. Hershel Schachter.[11] Others, however, ruled that *Sheheḥeyanu* was indeed warranted. This was the position of R. Rimon, and this was my practice as I saw friends and family for the first time after weeks apart during Covid-19 shutdowns.

I think it is preferable to prioritize in-person relationships, highlighting that, at least for most people, there are benefits to these kinds of friendships. To institute a blessing for virtual interactions is to give in to a culture where people would rather text with friends who are not present than speak with friends sitting next to them, and to forbid saying the blessing upon seeing those with whom one has been in contact overlooks the benefits real interactions add to our relationships. More importantly, the experience of Covid-19 indicated that many people still believe that in-person relationships cannot be replaced. However, as these blessings are based on one's personal feelings, one for whom this is not true need not or should not recite the blessing.

Will This Always Be True?

While I think the majority of people and *posekim* would still propound that communicating through various forms of media is not a replacement for face-to-face conversations, I am not sure what the future will hold. As virtual experiences improve, it is possible that the norms of communication will no longer be limited to talking through screens. Perhaps we will have holograms so that it will be as if our friends are in the room. Perhaps technology will advance to allow for "virtual hugs," so that we will feel the embrace of loved ones who are thousands of miles away. As technology advances, halakhic authorities will have to re-examine the question of whether virtual experience of contact can ever be considered equal to actual presence, especially, as noted above, whether these blessings capture the feelings that people experience.

11. Email to the RCA, May 4, 2020.

Chapter 2

Social Media, Communication, and the "Classic" *Aguna*

Can Anyone Become Lost in Our Interconnected World?

From *Meḥayeh HaMeitim* to the 9/11 *Agunot*[1]

In our discussion of *berakhot*, we noted that halakhot predicated on the dissemination of information will change more fundamentally in our interconnected world than laws based on relationships. Thus, regarding the question of whether one can say the *berakha* of *Meḥayeh*

1. Much of my analysis here is drawn from the excellent book put together by the Beth Din of America dealing with halakhic and philosophical perspectives on the 9/11 attack on the Twin Towers. See Michael J. Broyde, ed., *Contending with Catastrophe: Jewish Perspectives on September 11th* (New York: Beth Din of America Press and K'hal Publishing, 2011). Specifically, the introductory article by R. Michael Broyde and the summary article by R. Chaim Jachter are particularly helpful. Also, many of the central responsa on the issue have been translated for that volume. A version of R. Jachter's article can also be found here: https://static1.squarespace.com/static/52a75d36e4b06a3e88b21253/t/52eabe6fe4b07b90a848dcc2/1391115887699/The+Beth+Din+of+America+ruling+about+the+World+Trade+Center+agunot.pdf.

HaMeitim in the digital age, most rule that it can rarely be said. The *berakha* is predicated on a reality in which, after not being in touch with a friend for a year, one must worry that the friend was dead. Upon discovering that the friend is alive, one blesses God. To put it differently, the recitation of *Meḥayeh HaMeitim* is based on the possibility of "losing someone." However, most authorities assume that in the ever-connected world created by communication technology, there are very few cases in which one would assume that a friend is not alive without having heard news.

The question of whether someone can become lost in the world appears in a slightly different form in the world of *ishut,* marital status. The law, as outlined in the first mishna in Kiddushin, is that a marriage can end in one of only two ways: divorce or the death of the husband. If the husband is known to have died, then his wife is free to remarry.

However, if a husband disappears and his whereabouts are unknown, in many cases his wife becomes an *aguna,* a chained woman.[2,3]

Another treatment of the issues can be found in "*Heter Agunot Migdalei HaTeomim,*" *Yerushrun,* vol. 11 (5762), by Rabbis Shmuel Mordechai Gersten, Eliyahu Levin, and Avraham Bromberg.

2. The word *aguna* is often used in modern parlance to refer to the wife of a "recalcitrant husband," a husband who refuses to grant his wife a *get,* a bill of divorce, even though they are in a dead marriage or have been separated for years. As halakha requires a husband to initiate the *get* proceedings uncoerced, it is often difficult to solve this problem. Many attempts have been successful at minimizing the problem, such as the RCA Halakhic Prenuptial Agreement and similar documents in Israel and Canada; enforcement mechanisms that are open to the rabbinic courts in Israel; and public shaming of husbands by organizations such as ORA, the Organization for the Resolution of Agunot. This issue is important, but the classic term refers, as mentioned here, to a wife whose husband is missing. The issue of public shaming, using social media to pressure a husband into granting a *get,* is an important topic and will be discussed in a later chapter.
3. In halakha, the reverse case is much more easily solved, as from a biblical perspective, men may marry more than one wife. Polygamy is prohibited by the *ḥerem* of Rabbenu Gershom only. Thus, it is easier to permit a man whose wife has disappeared to remarry (see *Pitḥei Teshuva, EH* 1:14). R. Jachter, in the context of the 9/11 cases, noted therefore that:

   > R. Yonah Reiss, the administrator of the Beth Din of America, informed me that a number of husbands called the Beth Din of America regarding their wives who were missing after the World Trade Center attack. R. Reiss told me

Without certain knowledge that her husband is dead, she cannot remarry. If she does, she risks violating the prohibition of adultery – and if there are children, causing them to become *mamzerim*. Thus, the sixteenth chapter of Yevamot discusses various cases in which the status of a husband is unknown and the methods we use to establish whether or not he is dead.

The category we will be exploring in this chapter is that of *mayim she'ein lahem sof*, endless waters (i.e., a body of water whose furthest extent is not visible). This refers to a set of cases in which the husband is known to have been in a dangerous situation, such as seemingly drowning in a body of water. If there is no way of finding out whether the husband has died, the woman is stuck. In the classic case, because the far shoreline is not observable, we must be concerned that the husband has not died, but rather emerged on the other side of the body of water. Though we have not heard anything, the Talmud assumes that we must at least be concerned that the lack of news regarding him is not evidence that he has in fact drowned.

However, starting in the Gemara, many authorities wonder whether there might be a situation in which communications are so good that not hearing from the husband for a certain period would give us good reason to presume him dead, thus giving the court a reason to permit his wife to remarry. As we will see, there has been a chain of authorities making arguments along these lines after each advance in travel or communication technology. Though this type of argument is rarely used as the only reason to permit a woman to remarry, it persistently appears. Most recently, we will see how several rabbinic authorities use a version of this argument to permit remarriage for some of the women whose husbands were trapped in the Twin Towers on 9/11.

Mayim SheEin Lahem Sof in the Mishna and Gemara

To deal with this question, we must start from the central discussion in the Talmud. The passage is as follows:

that the Dayanim followed the ruling of the Gesher Hachayim who rules that a husband may remarry if there is adequate evidence that a wife was at the place where a tragedy occurred and that most people who were in her location and situation perished.

> **MISHNA:** If a man **fell into the water** and did not come out, **whether** the body of water **has** a visible **end or does not have** a visible **end, his wife is prohibited** from remarrying. There is no absolute proof that the man died, as it is possible that he emerged from the water some distance away. **Rabbi Meir said: An incident** occurred **involving a certain** person **who fell into the Great Cistern and emerged** only **after three days.** This is evidence that sometimes one may survive a fall into water, even when everyone assumes he is dead....
>
> **GEMARA: Rav Ashi said: That which the Sages said,** that if a man fell into **an endless body of water, his wife is prohibited** from remarrying, **applies** only **to an ordinary person** who is not well known and could slip away secretly and live in anonymity, hiding the fact that he survived. **But** it does **not** apply to **a Torah scholar,** because **if he would emerge** from the water, **publicity would be** generated and the news of his survival would spread. The Gemara rejects this: **That is not so. It is no different** for **an ordinary man and it is no different** for **a Torah scholar. After the fact,** i.e., if she remarried, **yes,** she may remain with her new husband, but she may **not** remarry ***ab initio.*** (Yevamot 121a)

The Mishna introduces the category of *mayim she'ein lahem sof* and assumes that if a body of water does not have a visible end, we cannot assume that a husband who fell into it has drowned, as Rabbi Meir illustrates with his story of a man who seemed to have drowned, only to turn up alive several days later. Thus, the Mishna seems to assume that, at least in the ancient world, we must be concerned that a husband could become lost. The ruling in *Shulḥan Arukh* (*EH* 17:32, 34) based on this is that a woman cannot remarry simply because it is known that her husband fell into endless waters, and testimony that a man has fallen into such waters is therefore not evidence that he is dead.

However, as the Gemara goes on to say, this is only true *ab initio*. If, however, a woman remarries because her husband has probably drowned in such a situation, she would not be forced to divorce her new husband as the prohibition for her to remarry is only rabbinic. *Beit*

Shmuel notes (*EH* 17:102) that on a biblical level, we rely on *rov*, majority. Thus, as most husbands who have fallen into a body of water in this way will die, on a biblical level she may remarry. Rashba (Ketubot 3a, s.v. *kol*) notes that the Rabbis are apparently quite concerned about this possibility, as though there are cases in which the Rabbis "uproot" marriages retroactively to prevent cases of *igun*, chained women, this is not one of them. Nevertheless, as this law is only rabbinic, if the woman does remarry, the court does not force her to divorce.

Rav Ashi and the Case of the Torah Scholar

The Talmud already raises the possibility that there are cases in which, if we do not hear from the husband, we may assume that he is dead. While it is true that communication was not great in the talmudic period, Rav Ashi assumes that as Torah scholars are well known, were a scholar to float up on the other side of a body of water, word would reach his wife's town. If it does not, this is evidence that the husband has drowned and died. Thus, he allows the wife to remarry.

However, this position is rejected by the Talmud. The question we must ask is why. There are two possibilities: The first is that Rav Ashi assumes that theoretically, there are cases where hearing no news about someone may contribute evidence to our belief that he is dead. However, the majority opinion rejects this totally. It is possible for a person to appear on the other side of the ocean and lose contact with his hometown, no matter who he is. Thus, lack of news is never evidence of the husband's death. Were this the case, the law would never change, no matter how good communication becomes.

However, one might argue that this is a question of degree – namely, everyone agrees that theoretically there could be a situation in which there is a presumption that if someone is alive, we would hear about it, and if we don't, that may lend credence to the assumption that he is dead. However, they argue that the husband being a Torah scholar is not enough. This opens the possibility that in other circumstances, even the majority position would accept a view akin to that of Rav Ashi.

The majority view accords with the former view, as reflected in the ruling in *Shulḥan Arukh* in the passages mentioned above. However,

R. Yisrael Isserlein (Germany, fifteenth century) argues that the latter view is correct (*Terumat HaDeshen,* Pesaḥim 139). He contends that the majority view in the Talmud only rejects the opinion of Rav Ashi because being a scholar is insufficient reason to assume that a husband's death will become known; however, in other cases, they would agree. Thus, he argues that if a husband known to have been in a life-threatening situation vanishes, we can allow his wife to remarry after several years. He notes that in the Diaspora, Jews are scattered all over the world; as Jews tend to be connected, if the husband were to show up even "two hundred or three hundred *parsa* [away]" – over a thousand miles – we would hear about it. The fact that we have not heard means that the court can permit the wife to remarry.

Is This Position Actually Rejected?

However, the fact that most authorities do not accept R. Isserlein's opinion does not mean that the story ends. As above, there are two ways of taking the rejection of his opinion. The first is that the majority position maintains that there is no circumstance under which lack of news may be used as proof of a husband's demise. The second is that in principle, this absence of evidence may have weight, but in practice, the authorities felt that this threshold had not been reached during the time of R. Isserlein. However, perhaps in later generations, in which communications and travel technology make the world an even smaller place, this argument would be accepted.

What emerges from a survey of later halakhic literature is that many accept the latter argument, though some, like the *Ḥazon Ish,* tended toward the first position.[4] After every expansion of humanity's technological abilities, major authorities argue that even if it were not true in the time of R. Isserlein, now that we have X form of technology, the world is so connected that lack of news is proof of the husband's death. R. Moshe

4. *Ḥazon Ish* (*EH* 31:7) tends to completely reject the *Terumat HaDeshen,* though he admits that many *posekim* advanced versions of the lenient ruling. However, noting that they usually only cite it as one of many arguments, he thinks that the fundamental position is to reject the *Terumat HaDeshen.* See "*Heter Agunot Migdalei HaTeomim,*" especially the section by R. Shmuel Mordechai Gersten.

Sofer (*Responsa Ḥatam Sofer, EH* 58, cited in *Pitḥei Teshuva, EH* 17:135) makes this argument in the early nineteenth century, noting the presence of post offices in every city. Thus, were the husband alive, he would have contacted his wife. A few years later, R. Haim Palagi (*Responsa Ḥayim VeShalom* 1) writes that with the fast transportation provided by boats, one could apply the *Terumat HaDeshen* argument in his time.

This argument is also made by several modern authorities. R. Yitzchak HaLevi Herzog, the first Ashkenazi chief rabbi of the State of Israel, cites this argument in the mid-twentieth century *Shu"t Heikhal Yitzḥak* (*EH* 2:9). R. Moshe Feinstein (*Responsa Iggerot Moshe, EH* 1:43) makes this argument as part of his attempt to permit remarriage for women whose husbands went missing during the Holocaust. He argues that even if one could not make this argument in the time of R. Moshe Sofer, the situation is different now:

> And all the more so in our times, with the number of post offices, the speed of information [flow] in the entire world has increased exponentially when compared to the year 5571 [1810–1811], in which *Ḥatam Sofer*'s responsum was written. Also, newspapers have proliferated in every country. Due to the pressure, the great poverty, and the persecution everywhere, each Jew who remains alive is seeking his relatives here in America, whom the Holy One, Blessed be He, in His mercy, left as a remnant. One writes to them, as well as to distant people. [In such a case,] it is a very well-established presumption that the fact that we have not heard from him [means] that he has died. And since every person has this presumption, one cannot argue "we do not distinguish," and we may permit even *ab initio*.

R. Feinstein notes the increase in the desire and ability to communicate, so that even those who reject the arguments of *Terumat HaDeshen* and *Ḥatam Sofer* might agree that under current circumstances, lack of news could be considered proof.

In 2001, this argument was cited again by the authorities dealing with the tragic *aguna* issues that arose in the aftermath of the attack on the Twin Towers, such as R. Ovadia Yosef (*Shu"t Yabia Omer, EH* 10:18).[5] He notes that though there is much controversy regarding the position of *Ḥatam Sofer*, and even some who argue that R. Sofer retracted it in later responsa, R. Yosef is willing to accept it. Again, here we find an argument of the form: Even if was not true then…

> according to my humble opinion, since the very essence of *Ḥazal*'s decree regarding endless waters is due to survivors being the minority and uncommon, in our times, as many media outlets have been added, as above, the concern that he may be found among tent-dwellers or the wild ones of the desert represents a minority of a minority….
>
> This becomes true even more so in our times, with the great development of media – telephone, wireless [Internet], telegram, newspapers, radio, television – which have gone out to the whole world and fill the ends of the earth. Also, there are planes flying from one end of the world to the other, every day, every morning anew.

R. Nota Greenblatt, in his responsum, writes similarly:

> [I]t seems there is another compelling reason to permit [the *aguna*] based on the extreme changes which have arisen in recent years with the way life is managed in this country and in all other developed countries. At this time it is not possible that a person can disappear and not know where he is. Even those that wander and sleep in the streets have a social security number registered with the government in order to receive benefits and to be treated by a doctor or in the hospital, etc.[6]

5. This responsum was originally sent to the Beth Din of America and published in Yeshiva University's journal *Kol Tzvi*. It can be accessed here on www.yutorah.org under *Hatarat Aguna MiBinyanei HaTeomim BiArtzot HaBerit*, https://tinyurl.com/23bssc5a. It was later published in the tenth volume of *Yabia Omer*. A translation can be found in *Contending with Catastrophe*.
6. See R. Broyde's introductory article in the above volume.

R. Eliyahu Levin argued similarly (the translation is my own):

> However, it seems that in a country like this, like the United States of America, it is not only for the lack of information or knowledge from him [that we are lenient]; rather, the issue is based on the normal way of life of a living person, who is employed in the common way of employment only by giving his details to his employer, and only then are the places of work open to him, especially if he has a profession like Rabbi A. When he gives his details to his employer, he is checked in the central police offices, and then it would be made known that he is missing. Thus, to live with fraudulent identification details of someone else would be especially hard for an American, with an American nature, who cannot live like this, for fear of danger from the government and out of concern for endangering his ability to exist financially....
>
> Similarly... in our days, a person must identify himself at places of work and in a bank, and if he does not come to these places, it will seem suspicious, and the government will seek to have him identify himself.... Furthermore, his family receives payment from the insurance company for the catastrophe that happened to him, and if his identity would become known, the information would be given over to the authorities, and the media would publicize it; thus silence concerning knowledge about him is a the silence of the masses.

It is important to reiterate that this leniency is rarely used by itself, as R. Chaim Jachter notes in his summary article in the Beth Din of America's book on the 9/11 tragedy:

> We should note that Poskim do not rely on this line of reasoning alone, as it virtually eliminates a rule from the Gemara, something Poskim are loath to do.

Still, even if this argument is only used in conjunction with other reasons, it indicates a recognition by *posekim* of the effect that communication technology has on halakha. One can only imagine that soon authorities will be making the argument that even if this was true before the prevalence of social media, now....

Why This Argument Works: The Concern Is Only Rabbinic

It is important to note that the reason this kind of argument is entertained is because, as mentioned above, the entire concern here is only rabbinic in nature. From a biblical perspective, the fact that most people who look like they are drowning and seem to have drowned do indeed drown is enough to permit the wife to remarry. This is based on the halakhic principle of following the *rov* (majority), which allows us to assume that what happens in most cases has happened in a specific case as well. This is evident in the Rashba's responsum that we saw earlier, and it is explicitly articulated in the positions of many *posekim* (see, for example, R. Herzog above).

Time Limit

Another avenue for leniency that is similarly built on the recognition of the power of communication is that of R. Eliezer of Verdun, in the later medieval period, cited by *Mordekhai* (Yevamot 92). R. Eliezer contends that when the Talmud states that the woman whose husband is lost is forbidden, it does not mean she is forbidden forever. Rather, after several years have passed without any communication, even the rabbis in the Talmud who challenge Rav Ashi would agree that the woman can remarry.

This position is greatly disputed. *Mordekhai* cites several authorities who vigorously reject this, maintaining that one who relies on it should be excommunicated and warning against inventing baseless time limits. R. Yosef Karo agrees (*Beit Yosef, EH* 17). However, historically, many authorities were willing to accept it, including R. Moshe Feinstein in his above discussion of post-Holocaust cases; R. Ovadia Yosef utilized it as one of his reasons to be lenient in his responsum concerning the 9/11 *agunot.*[7] R. Eliezer Waldenberg (*Shu"t Tzitz Eliezer* 15:59) notes

7. R. Jachter notes that the authorities who approve of utilizing this argument include *Shu"t Mahari Beirav* 13; *Shu"t Mabit* 1:187; *Shu"t Noda BiYehuda* 2, *EH* 47; and *Shu"t Iggerot Moshe, EH* 1:43.

that various lengths of time are put forth by *posekim* to qualify for this leniency, ranging from one year to four years. In the case of 9/11, R. Yosef advised the Beth Din of America to wait a year before allowing the *agunot* to remarry.

Again, while neither this leniency nor the previous one is used by itself, they are both based on the belief that it is hard for a person to disappear when advanced communication technology exists, and the better the technology, the harder it is to disappear.

What If the Husband Wants to Disappear?

All of this, however, assumes that we have no reason to believe that the husband wants to disappear. All the above cases deal with a husband who has no desire to go off the grid and evaporate. On the contrary, we have every reason to believe that if he were alive and well, he would return to his wife. The fact that he has not acts as an indication that he has died, when coupled with the knowledge that he was in a life-threatening situation which most people do not survive.

However, what if we have reason to believe that the husband did want to escape? What if he was known to be having marital problems, job problems, or any other reason to escape his life? In such a case, being in a situation where people would assume that he died would give him the perfect cover to disappear and rebuild his life elsewhere. Despite how hard it is to escape the world, modern technology has, in some ways, made it easier for someone who wants to start fresh to do so. With enough money, he can get plastic surgery and pay to take on a new identity.

For this reason, R. Yechezkel Landau (*Shu"t Noda BiYehuda* 2, *EH* 47) notes that we only seek out leniencies and utilize the arguments mentioned above when we have a reason to believe that the husband is not the kind of person who wanted to vanish. If, on the other hand, we have reason to believe that he was looking to abscond, we don't look for reasons to permit his wife to remarry:

> All the leniencies that I will speak about for this woman are on condition that this man, Rabbi Shimon, who as mentioned, lived with his wife in the way of the land, and there was no hatred

between them that would make us think that he wanted to distance himself, wander from her, and leave her as an *aguna*. Rather he lived with his wife in peace, and his way was to travel and do business for a few days and then return home. If this is the case, there is at least support for the claim that he is not alive, for if he were alive, he would come to his home. Even though this does not suffice to permit her, nevertheless, it is then worth searching for leniencies.[8]

---

8. The question of why it is legitimate for a *posek* to enter into a discussion with a preconceived notion, namely that he wants to provide a leniency, is beyond the scope of this discussion. However, it is worth noting that throughout halakhic literature, we find the notion that extenuating circumstances legitimate searching and relying on even tenuous reasons to be lenient. This type of argumentation is particularly common in cases of *aguna*, where the Talmud itself notes that we prefer to be lenient if possible.

For a brief discussion on the topic, see this author's post here: https://shaashuim.wordpress.com/2013/12/22/halachic-decision-making-in-extenuating-circumstances-part-1-halachic-methodology-part-9/.

Also see my *shiur* and sources here: https://www.yutorah.org/lectures/lecture.cfm/802192/_Jonathan_Ziring/Halachic_Decision_Making_in_Extenuating_Circumstances.

The words of *mori verabbi* HaRav Aharon Lichtenstein *zt"l* are particularly enlightening:

> What is the halakhic basis of such license? That the basis must indeed be halakhic is beyond question. No committed halakhist can seriously countenance the simplistic socio-economic interpretation that, under pressure, the Halakhah just periodically capitulates. For one thing, the image – or rather the reality – of Halakhah and its masters which he envisions simply does not correspond with this theory. For another, if *posekim* or their constituents have always been bent, consciously or subconsciously, upon adjusting the Halakhah to suit social or economic needs, they have certainly made a terrible botch of things. In one area after another, they have "modified" one injunction only to leave untouched a dozen far more stringent. Pressures of circumstance no doubt make themselves felt, but they generally operate within halakhic limits and to the extent that they are accorded halakhic recognition. Interpretations of the Halakhah's past – or projections of its future – that ignore its fundamental objectivity distort its very essence. Least of all, will the halakhist accept the contention that, under pressure, the Halakhah *should* capitulate...
>
> For the Jew, therefore, it is Halakhah and Halakhah alone that determines what it can exact from him. Hence, if straitened circumstances can justify a degree of leniency, the rationale must be grounded in – must, in a sense, constitute – a

As R. Jachter notes:

> This line of leniency underscores the importance of the Beth Din accurately establishing that the husband and wife were on good terms before the husband's disappearance, to reduce the possibility that the husband has taken advantage of the tragedy to disappear and establish a new identity.

Conclusion

We have discussed two arguments for leniency in permitting *agunot* to remarry, both of which are predicated on the power of communication. R. Eliezer of Verdun argues that even in the Talmud, Rav Ashi only disagrees about how long it would take for a husband to disappear and be presumed dead. Rav Ashi assumes that when dealing with a Torah scholar it would take a short period of time, while the majority position argues that for all people it takes more time (a year, two years, four years, etc.) This argument by itself is not utilized, and some *posekim* reject it altogether, but many authorities cite it as part of their argument.

The central argument we have focused on is that as communications and travel technology improve, the world becomes a smaller and

---

> halakhic principle. This rationale is based upon two premises. The first is the obvious desire and duty to employ every possible means to assist those in need.... It impinges upon the process of *pesak* as well. In cases of genuine difficulty, the imposition of possibly needless burdens is not merely neutral. It violates the letter as well as the spirit of Halakhah. Or, to put it more positively, within the limits of flexibility, the exercise of ingenuity in an effort to relieve potential hardship becomes a matter of the highest duty. Of course, ingenuity alone does not suffice. It can only be used in conjunction with erudition and commitment, and the number of those possessing the religious and intellectual qualifications for halakhic decision can never be very large....
>
> The obligation to compassionate leniency is imposed by *caritas*. The opportunity is provided by a pluralistic conception of Halakhah. So long as Halakhah is defined in purely monistic terms, every text being subject to only one correct interpretation and every problem amenable to only one solution, it is difficult to justify such leniency. However, the Rabbis interpreted Halakhah in somewhat more flexible terms.

See HaRav Aharon Lichtenstein, "'*Mah Enosh*': Reflections on the Relation between Judaism and Humanism," *Torah u-Madda Journal* 14 (2006–2007): 44–45.

smaller place. Thus, when we have reason to believe that a husband would not want to vanish, if he was in a situation in which he might have died and then he fails to reach out to his wife, we assume that is evidence of his death. While, as we noted above, neither of these arguments is used by itself to permit an *aguna, posekim* do utilize them in conjunction with other arguments.

As in the case of *Meḥayeh HaMeitim,* the *posekim* recognize that the world we live in is significantly more connected than that of the Talmud or any other early authority. Thus, in each generation, *posekim* wonder about the implications of this increase in communication technology. While in previous generations, lack of news may not have indicated anything, in the modern world, the silence from a husband who would presumably want to return home is meaningful. Unless we have reason to believe the husband would want to hide, we assume that he could not just become lost.

And, as we saw, in each generation, *posekim* thought that they had reached a state which represented a leap forward from that of previous authorities. Whether it was the presence of Jews around the world in the time of R. Isserlein, post offices for R. Sofer, steamboats for R. Palagi, newspapers for R. Feinstein, or cellphones and the internet for R. Yosef, each *posek* reflects the conviction that at some point, the world must reach a state at which silence and lack of connection can best be explained by death.

While none of these halakhic authorities speak about social media, I can imagine that in the next tragedy that strikes, they will make use of it. When the Facebook apps on our phones ask us whether we want to "check in" at each location, when anyone in the world can be contacted in an instant, there is even more reason to assume that someone who wants to connect would do so.[9]

9. The development of apps to help with contact tracing during Covid-19 further points to how effective modern technology can be at locating and tracking people.

Chapter 3

The Videoteleconference *Get*

Defining Direct Communication

In our chapter on *berakhot,* we saw that the *posekim* debate whether talking on the telephone or through a computer or television screen could be considered similar to "in-person" interactions. One of the most important questions that is related to this arises in another marriage issue. The writing and delivery of a *get* (bill of divorce) must be done either by the husband or his agent. To appoint an agent, the husband must directly instruct someone to write and deliver the bill of divorce to his wife. In the last 150 years, *posekim* have examined whether these instructions can be delivered by telephone or, more recently, videoteleconference. Is such communication direct or not?

For this issue, we will be drawing heavily on R. Chaim Jachter's excellent treatment of this topic in his article "The Use of a

Videoteleconference for a Get Procedure" in the *Journal of Halacha and Contemporary Society* XXVIII.[1]

The Problem

R. Jachter notes that the motivation for allowing use of videoteleconferencing for the husband to appoint the scribe and witness to write a *get* is primarily to ease the process in cases where either the husband or wife lives a great distance from a Jewish court that can supervise the proceeding. While in normal circumstances, all parties will be present in court (or at least on the husband's side), when this is not the case, halakhic authorities have offered many mechanisms to ease the process.

Tzivui HaBaal: The Husband's Instructions

The Talmud in Gittin cites a *baraita* which states that the scribe and witnesses cannot write or sign a *get* unless they are told to do so by the husband. This concept is codified as *tzivui habaal*:

> If **the scribe wrote** the bill of divorce **for her sake and the witnesses signed it for her sake** then **even though they wrote it, and they signed it, and they gave it to** the husband **and he gave it to** his wife, **the bill of divorce is void until they hear** the husband's **voice when he says to the scribe: Write** the document for the sake of my wife, **and to the witnesses: Sign** the document for the sake of my wife. (Gittin 72a)

As the Talmud explains, this means that the husband cannot tell someone to instruct others to write the *get*. This is accepted in *Shulḥan Arukh* (*EH* 120:4).

The consensus is that the appointment itself cannot be done though a third party, but the *posekim* debate whether the husband can appoint the scribe and witnesses directly, but without their being present, and then inform them through a third party. Both positions are cited by

1. The updated version has been published on YUTorah: https://www.yutorah.org/lectures/lecture.cfm/736614/rabbi-chaim-jachter/the-use-of-a-videoteleconference-for-a-get-procedure/.

the *Beit Shmuel* (*EH* 120:7), *Ḥelkat Meḥokek* (*EH* 120:12), and *Peri Ḥadash* (*EH* 120:6). R. Jachter summarizes the current approach of *posekim*:

> Almost all great Halachic authorities of the past two centuries have ruled leniently in cases where it would otherwise be impossible to obtain a Get on behalf of the wife. Generally speaking, these authorities either adopted the approach of the Maharim Mi'Brisk or ruled that a written appointment is valid if no viable alternative exists.
>
> A small minority of decisors do not accept the use of this procedure even in the most dire circumstances. These include Pri Chadash (Even Haezer 120:6) and Chazon Ish (Even Haezer 85). However, R. Eliezer Waldenburg (Tzitz Eliezer 10:43) of the Bait Din Hagadol in Yerushalayim notes that "virtually all" Batei Din in Israel permit an authorization in writing in cases of very urgent need. R. Gedalia Schwartz, the head of both the Bait Din of the Rabbinical Council of America and the Bait Din of Chicago, reports that, generally speaking, this is also the practice of Batei Din in North America. This author adds that this is especially true in a situation where it is highly doubtful that the couple's marriage was Halachically valid, such as when the couple married only in a civil ceremony.

Conceptual Background

Why must the husband directly appoint the scribe to write the *get*? Even the more lenient approach believes that the appointment must be done directly, even if it permits informing the scribe and witnesses indirectly. Several models can be suggested. First, this could be a general instance of *sheliḥut* (agency). The husband, not the scribe or the witnesses, is divorcing his wife. Thus, the creation of the *get* must be done by the husband or his agents. This position is taken by several Rishonim, such as R. Yitzchak of Dampierre (Tosafot, Gittin 9b, s.v. *af al pi*).[2]

Other Rishonim, such as Tosafot (Gittin 22b, s.v. *veha*), take the position that this is a function of *lishmah*. Throughout Gittin,[3] it emerges that a *get* must be written for its intended purpose – that it be used for

---

2. See also Tosafot, Gittin 22b, s.v. *veha,* who raise this possibility.
3. See especially the third chapter.

this man, to divorce this woman. Perhaps the requirement that the husband directly instruct the scribe and witnesses stems from this higher level of intent that is necessary to create a *get* and effectuate a divorce.

Nimukei Yosef (Bava Batra 168a, s.v. *vekhatav venatan*) suggests, even more straightforwardly, that this is the way to create a situation in which the husband is "having the *get* written."

These latter two formulations seem to point in a direction developed extensively by *mori verabbi* HaRav Aharon Lichtenstein *zt"l* – that divorce is not simply a legal procedure. Rather, the laws of *gittin* are meant to encapsulate the existential divide that it represents. Thus, the husband must be intensely and intimately involved in the process for it to work. [4]

The *Ḥazon Ish* (*EH* 85) seems to take this approach as well, arguing that we need the will of the husband, the scribe, and the witnesses to be united at one moment.

R. Moshe Feinstein (*Iggerot Moshe, EH* 1:117) raises a radically different possibility. In general, the gold standard of evidence in halakha is a pair of two valid witnesses. However, R. Feinstein suggests that it is only courts that are required to accept testimony as evidence. Thus, the scribe and witnesses must know that the husband wants to divorce his wife. However, they are under no obligation to believe anyone, even valid witnesses, as to the husband's intent. Thus, the Torah requires that they receive their instructions directly from the husband, so there can be no doubts as to whether he desires them to initiate the divorce proceedings.[5]

The question that the *posekim* contend with is what counts as direct instruction.

Written Instructions

The first question we must deal with is whether the husband can instruct the scribe and witnesses in writing. This issue begins with a mishna (Gittin 7:1, BT Gittin 67b):

4. See R. Assaf Bednarsh's article, *BeInyan Tzivui HaBaal LiKhtov et HaGet,* in which he develops this approach thoroughly: https://tinyurl.com/mtv6t6wm.
5. This approach follows the position that the scribe and the witnesses must be informed, not just appointed, directly.

> In a case where the husband **became mute, and** two people **said to him:** Shall **we write a bill of divorce for your wife, and he nodded his head** indicating his agreement, **they examine him** with various questions **three times. If he responded to** questions that have **a negative** answer: **No, and** responded **to** questions that have **a positive** answer: **Yes,** indicating his competence, **they shall write** the bill of divorce **and give** it to his wife based on the nod of his head.

In this passage, we find the first indication that the husband does not need to convey his wishes *verbally,* as we allow a mute person to divorce his wife after we have established competence.[6] We seem to require only confirmation that this is the husband's will (Tosafot, Gittin 72a, s.v. *kolo*).

From this mishna, Rav Kahana (Gittin 71a) derives that *tzivui habaal* can be done through writing even for a deaf-mute:

> **Rav Kahana says** that **Rav says:** With regard to **a deaf-mute who can express** himself **through writing,** the judges of the court may **write and give a bill of divorce to his wife** based on his written instructions. **Rav Yosef said: What is he teaching us? We** already **learned** in the mishna: In a case where the husband **became mute, and** the members of the court **said to him:** Shall **we write a bill of divorce for your wife, and he nodded his head** indicating his agreement, **they examine him** with various questions **three times. If he responded to** questions that have **a negative** answer: **No, and** responded **to** questions that have **a positive** answer: **Yes,** indicating his competence, **they shall write** the bill of divorce **and give** it to his wife based on the nod of his head.

---

6. In talmudic times, a deaf-mute was considered to lack legal competence. The status of deaf-mutes in modern times has been heavily debated. See R. J. David Bleich, *Contemporary Halachic Problems* II, 368–375, available here: https://www.sefaria.org/Contemporary_Halakhic_Problems%2C_Vol_II%2C_Part_II%2C_Chapter_XVIII_Status_of_the_Deaf_Mute_in_Jewish_Law?lang=bi.

However, the Gemara goes on to reject the position of Rav Kahana. The Rishonim debate whether the Talmud simply rejects his *application to a deaf-mute* who is considered legally incompetent or rejects *the possibility of issuing a written tzivui habaal.*

The Gemara, though, subsequently cites a *baraita* that conclusively rejects this.

Rambam (*Hilkhot Geirushin* 2:16) adopts the former approach, thus validating a written *tzivui habaal.* Many Rishonim, however, invalidate such written instructions.[7]

However, if writing is not sufficient, then why is nodding one's head in assent, which is explicitly accepted by the mishna above? The Rosh (Gittin 7:19) addresses this and contends that "nodding is better because he shows it with his body." R. Jachter cites R. Zalman Nechemia Goldberg, who interprets the view of the Rosh as follows:

> ... although writing is a bodily act, one cannot discern the writer's intention from the act of writing itself. Nodding the head is analogous to speech, on the other hand, because one can discern the intent of the husband from his bodily action alone. (Jachter, n. 4)

Thus, according to this latter group of Rishonim, we maintain that the *tzivui habaal* can only be done verbally or with a direct physical act that is legally equivalent. In *Beit Yosef* (*EH* 120) and *Shulḥan Arukh* (*EH* 120:5), R. Yosef Karo cites both views, though he indicates that he regards the stringent position to be normative. However, *Ba'er Heitev* (120:10) and *Get Pashut* (120:26) both rule that in cases of great need, one may be lenient.

Telephone

Can the appointment be done by telephone? There are two potential problems:

---

7. See Rosh, Gittin 7:19; *Ḥiddushei HaRashba,* Gittin 72a, s.v. *kolo*; Ran, Gittin 33a (Rif), s.v. *ḥeresh; Mordekhai,* Gittin 417; and *Hagahot Maimoniyot,* Gittin 2:16:200.

1. Without the physical presence of the husband, the scribe and witnesses cannot be sure of the speaker's identity.
2. As mentioned, the case of *tzivui habaal* requires a unique level of direct communication, at least according to many. Does a telephone call qualify?

Many *posekim* feel it is permitted. They note that in many areas of halakha (see Gittin 23a, for example), voice recognition counts as proof of identity. As for the second issue, they assume this is considered direct communication. R. Melech Schachter formulates the issue as follows: The command must be direct from the husband to the scribe and the witnesses, and in this case, *they hear the command from his mouth, literally!* (translation and emphasis mine). He further writes that he asked R. Moshe Feinstein and R. Joseph Soloveitchik, and they both agreed.[8]

Some authorities object simply because of evidentiary issues.[9] Others, however, take issue with R. Schachter's view cited above. They contend that speaking to someone on the telephone is *not considered direct communication.* Thus, even if we have *no doubt that the husband is on the telephone, his instructions do not count.* This is how R. Eliezer Waldenberg understands the view of R. Yitzchak Schmelkes.[10] R. Menasheh Klein (*Shu"t Mishneh Halakhot* 14:113) argues that this is the case because in all areas of halakha, we do not consider a voice transmitted through a telephone or similar media to be the person's voice.

Videoteleconference

R. Jachter writes that though no consensus has emerged regarding telephones, a *tzivui habaal* done by videoteleconference should be acceptable according to all authorities. Surprisingly, this possibility was already raised by R. Schmelkes over one hundred years before the technology was invented. In the 1860s, he raised the question of whether *tzivui habaal* could be accomplished through a telegraph, which R. Schmelkes was

8. See the article here: https://tinyurl.com/2wv2pktw.
9. See R. Jachter's article for a summary.
10. See *Shu"t Beit Yitzḥak, EH* 2:53. His position is debated by more recent authorities. See *Shu"t Tzitz Eliezer* 10:47 and *Shu"t Minḥat Asher* 2:96.

not inclined to accept. However, he added two addenda to this responsum, one about telephones as noted above, and another about videoteleconferences. R. Shlomo Brody argues that R. Schmelkes wrote this addendum as the possibility of such technology became popularized through science fiction. He notes that R. Schmelkes referred to this technology as a "telephone or *teletascope* machine in which one can also see the speaker's image through a photograph" and noted that there would be more room to allow *tzivui habaal* with such technology. The word "*teletascope*," he contends, is a

> Yiddish version of the word "telectroscope" (or "telephonoscope") that was regularly used then by both scientists and science-fiction writers in America and Europe to depict how the telephone could evolve. This April 3, 1898, headline from *The New York Times*, for example, depicted the novel ideas of the Polish inventor Jan Szczepanik.
>
> That year, Mark Twain would write about Szczepanik in his fictional short story, "From the 'London Times,' 1904." He depicted the telectroscope as connecting with "the telephonic systems of the whole world. The improved 'limitless-distance' telephone was presently introduced and the daily doings of the globe made visible to everybody, and audibly discussable too, by witnesses separated by any number of leagues." These predictions would come true, of course, but not by 1904. In any case, Schmelkes was apparently aware of these discussions and therefore added that should this concoction come to fruition, Jewish law could integrate its use for certain legal purposes.[11]

Building on R. Schmelkes, R. Jachter argues that this will solve the potential evidence problems raised above (though perhaps not entirely). More importantly, he cites R. Zalman Nechemia Goldberg as ruling that this will solve the "direct communication" issue as well:

---

11. https://www.tabletmag.com/sections/belief/articles/history-of-zoom-dilemma.

> R. Goldberg also points out that the *Ḥazon Ish* and R. Moshe Feinstein interpret the Ramban's position very differently than R. Schmelkes. The *Ḥazon Ish* (*EH* 85) writes that the Ramban requires "that the will of the husband and the will of the scribe and witnesses should be unified in one moment, and that the husband should be aware of the will of the scribe, and the scribe should be aware of the will of the husband, and it all should occur simultaneously." This requirement seems to be fulfilled if a husband appoints the scribe and witnesses via videoteleconference.
>
> He further notes that according to R. Feinstein, who thinks that the entire issue of *tzivui habaal* is based on the scribe's not needing to believe the witnesses, this should surely be fine.

In an addendum published in 5761, R. Jachter writes as follows:

> Since the time I first published my proposal regarding the use of videoteleconferencing for a Get, Poskim have had a mixed reaction. R. Zalman Nechemiah Goldberg, R. Hershel Schachter, and R. Mordechai Willig support the idea, whereas R. Yosef Shalom Elyashiv, R. J. David Bleich, and R. Elazar Meir Teitz reject the proposal. Accordingly, this proposal cannot be implemented as no rabbinical consensus has emerged regarding this issue. Perhaps it can be relied upon in a situation where it is highly doubtful whether a Get is necessary, such as when the couple was married only in a civil ceremony and never had a Chuppah. Those who rule strictly are concerned that the videoteleconference appointment is unacceptable according to the Ramban and still has potential for fraud.

R. Shlomo Weissman told this author that the position of the Beth Din of America is to avoid this if possible, but in cases of *igun,* they would accept it. R. Michoel Zylberman told this author that the Beth Din of America will usually use a combination of a telephone call and an ad hoc *beit din.*

Note that for reasons that are beyond the scope of this book, often courts will combine methods, requiring letters plus telephone calls, or similar arrangements.

Connecting This to the World of *Berakhot*

When we studied the laws of *Sheheḥeyanu* and *Meḥayeh HaMeitim,* we saw various positions as to which interactions are intimate enough to warrant blessings or to prevent the build-up of emotion to require a blessing upon reuniting in person. In the issue of *mayim she'ein lahem sof,* similar principles can be found in the world of *ishut.*

We saw that R. Ovadia Yosef claims that telephone conversations or communication across screens does not count, because "the excitement and emotional animation that one gets when he sees his friend face-to-face is with much greater power and strength." On the other hand, we saw that R. Yaakov Toledano feels such connection can be created when communicating through screens.

In this context, the unique requirements of *tzivui habaal* demand, according to the *Ḥazon Ish,* following the view of the Ramban, "that the will of the husband and the will of the scribe and witnesses should be unified in one moment, and that the husband should be aware of the will of the scribe, and the scribe should be aware of the will of the husband, and it all should occur simultaneously." While this is not an emotional claim, it does highlight the need for true human interaction. Indeed, in this context, we also saw a dispute as to whether telephone or video conversations could rise to that level.

Of course, one could distinguish in one of two directions. One could argue that formally, neither telephones nor videoteleconferences can create the *emotional response* of an in-person interaction, but they can be formally sufficient to create the meeting of the minds needed for *tzivui habaal.* On the flipside, one could argue that while there is no true meeting of the minds, friendly interactions can be as meaningful even without physical presence. All of this sidesteps the issues of evidence unique to *ishut.*

Nevertheless, it remains true that the same kinds of questions as to the nature of human interactions are raised in both areas of halakha, and thus a full understanding of the halakhic perspective on communication technology requires a thorough analysis of both.

As for the evidentiary concerns, this is also something we have seen before. In general, *posekim* are quicker to consider that laws may be changed if they are information-based. While the *posekim* debate whether voice recognition or even seeing someone in a videoteleconference may be trusted or is suspect due to concerns of falsification, in principle, they are open to the idea that technology might solve this issue. This again parallels the wider consensus that the laws of *Meḥayeh HaMeitim* have changed with the advent of communication technology, as well as the discussion we saw concerning *mayim she'ein lahem sof.*

The last few chapters should bolster our contention in the introduction to this book: to assess the ways in which communication technology has affected or can affect halakha, it is important to start by asking about the ways in which this technology has affected our lives. From there, we can look for the areas of halakha that are impacted by these changes, and we will find the implications in widely varying areas of law.

Chapter 4

"Visiting" the Sick and Comforting the Mourner

The question of the extent to which virtual relationships are the equivalent of in-person ones appears in a vivid way regarding the commandment to visit the sick, and in fact, this is one of the earliest cases in which halakhic authorities examined the question of whether videoconferencing counts for mitzva performance, building on our previous discussion in the case of *gittin*. A similar question is raised with regard to comforting mourners. We will not explore the topic exhaustively, but focus on the relevance for our issue.[1]

Background

On the one hand, visiting the sick is part of the general obligations of kindness under the rubric of *ve'ahavta lere'akha kamokha*, the dictate to love your fellow as yourself:

1. For a full analysis of the mitzva, see R. Daniel Feldman, *Divine Footsteps: Chesed and the Jewish Soul* (Yeshiva University Press, 2008), ch. 2.

> It is a rabbinic positive precept to visit the sick, comfort the mourners, escort the dead, dower the bride, accompany the [departing] guests – as well as to cheer the bride and the groom, and to assist them in whatever they need. Even though all these precepts are of rabbinic origin, they are implied in the biblical verse: "You shall love your neighbor as yourself" (Lev. 19:18); that is, whatever you would have others do to you, do to your brothers in Torah and precepts. (Rambam, *Hilkhot Avel* 14:1)

While some understand the Rambam to mean that visiting the sick is rabbinic in origin,[2] it seems more likely that this means it is a rabbinic expression/formalization of a biblical principle.[3]

It is also part of the correlated category of *vehalakhta biderakhav,* walking in the ways of God, *imitatio dei.* The Talmud (Sota 14a) notes that just as God clothed the naked, as He did with Adam and Ḥava in the Garden of Eden, people should clothe the naked; just as God visited Avraham when he was sick after his circumcision (Gen. 18:1), so too should people visit the sick; just as God comforted Yitzḥak after Avraham passed away, people should comfort mourners.

On the other hand, others count it as an independent mitzva. For example, the *Sefer Mitzvot Katan* (*Semak* 46), counts *gemilut ḥasadim,* performing acts of kindness as mitzva 46, while mitzva 47 is visiting the sick. R. Elazar of Metz (*Yere'im* 220) counts a separate mitzva to comfort mourners and visit the sick.

The Talmud does provide an independent source for visiting the sick, although not in imperative form, but rather by implication:

> **Reish Lakish said: From where** is there **an allusion from the Torah to visiting the ill?** It is **as it is stated: "If these men die the common death of all men, and** be visited after **the visitation of all**

2. See *Halikhot Bein Adam LaḤaveiro, Niḥum Aveilim* 1, n. 4.
3. See, for example, R. Joseph B. Soloveitchik, *Shiurim LeZecher Abba Mari z"l, Kibbud VeOneg Shabbat,* 75, and "Tzedaka: Brotherhood and Fellowship," in *Halakhic Morality* (Maggid, 2017), 123–180. This issue is addressed from several angles throughout the chapter.

> **men,** then the Lord has not sent me" (Num. 16:29). The Gemara asks: **From where** in this verse **may** visiting the ill **be inferred? Rava said** that this is what Moshe is saying: **If these men,** the congregation of Koraḥ, **die the common death of all men, who become ill, and are confined to their beds, and people come to visit them;** if that happens to them, **what do the people say?** They say: **The Lord has not sent me for this** task. (Nedarim 39b)

Torah Temima (Num. 16:29) understands that the Talmud is using this verse to prove that visiting the sick is part of the natural way the world works. Others, however, note that this verse proves that visiting the sick is greater than a mere commandment, as it was practiced by the descendants of Avraham even before the Torah was given.[4]

Elsewhere, the Talmud (Bava Metzia 30b) sees this as part of the advice that Yitro offered to his son-in-law, Moshe, identifying his phrase "they shall walk" to refer to visiting the ill. The Talmud then asks:

> **That is** a detail of **acts of kindness;** why does the *baraita* list it separately? The Gemara answers: The reference to visiting the ill is **necessary only for the contemporary of** the ill person, **as the Master said:** When **one who is a contemporary** of an ill person visits him, he **takes one-sixtieth of his illness.** Since visiting an ill contemporary involves contracting a bit of his illness, a special derivation is necessary to teach that **even so, he is required to go** and visit **him.** (Bava Metzia 30b)

Purpose of the Commandment

There are several purposes identified for this mitzva:

1. Provide emotional support for the sick person.[5] Included in this seems to be conversation.[6]

4. R. Yitzchak Zev Yadler, *Tiferet Tziyon,* Nedarim, 191–192.
5. See, for example, *Ramban, Torat HaAdam, Shaar HaMiḥush.*
6. See R. Shimon ben Tzemach Duran, *Mitzvat Aseh 25, Zohar HaRakia, Mitzvot Aseh HaTeluyot BaFeh* 47.

2. Provide physical aid to the sick person, both during the visit and after.[7] *Arukh HaShulḥan* (*YD* 335:3) identifies this as the primary reason for visiting, on the basis of the following story from the Talmud:

> **Rabbi Akiva entered to visit him** and instructed his students to care for him. **And since they swept and sprinkled water on the** dirt **floor before** the sick student, **he recovered.** The student **said to** Rabbi Akiva: **My teacher, you revived me. Rabbi Akiva went out and taught:** With regard to **anyone who does not visit the ill, it is as though he is spilling blood,** as it could be that the sick person has no one to care for him. If there are no visitors, no one will know his situation and therefore no one will come to his aid. (Nedarim 40a)

3. Pray for the sick person. Ramban (*Torat HaAdam*) writes that without prayer one fails to fulfill this commandment, and this is cited by *Tur* (*YD* 335) and Rama (ibid., 4).[8]

These rationales shape the laws themselves. For example, the Talmud (Nedarim 40a) rules that one should not visit the sick during the first three hours of the day, though this may only be an ideal when possible.[9] *Shulḥan Arukh* (*YD* 335:4) understands this to be a function of the centrality of prayer, arguing that in the morning people often feel better, and thus seeing the sick person then will not cause the visitor to pray as much as necessary. Others (such as Rambam, *Hilkhot Avel* 14:5), on the other hand, believe that this is when the sick is being tended to and visits may be practically detrimental rather than helpful. Other practical limitations include avoiding visiting those suffering from gastrointestinal

---

7. See summary in *Shulḥan Arukh*, *YD* 335.
8. Based on Ramban and *Tur*.
9. *Arukh HaShulḥan*, *YD* 335:8; *Ahavat Ḥesed* 3:3. See also *Responsa Salmat Ḥayim*, *YD* 185, who argues that when there are hospital visiting hours established for the good of the patients; that slot becomes the new ideal time.

disorders to avoid embarrassment to the patient, or those suffering from diseases that make conversation difficult.[10]

Those who focus on the emotional elements may rule that there is no mitzva to visiting an infant who does not appreciate the visit. On the other hand, the other elements are present, and thus the mitzva may be fulfilled.[11] (There may also be value in providing comfort to the parents.[12]) Noting the centrality of conversation to the visit, R. Chaim Yosef David Azulai argues that one should try to visit when no one else will be there and the patient would otherwise be alone.[13]

Phone call

Does one fulfill the mitzva by calling or through FaceTime or any other videoconference technology?

Some argue that while valuable, it does not fulfill the formal mitzva as one does not "visit." This is the position of R. Asher Weiss (*Minḥat Asher, Bereshit* 20). However, during the Covid-19 pandemic, he did encourage using this method rather than risk getting sick, implying there is a partial fulfillment of the mitzva.[14] Others note that the Talmud derives the mitzva from the word *yelkhu,* "they shall walk," implying that physical presence is necessary.[15]

Many, however, rule that it depends on the rationale. R. Yaakov Breisch[16] and R. Yaakov Haim Sofer[17] are worried that one will not be able to help the patient over the phone. R. Yitzchak Hutner, on the other hand, rules precisely the opposite, arguing that one can ensure that needs of the patient will be "looked into" (from the word *bikkur*), even over the phone, and thus rules that one does fulfill the mitzva.[18]

10. Nedarim 41a; *Shulḥan Arukh, YD* 335:8.
11. See *Responsa Rivevot Efrayim* 8:291, *VeEin Lamo Mikhshol* 6, 212, *Mitzvat Bikkur Ḥolim* 195.
12. *Respona Avnei Yashfei* 1:230.
13. *Yosef Ometz,* section 2, *Perek Bikkur Ḥolim.*
14. *Heviani Ḥadarav* (Makhon Hotzaat Sefarim Tzuf, 2020), 68. See, however, R. Mordechai Gross (ibid.), 319.
15. See *Responsa Mahari Shteig* 294 and *Responsa Avnei Ḥoshen* 3:497 citing R. Y. S. Elyashiv.
16. *Responsa Ḥelkat Yaakov, YD* 188.
17. *Zera Ḥayim* 2.
18. *Paḥad Yitzḥak, Iggerot UKetavim* 33.

R. Yisrael David Harfenes is concerned that without physical presence, the visitor will not be inspired to pray.[19] R. Moshe Feinstein (*Responsa Iggerot Moshe* 1, *YD* 223) argues that the primary mitzva is prayer and this can be fulfilled, though as there are other aspects to the mitzva, it will not be a complete mitzva. R. Ovadia Yosef (*Responsa Yeḥaveh Daat* 3:83) concurs, though noting that even the prayer is more powerful in the presence of the sick person. R. Eliezer Waldenberg argues similarly, noting that one can provide emotional support and prayer even when "visiting over the phone."

R. Yitzchak Weiss (*Responsa Minḥat Yitzḥak* 2:84) was the first to address the question of videoconferencing, or as he writes it, "television." He builds on the analysis regarding telephones, as well as R. Yitzchak Schmelkes's position regarding the instruction of a husband for the writing of a *get.* He argues that even with a videoconference, there are things that can be missed and one will be unable to know what the sick person truly needs. However, if one visits in person once, subsequent visits can be done by video teleconference. R. Shlomo Brody notes that this responsum was less theoretical than that of R. Schmelkes, but equally weighs in on what can and cannot be accomplished through communication technology:

> [I]n contrast to the case of Schmelkes, Weiss' theoretical discussion materialized a couple of weeks later. On Aug. 23, 1956, AT&T presented a primitive videophone system at a meeting of the Institute of Radio Engineers, previewing what would become the "picturephone" that was featured at the 1964 World Fair in New York.
>
> While brief and inchoate, the deliberations of Schmelkes and Weiss remain enlightening because they raise the immediate societal dilemmas presented by videotelephony. We can see people through a webcam but still miss their presence. Perhaps visual contact is sufficient for legal declarations before a court, or even to facilitate kashrut supervision by a rabbi in Brooklyn for a production plant in Thailand or a farm in Idaho. Yet it is not

19. *Responsa VaYevarekh David* 1, *YD* 106 in footnote.

> ideal when it comes to comforting the bereaved, and entirely inadequate for creating a community of worshippers that brings God's presence into a sanctified place. Videotelephony provides a lot of convenient services and ad hoc solutions for many problems. Yet if there is one good thing that the coronavirus experience may have taught us, it's that a "virtual community" is no replacement for a real community. As Schmelkes and Weiss noted long before Zoom and Skype became household names, seeing each other is not the same as being with one another.[20]

A similar question is raised as to whether one can fulfill the mitzva by writing a letter. R. Yonatan Shteif (*Responsa Mahari Shteif* 294) assumes that the question depends on whether writing is legally considered speech. R. Daniel Feldman summarizes the problem with this line of thinking:

> As R. Y.D. Harfenes notes, this premise is difficult to understand as *bikur cholim* is not a *mitzvah* that by definition requires speech. However, one might indeed question the effectiveness of a letter in that it does not provide an opportunity for immediate feedback from the patient (a concern reduced, but not eliminated, with the use of e-mail). Thus it would seem that a letter is similar to a phone call in that it does not accomplish all of the goals of a personal visit, although a letter would seem to accomplish less than a phone call would.[21]

Others raise the question of sending a messenger. R. Moshe Binyamin Tomashoff (*Responsa Avnei Shoham* 4:56) notes that practically, this may not work, as the messenger will be performing the mitzva for himself, not for the person who sent him. R. Yaakov Traube (*Responsa Avnei Yaakov* 217) makes a related point. He notes that as the goal of *bikkur ḥolim* is to help the patient, practically and emotionally, the question is really whether this is accomplished through a messenger or not. He notes that

20. https://www.tabletmag.com/sections/belief/articles/history-of-zoom-dilemma.
21. *Divine Footsteps,* 69–70.

in general, a single emissary can perform a mitzva for a group of people. However, in the case of visiting the sick, the experience of having ten people visit the sick person or having ten people send a single emissary is distinct. This makes it difficult to rule that one can send a messenger. R. Avraham Binyamin Sofer (*Derashot Ketav Sofer,* 139) argues that the visitor is supposed to be moved to repent by seeing the sick person, and this cannot be accomplished by a messenger.[22]

Niḥum Aveilim

As with visiting the sick, comforting mourners is an expression of the biblical values of *ḥesed*[23] and *imitatio dei,* though it may also have stand-alone value. Rambam (*Hilkhot Avel* 14:1) argues that it is one of the rabbinic mitzvot that expresses these larger biblical values. Some identify it as a separate biblical mitzva, such as *Yere'im* (219) who identifies a biblical mitzva to visit the sick and comfort mourners.[24]

Despite the conceptual connection between visiting the sick and comforting mourners, the latter has unique elements. For example, the Rambam writes:

> It appears to me that comforting mourners takes precedence over visiting the sick. For comforting mourners is an expression of kindness to the living and the dead. (*Hilkhot Avel* 14:7)[25]

The exact kindness for the dead is unclear. R. Daniel Feldman[26] suggests that the soul itself receives comfort, as according to the Talmud, the soul mourns its own death for the first week:

---

22. See discussion by Feldman, 71, and *Natan Piryo,* Nedarim, 92.
23. See, for example, Rabbenu Yona, Berakhot 11b.
24. See also *Ahavat Ḥesed* 3:3:5 and *Biur Halakha, OḤ* 72:4.
25. See, however, *Mishnat Yaavetz, YD* 37 regarding *niḥum aveilim* on Yom Tov, when he claims that the mourning is finished from the vantage point of the mourners, but there is still value from the perspective of the deceased. However, as in that case there is only one element to the mitzva, visiting the sick takes precedence even for the Rambam.
26. *Divine Footsteps,* ch. 3, p. 80.

> **Rav Ḥisda said: A person's soul mourns for him** during **all seven days** of mourning following his death, **as it is stated: "And his soul mourns over him,"** and **it is** also **written: "And he mourned his father seven days"** (Gen. 50:10). (Shabbat 152a)

This seems to emerge from the immediately following passage:

> **Rav Yehuda said:** In the case of **a deceased person who has no comforters,** i.e., he has nobody to mourn for him, **ten people should go and sit in his place** and accept condolences. The Gemara relates the story of **a certain person who died in Rav Yehuda's neighborhood** and **who did not have** any **comforters,** i.e., mourners; **every day** of the seven-day mourning period, **Rav Yehuda would take ten** people **and** they would **sit in his place,** in the house of the deceased. **After seven days** had passed the deceased **appeared** to **Rav Yehuda in his dream and said to him: Put your mind to rest, for you have put my mind to rest.** (Ibid., 152b)[27]

As Maharal notes, if the soul is mourning, then it receives comfort when people come to console the ten people who are the "mourners." Meiri (Shabbat 152a) assumes that comforting the mourners provides honor to the deceased, and presumably this is true in all cases, not just the unique situation where there are no relatives. R. Aharon Yehuda Grossman[28]

---

27. While Rambam (*Hilkhot Avel* 13:4) accepts as law that ten people need to sit for the week as mourners, Raavad challenges it as having no source. It is not clear exactly what he rejects. The *Migdal Oz* implies that the Raavad was simply mistaken, as the Gemara is clear that in the absence of family, ten people mourn in the home of the deceased. Radbaz suggests that the Rambam implies that the ten people need to establish themselves as consistent mourners for the entire week, and the Raavad rejected this implication, arguing that you only need them to sit there once in the morning and once in the evening. Radbaz thinks that the Rambam may agree with that, regardless of whether the Raavad understood him that way. The *Leḥem Mishneh* argues that the ten people do not accept condolences as mourners, but merely go to the home of the deceased, and it was the implication that they accept condolences that was rejected by Raavad.
28. *VeDarashta VeḤakarta al HaTorah,* vol. 4, 149.

cites the *Pnei Menaḥem* of Ger, suggesting that while a dead person can no longer perform mitzvot, he can be rewarded for being the cause of mitzvot, such as the comforting of mourners, and this is the kindness for the dead.

Based on this dual nature to the mitzva, R. Moshe Feinstein (*Responsa Iggerot Moshe, OḤ* 4:40:11) argues that: 1) One cannot fulfill the aspect for the dead from afar. 2) One can provide partial, though not complete, comfort to the living, and thus one fulfills that mitzva but not in its ideal form. This is accepted by many authorities (see *Ḥazon Ovadya Niḥum Aveilim* 1:1 for a summary). R. Yitzchak Hutner (*Paḥad Yitzḥak, Mikhtavim* 33) went farther, arguing that while *bikkur ḥolim* could be fulfilled at some level via telephone, comforting mourners requires a certain structure (as proved by the detailed instructions as to where people stand/sit during the mourning process) that necessarily entails physical presence. Without that, one does not fulfill the mitzva at all.

Others distinguish between visiting the sick and comforting mourners for more technical reasons. R. Harfenes (*Responsa Sho'alin VeDorshin* 5:79:4) argues that as the mourner must open the conversation, calling may be problematic because the comforter is opening the visit. However, this only makes it less than ideal, but does not negate its value when there is no other option.[29] Others simply write that one should wait for the mourner to speak first.[30]

Some argue that one can even fulfill the mitzva by writing a letter. R. Moshe Sternbuch (*Responsa Teshuvot VeHanhagot* 2:587) cited R. Yitzchak Zev HaLevi Soloveitchik (the Brisker Rav) as writing that one can fulfill this mitzva this way. R. Sternbuch suggests, parallel to R. Feinstein above, that one cannot accomplish the aspect that relates to the deceased, as this requires physical presence, and even for the living mourners this is a non-ideal way of accomplishing the mitzva and should only be used when visiting in person is not possible. R. Soloveitchik is further quoted as saying that this is legitimate because in this case, there is no specific commandment to *speak,* and thus the question of whether

29. See *Responsa Yabia Omer* 10, *YD* 48.

30. See Feldman, 104.

writing or speaking are legally equivalent is irrelevant. The goal is to comfort the mourner. This is cited by R. Gavriel Zinner (*Nitei Gavriel Aveilut* v. 1. 25:11) and R. Ovadia Yosef (*Ḥazon Ovadya Aveilut* 1:1) as well. The Lubavitcher Rebbe is cited as permitting any of these methods, as this is not considered a mitzva that must be done with one's body.[31]

R. Feldman notes that several authorities prefer letters to phone calls:

> Assuming that one is unable to come in person and is seeking an alternate method of *nichum aveilim*, R. Yitzchak Shmuel Schechter suggests a distinction between a phone call and a letter. A conversation on the phone may be more effective when the one consoling is an actual friend or acquaintance of the mourner, and the give-and-take of the conversation will allow the caller to gauge the mourner's mindset and adjust his efforts appropriately. If the one consoling is a prominent personality who is interested primarily in showing honor to the deceased, this may be done more effectively with a letter, which can be crafted with the inclusion of words of Torah, and which the bereaved can keep as testimonial.[32]

He notes that some generalize and prefer letters to phone calls for this reason.

(Although the mourner is supposed to open the conversation, some argue that by opening the letter, the mourner, rather than the writer, is considered to have initiated the interaction.[33])

Similarly, some rule that one can fulfil this mitzva even by sending a messenger.[34]

As R. Tzvi Reisman (*Ratz KaTzvi* 2:4) notes, the question in both *bikkur ḥolim* and *niḥum aveilim* is whether the mitzva requires presence of *gufo,* one's body, oneself. As we have seen in the case of *berakhot* and

31. *Noam* 24: 227–228.
32. *Divine Footsteps,* 104–105, with notes 115–116.
33. See *Shaarei Halakha UMinhag,* vol. 3, 367, cited in *Halikhot Bein Adam LaḤaveiro, Niḥum Aveilim,* n. 12.
34. See *Nitei Gavriel Aveilut,* ibid., citing *Shaarei Halakha UMinhag, YD* 137.

tzivui habaal, while at some level these technologies can accomplish things in a way similar to physical interaction, there are many authorities who assume that physical presence and connection can never be truly replaced by these technologies. On the other hand, some rule that it is sufficient for some scenarios and not others. As R. Brody noted above, the fact that R. Yitzchak Weiss directly draws his analysis for the performance of these mitzvot from the case of *tzivui habaal* highlights how these issues are not endemic to the local laws, but rather speak to much broader questions as to how relationships change, or do not, due to communication technologies. To this end, we now turn to *teshuva* and apologies.

Chapter 5

Teshuva and Social Media

Facebook Apologies

The Facebook Apology on Erev Yom Kippur

For years I was bothered (and still mostly am) by the insincerity of apologies offered on Erev Yom Kippur. People go over to their friends, whom they likely have not egregiously offended, and ask them for *meḥila* (forgiveness). Perhaps they wait for a formal "I am *moḥel* (forgiving) you," and don't suffice with a "Don't worry about it" or a nod of the head and wave of the hand.

As pro forma as this has always felt to me, I have been even more bothered by the mass-text apology or the generic request for forgiveness on Facebook. The use of social media to quickly reach all those whom one might have slighted feels pointless at best; at worse, it devalues the notion of *teshuva*.

Moreover, those whom we have hurt the most are those who are least likely to be our friends on Facebook or to receive our WhatsApps; they are probably no longer in contact with us on social media. As the High Holy Days are about heartfelt change, this type of activity does not seem to fit the bill.

However, while this is still my general feeling, I have found some value in these actions. To explain, in halakhic language, why these apologies are incomplete but may nevertheless add to the experience of Yom Kippur, we must turn to the nature of the requirement to ask for forgiveness.

Obligation to Appease

The Mishna in Yoma (8:5–6) outlines the requirements for achieving full atonement, explaining which approaches to *teshuva* are critically flawed:

> **Repentance** itself **atones for minor transgressions, for** both **positive** mitzvot **and negative** mitzvot. **And** repentance places punishment **for severe** transgressions **in abeyance until Yom Kippur comes and** completely **atones** for the transgression. With regard to **one who says: I will sin and** then **I will repent, I will sin and I will repent,** Heaven **does not provide him the opportunity to repent,** and he will remain a sinner all his days. With regard to one who says: **I will sin and Yom Kippur** will **atone** for my sins, **Yom Kippur does not atone** for his sins. Furthermore, for **transgressions between a person and God, Yom Kippur atones;** however, for **transgressions between a person and another, Yom Kippur does not atone until he appeases** the **other** person.

As the Rambam codifies in chapter 2 of *Hilkhot Teshuva,* repentance requires abandoning and regretting the sin, committing to avoid the sin in the future, and confessing the sin. These elements suffice to atone for "regular" sins between man and God. As the Mishna and Talmud detail, more severe sins may require Yom Kippur, suffering, and even death to achieve full expiation.

However, even if one later goes through this process, one may undermine the whole endeavor by planning to sin and repent, thus making *teshuva* itself the justification for sin.

In this context, the Mishna adds that merely repenting for interpersonal sins without gaining forgiveness from the person who was wronged is ineffective.

There is a celebrated dispute among the commentaries as to whether or not failing to appease one's victim prevents the perpetrator's being forgiven for other sins or at least the man-God component of all interpersonal mitzvot.

The final mishna in Yoma records:

> Similarly, **Rabbi Elazar ben Azarya taught** that point from the verse: **"From all your sins you shall be cleansed before the Lord"** (Lev. 16:30). For **transgressions between a person and God, Yom Kippur atones;** however, for **transgressions between a person and another, Yom Kippur does not atone until he appeases** the **other** person. In conclusion, **Rabbi Akiva said: How fortunate are you, Israel; before Whom are you purified, and Who purifies you?** It is **your Father in Heaven, as it is stated: "And I will sprinkle purifying water upon you, and you shall be purified"** (Ezek. 36:25). **And it says: "The ritual bath of Israel is God"** (Jer. 17:13). **Just as a ritual bath purifies the impure, so too, the Holy One, Blessed be He, purifies Israel.** (Yoma 8:9)

R. Yoshiya ben Yosef Pinto (Rif on *Ein Yaakov*) contends that according to Rabbi Elazar ben Azarya, if the sinner does not receive forgiveness from the victim, the perpetrator is not forgiven for *any of his or her sins against God,* deriving this from the phrase "from *all* your sins." Many *posekim* follow this position. However, as R. Ovadia Yosef notes, R. Pinto himself thinks that Rabbi Akiva disagrees with this conclusion, ruling that one may be forgiven for the sins between man and God even without achieving atonement for interpersonal offenses. R. Pinto rules in accordance with this latter position, though he is often misquoted as ruling in accordance with his interpretation of Rabbi Elazar ben Azarya, and many rule accordingly. (For a summary of both sides, see *Responsa Yeḥaveh Daat* 5:44.)

Others, such as *Peri Ḥadash* (*OḤ* 606:1) citing R. Shmuel Ghermezian, argue that at the very least, without appeasing the victim of a crime, the perpetrator will not be forgiven for the aspect of that interpersonal sin that is between man and God.

Regardless of the exact consequences of not gaining this appeasement, it is clear that full atonement for interpersonal sins requires gaining forgiveness from one's fellow.

Is It About Apologizing or Being Forgiven?

There are two ways of conceptualizing this requirement:

1. Apologizing is merely a means to achieving the forgiveness of the victim.
2. The process of apologizing is intrinsically important. This could be because the act of apologizing itself rebuilds the relationship, or because the act is embarrassing and thus forces the sinner to humble himself or herself. It could also be that the embarrassment itself is a mild form of suffering that aids in atonement.

The most obvious practical difference would be whether one needs to apologize if the victim has forgiven the crime without the apology.[1] The less obvious difference might be whether the apology must be delivered directly or may be delivered in ways that avoid face-to-face contact.

In the Bavli

We will begin with the two central passages in the Talmud that the commentaries bring to bear on this discussion. The first is from the Bavli (Yoma 87a):

> **Rabbi Yitzḥak said: One who angers his friend, even** only verbally, **must appease him, as it is stated: "My son, if you have become a guarantor for your neighbor, if you have struck your hands for a stranger, you are snared by the words of your mouth…. Do this now, my son, and deliver yourself, seeing you have come into the hand of your neighbor. Go, humble yourself [*hitrapes*] and urge [*rehav*] your neighbor"** (Prov. 6:1–3). This should be understood as follows: **If you have money** that you owe him, **open the palm of [*hater pisat*]** your **hand to** your neighbor and pay the money that you owe; **and if not,** if you have sinned against him verbally, **increase [*harbe*] friends for him,** i.e., send many people as your messengers to ask him for forgiveness.

In this passage, the Gemara raises the possibility of having intermediaries involved in achieving forgiveness. However, it is not clear whether these intermediaries are meant to set the groundwork for the personal apology,

1. See, for example, *Responsa Divrei Yatziv, OḤ* 258.

making it more likely that the apology will be accepted, or to take the place of the sinner who offers a personal apology. Alternatively, they may be used only as a last resort if one fails to achieve appeasement alone. The understanding that the intermediaries are not issuing the apology is supported by the following statement, in which Rav Ḥisda encourages the sinner, if necessary, to apologize in the presence of three rows of three people:

> **Rav Ḥisda said: And one must appease the** one he has insulted **with three rows of three people, as it is stated: "He comes [*yashor*] before men, and says: I have sinned, and perverted that which was right, and it profited me not"** (Job 33:27). Rav Ḥisda interprets the word *yashor* as related to the word *shura*, row. The verse mentions sin three times: I have sinned, and perverted, and it profited me not. This implies that one should make three rows before the person from whom he is asking forgiveness.

This seems to indicate that the outsiders are part of the process, but they do not replace the need for a personal apology; however, the Gemara does not weigh in on whether they can set the groundwork for the sinner to express his or her contrition. The Gemara then notes that if after this effort the injured party does not forgive the sinner, the sinner need not continue to seek forgiveness (unless the victim is the sinner's teacher):

> **Rabbi Yosei bar Ḥanina said: Anyone who asks forgiveness of his friend should not ask more than three times, as it is stated: "Please, please forgive** the transgression of your brothers and their sin, for they did evil to you. **And now, please** forgive" (Gen. 50:17). The verse uses the word "please" three times, which shows that one need not ask more than three times, after which the insulted friend must be appeased and forgive.

The idea that the outsiders are part of the process of apologizing primarily undertaken by the sinner himself or herself is further supported by the final law in this series of statements, which dictates that if the wronged party passes away before the sinner appeases the victim, the sinner must bring an audience of ten to the grave to ask for forgiveness.

> **And if** the insulted friend **dies** before he can be appeased, **one brings ten people, and stands them at the grave** of the insulted friend, **and says** in front of them: **I have sinned against the Lord, the God of Israel, and against so-and-so whom I wounded.**

In the Yerushalmi

The second passage is found in the Yerushalmi (Yoma 8:7):

> Shmuel says that one who has sinned against his friend must say to him, "I have wronged you." If he accepts, good. If not, [the sinner] must bring ten people to appease him in front of them....
>
> And if he died, he must go to his grave.

Here, the simple reading of the passage again assumes that the primary actor in the apology must be the sinner himself, directly.

Two commentaries on this passage of the Yerushalmi debate whether this is, in fact, the case. The *Ein Yaakov* argues that it is:

> From here it seems that it is a mistaken custom that many in our days observe, that if someone sins against another and provokes him with words, an intermediary peacemaker enters between them and speaks with the offended one to mollify him to accept the appeasement of the offender. After this introduction, the offender comes to ask for forgiveness from him.
>
> This is not intent of Shmuel. Rather, the offender should go himself before the offended and say, "I have wronged you." If he does not accept, then he may bring people with him to entreat his favor in front of them to forgive him. A precise reading of Shmuel's language indicates this, as the corresponding line indicates: "And if he died, he must go to his grave"....
>
> Rather the offender must go himself to appease the offended, and this embarrassment and degradation will atone for him for sinning against his friend.

The *Ein Yaakov* argues that it is the *process* of asking for forgiveness that is necessary for atonement. Thus, one cannot save face by sending a middleman to ask for forgiveness, which removes the awkwardness. One could suggest that this is why one who must ask for forgiveness after the death of the wronged party must bring ten people, so that the admission of wrongdoing will be public and entail similar humiliation.

One could make a parallel argument and claim that the issue is not embarrassment per se, but the humbling of the sinner that is critical. This would be bolstered by the verses from Proverbs that are cited by the Bavli, which emphasize the importance of humbling oneself.

The position of the *Ein Yaakov* is accepted by the *Baḥ* (*OḤ* 606), *Sheyarei Knesset HaGedola* (*Tur, OḤ* 606), *Matei Moshe* (808), R. Ovadia Yosef (*Yeḥaveh Daat* 5:44), and others.

On the other hand, *Yefei Mareh* argues in his comments on the above *Ein Yaakov*:

> I have found nothing necessitating that which he says, that the offender must go himself; in the end he goes to appease him, so what difference does it make? Either way, the victim is mollified. And even if the offended were to be appeased without the offender ever going to him at all, that would be fine. What need is there for embarrassment and degradation to atone for him, once the offended has forgiven him anyway? For it depends on [the victim].

Yefei Mareh rejects not only the need for the sinner to apologize in person first; rather, he negates the fundamental need for an apolgy. It is merely a means to achieve the forgiveness of the offended party – which theoretically could happen due to the offended's good nature, an intermediary, or other reasons. Presumably, attitudes like this explain the custom of forgiving others (whether or not they have asked for forgiveness) nightly before going to sleep, or as part of *Tefillat Zaka* before the start of Yom Kippur. (See *Peri Ḥadash, OḤ* 606, who agrees.)

This position is supported by *Avot DeRabbi Natan* (ch. 12), which describes how Aharon HaKohen would arrange to make peace between people in a feud. However, based on this, one might suggest that third parties could set the groundwork for a personal apology, constructing a position between those of *Yefei Mareh* and *Ein Yaakov* – the sinner need not apologize without any help, but must still humble himself or herself enough to face the victim at some point in the process.

There are some *posekim* who accept intermediate positions. One example is the view that it is best to go in person, presumably for the reasons outlined above, but if this is too hard or will not be effective, one may send a third party, especially if the third party is an important person whose presence will dignify the wronged party. This, for example, is the position of the *Mishna Berura* (*OḤ* 606:2) and the *Kaf HaḤayim* (*OḤ* 606:11).

Impersonal Apologies

This debate, I think, sheds light on the value of apologies through media that allow one to save face. With phone calls, one may avoid eye contact, limiting the necessity to humble oneself and minimizing the embarrassment, without eliminating these elements totally. Letters, emails, or text messages minimize both of these even further. A mass text, WhatsApp, or Facebook post requires no real admission of guilt, no looking in the eyes of the injured party; this eliminates almost all the cathartic qualities of the process.

Thus, it seems that *Yefei Mareh* would have no problem with any of these methods if they actually achieve forgiveness, though mass apologies usually do not. *Ein Yaakov*, on the other hand, would fundamentally oppose hiding behind these less direct forms of communication. Practically, I would assume that the *Yefei Mareh* would oppose the mass-text or Facebook apologies, as there is no way of ensuring that every victim has forgiven the perpetrator. However, individual messages would suffice.

R. Dov Lior follows this general approach and writes that if the wronged party responds that he or she forgives the sinner, a Facebook apology is sufficient.[2]

R. Ovadia Yosef, on the other hand, follows the general approach of the *Ein Yaakov*. He rules that it is ideal to apologize in person, not

2. Available at: https://www.yeshiva.org.il/ask/59843.

through an intermediary or letter (or any other form of communication, presumably, though phone calls may be different). However, like the *Mishna Berura,* he believes that if sending a third party will be more effective, it is permitted. His son, R. Yitzchak Yosef, concurs (*Yalkut Yosef, OḤ* 606:10).

R. Moshe Harari (*Mikra'ei Kodesh, Hilkhot Yom HaKippurim* 2:36, n. 9) cites the view of R. Mordechai Eliyahu, who rules that one may not discharge the obligation of *teshuva* by apologizing on the phone, even if others are present for the phone call. However, like the *Mishna Berura,* he rules that if one has no choice, one may discharge the obligation by apologizing in this fashion, even if the embarrassment to the offender is now minimal. However, R. Yitzchak Yosef writes that if victim is not in the city, the sinner may commit to apologize when he gets the opportunity to see the offended party in person.

If there are *posekim* who eschew personal letters and phone calls, how much more so would they reject mass texts and Facebook posts!

Confession vs. Apology

Sherry Turkle, in her excellent book *Alone Together*[3] about how technology has changed the nature of human relationships, offers an insightful comment about such apologies. She notes that "apologies" offered on social media are more properly termed "confessions," and for many, they fall short. They feel that these apologies

> are more like confessions because a real apology has to deal more directly with the person you have wronged. Maria, the thirty-three-year-old financial analyst who said that the intensity of Second Life could be exhausting, does not like it when people try "to make things right" by e-mail. She thinks apologies must be made in person. "...When people confess on the computer, they think they have done their job and now it is up to others to respond. But I think if you have hurt me, why should it be my job to come tell you that it is all right?" Recall sixteen-year-old

3. Sherry Turkle, *Alone Together: Why We Expect More from Technology and Less from Each Other* (Basic Books, 2011).

> Audrey's derisive account of an online apology: "It's cheap. It's easy. All you have to do is type 'I'm sorry.'"... Sydney, twenty-three, a first-year law student, takes exception: "Saying you are sorry as your status... that is not an apology. That is saying 'I'm sorry' to Facebook."

These two actions are not the same. Mere confession, as we have noted above, lacks the ability to heal the relationship that has been harmed:

> The elements of an apology are meant to lay the psychological groundwork for healing – and this means healing both for the person who has been offended and for the person who has offended. First, you have to know you have offended, you have to acknowledge the offense to the injured party, and you have to ask what you can do to make things right.
>
> Technology makes it easy to blur the line between confession and apology, easy to lose sight of what an apology is, not only because online spaces offer themselves as "cheap" alternatives to confronting other people but because we may come to the challenge of an apology already feeling disconnected from other people. In that state, we forget that what we do affects others.

Turkle notes that this is not only true of statements made on Facebook or the like that are not directed to the person who has been hurt. Technology allows even "direct" encounters to be shallower, affecting the effectiveness of apologies. She notes that many feel that it is impersonal, as one does not hear the voice of the one speaking. Furthermore, by text, tone of voice is lost, leaving open the possibility that seemingly sincere apologies were delivered sarcastically.

> The other agrees: "It's harder to say 'Sorry' than text it, and if you're the one receiving the apology, you know it's hard for the person to say 'Sorry.' But that is what helps you forgive the person – that they're saying it in person, that they actually have the guts to actually want to apologize." In essence, both young

> women are saying that forgiveness follows from the experience of empathy. You see someone is unhappy for having hurt you. You feel sure that you are standing together with them. When we live a large part of our personal lives online, these complex empathetic transactions become more elusive. We get used to getting less.

In her more recent *Reclaiming Conversation,* Turkle returned to this idea, noting that when one apologizes face to face, one is forced to see how he or she hurt the other person, see how they are upset. Realizing the hurt one has caused is necessary to begin the process of apologizing. However,

> none of this happens with "I'm sorry," *hit send.* At the moment of remorse, you export the feeling rather than allowing a moment of insight. You displace an inner conflict without processing it; you send the feeling off on its way. A face-to-face apology is an occasion to practice empathic skills. If you are the penitent, you are called upon to put yourself in someone else's shoes. And if you are the person receiving the apology, you, too, are asked to see things from the other side so that you can move toward empathy. In a digital connection, you can sidestep all this. So a lot is at stake when we move away from face-to-face apologies.[4]

Turkle's comments and records of people's own experiences mirror much that emerges from the position of *Ein Yaakov.*

The Potential Value

However, even for *Ein Yaakov,* there may still be value in such communications. For example, R. Ben-Tziyon Algazi suggests that mass texts work to ask forgiveness out of courtesy, from people whom one probably has not wronged. However, one must issue personal apologies to those people whom one knows he has wronged. Though he does not explain the exact argument, perhaps it is as follows:[5]

4. Sherry Turkle, *Reclaiming Conversation: The Power of Talk in a Digital Age* (Random House, 2015), 62.
5. Available at: https://www.inn.co.il/News/News.aspx/209200.

While the simplest understanding for the custom to apologize on Erev Yom Kippur is because it is the final chance to gain forgiveness for the year, there is another aspect. Several Rishonim cite midrashic sources which indicate that one of the central motifs of Yom Kippur is that we try to be like angels. For this reason, we don't eat or drink, we stand, etc. Some Rishonim add (see, for example, *Or Zarua, Hilkhot Yom HaKippurim* 277, based on *Pirkei DeRabbi Eliezer* 46, *Tur, OḤ* 606) that a component of this is that "just as angels have peace among them, so too, to be angelic, we need to have peace among us." From this perspective, it is undeniable that the half-hearted/well-meaning apologies do create a sense of goodwill. Even with our friends, we have minor disagreements, tensions, and grudges. When Erev Yom Kippur comes, we are ready to forgive and forget. Together we seek forgiveness and a relationship with God, as individuals and as a community.[6]

Conclusion

As we saw in previous chapters, social media communications should not replace in-person interactions. Especially when it comes to asking for forgiveness, face-to-face conversation is critical for rebuilding relationships. While the access to phones, email, and the like allows us to communicate with those far away, we should approach those whom we have hurt in person, if possible, to show that we have changed. However, mass texts and Facebook messages can help create the atmosphere of forgiveness and friendship that we want as we enter Yom Kippur. As with the case of visiting the sick and comforting mourners, communication technology is valuable in forming and maintaining relationships, even if it cannot replace in-person meetings.

6. It is worth noting that R. Dr. Asher Meir argues that *Tur* has a different perspective on *teshuva* in general. He argues that *Tur* believes that the purpose of apologizing in general is to bring peace. Based on this, he writes that one should apologize even if one is unsure whether he has harmed someone else, in order to generate peace. However, it seems more likely that this aspect is unique to Yom Kippur and not a general law in *teshuva*. See https://outorah.org/p/5629/.

Chapter 6

Prayer for the Sick: Connected Only by a Facebook Post

Introduction: The Importance of Really Caring in Prayer

Social media allows us to contact countless people in an instant. At its best, it allows us to share valuable information, encourage others to engage in positive activities, generate compassion for worthy causes, and generally involve larger circles of people in constructive efforts.

One expression of this which perhaps strikes us as obvious is the (all-too-often) urgent request to pray on behalf of a sick or injured person whom we have never met and are in no way directly connected to. Undoubtedly, the impulse to get large numbers of people to care about strangers and entreat God to help them is praiseworthy. However, there is a danger: people may pray without caring. While this may seem like a small cost, the importance of praying out of true identification, sympathy, and perhaps even empathy is often overlooked. To frame the issue, let us begin with a quote from R. Shlomo Zalman Auerbach.[1] I think

1. My thinking on this subject has been influenced by R. Mordechai Torczyner in his *shiur* here: https://www.yutorah.org/lectures/lecture.cfm/915958/rabbi-mordechai-torczyner/davening-for-the-terminally-ill/, as well as in subsequent exchanges with him.

it is critical for how we think about this issue, especially if we intend to undertake to pray for strangers.

In *Halikhot Shlomo* (*Hilkhot Tefilla,* ch. 8, n. 60), R. Auerbach's students record the following:

> Our master customarily said that one should not pray for an ill person during the *Amida* unless one has some connection to him, and one feels his pain, for one should not come to the King – the King of kings, God – without a reason and justification for pushing to ask for someone else.
>
> He would tell of the Maharil Diskin, that once someone asked him to pray for an ill person, and he agreed [after instructing him, as was his practice, to contribute a particular sum to the orphanage], and after some time the Maharil met him and asked after the ill person's welfare, and he replied that the person had already become healthy, with God's help. The Maharil thundered at him for not telling him of this, and burdening him with praying for that person all this time, saying, "Is it light in your eyes, making such a request in prayer? One must seek and find a reason to pray each time!" (And our master also thundered regarding this, and once he rebuked a student who delayed telling him about his salvation through God's generosity. He said: Three times each day I pain myself and feel your suffering, and why did you only now decide to tell me?)[2]

What is clear from this passage is that the Maharil Diskin and R. Auerbach feel that to pray is to express genuine care and concern. When we agree to mention strangers in our prayers, this consideration should give us pause and remind us what such an endeavor entails. But what is the source for this attitude?

The History of Personal Requests

Let us begin with the Abudraham's summary of how we have arrived at the text of the *Amida* that we currently recite thrice daily:

---

2. Translation from Torczyner above.

> There is a positive biblical commandment to serve God through prayer.... And the Torah has no [required] number of prayers. Rather, everyone may pray with full intent whenever he wants. Whether a little or a lot, it will go up with grace and be accepted.
>
> This was how things were from the time of Moshe Rabbenu until the time of the destruction of our holy and glorious Temple, when the Jews were exiled among the nations because of their sins and actions and were mixed among the nations.... And children were born in these lands, and those children who arose after them had confused and mixed-up language, [comprised of] foreign languages, Moabite, Ammonite, Zidonite, and Hittite, as it says (Nehemia 13:24): "And a good number of their children spoke the language of Ashdod and the language of those various peoples, and did not know how to speak Judean." And they could not pray or speak as was necessary in Hebrew, but only with confusion and a mix of foreign languages, and the true language was destroyed, cut down, and extinct from the land.
>
> When the Men of the Great Assembly saw this evil sickness, they said, "Let us go in the light of our God, 'and let our lips replace the bulls [of sacrifices]' (Hosea 14:3), us and all of our congregation, and institute prayer which is called 'service,' which is heavy on the tongue, in a clear language and with brevity – pure, clear, and straight, purified from the illness of the foreign language, so that it will be easy and fluent in people's mouths, under which we all pray, with one language and with one tongue."
>
> And they all gathered, and instituted to pray the *Amida* before the Eternal One, every day, three times. (*Abudraham, Tikkun HaTefillot* 2)

The original biblical value of prayer[3] was for each person to express his or her own personal needs in eloquent Hebrew; the current formalized

3. According to the Rambam (*Sefer HaMitzvot, Aseh* 5; *Hilkhot Tefilla*, ch. 1), the daily requirement of prayer is a biblical command. The Ramban (Mitzva no. 5) disagrees,

prayers emerged when people were unable to do that. However, what is clear is that the goal of standardized prayer is to help facilitate true *kavana* (intention) – not, as is all too often the case, get in the way.

The first three and last three *berakhot* of the *Amida,* those of praise and thanks, are mostly formalized and can rarely be changed (see Berakhot 34a and *Beit Yosef, OḤ* 119 for exceptions). However, to maintain the centrality of personal *kavana* in prayer, *Ḥazal* allow, encourage, and perhaps mandate adding personal requests to the middle blessings, those of petition:

> With regard to the halakhic ruling, **Rav Yehuda says** that **Shmuel says:** The ***halakha*** is that **a person requests his own needs** during the *Amida* prayer **in** the blessing ending: **Who listens to prayer. Rav Yehuda, son of Rav Shmuel bar Sheilat, says in the name of Rav: Although** the Sages **said** that **a person requests his own needs in** the blessing ending: **Who listens to prayer,** that is not the only option. **Rather, if he wishes to recite at the conclusion of each and every blessing** personal requests that **reflect the nature of each and every blessing, he may recite** them.
>
> Similarly, **Rav Ḥiyya bar Ashi says** that **Rav says: Although** the Sages **said** that **a person requests his own needs in** the blessing ending: **Who listens to prayer, if he has a sick person in his house he recites** a special prayer for him **during the blessing of the sick. And if he is in need of sustenance, he recites** a request **during the blessing of the years.**
>
> **Rabbi Yehoshua ben Levi says: Although** the Sages **said** that **a person requests his own needs in** the blessing ending: **Who listens to prayer; but if one wishes to recite** prayers and supplications **after** finishing **his** *Amida* **prayer, even** if his personal requests **are as long as the order** of the confession of **Yom Kippur, he may recite** them. (Avoda Zara 8a)

---

arguing that prayer is a privilege, except perhaps in cases of dire need. For these purposes, I will elide the differences.

The Gemara offers several places where personal requests can be made – during the relevant blessings (such as praying for the sick during the blessing of "*Refa'einu*," "Heal us"), the blessing of "*Shema Koleinu*" ("Listen to our voice…Who listens to prayer," the generic blessing), and at the end of the *Amida*. What is the distinction among these?

Rabbenu Yona (Berakhot 22b) suggests the following based on a careful reading of the above passage:

1. In *Shema Koleinu,* one may add any request.
2. At the end of each topical blessing, one may make a relevant request, but only in communal language.
3. One may use personal language *in the middle of the topical blessings* if he or she has a specific personal need, such as someone sick in his or her home.
4. At the end of the *Amida,* before or after "*Yehi ratzon,*" one may make any requests one desires, personal or communal.

The *Beit Yosef* (*OḤ* 119) understands that the Rosh disagrees, and allows making both communal and personal requests, both in the middle and at the end of the topical blessings. However, in *Shema Koleinu,* one may make any request, as it is a catch-all blessing. He assumes that the Rambam (*Hilkhot Tefilla* 6:2–3) similarly rejects Rabbenu Yona's distinctions.

Tosafot (Avoda Zara 8a, s.v. *im ba*) argues that the only distinction is length; in the topical blessings, as well as *Shema Koleinu,* one may make short requests. At the end of the *Amida,* one may add as much as he or she wants, even as long as "the confession of Yom Kippur." The Meiri (Avoda Zara 8a, s.v. *kevar yadata*) argues that in the middle blessings one may only add requests for that which one *needs,* while in *Shema Koleinu* one may make requests for what one *wants.* The Arizal (cited in *Birkei Yosef*) argues that in the topical blessings one should think about one's requests, but only verbalize them in *Shema Koleinu.*

Ran, on the other hand, understands that this is not about allowances, but requirements. If one has a sick person at home to pray for, one *must pray for the ill in Refa'einu.* If one does not, then one may do so in *Shema Koleinu.*

This position emphasizes the extent to which prayer is not meant to be a set text, but a true expression of our needs. However, even according to the other positions, *Ḥazal* want our prayers to continue to express the original values of *tefilla*: to convey our desires and requests to God. This explains all the various places within *tefilla* in which we may, in different ways, add our requests. This point is made by the *Piskei Teshuvot* (*OḤ* 119) in his introduction to the above laws:

> Extra importance is evidenced in those requests that a person adds in his prayer, for prayer is a biblical commandment that requires intention of the heart. In our great iniquity, since a person is habituated to it, his mouth speaks and his heart is not with him. The personal requests that a person adds based on his requests that arise anew daily, for health, sustenance, and success in Torah – that it should not desert his mouth or those of his children and descendants – and so too all his other needs, flow in general from the walls of the heart.

Where to Pray for the Sick

The simple reading of the Gemara in Avoda Zara indicates that one only prays for the ill in *Refa'einu* if the sick person is in one's own household – a relative or close friend. R. Ben-Tziyon Abba-Shaul (*Responsa Or LeTziyon* 2:7:33) assumes that this is indeed specific. He rules in accordance with the position that communal prayers may only be said in *Shema Koleinu* and argues that praying for anyone who is not a member of one's household is like praying for the community and thus must be relegated to *Shema Koleinu.*

Mishna Berura (*OḤ* 116:3, *Shaar HaTziyun* 5) disagrees, following the position of *Eliya Rabba, Magen Gibborim,* and *Birkei Yosef.* R. Auerbach concurs (*Halikhot Shlomo* 8:16). It is in this context that his students add the note that we began with.

R. Abba-Shaul adds that one should request that a certain sick person be cured in, at most, two out of three prayer services a day, to avoid the petition becoming a rote request.

The Conceptual Underpinning

These halakhic disputes seem to capture the sentiment we began with. Prayer is serious business, to put it simply. R. Abba-Shaul thinks that the topical blessings are only for personal requests, and he cannot conceive that praying for someone who is not part of one's family (perhaps close friends?) could be personal. Thus, he relegates such a request to *Shema Koleinu*, the standards of which are looser. While most authorities disagree, as R. Auerbach illustrates, they do not disagree with the principle that what justifies (or obligates) prayer is true identification with the need. As the anecdote from the Maharil indicates, he believes that one could come to care about a stranger to the extent that the well-being of the other becomes one's own concern. This is the standard.

The Challenge

As we noted at the beginning, it is undeniable that caring for others – family, friends, strangers – should be ethically and religiously meaningful. Prayer is a way of expressing this concern. However, prayer must be taken seriously. When we are flooded with requests to pray for strangers, it is a beautiful thing to take it upon ourselves to pray for them. With social media, mass emails, and other forms of communication, those requests may come from people many steps removed from us.

As R. Auerbach captures, to accept to pray is to accept to care. This may be uplifting, but it is not easy. Simply adding the name without taking the time to internalize that we are actually beseeching God to aid someone we have come to care for empties the prayer of its meaning.

R. Abba-Shaul seems not to believe that it is possible to really care that personally about an outsider, and therefore he pushes such requests to the generic blessing of *Shema Koleinu*. He further instructs that we ensure that such personal requests not become rote by only saying them at some prayer services. This prevents the name of some stranger from becoming just more words that we mutter. Whatever exact halakhic position we accept, the challenge to pray only if we can muster deep emotional concern seems to underlie all the positions we have seen. If that means not simply adding a list of sick people to every prayer, but rather alternating so that we remember that there are real people behind the names, then this is what we should do. If that means putting the petition in *Shema Koleinu*, as per R. Abba-Shaul, to remind ourselves that this prayer is not as personal as petitions for ourselves and those close to us can be, then so be it. This analysis is not meant to discourage people from turning to the world to pray for their relatives and friends; it challenges us to internalize what we are obligated to do in order to take that responsibility seriously.

Using the Name of the Sick Person

The Gemara records that when Rabbi Elazar would visit the sick, he would pray for them in Aramaic. The Gemara asks how this is possible:

> The Gemara asks: **How did he do this,** pray in Aramaic? **Didn't Rav Yehuda say: A person should never request** that **his needs** be met **in the Aramaic language? And,** similarly, **Rabbi Yoḥanan said: Anyone who requests** that **his needs** be met **in the Aramaic language, the ministering angels do not attend to him** to bring his prayer before God, **as the ministering angels are not familiar with the Aramaic language,** but only with the sacred tongue, Hebrew, exclusively. The Gemara responds: **A sick person is different.** He does not need the angels to bring his prayer before God because **the Divine Presence is with him.** (Shabbat 12b)

The Ramban (*Torat HaAdam,* 18) cited by the *Beit Yosef* (*Tur, YD* 335; *Shulḥan Arukh, YD* 335:5), accepts this distinction. The *Taz* (ad loc. 4), however, notes that according to many Rishonim, one may pray in any language aside from Aramaic, which is uniquely inscrutable to the angels. Based on the limitations of praying not in the presence of the sick person, the *Eliya Rabba* (*OḤ* 116), whose view is accepted by the *Mishna Berura* (ibid., 3), rules that when one prays in the presence of the sick person, one need not use the sick person's name. However, when the sick person is not present, just as one must be more precise in the language used, one must use the name of the sick person. The *Ḥatam Sofer* (*Ḥiddushim,* Nedarim 40b, s.v. *ve'ahavta*) further argues that, for this reason, it is better to pray for a sick person in his or her presence than from afar, as using the name of sick person causes God's attributes of justice to be turned against the sick person. Thus, the prayer is less efficacious.

These concerns are true anytime that we pray for someone not in his or her presence. However, the more we are asked to pray for strangers, the more likely it may be that we forget the halakhic details, settling to pray for "the person that X requested we pray for on Facebook." However, as this rule indicates, such a formulation is not sufficient. Ideally, part of taking prayer seriously is giving attention to the minutiae. This is also part of showing that we care, and that we understand the gravity of approaching God with petitions.

Conclusion

The goal of this chapter, I hope it is clear, is not to claim that there is a problem with our tendency to get as many people to pray for those in need as possible. It is rather a reminder that prayer requires genuine concern and attention to detail. These elements are often lost in the flood of requests to pray. However, we can all remember cases where such requests are met with real care. The number of people who remember the names of those captured soldiers whom we pray for in *shul* every week, and care that they one day be returned to their families, indicates that we are capable of mustering that level of empathy. The challenge is to achieve that concern for every person, no matter how far removed, when we agree to integrate them into our deepest requests of God.

Chapter 7

Mara De'atra in the Globalized World

Defining Community

In the last several chapters we have focused on how communication technology has affected interpersonal relationships, focusing on individuals. We now transition to several issues that relate to the defining of community.

The Local Rabbi in the Globalized World

> The Chief Rabbinate of Israel will soon take up the question of whether to confer Rabbinic ordination upon the search engine Google, since it provides information on Jewish law at least as accurately and reliably as any human who has earned that title, a spokesman for the office announced today.[1]

1. http://www.preoccupiedterritory.com/rabbinate-considers-granting-ordination-to-google/.

The above quote is taken from a satirical piece of "Purim Torah." However, as with any good satire, it reflects a truth – in this case, about the way that the internet has changed the way people ask, or don't ask, halakhic questions. Some people rely on "Rabbi Google," searching for the range of answers available online. However, others prefer to rely on people, though they use phones and the internet to expand the reach of whom they can consult. Using synchronous technology to reach out to a rabbi with whom one has a relationship is easy – just call or FaceTime your rebbe from yeshiva. Or, instead of turning to rabbis with whom one has a direct, personal connection, there is a plethora of authorities who can be consulted through *Shu"t* SMS, *Shu"t* WhatsApp, and the like. Others rely on many Facebook groups devoted to crowdsourcing halakhic material.

This phenomenon has been tackled from many angles. For example, R. Elli Fischer has explored the "End of Expertise" phenomenon, or the breakdown of top-down authority.[2] Others have warned about the prevalence of flawed material that is available.

However, here we will focus on a different perspective. Halakhic authorities were traditionally regional or geographic. The local rabbi was the authority for the community. If he chose to consult with greater experts, the laymen relied on his choice of expert. These experts as

2. R. Fischer argues that there are four ways in which rabbinic authorities have dealt with maintaining influence in the internet age. Some, such as R. Hershel Schachter, have argued that a halakhic authority must know Torah without relying on search engines, thus arguing that, by definition, any method of accessing halakhic information that does not rely on personal expertise is worthless.

Others have become experts at organizing the vast amount of accessible material, thus gaining influence through their ability to guide others through the overload that the internet may cause. R. Fischer points to R. Yosef Zvi Rimon as an example.

Others provide philosophical frameworks that help ground the details in the bigger picture, thus making their halakhic writing inspirational and holistic, and worth reading over the rest of halakhic material that is available. R. Fischer points to R. Eliezer Melamed as an example of this model.

Finally, R. Fischer notes that *posekim* such as R. Asher Weiss present their positions with such common sense that they resonate in a way that much halakhic writing does not. See https://www.yutorah.org/lectures/lecture.cfm/894989/rabbi-elli-fischer/r-e-fischer-the-end-of-expertise-psak-halachah-in-the-digital-age-2-4-18/.

well were often chosen geographically.[3] Communication technology has made geography almost irrelevant – people will ask questions from whomever they want to, wherever they live. How does this affect the notion of authority? The most poignant concept that must be addressed is that of *mara de'atra* (master of the place), the terms used by the Talmud to refer to the local rabbinic authority to whom all halakhic decisions are to be addressed.

This question must be addressed on two levels. First, we will discuss the breakdown in classic notions of *mara de'atra.* Next, we will discuss the ways in which our ever-shrinking world has managed to recreate a similar dynamic along lines of identity, rather than geography.

The Right to Rely on the *Mara De'atra*

The notion of a *mara de'atra* has many implications. From the perspective of a layperson, perhaps the most surprising is the right of a community to follow its rabbi, even against the majority opinion. The Talmud seems to celebrate this right. The Mishna in the beginning of the nineteenth chapter of Shabbat records a dispute as to what can be done to prepare for a circumcision on Shabbat. While all opinions agree that a *brit mila* which is performed on the eighth day overrides Shabbat, the majority position is that one cannot violate Shabbat to prepare tools for the circumcision. However, Rabbi Eliezer permits it. Commenting on this, the Talmud (Shabbat 130a)[4, 5] states:

> With regard to this issue, **the Sages taught** in a *baraita*: **In the locale of Rabbi Eliezer,** where they would follow his ruling, **they would** even **cut down trees** on Shabbat **to prepare charcoal** from it in order **to fashion iron** tools with which to circumcise a child **on Shabbat.**

---

3. In truth, geography may have been less important than culture, though the two overlapped. This point has been demonstrated by R. Elli Fischer and Moshe Schorr using metadata analysis of the responsa of many prominent authorities. See their work at https://blog.hamapah.org/, especially this post: https://blog.hamapah.org/mapping/once-a-galitzianer/.
4. All translations taken from the Koren edition.
5. See also Ḥullin 116a.

The Talmud thus records, without qualms, that those living in the city of Rabbi Eliezer would follow his minority position. The Talmud then continues with the story of Rabbi Yosei HaGelili who ruled, again as a minority position, that it was permitted to eat poultry with milk, and whose followers practiced in accordance with his opinion:

> **In the locale of Rabbi Yosei HaGelili they would eat poultry meat in milk,** as Rabbi Yosei HaGelili held that the prohibition of meat in milk does not include poultry. The Gemara relates: **Levi happened** to come **to the house of Yosef the hunter. They served him the head of a peacock [*tavsa*] in milk** and **he did not eat. When** Levi **came before Rabbi** Yehuda HaNasi, the latter **said to him: Why did you not excommunicate** these people who eat poultry in milk, contrary to the decree of the Sages? Levi **said to him: It was** in **the locale** of **Rabbi Yehuda ben Beteira, and I said: Perhaps he taught them** that the *halakha* is **in accordance with** the opinion of **Rabbi Yosei HaGelili,** who permits the eating of poultry meat in milk.

The Talmud then goes further, recording that those who followed these minority positions were rewarded for their commitment to their rabbis' rulings, though according to the majority of rabbis they were violating significant prohibitions!

> **Rabbi Yitzḥak said: There was one city in Eretz Yisrael where they would act in accordance with** the opinion of **Rabbi Eliezer** with regard to circumcision, **and they would die at their appointed time** and not earlier, as a reward for their affection for this mitzva. **And not only that, but on one occasion the wicked empire,** Rome, **issued a decree against the Jewish people** prohibiting **circumcision; but against that city it did not** issue the **decree.**

Why does the authority of the local rabbi override the normal rule of the majority? R. Yom Tov Asevilli (Ritva) cites (Shabbat 130a, s.v. *hayu meitim*) R. Avraham of Posquières (Raavad), who makes two critical points.

The first is that the Talmud's discussion is limited to cases where there has not been a formal vote to establish the accepted law. If there has been, then the local rabbi must yield. This solves the formal problem of the Torah's requirement "*Aḥarei rabim lehatot*," "Follow the majority" (Ex. 23:2; Bava Metzia 59b).[6]

Secondly, he argues that members of the town are *obligated* to follow their rabbi under the prohibition of "*Lo tasur*," "Do not veer [from the words of the rabbis]" (Deut. 17:11; Shabbat 23a). If they are so obligated, they are obviously entitled to do so even against the majority. This position is quite novel, as this verse is usually limited to the rulings of the Sanhedrin, the supreme rabbinic court, or perhaps the consensus of legal authorities that takes its place when the Sanhedrin does not exist.[7]

Regardless of exactly where the authority comes from, the Talmud clearly expects the average person to follow his or her local rabbi.

---

6. The issue of whether majority rulings require a vote is complex. See my discussion here: https://www.yutorah.org/lectures/lecture.cfm/802192/_Jonathan_Ziring/Halachic_Decision_Making in Extenuating_Circumstances.
7. A summary of these positions can be found in my lecture here: https://www.yutorah.org/lectures/lecture.cfm/821702/rabbi-jonathan-ziring/lo-tasur-and-daas-torah-1-the-role-of-baal-habatim-in-psak-6/. The *Minḥat Ḥinnukh* (496) notes that the simplest understanding of the verse is that it is limited to the Sanhedrin. The *Sefer HaḤinnukh* (495) expands it to include the central authority in every generation. However, in the following mitzva (496), he refers to the great sages of each generation, but does not limit it to a central authority, which perhaps indicates that he may be taking a view closer to that of Ritva. R. Yehuda Herzl Henkin seems to go in this direction. He suggests that whether it is prohibited to present a rabbinic law as biblical depends on if one extends *Lo tasur* to later rabbis. He does not distinguish between the central authorities or individual ones. Rabbis Aryeh and Dov Frimer summarize his discussion of this issue, both in his written responsa and in their correspondence with him. See R. Aryeh A. and R. Dov I. Frimer, "Women's Prayer Services – Theory and Practice," *Tradition* 32:2 (Winter 1998): 5–118, Addendum, part 5.

   Rambam similarly grounds rabbinic authority in each generation in this verse (see, most expansively, his introduction to *Mishneh Torah*). Ramban rejects this expansion, though how he explains the source of rabbinic power is unclear. See the discussion, for example, in R. Elchanan Wasserman's *Kovetz Divrei Soferim,* chapter 1. However, none of these authorities take the position expressed by Ritva, that this verse gives power to every individual rabbi, rather than the leading authorities.

Rabbinic Respect for the Local Authority

Elsewhere, the Talmud notes that rabbis would refrain from ruling in places where there was a ruling rabbi. For example, the Talmud (Pesaḥim 30a) records that Rav refrained from publicly disagreeing with Shmuel where Shmuel had authority. Elsewhere (Eiruvin 94a), the Talmud records that Rav once turned his face away when Shmuel ruled that something was permitted that Rav ruled was forbidden. The Talmud states that Rav needed to turn away so that it would be clear that he disagreed with Shmuel, but he did not verbalize his opposition out of respect for Shmuel's local authority. While Meiri explains that Rav only did this because the prohibition in question was rabbinic, Ritva contends that in any case where a rabbi does not believe his colleague has made an outright error, but rather an error in judgment in a case that is not black and white, he is not allowed to challenge the local authority.[8]

While the exact scope of the local rabbi's authority is unclear, its existence is unchallenged. Rema (*YD* 245), citing Maharik (*Shu"t Maharik* 169), adds several restrictions. For example, he writes that a visiting rabbi cannot perform any rabbinic functions that would deprive the local rabbi of his livelihood; nor may he issue ritual rulings, offer sermons, or take rabbinic prerogatives. On the other hand, Rema writes that a qualified rabbi may set up his own rabbinate in the area. The full implications of this principle are beyond the scope of this discussion, but these examples should be sufficient to indicate the importance of the category.

Several rabbinic writers used this category to claim that the Chief Rabbinate of Israel has legal authority over Israel.[9] While in theory this could be true, as HaRav Aharon Lichtenstein has noted, there would have had to have been an acceptance of their authority as such.[10] In reality, the number of people who feel bound to the authority of the Chief Rabbinate is small, thus vitiating this argument, even if it is theoretically plausible.

---

8. For a discussion of these positions, see Aaron Kirschenbaum, "*Mara De-Atra: A Brief Sketch*," *Tradition* 27:4, available at: https://traditiononline.org/mara-de-atra-a-brief-sketch/.
9. For the most thorough presentation, see R. Shaul Yisrael's *Amud HaYemani*, ch. 6.
10. See "The Israeli Chief Rabbinate: A Current Halakhic Perspective," *Tradition* 26:4 (Summer: 1992): 26–38, reprinted in *Israel as a Religious Reality*, edited by Chaim Waxman (Aronson, 1994), 119–137; *Leaves of Faith*, vol. 2 (2004), 261–277.

The Breakdown

However, the intense control the local rabbi had has mostly broken down. Dr. Aaron Kirschenbaum[11] outlines several reasons for this:

> First and foremost, the alienation of the masses of our people from Halakha has diminished the "locality" over which the local rabbi is "master" from the autonomous judicial community (*kahal*) of the Middle Ages to the particular (Orthodox) synagogue from which he draws his salary. But even for the halakhically observant Jew, the telephone and automobile have rendered "city" a meaningless term; and "locality," which is now limited to the individual synagogue, may paradoxically also refer to a huge geographic expanse.
>
> In the British Empire and in the State of Israel, the maintenance of a chief rabbinate has decreased significantly the role of the traditional *mara de'atra*. Indeed, the chief rabbis themselves are often viewed as the *mara de'atra* of the entire country. Also, specialization has overtaken the modern rabbinate so that rabbi (*rav*), rabbinical judge (*dayan*), teacher (*moreh*), and communal leader (*manhig tzibburi*) are seldom incorporated in one man.
>
> Finally, the emergence of *rashei yeshiva* as halakhic decisors whose authority transcends geographic boundaries and, even more so, the walls of the individual yeshiva, has contributed much to the near demise of the traditional *mara de'atra*. Not only do their disciples (*talmidim*) turn to them, not only do the laity turn to them – but the communal rabbi, the local *mara de'atra* himself, as a former *talmid*, also turns to them for *pesak* and guidance. Indeed, the telephone has done much to undo the role and stature of the old-time *mara de'atra*.
>
> It would therefore appear that the *mara de'atra* in the traditional sense survives today chiefly in small communities or in communities far removed from the main centers of contemporary Judaism, i.e., in Israel or in urban America. It is hazardous to predict the future of the *mara de'atra*. Nevertheless, it would

---

11. See above, note 8.

> appear that there are no significant factors on the horizon in contemporary Jewish life that could stop the historical, sociological, and technological processes that are bringing this concept to the vanishing point.

Dr. Kirschenbaum notes that the general lack of commitment to halakha has weakened the power of the rabbinate. For our purposes, however, his point that advanced communications have made location a "meaningless term" cuts to the heart of our issue. The fact that people can communicate with whomever they want means that *they will.* R. Yaakov Ariel is similarly cited as saying:

> The concept of *mara de'atra* in our days is very problematic, because people move and wander from place to place, and there are telephones and other means of communication which allow communicating with different rabbis.[12]

Dr. Kirschenbaum made his comments in 1993. As he predicted, the forces that would break down the geographic authority of rabbis have only increased.

However, this has not created a power vacuum. On the contrary, as Dr. Kirschenbaum notes, the increase in communications has enabled the rise of a different kind of authority. Dr. Kirschenbaum defines this as the authority of the *rosh yeshiva*.

However, I think the critical category at play is identity. Historically, the local rabbi gained his power due to accessibility. Now, as the world is so connected, people choose whom they ask based on whom they like or identify with. In the past, while people may have wanted to access such rabbis, it was often impossible, or at least difficult. The ease of communication allows and encourages the creation of ideological communities in general, and this expresses itself in who is given halakhic authority.

12. This quote is from an article that is no longer available online. However, in other pieces, R. Ariel denies this position, and argues that, at least for communal issues, the rabbi of the city is the legitimate and binding authority. See: https://www.yeshiva.org.il/ask/107778.

The Recreation of the *Mara De'atra:* From Geographic Authority to Ideological Identification

While communication technology has led to the breakdown in classic models of halakhic authority that were based on location, specifically the *mara de'atra* (master of the place), the local rabbi, the nature of that breakdown has opened the doors to a replacement: the ideological *mara de'atra*.

We cited Dr. Aaron Kirschenbaum, who writes:

> [T]he emergence of *rashei yeshiva* as halakhic decisors whose authority transcends geographic boundaries and, even more so, the walls of the individual yeshiva, has contributed much to the near demise of the traditional *mara de-atra*. Not only do their disciples (*talmidim*) turn to them; not only do the laity turn to them; but the communal rabbi, the local *mara de-atra* himself, as a former *talmid*, also turns to them for *pesak* and guidance. Indeed, the telephone has done much to undo the role and stature of the old-time *mara de-atra*.

However, as Dr. Kirschenbaum notes, rabbinic authority is still sought after. The difference is that people turn to those authorities with whom they have a relationship, or with whom they identify ideologically. Does halakha vest the authority of *mara de'atra* in such a figure? As we will see, there is evidence that it does.

Rashba: Communities Who Have Accepted Rif and Rambam

The first authority to recognize this new kind of *mara de'atra* is Rashba (*Responsa* 1:253). He first highlights the extent to which the Talmud respects local authority and the right of constituents to follow their rabbi, even against the majority opinion:

> In Rabbi Eliezer's region, they would cut wood [on Shabbat] to make charcoal to make the knife [for circumcision], and the Sages did not protest as they were acting like their teacher (Shabbat 130a). And in the chapter *Kol HaBasar* (Ḥullin, ch. 8, 116a) it says:

> Levi visited the town of Yosef the Fowler. They served a head of fowl cooked in milk. He did not eat, and said nothing. When [Levi] returned to Rav, he said, "Why didn't you excommunicate them?!" He replied, "That is the town of Rabbi Yehuda ben Beteira. I thought perhaps he expounds like Rabbi Yosei the Galilean's opinion, who says: 'Poultry meat is excluded [from the prohibition of meat and milk] for it does not produce milk.'"
>
> And so too in many cases.

However, he notes that in his time, people had begun to treat great authorities of the past with the same deference as they would their local rabbi:

> In a similar way, people who have accustomed themselves based on one of the great authorities, [such as] the places where they act in all their actions based on the laws of Rif *z"l*, and the places where they always act based on Rambam's code – they have made these great ones their teachers.

Rashba seems to accept this model: an ideological *mara de'atra*. However, he qualifies this and argues that while it is similar to the classic model, it is not identical. Assuming that a community has a rabbi, he can rule against the authority the community normally follows:

> However, if there is a sage worthy of ruling, and he sees a proof to forbid what they permitted, he can forbid it, for this [deceased figure] is not actually their teacher, and if they were to act differently than their actual teacher in his place, it would be lessening the honor of their teacher in his place....

Thus, Rashba creates a category that is akin, though not identical, to *mara de'atra*. However, it should be noted that this does not get us all the way to the level of an individual who chooses to be part of an ideological community. The Talmud's examples of *mara de'atra* are the leaders of communities. While Rashba does accept the possibility that the rabbi can be virtual rather than real, so to speak, he still discusses geographic communities in terms of who accepts said authority. While he begins to point in the direction Dr. Kirschenbaum mentions above, he does not actually discuss the possibility that both the rabbi and the community may be defined by ideological identification rather than geography.

At any rate, the model created by Rashba is used by later *posekim* to explain the emergence of Ashkenazic communities who follow the positions of R. Moshe Isserles (Rema) and Sephardic communities who follow the positions of R. Yosef Karo in *Shulḥan Arukh.*[13] Many Aḥaronim assume that this is an absolute obligation, as the world has accepted these two authorities for the two communities.

For example, R. Yonatan Eybeschütz writes that any position not mentioned by R. Yosef Karo or Rema need not be considered, as the sages of the generation have accepted to follow the pithy formulations of these two *posekim*. He further states that God approved of this acceptance, and that while the Aḥaronim try to argue with these two authorities, their questions are never unsolvable.[14]

However, in the original context, the communities who were accepting these rabbinic authorities were geographic. Ashkenazic Jews lived in certain parts of Europe[15] and Sephardic Jews came from mostly the Middle East. Even under these circumstances, there were *posekim* who felt that this pseudo *mara de'atra* could not allow the people following minority opinions to be lenient concerning biblical laws (*Responsa Mahari ben Lev* 1:75). Still, the majority of *posekim* treat this category almost like *mara de'atra,* even when it allows leniency.

Shakh (*YD* 242:4) notes that a similar model has allowed people to have more than one "main teacher," instead choosing different rabbis

13. See, for example, *Responsa Ḥayim Bad* 108; *Shem Gedolim, Maarekhet HaSefarim, Bet "Beit Yosef"*; *Urim VeTummim*, ch. 25 in *Kitzur Tokfo Kohen*, 123–124. For a full discussion of the acceptance of *Shulḥan Arukh*, see "The Reception of the *Shulḥan Arukh* and the Formation of Ashkenazic Jewish Identity" by Joseph Davis in *AJS Review*, vol. 26, No. 2 (November 2002): 251–276. Maoz Kahana has further written about the role that the *Ḥatam Sofer* and *Noda BiYehuda* had in this process. See his book, *Halakhic Writing in a Changing World: From the Noda BiYehuda to the Ḥatam Sofer, 1730–1839* [Hebrew].
14. See previous note.
15. Whom the Rema was meant to bind has been a dispute since the time of Rema. See *Vikuaḥ Mayim Ḥayim*. Maoz Kahana writes about this extensively.

to rule on the areas of halakha in which they have expertise. While he accepts this pragmatic division of the authority of the rabbi, he notes that one must avoid the danger of searching for the most lenient position in all circumstances.

In the twentieth century, *posekim* begin to write extensively about "Ashkenazim" and "Sephardim" as ethnic groups who *originated* in particular geographic areas, though they no longer lived there. While there are indications that some people treated the terms in this way earlier,[16] the phenomenon increased as the upheaval of the twentieth century brought many Jews from around the world to joint communities such as Israel and North America. At that point, *posekim* begin to write about customs of *edot* (ethnic communities) as if they were geographic ones, applying the talmudic rules from the latter to the former.[17] While the exact justification for that is unclear, for our purposes it is sufficient to note that this tendency has been widespread among *posekim*.[18] We return to this below.

Ideological Communities

The next logical step is to argue that communities can be forged around ideological identification and halakhic authorities chosen accordingly. R. Nathaniel Helfgot has summarized the more general position as it emerges from an expanded understanding of Rashba as follows:

---

16. See, for example, *Responsa Re'em* 78 and Davis above.

17. It is also possible that the original geographic Ashkenazic and Sephardic communities were defined by culture rather than strict geography. R. Elli Fischer and Moshe Schorr have offered evidence for this using analysis of metadata, at least in the case of the authority of certain *posekim* such as R. Shlomo Kluger and Maharsham. See https://blog.hamapah.org/. See also the introduction of *Sema,* who seems to go in this direction. See Davis above.

18. See *Responsa Shevet HaLevi* 6:59, *Responsa Iggerot Moshe, YD* 2:75, and *Responsa Siaḥ Naḥum* 30. Each have slightly different understandings of this, but they all urge following this model. R. Ovadia Yosef writes about this more than any other *posek* in the modern period. As R. Dr. Binyamin Lau has documented, R. Ovadia devoted his life to bringing Sephardim back to the rulings of *Shulḥan Arukh*. This was despite the fact that many authorities, such as R. Mordechai Eliyahu and R. Shlomo Mesas denied that all communities among *Edot HaMizraḥ* (Eastern communities) had followed *Shulḥan Arukh*. They instead followed their own authorities, such as *Ben Ish Ḥai*. See Lau's book, *MiMaran ad Maran* (Hebrew).

> This ruling of Rashba moves the concept beyond the limitations of specific time and place and makes the ideological and halakhic affiliation with a particular authority's rulings the center of the mandate. One can plausibly extend this concept beyond the boundaries of any reference to geographic area as well. Once one claims that the concept of following the view of an individual scholar extends beyond his death or his actual place of domicile, the road is clear to an expansive reading of this notion. Thus, a Belzer Hasid who lives in Cape Town, South Africa, or a transplanted Washington Heights *yekke* who was a member of Kehillath Adath Jeshurun and was now living in San Jose could continue to follow the practices and *pesakim* that they felt loyalty to, in their day-to-day life.[19] [20]

R. Helfgot's presentation was propounded by HaRav Aharon Lichtenstein before him to explain why the Modern Orthodox community needed and was able to find its ideological justification in the personality of R. Joseph B. Soloveitchik:

> The definition of the relevant community, however, is murky. The Gemara speaks of locale, but it seems strange that geography should be the sole determinant. Would an enclave of Judean emigres in Galilee be permitted to eat chicken fried in butter? Would only residents of twelfth-century Egypt be entitled to rely upon the Rambam's minority *kulot*? It seems far more likely that other factors – ethnic identity or, above all,

---

19. R. Nathaniel Helfgot, "Minority Opinions and their Role in Horaah," *Milin Havivin*, vol. 4.
20. R. Helfgot does note that within a given *shul*, one may still be required to follow the geographic custom rather than his ideological one. See note 39:

> It would seem, however, that public manifestations of a practice that fly in the face of the accepted custom of a specific town or in our contemporary contexts, synagogue, would not be sanctioned. Such actions would contradict the principles outlined in the fourth chapter of Pesaḥim that require one who moves to a new locale to accept the public practices of the community that one is now residing in, especially when public actions to the contrary would cause discord and strife.

> spiritual and ideological fealty – should carry no less weight. I believe this is clearly suggested by the Rashba: In this vein, if they have been accustomed to act consistently in accordance with the Halakhot of the R. Alfassi *z"l*, or, in places which have become accustomed to act consistently on the basis of the codex of the Rambam *z"l*, they have, in effect, established these *gedolim* as their *rebbe*. Physical proximity is obviously not intended here. What is envisioned is, evidently, rather, a principled and consistent attachment. Its basis is left open; the places cited could have come to be "accustomed to doing all their actions" in accordance with the dicta of the Rif or the Rambam as a result of either accident or choice. The point is, however, that spiritual commitment rather than geographic contiguity is the determinant factor. A Sephardi congregation in Warsaw could still be bound by the rulings of the *Rishon Le-tzion*. Would a Gerer chasid cease to be part of the Beth Israel's community just because he had moved to Paris?[21]

R. Lichtenstein goes on to explain that for him, it is this model that was adopted when Modern Orthodoxy accepted R. Yosef Dov Soloveitchik as its guiding light, thus granting legitimacy to the worldview the community represents.

What makes this notion so appealing and so practical is communication technology. Whether by telephone or email, accessing rabbinic counsel from anywhere in the world is simple. Now, people often receive guidance from halakhic websites they trust. People buy the practical halakha guides from the community they feel a part of. And, more recently, people join Facebook and WhatsApp groups to gain halakhic advice from peers or teachers they identify with, whether or not they have ever met.

---

21. "Legitimization of Modernity: Classical and Contemporary," in *Engaging Modernity: Rabbinic Leaders and the Challenge of the Twentieth Century*, edited by Moshe Z. Sokol (Aronson, 1997), 3–33. Reprinted in *Leaves of Faith*, vol. 2 (2004), 279–308, specifically 289–290.

Dangers

However, relying on this type of *pesak* alone has dangers. R. Yosef Eliyahu Henkin (*Ezrat Yisrael* 70) already warns against issuing halakhic rulings over the telephone, as it does not lend itself to a relationship between the *posek* and the person asking the question. This often leads to mistakes. While this fear is not accepted by most and may be ameliorated when communication technology is used to reach authorities with whom one is close, the more anonymous modes of receiving halakhic guidance do often fail on this plane.

As *Shakh* noted above, once one has access to many authorities, one must still have integrity and follow the position dictated by his commitments. This insight is particularly poignant in the context of virtual ideological communities. It is too easy to remain part of a community with a set of halakhic leaders until a single position or issue that is at odds with one's desire. While virtual communities may not be able to apply social pressure the way geographic communities can (though in some cases they can apply more), individuals must maintain their own standards. If they indeed have accepted a group of *posekim* as their ideological *marei de'atra*, they should not jump ship every time they receive an answer that is not to their liking.

R. Shlomo Brody has also noted that the same dynamics that have allowed *pesak* to travel so freely carry a downside from the perspective of the *posek*. Traditionally, *posekim* could feel comfortable issuing rulings for individuals, without assuming that every word they said would become globally known. However, every *posek* now knows that within minutes, his position can be publicized to the world via social media. This will often constrain *posekim* from issuing rulings that they feel are right for an individual, but not for the global community. He wrote this in the context of the sensitive issue of women wearing tefillin:

> These arguments also raise the question of whether legal rulings (particularly those of great social sensitivity) can and should take into account individual situations, which may (or may not) impact a given ruling. R. Melamed and R. Henkin discuss one potential situation: where a generally pious woman insists that this would be beneficial for her religious growth and is willing to don *tefillin* in private. Other complex situations might include school or other educational environments, pluralistic institutions like Hillel Houses,

potential *kiruv* opportunities or challenges, keeping someone from leaving Orthodoxy, and a host of other questions. One could argue that all *psak* (legal rulings to specific questions) must remain local and individualized, thereby preventing a given individual's needs from being overlooked in the face of a larger legal and social battle (in which the individual may have no stake or interest). One might counter, however, that in our hyper-connected world, the notion of a fully individualized *psak* is not feasible, especially in sensitive areas of halakha. One must assume that any *psak* given to an individual will be (mis?) interpreted as a global statement or taken as a precedent for others. The brouhaha created in the current case points to the great difficulty of issuing individual rulings, particularly when *tefillin* are worn in a public context.[22]

Qualification

However, this is not to say that communal rabbis do not still maintain much power. Often, there are many synagogues in an area, and people will choose the one with the rabbi they identify with. Thus, while the *shul* is chosen for ideological reasons, their rabbi will be local.

Furthermore, there are many questions that will remain local, such as the customs of the *shul*. It seems, anecdotally, that even people who turn to other rabbis for general halakhic questions will turn to the local rabbi for these kinds of issues.

Third, local rabbis have taken on an even more central pastoral and inspirational role than they did in the past, and often this is more important to their function than being a halakhic authority. Dr. Kirschenbaum describes this aptly, and throws down the gauntlet, challenging rabbis to recognize the change that modern society has brought to their role and embrace it:

> The local rabbi, especially in American Centrist Orthodoxy, has been transformed into a modern clergyman, the spiritual leader of his congregation. He, too, faces a challenge as a result of the revolution

22. See R. Shlomo Brody's article at: http://www.torahmusings.com/2014/02/women-tefillin-and-the-halakhic-process/.

> in modern society. Indeed, it is a greater challenge than even before. Does he possess the religious integrity, the Torah learning, the social grace, and the personal charisma to create the respect due his authority? Although no longer the *mara de'atra* in the traditional, historical meaning of the concept, can he, in his relatively new role, serve the needs of his community as his predecessors did in the past?

Thus, even if our analysis is correct, it only shifts the importance of the local rabbi, rather than eliminating it.

Conclusion

The ever-increasing ways that we communicate encourage the creation of global ideological communities. Often, defining ourselves as part of such communities gives us access to halakhic authorities we trust more than those who happen to live nearby. To the extent that halakha recognizes the creation of such communities, we may use social media to strengthen our connections and disseminate (uniform?) halakhic positions instantly across the world.

However, as *posekim* have noted, these communities and the authorities they rely on cannot always replace the pastoral and practical guidance of an in-person guide, whether or not that person is as ideologically in sync with the questioner. People who would rather find their *pesak* in an ideological community must also recognize the potential obligations that entails. Just as the ruling of *mara de'atra* is binding, if the above analysis is correct, the ruling of the leading authority in a given group may hold the same power.

Lastly, the globalization of *pesak* may actually hinder necessary individuation in *pesak*. Nevertheless, it is not possible to turn back. The dangers are present, but the reality is that many people are more part of their global ideological communities than they are of those in their physical vicinity. Thus, we must recognize the potential halakhic opportunities and costs that our current situation offers.

Addendum on Customs

While we cannot fully explore the development of familial and ethnic customs, it is worth briefly highlighting the treatment by R. Dr. Norman

Lamm who was one of the first to write about this phenomenon and its tenuous basis.[23] He suggests three ways of relating to the breakdown of community for the purpose of customs:

1. To assume that customs are indeed geographic, and thus the notion of custom of *edot* is incorrect and should be rejected.
2. To assume that geography was never the real category. Rather, customs devolve on communities. The most important are those accepted by the entirety of the Jewish people. Customs of geographic locations were essentially similar to these customs on a smaller scale. However, with the breakdown of geography as the primary category, we can naturally turn to other models of association, such as families.
3. To assume that there is no *fundamental obligation* to relate to ethnic or familial groups for the purpose of custom, but justify doing so as *voluntary association.* This is based on the Talmud's assumption that professional guilds can be created that bind their members to specific codes of action. When people join a synagogue, they commit to be part of that community (Bava Batra 8b–9a).

This latter model is briefly mentioned by R. Eliyahu Mizrachi (*Responsa Re'em* 78) in the fifteenth–sixteenth century. R. Baruch Simon[24] notes there are several problems with this position. First, it is not clear that one who chooses to pray in a synagogue has any intent to accept its customs. Second, even if one does, it would seem that those customs would be limited to those that relate to prayer in the synagogue.

Regardless, his analysis, and that of those who otherwise justify the acceptance of ethnic customs, highlights the extent to which the nature of community has been redefined, transitioning from geographic to social/ethnic associations. In the case of customs, as noted, much work must be done to justify the move. However, as with the case with *mara de'atra,* its de facto acceptance by many shapes the contours of halakhic practice in our globalized world.

23. *Tokef Minhagim al pi HaHalakha* (*Beit Yitzchak, YU,* 5748). Available here: https://tinyurl.com/2p9cfj47.
24. *Imrei Barukh: Tokef HaMinhag BeHalakha* (*Makhon Be'er HaTorah,* 5775), 77.

Chapter 8

Social Media-Driven Fundraisers in Halakha

Introduction

Communication technology has radically changed the way we think about charity. While classically, charity may have been donated to the poor person who knocked on the door, or through local organizations, now raising money from across the globe is the norm. Through websites like CauseMatch and Charidy, many charities have campaigns that are social media-driven, in which people reach out to their friends, families, and acquaintances, asking them to support the causes important to them.

While this impulse is no doubt praiseworthy, it raises halakhic issues. As we will see, halakha gives precedence to charities that are connected to the giver, either through familial or geographical ties. These social media-driven campaigns, however, specifically attempt to attract donors who are *outside* the immediate circle of the cause. What does halakha say about this?

Moreover, as we discussed in our treatment of *mara de'atra,* the notion of community, while once primarily geographic, is now often defined along identity, social lines, by association. Might a similar phenomenon occur concerning our philanthropic commitments? If so, what might that look like?

While we will focus on charity, these principles may guide all our interpersonal commitments. R. Yisrael Meir Kagan assumes that the same rules that guide the laws of *tzedaka* guide all laws of kindness (*Ahavat Ḥesed* 1:6). It must be noted that in some cases, the rules are equivalent for individual charity and funds distributed by organizations; in other cases they are not. Critically, as R. Moshe Feinstein (*Responsa Iggerot Moshe, YD* 1:144) notes, an individual, even when guided by the principles, may maintain more discretion than one distributing communal funds.

The Concentric Circles of Charity Obligations[1]

Priorities in charity are a practical necessity. As R. Daniel Feldman notes, "Since resources that are bestowed in one place cannot be bestowed elsewhere, the halakhah has formulated principles to guide the maximal fulfillment of the crucial *mitzvah* of *tzedakah*."[2] So what are these principles and what are their sources?

We derive many of the laws of charity from the commandment to lend money to those in need. The Torah frames this mitzva in the context of giving to other Jews: "If you lend money to My people, to the poor among you, do not act toward them as a creditor; exact no interest from them" (Ex. 22:24, JPS translation).

However, the Gemara does not limit charity to only Jews. Gittin 61a outlines the obligations of charity and kindness that are extended to both Jews and non-Jews due to *darkhei shalom*, the ways of peace.[3] However, the Gemara does contend that one's obligations first extend to Jews, and only afterward to non-Jews. Similarly, the Gemara draws several concentric circles, arguing that "charity begins at home" with one's family, then expands to one's city, and only then includes those from other places:

1. The moral argument for preferring those within one's concentric circles seems to lie at the heart of Adam Smith's moral philosophy. See James Otteson's *Adam Smith's Marketplace of Life* (Cambridge University Press, 2012).
2. *Divine Footsteps,* ch. 9, "Making a Difference: Priorities in *Tzedakah and Chesed,*" 211.
3. The commentaries are divided as to whether this is a fundamental value of pragmatic concern. See my *shiurim* here: https://www.yutorah.org/search/?s=darkei+shalom+ziring&sort=1.

> **There are** those **who teach that which Rav Huna** said in connection with **that which Rav Yosef taught:** The verse states: **"If you lend money to any of My people, even to the poor person who is with you"** (Ex. 22:24). The term "My people" teaches that if one of **My people,** i.e., a Jew, **and a gentile** both come to borrow money from you, **My people take precedence.** The term "the poor person" teaches that if **a poor person and a rich person** come to borrow money, **the poor person takes precedence.** And from the term: "Who is with you," it is derived: If **your poor person,** meaning one of your relatives, **and** one of **the poor of your city** come to borrow money, **your poor person takes precedence.** If it is between one of **the poor of your city and** one of **the poor of another city, the** one of **the poor of your city takes precedence.** (Bava Metzia 71a)

The Gemara has a more truncated discussion of these laws in the context of charity specifically:

> With regard to the mitzva of giving charity and granting loans, it is written: "For the poor shall never cease out of the land; therefore I command you, saying: **You shall open [*patoaḥ tiftaḥ*]** your hand to your poor and needy brother in your land" (Deut. 15:11). **I have** derived **only** the obligation to give charity **to the poor** residents **of your city. From where** is the obligation to give charity **to the poor** residents **of another city** derived? **The verse states: "*Patoaḥ tiftaḥ*,"** to teach that you must give charity to the poor **in any case.** (Bava Metzia 31b)

This appears in the *Sifrei* (Deut. 116) as well.

Most authorities understand this to mean that relatives take precedence over those in one's city, even if the relatives do not live close by. They note, however, that this is only true of the one distributing his own funds, not a disburser of communal funds who cannot prioritize his relatives (*Shulḥan Arukh, YD* 254:10). However, Meiri (Ketubot 85b) argues that the precedence of relatives is only when they live in the same city; otherwise, the poor of your city is the primary rule that governs the distribution of charity. A similar position is cited by *Pitḥei Teshuva* (251:2) from *Responsa Shemesh Tzedaka* (19) of R. Shimshon Morpurgo, arguing that the precedence of a scholar is only when judging among people in the same city.[4] However, it is worth noting that in the original responsum, R. Morpurgo, while dealing with a case in which the relevant issue was weighing scholarship and proximity, like Meiri seems to give this rule absolute precedence: "There is nothing that stands before the poor of your city except the redemption of captives." Regardless, the majority view (*Shulḥan Arukh, YD* 251:3) is that relatives take precedence over those who merely live in one's city.

Within the family unit, there are also orders of precedence. For example, one's young children (under the age of six) seem to have precedence over other relatives (Ketubot 50a; *Beit Yosef, YD* 251). The obligation to take care of one's relatives is so fundamental that the communal charitable funds need not support those with wealthy relatives who can take care of them (*Shulḥan Arukh, YD* 257:8).

The Rema (*YD* 251:3) notes that even before one's relatives, one must support oneself. Thus, one must first see to one's own needs before disbursing charitable funds.

We might understand all these laws as pragmatic: each person ought to take care of those closest to him or her, for the sake of utility.[5] Slightly differently, R. David Ariav (*LeRe'akha Kamokha* 2: *Kuntres HaBiurim* 8) argues that the Torah is trying to maintain peace and harmony. This is best accomplished if one gives precedence to those with whom one interacts most.[6]

Alternatively, we could understand this as moral: one fundamentally owes more to those in his or her inner circle than those outside it. My teacher, R. Aharon Lichtenstein, assumes that this is a

4. R. Avraham Sofer in n. 8 on the Meiri equates these positions, though R. Feldman, p. 222, seems to take the Meiri as more expansive: "The Meiri maintains that this is the overriding priority, and all other factors are evaluated only within this context."
5. This seems to emerge from R. Avigdor Nevenzahl, *Siḥot LeSefer Vayikra* 209–210, arguing that in general, relationships are built in concentric circles because of the limitations of human beings. However, he may be hinting at more fundamental claims as well.
6. See Feldman, 225.

fundamental value, though he does not explain the rationale.[7] R. Dovid Cohen argues that the precedence for family members comes from both a biblical decree as well as recognition of gratitude, as one usually owes more to his relatives.[8] R. Joseph Soloveitchik explores these themes in *Halakhic Morality*[9] in the chapter "*Tzedakah*: Brotherhood and Fellowship."

R. Daniel Feldman formulates a particular angle based on comments of R. Shimon Shkop:

> R. Shimon Shkop, in the introduction to his *Sha'arei Yosher* suggests a novel interpretation of the statement of Hillel: "*Im ein ani li, mi li? U-ke-she-ani le-atzmi, mah ani?*" The common understanding of this phrase is that it represents the tension between necessary self-interest and communal concern.... R. Shkop understands the phrase slightly differently. As human beings, concern for oneself is understandably the starting point. However, the measure of a person is in how expansively one chooses to define the concept of "myself": me the individual; me and my family; me and my city; me and the Jewish people; me and the world? Thus, the phrase is interpreted: If I am not for myself, who will be?; but, if I define "myself" as only me the individual, then I am, in actuality, very small.
>
> With this foundation, we can understand the preference of *aniyyei irekha*. The notion of kindness to others develops from a core of self-concern, moving outward; it is only logical that the closest will get the highest priority.[10]

In addition to the above considerations, the *Shulḥan Arukh* (*YD* 251:7–8) rules that the order of precedence for saving people listed in Mishna Horayot (3:7–8) applies to charity as well, thus giving precedence to men over women, *kohanim* over Levites, and Torah scholars over the

7. *Minḥat Aviv*, 110.
8. *Birkat Yaavetz*, vol. 1, 51–52.
9. *Maggid Books, 2017.*
10. *Divine Footsteps*, 224–225.

unlearned. Some argue that this is only relevant for communal funds, but individuals are not bound to the latter detail, or at least only in mitigated ways.[11] However, R. Avraham Yitzchak Kook (*Responsa Daat Kohen* 131) argues against using this latter category in the contemporary context, instead opting to show compassion to all.

R. Asher Weiss (*Minḥat Asher,* Deut. 21) notes that it is unclear whether these rules are a matter of strict law, or simply positive values that are not firmly binding. R. Chaim Kanievsky notes that despite these rules, each case needs to be judged independently (*Derekh Emuna, Matanot LeAniyyim* 10:19). R. Daniel Feldman further notes that from several sources it emerges that even when the halakhic principles must be considered, they will not always determine exactly how money should be distributed, despite the fact that the existence of personal discretion is usually "incompatible with regulation."

This is despite the fact that "*tzedakah* is a concrete religious obligation.... When all is said and done, individual judgment will steer the course."[12] He further argues that:

> The Vilna Gaon is quoted as having homiletically understood the verse, "*lo tikpotz et yad'kha mei-achikha ha-evyon,* you shall not...close your hand against your destitute brother" (Deut. 15:7), as an instruction about the evaluative responsibility contained within the *tzedakah* imperative. When the hand is closed in a fist, all the fingers appear to be the same size. However, when the hand is open, it becomes clear that the fingers are all of different lengths. Similarly, the appearance of objectivity in *tzedakah* standards is deceptive. In real life, appropriate giving will always require a judgment call based on the subjective elements.[13]

---

11. See, for example, *Responsa BeTzel HaḤokhma* 3:23. See R. Akiva Eigar (*YD* 251:3) and *Responsa Ḥakham Tzvi* 70 as to whether one can give precedence to all relatives over Torah scholars, or only fathers. See also *Ḥokhmat Adam* 145:4.
12. Feldman, 212.
13. Feldman, 213, based on *Responsa Teshuvot VeHanhagot* 1:567.

Geography or Identity

The question of what defines someone as part of the giver's city will help clarify the nature of this obligation. The *Tur* (*YD* 251) cites Ri bar Baruch as ruling that even a visitor who asks for charity is considered "a poor person of your city." One could argue that this follows a very pragmatic understanding, that one is obligated to give to the closest poor person. More formally, R. Natan Gestetner (*Responsa LeHorot Natan* 13:72) argues that this is based on *ein maavirin al hamitzvot,* the prohibition to give up the opportunity to perform a mitzva in the present for the sake of one to be done at later time or in a farther place. R. Ariav's claim that the rules of precedence are meant to maintain peace might also help explain this position.

However, this position is rejected by *Tur* (ibid.) and Rama (ibid., 3). Thus, technical rules are established to determine who is considered a resident, such as living in the city for twelve months or acquiring a place of residence.[14] This forces us to consider the more fundamental options mentioned above that highlight a fundamentally greater level of obligation to those in one's inner circles, defined more objectively. One owes more to the members of his city and they are fundamentally closer to him, regardless of whether they happen to be in front of him at the moment. Similarly, a visitor does not gain a moral claim simply by showing up in a city for a day.

Many *posekim* assume that neighbors have precedence over others in one's city. However, they are divided as to whether this refers merely to those who physically live closer, or those with whom one often interacts (*Derekh Emuna, Matanot LeAniyyim* 9:13). The Gra (*YD* 251:4) assumes that one's immediate neighbors come before those on one's street.

This turns on a critical question – is community defined geographically or socially, by association and interaction? R. Yehuda Zoldan contends that we may understand this not in geographical terms, but in terms of community: With whom does one identify?[15] He sides with the notion that these halakhot are aimed at encouraging people to support those with whom one feels a sense of community and functions

---

14. See *Ahavat Ḥesed* 6:2; *Tzedeka UMishpat* 3, n. 35; and *Ahavat Tzedaka,* 323–324.
15. *Tzohar Journal,* vol. 37, 42.

as such. He cites the *Sheyarei Knesset HaGedola* (*YD* 251:3), who argues that in a community with multiple subgroups, one gives precedence to one's own subgroup.

R. Zoldan then moves beyond this. He suggests that the halakhic orders of precedence assume that the poor rely on those in their geographical area. However, now people specifically turn to those, anywhere in the world, who are part of the same ideological community. Hence, universities and yeshivas turn to those, wherever they may be, who share the vision of their institutions. He further notes that in many yeshivas, the students actually live in dormitories and are not local. Thus, the local population may not know anyone in the yeshiva. R. Asher Weiss (*Minḥat Asher,* Deut. 21) specifically justifies this based on global communication:

> Even though the *posekim* have promulgated rules concerning the precedence of charity, one must understand the situation based on the reality of the time and place. For it is clear, in my humble opinion, that even though *Ḥazal* write that "the poor of your city come first," this was only in their days when it was the people of the city who had to concern themselves with the poor of the city and there was no one else who would care for them. However, in our times, with transportation and mass communication, a poor person may travel to the ends of the earth to collect donations; alternatively, there are rabbinic organizations or charitable organizations who collect for the poor with much publicity which crosses borders and vast distances. Thus, the poor person is no longer included in "the poor of your city."

R. Zoldan uses this shift away from geographical concerns to endorse supporting a yeshiva one identifies with over one that happens to be located closer to his home. Again, this phenomenon mirrors the shifts we identified in several other issues, such as *mara de'atra.* In fact, R. Eliyahu Mizrachi (*Responsa Re'em* 53), who makes arguments to that effect in the context of communal customs (see above), also assumes that communities within a city are considered "the poor of your city," and those who are part of other communities are considred the poor of other cities. R. Shmuel Wosner (*Responsa Shevet HaLevi* 5:135) questions whether for

R. Mizrachi those who are part of other communities would be given any precedence over those from other cities.

R. Moshe Heinemann of Baltimore seems to take the approach that the precedence of the poor of one's own city is due to moral reasons. Thus, he equates the poor of one's city with those institutions to which one has a moral debt. Here are some of his suggestions for allocating charitable funds:

> In allocating and disbursing Tzedakah funds one should divide the amount of Tzedakah into thirds. The first one-third should be given to needy individuals or institutions in town. A second third should be used to satisfy one's moral obligations whether they be in town or elsewhere. In the event that one's moral obligations are all in town then at least two-thirds of one's Tzedakah would be distributed in the Baltimore area. The final third may be given to any qualified individual or institution including those out of town, provided that the requirement stated above, of assuring that over 50% of one's Tzedakah be distributed in town, has been satisfied.
>
> The following constitute moral obligations.
>
> 1. A needy relative or close friend.
> 2. A mosad in which you, your spouse, or your children received a Torah education without paying full tuition.
> 3. A mosad or needy individual from which you have direct benefit.
> 4. A mosad owned or directed by a relative or close friend to whom you feel a responsibility to help.[16]

From R. Heinemann's argument, however, it seems that he does not think that the notion of geographical community has been *replaced by the notion of an ideological one.* Rather, he thinks that *both notions of community are critical.* On an intuitive level, his suggestions make sense. When it comes to charity for needy people, the issue at hand is not primarily ideological. Rather, we want to ensure that all poor people who need

16. Accessed here: https://tzedakah.info/guidelines-for-giving/community-guidelines/.

money for food and clothing are provided for. The insistence that each community provide for their own seems pragmatic. Indeed, it would seem preferable to require each geographical community to provide basic sustenance for its poor, because relying on people to give to those they identify with would likely leave many without support. This notion seems to emerge from the Rambam's summary of these laws (*Hilkhot Mattenot Aniyyim* 9:1–3, Sefaria translation):

> Any city in which there is a Jewish community is obligated to raise up collectors of *tzedakah*, people who are well known and trustworthy, to go door-to-door among the people from Sabbath eve to Sabbath eve and to take from each and every one what is appropriate for them to give. [The amount] should be a set and clear matter for each person. They also distribute the money from Sabbath eve to Sabbath eve and give to each and every poor person enough food to last them for seven days. This method is called the *kupah* [the "coffer" for the charity fund].
>
> So also [the community] must enlist collectors to take [donations] on a day-to-day basis, from each and every yard, a main dish, other types of food, fruit, or money for anyone who would donate something at that time, and they distribute this collection in the evening among the poor and give to each poor person from it a day's sustenance. This method is called the *tamchui* [the "charity plate"].
>
> Never have we seen or heard of a Jewish community that does not have a *kupah*, but as for a *tamchui*, there are places whose custom it is to have it and places that do not. The widespread custom today is that the collectors of the *kupah* make their rounds each day [to collect the *tzedakah*], and they distribute it on each Sabbath eve.

Institutions like soup kitchens are clearly geographically dependent. As R. Heinemann presents it, this may indicate that issues of poverty should be dealt with on a local level, perhaps, we can suggest, to prevent people from falling through the cracks due to the lack of a social network. On the other hand, concerning charity to educational institutions and the like, it makes sense to give precedence to those schools which espouse the worldview one wants promulgated.

It should be noted that if the concern is that people take care of the poor in their own area, regardless of whether they identify with them, neither definition of community will be sufficient when rich people congregate into communities isolated from those less well off. In such circumstances, the rich may neither be part of the same geographic or social community as the poor. In fact, people on both sides of the political divide in the United States have noted that this reality is to the detriment of the poor and society as a whole. This is the central thesis in Robert D. Putnam's *Our Kids: The American Dream in Crisis* and Charles Murray's *Coming Apart.* In such cases, we would have to turn to criteria of need, discussed below.

The Poor of Israel

Another data point as to how to define communities comes from the laws pertaining to the poor of Israel. The *Sifrei* derives that those in Israel who are poor have precedence over those from outside Israel, and this is accepted as law (*Shulḥan Arukh, YD* 251:3). The *Baḥ* (*YD* 251:4) assumes that those who live in Israel precede those from other cities outside of Israel. However, those who live in one's own city precede the poor of Israel. Others, such as R. Avraham Yitzchak HaKohen Kook, argue that the poor of Israel are equivalent to the poor of one's own city (*Responsa Daat Kohen, Inyanei Yoreh De'ah* 133). The *Ḥatam Sofer* (*Responsa, YD* 234) assumes that those who live in Jerusalem are given precedence over those who live elsewhere in Israel.[17]

Why? *Ḥatam Sofer* (*Responsa, YD* 233–234) assumes that this criterion is similar to the precedence given to scholars. Thus, in the context of those in Jerusalem, he deals with the question of whether they should be considered great "*baalei maaseh* – people of [good] deeds." This seems to be related to the spiritual merit accrued by living in these holy places. *Pe'at HaShulḥan* (*Hilkhot Eretz Yisrael* 2:29) suggests that supporting the poor in Israel is a fulfillment of the mitzva to settle the Land of Israel. R. Lichtenstein argues this

17. See also *Torah Temima,* Deut. 15:7, n. 22.

is the case because *tzedaka* has an element which requires not just supporting the individual poor, but dealing with the problem of poverty in society. While this obligation may exist in every country, in Israel, it integrates into the value of settling the land, thus elevating the requirement.[18] R. Lichtenstein suggests that this is the meaning of the *Pe'at HaShulḥan,* though he acknowledges that he may have intended something less fundamental, namely that enabling a poor person to not leave Israel is valuable for settling the land. However, in his more fundamental formulation, R. Lichtenstein assumes that improving the quality of life for the poor in Israel would also fulfill this value, even if there was no danger of the poor leaving the land. As R. Lichtenstein notes, the above formulations shed more light on the unique nature of our obligations to Israel than the nature of charity and in many ways are parallel to other obligations that are distinct in their fulfillment between Israel and the Diaspora.

However, others, such as R. Kook, see this as an expansion of "the poor of your city" (*Responsa Daat Kohen* 133). This seems to push toward a non-geographic understanding of this principle, toward an understanding of community that is more about identification. R. Feldman offers two interpretations:

> On the one hand, it may be argued that the stake the entire Jewish nation has in the welfare of the Land incorporates the Land of Israel into the orbit of *irekha*; alternatively, the fact the whole world benefits spiritually from development in the Holy Land accomplishes the same status.[19]

These formulations focus on the nature of the mitzva of *tzedaka,* highlighting that the primary category may not be geographic proximity. R. Feldman notes that this is the position of R. Zevulun Charlop as well, with a modern twist:

18. See *Minḥat Aviv, "Tzedaka BeEretz Yisrael UVeḤutz LaAretz,"* 112–114.
19. *Divine Footsteps,* 226–227.

> The increasing development of the "global village" has, through technological advances, both diluted the significance of those in immediate geographic proximity, while enhancing the connection of faraway donors to those living in Israel.[20]

This question may also be relevant to whether those who are temporarily living in Israel gain the elevated status.[21] If it is part of the laws of charity, then it may require the residence requirements discussed above. If it is part of our obligations to the Land of Israel, then one would have to explore precisely what generates those obligations.

The Levels of Need

Complicating the matter is that there is also a hierarchy of needs. Based on the Yerushalmi (Pe'ah 8:8), the Maharik (128) rules that supporting a synagogue precedes supporting the poor. The *Shulḥan Arukh* brings this as a possibility (*YD* 249:16), though he notes that providing for children to study Torah, or for poor people who are sick, takes precedence over supporting a synagogue. This is cited by the *Beit Yosef* (*YD* 249). At the top of the list are issues of *pikuaḥ nefesh.* Thus, redeeming captives precedes other charitable causes (Bava Batra 8b; *Shulḥan Arukh, YD* 252:1). Providing for the sick, especially those facing deadly diseases, rises to the top of the list as well (*Ḥokhmat Adam* 145:7–8). Marrying off orphans is also deemed particularly important, with girls getting precedence over boys (Ketubot 67a–b; *Shulḥan Arukh, YD* 249:15). Providing food to the starving takes precedence over clothing those in need (*Shulḥan Arukh, YD* 251:6).

Posekim discuss various permutations of these issues. For example, R. Moshe Feinstein rules that if there are no halakhic authorities, precedence is given to providing for scholars over funding education for children. However, if there are halakhic authorities, one should first fund children's education (*Responsa Iggerot Moshe, YD* 3:94). Elsewhere he discusses whether education or *mikvaot* are funded first (*Responsa*

20. *Divine Footsteps,* 228.

21. See *Responsa Divrei Ḥayim, ḤM* 2:68 and *Responsa Minḥat Elazar* 4:8.

Iggerot Moshe, YD 2:115). *Posekim* discuss many different questions within this issue.[22]

Panim Yafot (Deut. 15:7) notes that that all these rules stand in tension with the precedence of community. Thus, he claims that basic needs come first, regardless of who the impoverished person is. Once the poor have been provided with those needs, the orders of communal and familial precedence apply. This is accepted by many authorities.[23]

It must be noted, however, that this may only be for those disbursing communal funds. Individuals may have more discretion.[24]

Giving to Multiple Causes

The Gemara in Eiruvin (63a) states that one who gives all his *teruma* to one *kohen* brings evil to the world. Based on this, many Rishonim, as recorded in *Shulḥan Arukh* (*YD* 257:9), rule that one should not give all the charitable funds to one person. However, there are those who question this analysis (*Responsa Imrei Yosher* 1:4). To justify extending this principle to all charitable donations, the author of *Sefer Ahavat Tzedaka* (ch. 9, *Millu'im* 5) suggests four reasons for this:

1. Based on *Baḥ* (*OḤ* 695), he suggests that this is more beneficial: one benefits one hundred poor people rather than one.[25]
2. Based on Rambam (*Commentary,* Avot 3:15), he argues that this is better from the perspective of virtue and ethics. The more acts of charity one is engaged in, the more charitable a person he becomes.
3. This way he ensures giving to the poor person who deserves it more (*Levush, YD* 257:9).
4. This way he does not cause pain to the other poor people by excluding them (ibid.).

---

22. For a collection of some of these, see http://olamot.net/ on *Kidimuyut BeTzedaka.*
23. See *Ḥiddushei Ḥatam Sofer,* Nedarim 80b; *Responsa Ḥatam Sofer, YD* 231; and *Responsa LeHorot Natan* 13:72.
24. See *Responsa Iggerot Moshe, YD* 1:144.
25. See also *Magen Avraham,* ibid., 12.

Based on this, we could argue that even if one were to accept a purely geographical or ideological notion of community, since we encourage people to donate to multiple causes, he or she can make sure to give to charities outside those limited circles as well.

The *Arukh HaShulḥan* (*YD* 251:4) pushes this further. He notes that a strict reading of the familial hierarchies would suggest that a poor person with no rich relatives might receive no charity, if all people devoted all their charitable resources to their inner circles. Thus, he suggests that while most of one's donations should be dispensed according to the rules recorded above, one should make sure to give to those in the outer circles who may not have others to support them.

R. Tzvi Spitz (*Responsa VeDarashta VeḤakarta, YD* 1:36) argues that the hierarchies should be followed exclusively. However, R. Aharon Yehuda Grossman (ibid., 35) argues that this cannot be. He cites R. Chaim Pinchas Scheinberg as arguing that it would be cruel for one to only give charity within his circles, however defined. The Talmud notes that there is a non-kosher bird known as the *ḥasida,* which means "kind." Nevertheless, its kindness is directed only at its own, which makes that kindness lacking. "**Rav Yehuda says: As for the *ḥasida,* this is the white *dayya.* And why is it called *ḥasida*? Since it performs charity [*ḥasidut*] for its fellows,** giving them from its own food" (Ḥullin 63a). Based on this, he argues that it is important to give some charity outside one's circles.

It is worth noting that depending which rationale one accepts, these rules of prioritization may or may not extend to cases in which administrators are distributing the funds. If the rationale is pragmatic or focuses on the good of the poor, these rules would be the same. However, if the reason is to develop the character of the giver, presumably these rules would apply differently when being distributed by funds.[26]

It is also possible that even if one prefers giving charity to multiple people, one should not do this so much that the gift is irrelevant.[27]

26. See *Responsa LeHorot Natan* 2:102; *Responsa Shevet HaKehati* 2:20; and the summary by Feldman, 215–216.
27. See *Responsa Minḥat Yitzḥak* 6:102; *Tzedaka UMisphat* 3, n.16; and the summary by Feldman, ibid., 216.

However, it is worth noting that there is a minority position that it is better to concentrate funds. R. Yaakov Emden (*Leḥem Shamayim,* Avot 3:15) argues that this is the case because 1) giving a larger sum is harder and thus changes one's character more and 2) it has a greater effect on the poor person. Maharal (*Netivot Olam, Netiv HaTzedaka* 4) rules similarly.

Immediacy

Another factor to consider is encountering need. The Gemara, in describing what generates the obligation to help an animal that has collapsed under a burden, emphasizes the following:

> **The Sages taught** in a *baraita*: It is written: **"If you see** the donkey of him that hates you collapsed under its burden...you shall release it with him" (Ex. 23:5). I **might** have thought one is obligated **even** if he sees the animal **from a distance;** therefore **the** previous **verse states: "If you encounter** your enemy's ox or his donkey going astray, you shall return it to him" (ibid. 23:4). **If** the Torah had written only: **"If you encounter,"** I **might** have thought that one is obligated to unload the burden only if there was **an actual encounter;** therefore, **the verse states: "If you see." And what is seeing in which there is** an element of **encounter? The Sages calculated** it as **one of seven and a half** portions, i.e., two-fifteenths, **of a *mil*, and that is** the measure of **a *ris*.**

As R. Mordechai Torczyner notes, this gemara introduces the notion that what obligates one to engage in *ḥesed* is the internal feeling generated by encountering the necessity:

> The Torah speaks of helping your neighbour's animal in two separate passages. In one it says to help "When you *see*" the animal. In the other it says to help "When you *encounter*" the animal. The Talmud (Bava Metzia 33a) blends the two verses to say that we are obligated to act on behalf of others when we *perceive* a need,

> with an intimacy that makes it an *encounter*. If we feel the impact, then we must be moved to act.[28]

Specifically as regards charity, the Torah seems to support this. In addition to the positive commandment to give charity, the Torah forbids closing our hand to the poor (Deut. 15:7). This seems to be a prohibition against ignoring an explicit request for charity, as it is an expression of emotional indifference. The Rambam (*Hilkhot Mattenot Aniyyim* 7:2) formulates it as follows:

> Anyone who sees a poor person begging and averts his eyes from him and does not give him *tzedakah* transgresses a negative *mitzvah*, as it is said, (Deut. 15:7) *[If, however, there is a needy person among you, one of your kinsmen in any of your settlements in the land that the LORD your God is giving you,] do not harden your heart and shut your hand against your needy kinsman.* (Sefaria translation)

It should be noted that in *Sefer HaMitzvot* (*Lo Taaseh* 232), the Rambam seems to rule that mere knowledge of the needy would make one violate the prohibition, contrary to his position here.[29] Rashba (Shevuot 25a), however, cites as authoritative the position that this prohibition only applies after being asked for charity. R. Yaakov Yeshaya Bloi (*Tzedaka UMishpat* 1, n. 3) notes that while some rule like the stricter position implied in the *Sefer HaMitzvot* (such as *Rishon LeTziyon, YD* 247:1), the majority seem to follow the implication in the *Mishneh Torah*.[30]

These two sources might suggest that if one feels connected to a charitable need, even from an outer circle geographically and ideologically, it would be proper to donate at least minimally to express concern. For example, the worthy outpouring of support

---

28. https://us7.campaign-archive.com/?e=&u=a4f176747199faeed32ae9a29&id=b31ca85cff.
29. See Ri Korkos and *Derekh Emuna* ad loc. See also *Responsa Yaḥel Yisrael* 6; *Responsa Shevet HaLevi* 5:131; and Feldman, 219–220. See *Reshimot Shiurim Inyanei Tzedaka* for conceptual parallels to *biah reikanit*, entering the *Beit HaMikdash* empty-handed.
30. See discussion in *Responsa Shraga HaMeir* 8:90:5:2 and Feldman, 219.

when there are natural disasters, terrorist attacks, wars, etc. seems to be an expression of this value – when people are moved by extreme and sudden need, they should concretize those emotions and support those who need it.

Benefit of Human Interaction

In a homiletic piece, R. Avraham Price (*Imrei Avraham, Naso 1*) notes that many of the passages in the Talmud about *tzedaka*, even when they instruct the giver to try to avoid knowing the identity of the recipient, assume that there is some interaction between giver and receiver. Based on this, he argues that to only donate through organizations, to the exclusion of giving directly to people who ask for money, is to hide from the poor, about which the Talmud (Bava Batra 10a) states, "**Anyone who turns his eyes away from** one seeking **charity is** considered **as if he worships idols.**" He harshly critiques organizations that encourage people to give only through them and feel exempt from providing for the poor. This becomes clear from the emphasis that is placed on giving charity with the proper attitude, providing psychological support to the poor, in addition to the financial support (see *Rambam, Hilkhot Mattenot Aniyyim* 10:4). In a world where we often donate online, through organizations and the like, it is important to remember that the human connection should not be eliminated.

Conclusion

In this chapter, I have not tried to outline firm guidelines for charitable distribution. However, what we have seen is that, as in other areas of halakha, there is room to understand the notion of community that drives the hierarchies of charitable giving in terms of identification either instead of or in addition to geographical considerations. Additionally, as one factor in charitable giving is the emotional pull, mere exposure to a wider network of people and causes should be relevant when considering to whom one donates. Social media and other forms of communication, therefore, have in many ways transformed the communities from which we fundraise. However, there are reasons not to fully abandon the geographical considerations that drive the formulation of the halakhot in classical sources.

Section 2

Responsibility for What Is Posted Online

Chapter 9

Responsibility for Facilitating Sin or Harm on the Internet: General Introduction

Halakha often holds people responsible for facilitating the sins of others. In the digital age, there has been much discussion of this, focusing on both the legal question of whether internet companies are responsible for what is published on their platforms, as well as the ethical questions of whether, and to what extent, those who host these platforms should care. In the last several years, these questions have been widely discussed, as false information shared on social media seems to have influenced recent elections in the United States and Great Britain and has affected the attitudes of many people with regard to Covid-19 restrictions and vaccines. The legal scholar Cass Sunstein recently published a book[1] addressing the legal and moral question concerning responsibility for false information and the harm it causes, and what internet companies have done and must continue to do to combat it. Considering the importance of these issues, it is well worth exploring the wisdom of the halakhic system to gain insight on these complex matters.

Legally, at least in the United States, internet companies are almost always immune to litigation based on what has been published on their platforms. This is based on Section 230 of the United States Communications Decency Act, which states, "No provider or user of an interactive computer service shall be treated as the publisher or speaker of any information provided by another information content provider." Jeff Koseff captures the importance of this law in the title of his recent book, *The Twenty-Six Words That Created the Internet.*[2] Koseff argues that this law enabled the development of the internet as we know it, further contending that it is the existence of this law in the United States that has made it home to the most successful internet companies, as had they been based in other countries, almost of all of which have more restrictive laws, they would have faced great difficulties.

While at first glance, the above might imply that there is a widespread feeling that internet companies should not be responsible for what they facilitate on their platforms, this is mistaken. Koseff notes that in the years preceding his book, several court decisions limited the freedoms implied by Section 230. In the years since he published, several bills have been introduced to scale back Section 230, such as the Eliminating Abusive and Rampant Neglect of Interactive Technologies (EARN IT) Act, Platform Accountability and Consumer Transparency (PACT) Act, and several others. More importantly, however, this presentation speaks only to the *legal issues*; it does not speak to the *ethical concerns.* In fact, one of the original motivations for Section 230 was, in the words of Rep. Chris Cox, one of the two authors of this section of the law, the hope that "the people who were in the best position to clean

1. Cass R. Sunstein, *Liars: Falsehoods and Free Speech in an Age of Deception* (Oxford University Press, 2021).
2. Cornell University Press, 2019.

up the Internet would do so."[3] Previously, by editing or moderating any content, the platforms could become liable for anything published, thus making moderation an all-or-nothing choice, giving them a perverse incentive to not moderate at all.[4] This is amply clear from the title of Section 230, Subsection C: *Protection for "Good Samaritan" Blocking and Screening of Offensive Material.*

Thus, as our interest is not in the secular legal question, we propose the following: While the US Congress and other governments may debate as to whether the best way to protect people from misuse of the internet is legislation or expectations of decency on behalf of internet companies, there is *an ethical intuition that seems widely shared. Even when a person or company is not harming someone, they may be responsible for the harm they enabled, or responsible to protect those who are being harmed.* From the charter of Facebook's oversight board, one can see that social media companies are indeed struggling with these questions as well.

> Freedom of expression is a fundamental human right. Facebook seeks to give people a voice so we can connect, share ideas and experiences, and understand each other.
>
> Free expression is paramount, but there are times when speech can be at odds with authenticity, safety, privacy, and dignity. Some expression can endanger other people's ability to express themselves freely. Therefore, it must be balanced against these considerations.[5]

---

3. Rep. Chris Cox, interview cited in Koseff, 60.
4. Take the following comments of the US Court of Appeals for the Ninth Circuit in the case of "Fair Housing Council of San Fernando Valley v. Roommates.com, LLC": Under the reasoning of *Stratton Oakmont,* online service providers that voluntarily filter some messages become liable for all messages transmitted, whereas providers that bury their heads in the sand and ignore problematic posts altogether escape liability.... In passing section 230, Congress sought to spare interactive computer services this grim choice by allowing them to perform some editing on user-generated content without thereby becoming liable for all defamatory or otherwise unlawful messages that they didn't edit or delete."
5. https://www.oversightboard.com/governance/.

As society explores the best way to achieve this goal, it is important for us to mine the halakhic system for insights that will give us the language to navigate these critical issues.

For this reason, while there is much halakhic discussion concerning whether or not a corporation is treated as a person, and whether a corporation is therefore subject to mitzva obligations, for our purposes we claim that the halakhic ethic will provide insight, whether or not halakha formally applies to a corporation as it would to an individual.

While much of the legal discussion has been focused on internet companies, we must also explore the extent to which participation in the culture of the internet or social media makes one complicit in the problematic usage of those platforms from a halakhic perspective, even if one personally uses them only for positive or neutral purposes.

The Case of Google in China

As noted, many believe that technology and social media companies do have some responsibility to ensure that their platforms are not misused, even if people will disagree about what is considered wrong and to what extent the companies must prevent this damage. This conviction is shared by many in the world of big tech as well. As evidenced from the story of Google's problems in China, there seems to be an intuition that moral culpability may extend to participation in a problematic culture.

For example, the Google security team has taken as a mantra "Do know evil!" This is an allusion to Google's one-time directive, "Don't be evil." As Steven Levy records, Google had difficulty living up to its own ideals when it entered the Chinese market. In his book, *In the Plex: How Google Thinks, Works, and Shapes our Lives,*[6] Levy details its challenges. Google's founders did not agree with the censorship that the Chinese government insisted on when it opened in China. They thought it was an "evil." Nevertheless, they thought it was better to somewhat open the world of the internet for the Chinese market, helping to bring some information and freedom, rather than let the perfect be the enemy of the good. Thus, they entered the market and tried to keep within their own

6. Simon & Schuster, 2011.

guidelines, which attempted to limit China's encroachments on people's freedom to search. But in 2010, they no longer saw this as feasible and effectively ceased operations there. Levy describes the problem:[7]

> "DO KNOW EVIL!"
>
> That was the legend on the back of the cool black T-shirts printed by the geeks, scientists, pager-bound technicians, and former break-in artists on the Google Security Team.
>
> But the failure to know evil – or more accurately, the failure to navigate around it without falling into its dark orbit – would come to haunt the company in its most serious moral crisis. When the revelation came that a security breach had compromised the company's intellectual property and additional attacks had exposed the Gmail accounts of dissidents critical of the Chinese government, Google's "China problem" became front-page news. After weeks of struggling with the issue, Google's Executive Committee, including Schmidt, Page, and Brin, finally agreed on the most significant and embarrassing retreat in the company's history. On January 12, 2010, they changed course in the country with the world's biggest Internet user base, announcing an effective pullout of their search engine from mainland China. Though the underlying issue of Google's China pullout was censorship, it was ironic that a cyberattack had triggered the retreat. Google had believed that its computer science skills and savvy made it a leader in protecting its corporate information. With its blend of Montessori naiveté and hubris that had served it so well in other areas, the company felt it could do security better. Until the China incursion, it appeared to be succeeding.

We can note several salient points:

1. Google's founders shared the general sentiment that they were at least somewhat responsible for how their search engine was used.

---

7. pp. 267–268.

2. The fundamental belief that a company is responsible for its product being used unethically is a general one, though the specifics of *what is considered wrong may vary depending on one's perspective.* Thus, while for illustrative halakhic purposes we will give examples of potential sins that are committed using these products and platforms, the general contours of our arguments do not depend on whether or not one accepts the sinful nature of our specific examples.
3. Attempts at avoiding such ethically compromised situations do not always succeed. While the general media may have not judged Google favorably for the way it handled China, there is clearly a distinction ethically and halakhically between attempting to avoid unethical behavior and failing, on the one hand, and making no attempt to avoid such behavior, on the other. This distinction is often lost.
4. Part of Google's calculus was that while they did not agree with China's censorship, they originally entered China believing they could bring about a net good. They ceased operations there when they decided that was not the case. What are the halakhic implications of such an assessment – that one is allowing and thereby (albeit hesitantly) endorsing problematic behavior for a greater good? Does that intent make it less problematic?[8]

As noted above, the question of liability has recently returned to Congress. For example, there have been several congressional hearings in which Mark Zuckerberg, founder and CEO of Facebook, was questioned and criticized for not stopping his platform from being misused. This indicates that there is growing consensus that such companies cannot allow their platforms to be used with abandon. The fact that Facebook has instituted new policies to deal with false information, for example,

8. See Sunstein, *Liars*, chs. 2–3, where he attempts to balance the importance of 1) state of mind, 2) magnitude of harm, 3) likelihood of harm, and 4) timing of harm, and lay out how different moral theories will assess these factors and the practical implications.

suggests that they accept this argument at a moral level, or at least are sensing the change in the legal realities, as evidenced by the recent legislation noted above.

The User

While most of the legal discussion has revolved around the responsibilities of tech companies, one philosopher addresses the role of the user.

Dr. S. Matthew Liao, in an op-ed in *The New York Times*,[9] notes that Facebook, from his perspective, has enabled many wrongs, such as spreading false information, connecting and spreading the propaganda of white supremacists, spreading other hate speech, and causing depression and anxiety among those who compulsively scroll through Facebook.

He believes that people who agree that the actions listed above are wrong should at least wonder whether they are complicit:

> Some people might think that because they mostly share photos of their cats on Facebook, such concerns do not apply to them. But this is not so, for three reasons. First, even if one does not contribute directly to the dissemination of fake news or hang out in echo chambers, simply being on Facebook encourages one's friends to stay on Facebook, and some of those friends might engage in such activities. This influence on others is known as a (positive) network effect, where increased numbers of people improve the value of a product.
>
> Second, by being on Facebook one serves as a data point for Facebook's social media experiment, even if one encounters none of Facebook's experimental manipulations. In doing so, one could be helping Facebook to refine its algorithms so that it can

9. Available at: https://www.nytimes.com/2018/11/24/opinion/sunday/facebook-immoral.html.

> better single out specific individuals for certain purposes, some of which could be ... nefarious ....[10]
>
> Third, using Facebook is not just an individual action but also a collective one that may be akin to failing to pay taxes. A few people failing to pay taxes might not make much of a difference to a government's budget, but such an action may nevertheless be wrong because it is a failure to participate in a collective action that achieves a certain good end. In a similar vein, choosing to remain on Facebook might not directly undermine democratic values. But such an action could also be wrong because we might be failing to participate in a collective action (that is, leaving Facebook) that would prevent the deterioration of democracy.

Liao continues to argue that those who are engaged in problematic activities are obviously obligated to leave Facebook (or, better yet, to stop engaging in those activities). In addition, Liao argues that "for those of us who do not engage in such objectionable behavior, it is helpful to consider whether Facebook has crossed certain moral 'red lines,' entering the realm of outright wickedness." Meaning, Liao takes it as a given that despite his arguments above, an individual user of Facebook would not be obligated to dissociate from Facebook had the company not engaged in evil. This is surprising, as toward the end of the piece, he writes:

> That said, we should not place the responsibility to uphold democratic values entirely on Facebook. As moral agents, we should also hold ourselves responsible for our conduct, and we should be reflective about what we say, react to and share when we are on social media.

By the same token, as moral agents we should at least consider the question as to whether Facebook users would be obligated to leave

---

10. Liao specifically singles out the purposes of Cambridge Analytica, a company that used data to target campaign ads to specific people during the Brexit vote and Trump election. Whether one objects to, or accepts, the specific goals of Cambridge Analytica is irrelevant to the overall argument.

Facebook if their presence allowed other individuals to be involved in problematic activities. While staying on Facebook would be a lower-level ethical violation, to be sure, this does not mean that it is not problematic at all.

Endorsements

Liao notes that there are more active ways in which social media users condone problematic behavior:

> Among Twitter users, a common refrain is "retweets are not endorsements." In a similar manner, one might also think that "sharing" or "reacting to" are not "endorsements." This is a mistake. By sharing or reacting to a post, even if one explicitly criticizes the post, one is amplifying the message of that post and signaling that the post warrants further attention.

As we will see, halakha may very well share this intuition – that reacting to or sharing a post is somewhat of an endorsement, and thus creates halakhic issues when the material shared is that of prohibited activity. But it is also likely that one can distinguish between "not endorsing" and criticizing or calling out activity. The latter may be critical to help root out problematic attitudes.

Thus, taken together, and leaving aside those who obviously misuse the internet to harm others, we must ask:

1. Are Facebook, Google, Twitter, and similar companies responsible for ensuring that their platforms are not misused? To what extent would they be responsible – to attempt to limit it, to make it impossible, or to do nothing at all?
2. If there is moral culpability, does this extend to the *users* of these platforms? Meaning, if we conclude that one is accountable for problematic content posted by others, does having a Facebook account make one a participant in sinful activity?
3. If people post evidence of problematic behavior, is it considered illicit support of that behavior to "like" a picture or offer encouragement, approval, or congratulations?

4. Is one obligated to actively express disagreement with such posts concerning problematic activities?

There are two halakhic axes upon which to assess these issues. The first is *lifnei iver* and its corollaries, which explore the moral responsibility for causing, enabling, or encouraging problematic behavior. The second is *lo taamod al dam re'ekha*, the prohibition of standing idly by when others are being harmed, focusing on the responsibility to protect victims, regardless of who is culpable for the creation and publication of the damaging material.

Chapter 10

The Parameters of *Lifnei Iver*

Lifnei Iver

Let us begin with the biblical prohibition of *lifnei iver*, its derivatives, and its corollaries. (The halakhic discussions in the following chapters are quite detailed. Some of these discussions appear with a gray background, for the benefit of readers who would prefer to skip them.)

Before discussing the details, it is important to explain how this phrase came to mean what it does.

It is written in the Torah (Lev. 19:14): "You shall not curse the deaf, and you shall not put a stumbling block before the blind. You shall fear your God; I am the Lord." Who is this blind person, and what is the stumbling block?

As R. Elchanan Samet notes,[1] building on the approach of Nehama Leibowitz,[2] there are four possible interpretations:

---

1. https://www.etzion.org.il/en/tanakh/torah/sefer-vayikra/parashat-kedoshim/kedoshim-you-shall-not-place-stumbling-block-blind.
2. Nehama Leibowitz, *New Studies in Vayikra – Leviticus* (The World Zionist Organization, 1993), 307–313.

1. **The literal interpretation:** According to this approach, the blind person is literally someone who cannot see, and the stumbling block is a physical obstacle. The Torah is prohibiting the tripping of a blind person. The Gemara (Nidda 57a, Ḥullin 3a) attributes this interpretation to the Kutim, those who reject the rabbinic interpretations of the Torah.
2. **The almost-literal interpretation:** This takes slight poetic license, contending that the "blind person" is simply someone who does not see the obstacle, and the stumbling block is any danger placed in their path. As R. Samet writes:

   > [T]his approach maintains virtually the same interpretation of the term "stumbling block," and only minimally expands the definition of the word "blind," to include a person with operative vision but who cannot see the stumbling block before him. The prohibition thus comes to forbid taking unfair advantage of not only the handicapped, but anyone in a situation where they cannot detect a given threat to their well-being.

   R. Samet notes that Onkelos's translation of this verse tends in this direction.
3. **"Blind" refers to someone who is unaware of certain information, and one is prohibited from taking advantage of that deficiency.** This is the explanation of the *Sifra*. Based on this, the *Sifra* forbids giving bad advice concerning both physical and spiritual matters. This explanation is accepted by the Rambam (*Sefer HaMitzvot, Lo Taaseh* 299; *Hilkhot Rotze'aḥ* 12:14) and *Sefer HaḤinnukh* (232).[3]
4. **The stumbling block is sin, and one is prohibited from enabling someone to sin.** This is the primary usage of this prohibition in halakha, and it is derived from a passage in Tractate Avoda Zara.

We will now discuss the fourth of the above interpretations.

3. As Nehama Leibowitz notes, the *Sifra* provides three examples that indicate three potential categories of bad advice: physical damage, material damage, and spiritual damage.

The Mishna at the beginning of Tractate Avoda Zara forbids commerce with idol worshippers[4] for the three days before their holidays. The Gemara adds that one also may not give animals to these idol worshippers during this period, and offers two reasons for this latter prohibition.

One is what the Gemara refers to as *harvaḥa*. Rashi (6a, s.v. *mishum harvaḥa*) assumes that this means that the idol worshipper will be so thankful for the animal that he will thank his god on his holiday, making the Jew responsible for the invocation of an idolatrous god.[5]

The other possibility raised is that the Jew is violating *lifnei iver* by giving the idol worshipper an animal that he might use as an offering on the upcoming holiday.

The Gemara proves the existence of such a prohibition from a statement of Rabbi Natan:

> **Rabbi Natan said: From where** is it derived **that a person may not extend a cup of wine to a nazirite,** who is prohibited from drinking wine, **and** that he may not extend **a limb** severed **from a living animal to descendants of Noah? The verse states: "And you shall not put a stumbling block before the blind"** (Lev. 19:14). (Avoda Zara 6a–b)

We saw earlier that according to the *Sifra*, the prohibition against placing a stumbling block includes being involved in someone else's sin. However, as in the first two levels of interpretation, the *Sifra* limits the prohibition to a case in which the victim is *unaware of, or,* in the words of the verse, *blind to,* the obstacle. How do *Ḥazal* extend this prohibition to cases in which one enables *a willing sinner* to engage in illicit behavior with *eyes open, literally and figuratively*? The Rambam solves this problem as follows:

4. The question of whether this refers to all non-Jews or only idol worshippers inspires an extensive discussion among the Rishonim and halakhic authorities, which is beyond the scope of our discussion.
5. Rabbenu Tam, Ritva, and Meiri have alternative interpretations, both of the mishna (2a) and the central discussion in the Gemara (6a–b). We will return to these explanations below.

> Anyone who misdirects a person, blind on any subject, by giving him wrong advice, or encourages a criminal, *who is blind and cannot see the way of truth because of his greedy lust*, transgresses a prohibition, as it is written: "You shall not put a stumbling block before the blind." (Rambam, *Hilkhot Rotze'aḥ* 12:14)

Meaning, the blindness being discussed is figurative, as when a person is blinded by passion. R. Jeremy Weider has suggested that one may extend the Rambam's description to the third interpretation as well. In other words, one may not put others in a situation in which they are likely to develop an emotional attachment that will make it difficult for them to make the "right" decision, even if no deception is involved.[6]

There is much discussion among the halakhic authorities as to whether the latter two interpretations offered by *Ḥazal* negate the first two interpretations, as R. Samet discusses at length.[7] For our purposes, we will be focusing on the fourth interpretation, based on the Gemara in Avoda Zara. Colloquially, it is this aspect of the prohibition that people refer to, though this interpretation is not meant to negate the others. As noted, it is standard among halakhic authorities to accept the third interpretation, namely the prohibition against offering bad advice, and several prominent halakhic authorities accept the binding halakhic nature of the first two interpretations as well, in addition to that presented by the *Sifra* and the Talmud.

---

6. Available at: https://www.yutorah.org/lectures/lecture.cfm/890788/rabbi-jeremy-wieder-rabbi-shmuel-maybruch/mental-health-in-dating-a-panel-discussion/. In context, R. Wieder cautions against waiting to reveal health issues to a potential spouse until the point at which the couple is so emotionally involved that it would be difficult to back out of the relationship.
7. For some opinions not discussed by R. Samet, see my *shiur*: https://www.yutorah.org/sidebar/lecture.cfm/906714/rabbi-jonathan-ziring/avodah-zarah-6-lifnei-iver-from-pshat-to-halachah-1-6a-b-/.

What Does It Mean to Cause Someone to Sin?

A critical element to consider in any situation is how directly linked must one be to the problematic behavior to be considered liable. To understand the scope of this issue, we must turn to the central discussion in the Talmud about *lifnei iver*. As we will see, many halakhic authorities distinguish between enabling a sin, meaning making it possible for someone who could not have committed the sin without one's help, and merely aiding a sinner who could have committed the sin regardless, albeit with more difficulty.

Enabling vs. Aiding: Two Sides of the River

As noted above, the central discussions of *lifnei iver* appear in the middle of the discussion of the prohibition to conduct business with idol worshippers for the three days before their holidays. The Gemara provides two possible reasons for this sin: *lifnei iver* and *harvaḥa*. The majority of Rishonim assume that if the issue is *lifnei iver*, the prohibition applies specifically to selling items that can be used for worship. According to the latter opinion – which as noted by Rashi means that we are concerned the non-Jew will be caused to thank his god for the business he did with the Jew – this limitation may not apply.

Although this distinction is accepted by some Rishonim, this is not what the Gemara focuses on. The Gemara presents the issues as follows:

> **A dilemma was raised before** the Sages: Is the reason for the prohibition against conducting business with gentiles in the days preceding their festivals **because** the gentile might **profit,** which will bring him joy, and he will subsequently give thanks to his idol on his festival? **Or perhaps** it is because this is a violation of the prohibition: **"And you shall not put a stumbling block before the blind"** (Lev. 19:14), as one who sells an animal to a gentile thereby aids him in engaging in prohibited idol worship.
>
> The Gemara explains: **What is the** practical **difference** between the two options? The practical difference is in a situation **where** the gentile already **has an animal of his own. If you**

> **say** that the reason for the prohibition is **because** he might **profit,** here too the Jew **causes him to profit.** But **if you say** that the reason for the prohibition is **due to** the prohibition: **"You shall not put a stumbling block** before **the blind,"** since the gentile **has his own** animal, the Jew is not helping him sin. (Avoda Zara 6a)

At this stage, the Gemara suggests that the difference between the two is as follows: If the issue is *lifnei iver,* the Jew sins only by enabling the non-Jew to sin. This will be so only in a case when the non-Jew has no other animals to offer as a sacrifice. If the non-Jew has an animal, the Jew is not the person responsible for the sin. Thus, the halakhic problem must be something else.

The Gemara, however, challenges this, noting that there are indications that one violates *lifnei iver* even in cases in which the sinner could have committed the sin without outside help:

> The Gemara challenges: **And** even **if he** already **has** his own animal, does **not** one who assists him **transgress due to** the command: **"You shall not put a stumbling block** before **the blind"? But isn't it taught** in a *baraita* that **Rabbi Natan said: From where** is it derived **that a person may not extend a cup of wine to a nazirite,** who is prohibited from drinking wine, **and** that he may not extend **a limb** severed **from a living animal to descendants of Noah? The verse states: "And you shall not put a stumbling block before the blind"** (Lev. 19:14). **But here,** in both cases, **if one does not give it to him, he can take it himself, and** yet the one who provides it to him **transgresses due to** the prohibition: **"You shall not put a stumbling block before the blind."** (Ibid.)

The Gemara cites a *baraita* that prohibits someone from handing a glass of wine to a *nazir,* who is forbidden by dint of his or her vow to drink wine. However, the Gemara at this stage assumes that the case is one in which the *nazir* could have reached the glass of wine unassisted. Thus, it seems that the initial distinction between enabling and aiding is false, as the *baraita* still forbids helping the *nazir* due to the prohibition of *lifnei iver*. To this, the Gemara responds:

> **Here we are dealing with** a case **where they are standing on** the **two sides** of **a river,** and therefore the recipient could not have taken it himself. Since his help was instrumental, the one who conveyed the item has violated the prohibition of putting a stumbling block before the blind. The Gemara adds: The language of the *baraita* **is also precise, as it teaches:** A person **may not extend, and it does not teach: One may not give. Learn from** the usage of the term "extend" that the *baraita* is referring to one located on one side of a river, who extends the item to the one on the other side. (Avoda Zara 6a–b)

The Gemara rejects the inference and returns to its initial assumption, that *lifnei iver* is violated only when one enables a sinner to perform a sin that could not have been committed without assistance. To explain the *nazir* case, the Gemara suggests that one violates *lifnei iver* only if the cup of wine is located out of reach of the *nazir,* such as on the opposite side of a river. Thus, by handing the cup to the *nazir,* one is indeed making it possible for the *nazir* to sin in a way otherwise impossible. By contrast, if they are both on the same side of the river, the one who hands the wine to the *nazir* is merely *aiding* him to sin, not *enabling* the sin.

This translation and elucidation of the Gemara's answer follow the understanding of Rashi and many Rishonim, who derive the enabling versus aiding distinction from this passage. As Rashi (s.v. *dekaima bitrei*) writes, one violates *lifnei iver* when "the idol worshipper is on one side and the Jew is on the other side, for if he had not given it to him, he could not have taken it." Among Aḥaronim, it is almost universally accepted that this is correct by Torah law. They often refer to this distinction as *trei avrei nahara* (or *denahara*) and *ḥad ever denahar* – "two sides of the river" or "on the same side of the river."

Before turning to the potential rabbinic prohibition that includes even aiding a sinner, we will explore a less-known opinion that rejects this distinction entirely.

The Rambam

The Rambam in many places ignores the distinction between enabling and aiding. For example, the Rambam prohibits buying stolen goods, without distinguishing between cases where the thief could have sold the property to someone else or would have stolen the item even had he not been able to sell it:

> It is forbidden to purchase a stolen item from a thief, and it is forbidden to assist in modifying the stolen item so that one will purchase it. Anyone who does this, and other things like this, strengthens the hands of transgressors and [doing so] transgresses "You shall not put a stumbling block in front of the blind" (Lev. 19:14). (*Hilkhot Gezeila* 5:1)

Similarly, building on *sugyot* later in the first chapter of Avoda Zara, the Rambam prohibits selling weapons to non-Jews, as well as to Jewish bandits. In the latter context, the Rambam writes:

> Whatever must not be sold to a non-Jew must not be sold to a Jewish bandit, since this will encourage a criminal and misdirect him.
>
> So too, anyone who misdirects a person, blind on any subject, by giving him wrong advice, or encourages a criminal, who is blind and cannot see the way of truth because of his greedy lust, is transgressing a prohibition, as it is written: "You shall not put a stumbling block before the blind" (Lev. 19:14), meaning that if a person comes to you for advice, you should give him advice fitting his needs. (*Hilkhot Rotze'aḥ* 12:14)

Here as well, the Rambam does not address the issue of whether or not the bandit could have obtained weapons elsewhere.

The Rambam does not address this distinction in any of his discussions of this prohibition (see, for example, *Sefer HaMitzvot, Lo Taaseh* 299).

Nevertheless, most Aḥaronim assume that the Rambam must have accepted this distinction, and provide numerous suggestions to explain why the Rambam never actually presents it (see, for example, *Responsa Divrei Malkiel* 1:103).

Rabbenu Ḥananel

R. Nachum Rabinovitch, however, notes that the straightforward understanding is that the Rambam does not accept this distinction, and notes that many other Rishonim do not mention this distinction either.[8] R. Rabinovitch points to the commentary of Rabbenu Ḥananel, a source that the Rambam would have used to understand the Gemara, which offers an alternative explanation of the distinction of one side versus two sides of the river.

While Rashi focuses on the location of the *object used in the sin and its proximity to the sinner,* Rabbenu Ḥananel suggests that the issue at hand is *the location of the sinner and his proximity to the helper.* When the two people are separated by a river, the potential helper cannot be forced into aiding the sinner. But when they are on the same side of a river, the sinner can force the other person to help him. For Rabbenu Ḥananel, one violates *lifnei iver* only if there is the possibility of opting out. If the sinner can force the other to help, then the sinner bears full responsibility. Presumably, the reason is because in such a case, the possibility of being coerced removes the agency from the helper and returns it fully to the sinner.

R. Rabinovitch suggests that the Rambam accepts this interpretation of the Gemara. He further argues, contrary to the conviction of many Aḥaronim, that this is a mainstream opinion among Rishonim. If this is the case, then many of the distinctions we will make between cases where the social media platform or user is enabling or at most merely aiding the sinner would not be relevant. The possibility that the latter cases are subject only to rabbinic law and are therefore guided by different principles than the former ones assumes the distinction as

8. See his extensive article *"Kol Yisrael Areivim Zeh BaZeh," Techumin* 11: 41–72. See also R. Baruch Weintraub, who proves this based on the Rambam's understanding of Bava Kama 117a, as recorded by Rambam in *Hilkhot Ḥovel UMazik* 8:3. His article is available at: http://www.etzion.gush.net/vbm/archive/yomyom/dafyomyomi/2010-08-20.php.

understood by Rashi. According to the Rambam's opinion, which R. Rabinovitch contends should be accepted, even cases in which one can be understood as only aiding the sinner, rather than enabling him, may be prohibited by Torah law.

Rabbis David and Avraham Stav[9] note that while the Rambam (*Peirush HaMishnayot,* Terumot 6:3) does recognize a distinction between *lifnei iver* (enabling) and *mesaye'a* (aiding), he seems to think that both are forbidden by Torah law, as R. Rabinovitch suggests. R. Natan Gestetner (*Responsa LeHorot Natan* 3:23) notes this as well, contending that the Rambam derives that aiding is prohibited based on another verse: "You shall not join hands with the guilty" (Ex. 23:1).

Easing

Rashi seems to make a distinction between enabling one to sin in a case in which it would have otherwise been *impossible,* and all other cases, and this is accepted by many halakhic authorities (see summary in *Yad Malakhi* 363). Yet, some Rishonim who accept his basic model still reject this extreme formulation. For example, the Meiri (Avoda Zara 6a, s.v. *kol shehu*) writes that if the sinner would be unlikely to obtain the item used in the sin due to *difficulty of access* (though not impossibility), then giving the sinner the item would constitute *lifnei iver* by Torah law. The *Ketav Sofer* (Responsa, *YD* 83) argues that even if the sinner does not yet own the item and would thus have to exert effort to obtain it, giving him the item would violate *lifnei iver* by Torah law. A similar stance is put forth by R. Yair Bacharach (*Responsa Ḥavot Yair* 185). According to these formulations, even if one rejects the view of the Rambam, many cases that according to a strict reading of Rashi would at most be by rabbinic law would be considered *lifnei iver* by Torah law.

9. *Avo Beitekha* (Maggid, 2017), 241–242.

What If Someone Would Need to Help?

The *Mishneh LaMelekh* (*Hilkhot Malveh VeLoveh* 4:2) argues that in a case in which the sinner could violate a prohibition without the help of anyone in particular, but not without the participation of someone, the specific person who *aids* the sinner is considered to be *enabling* him and violates *lifnei iver* by Torah law.

His example, derived from Bava Metzia 75b, is that a lender who accepts a loan with interest violates *lifnei iver*, in addition to an independent local prohibition. Though there are other possible borrowers, a lender cannot violate the laws of *ribbit* (interest) unless some Jew somewhere agrees to enter into the prohibited loan. The *Mishneh LaMelekh* cites the *Penei Moshe* (*YD* 108), who disagrees.

Whether or not this analysis is accepted is a dispute among the halakhic authorities. R. Eliezer Waldenberg summarizes this dispute in several responsa; sometimes he is more sympathetic to the opinion of the *Penei Moshe*, and sometimes less so. For example, in one responsum (*Responsa Tzitz Eliezer* 3:16), he argues that both broadcasters of and listeners to the radio in Israel on Shabbat violate *lifnei iver*. Despite the fact that there are other listeners, if all Jews in Israel would keep Shabbat, the radio would not broadcast on Shabbat. Thus, no listener can defend himself by saying someone else will listen, as the sin would not happen without some Jew being willing to facilitate the sin. By contrast, in another responsum (20:20) he provides several leniencies for a businessperson to enter into partnership with Shabbat violators, even if the company could not exist without some other Jew entering the partnership.[10]

Rabbinic Extensions: Aiding Without Enabling

Several of the Rishonim, while they accept Rashi's distinction between enabling and aiding, contend that even merely aiding a sinner may be

10. For more on this, see *Benei Ḥayil* (*ḤM* 34, *Hagahot Beit Yosef* 7), the Ḥida (*Darkhei Yosef*, *ḤM* 9:3), *Minḥat Ḥinnukh* (232:3), *Knesset HaGedola* (*YD* 159, *Hagahat HaTur* 11), *Responsa Ketav Sofer* (*YD* 83), and *Responsa Minḥat Yitzḥak* (3:79).

forbidden by rabbinic law. Tosafot (Shabbat 3a, s.v. *bava dereisha*),[11] for example, contend that even when the item used in the sin is on the same side of the river as the sinner, the facilitator of the sin violates a rabbinic prohibition. The same opinion appears in the Ran (Avoda Zara 1b [Rif], s.v. *minayin*).

Several other potential formulations emerge from the commentaries of Rishonim on the opening pages of Avoda Zara, though they are less often cited in later halakhic literature. For example, Rabbenu Tam (Tosafot, Avoda Zara 2a, s.v. *asur*; in more detail, *Ḥiddushei HaRitva* ad loc.) rejects Rashi's understanding of *harvaḥa*. As he notes, if *lifnei iver* in the case of selling to non-Jews before idolatrous holidays refers to giving them animals to sacrifice, and *harvaḥa* encompasses selling anything that might cause the non-Jew to thank his god on the holiday, the Gemara should have suggested a more fundamental difference between the rationales than one side versus two sides of the river. It should have stated that in terms of *lifnei iver*, it is forbidden only to sell items that can be used for worship, while in terms of *harvaḥa*, all business would be forbidden.

Based on this, Rabbenu Tam argues that according to both rationales, it is forbidden to sell them only items used in worship. *Harvaḥa*, which literally means an abundance, means that it is forbidden to sell animals even when the idol worshipper has animals, if this will make it easier for the idol worshipper to sacrifice better-quality animals (presumably this is true whether the animal he offers is from his own flock or the new animals being purchased). However, Rabbenu Tam rules in accordance with the explanation of the Gemara that the prohibition is due to *lifnei iver*, not *harvaḥa*, thus forbidding selling animals that can be used for worship only when the idol worshipper has no similar animals, even if he has other means of obtaining animals. Note that according to Rabbenu Tam, *harvaḥa* prohibits contributing to the performance of a sin even when the sin could have been done without his help.

11. See also *Tosafot HaRosh*, ibid. and Ran, ibid., 1a, s.v. *umakshu*.

The Ritva cites Rabbenu Tam, though he does not focus on the issue of quality, but rather of quantity. He writes that concerns of *harvaḥa* would forbid selling animals to the idol worshipper on the assumption that this would allow him to sacrifice more animals. This is quite a novel approach. Within the formulation of Rabbenu Tam in Tosafot it could be that one is not really helping the idol worshipper to sin, because the plan had always been for him to sacrifice one offering, which he still does, albeit of a higher quality. The Ritva's suggestion that it is not full-fledged *lifnei iver* even when the idol worshipper could have sacrificed fewer animals and can now sacrifice more is surprising, as one could have argued that each offering is independent, and the Jew enables the idol worshipper to sacrifice the additional animal. This is even more surprising considering that, like Rabbenu Tam, the Ritva argues that according to the Gemara's conclusion, this is permitted!

Tosafot Rabbenu Elḥanan (Avoda Zara 6b, s.v. *velo ketani*) argues against this possibility, maintaining that because a case may arise in which the idol worshipper would sacrifice both animals, this would be a violation of *lifnei iver* (though it is not clear whether he means that the prohibition applies by Torah law or by rabbinic law; either way it is prohibited). However, the argument that one does not violate *lifnei iver* by Torah law if the sinner could have committed the sin without one's help, even though now the sin is greater in scale, is rarely spelled out in practical halakhic rulings. Nevertheless, it is important to note that this model exists.

Rejection of the Lenient Opinion or Limitation of Its Scope?

As noted by the *Beit Yosef* (*YD* 151), there are several Rishonim who seem to permit such activity entirely, though admittedly the argument is one of silence – namely, unlike the Rishonim above, they do not state an addendum that such cases are prohibited by rabbinic law. This is how he understands the view of Tosafot (Avoda Zara 6b, s.v. *minayin*) and the *Mordekhai* (Avoda Zara, ch. 1, no. 795). The Rema (*YD* 151:1) cites both possibilities: that it is forbidden to sell to non-Jews items used in worship only if they have no others to use, and that it is forbidden even when they do have others. He claims that the custom is to be lenient, though one who is careful in halakhic matters should be strict. As the *Ḥavot Yair* (no. 185) notes, this means that in principle the Rema agrees with the lenient opinions.

Yet, not all halakhic authorities are willing to concede the existence of the lenient opinion. The *Beit Yosef* himself notes that the *Mordekhai* elsewhere (Shabbat 450) seems to accept the rabbinic prohibition of aiding even when not enabling. While one cannot conclusively demonstrate contradictions between different passages in Tosafot, as they are authored by different people, the *Beit Yosef* is bothered by the fact that Tosafot in Shabbat accept this rabbinic prohibition, while in Avoda Zara, Tosafot do not.

Thus, several halakhic authorities offer the following distinction: when one is causing a non-Jew to sin, it is prohibited only if one is enabling the sin, but it is forbidden by rabbinic law even to aid a Jew to sin, and this rabbinic extension applies only with regard to Jewish sinners. This is accepted by the *Shakh* (*YD* 151:6), though he excludes a *mumar*, who is a Jew who has rejected mitzvot and concerning whom we have limited obligations as a Jew. R. Yechezkel Landau (*Dagul MeRevava, YD* 151:6) argues that the intention of *Shakh* is that one never needs to stop an intentional sinner from sinning, contrary to the straightforward explanation of the *Shakh*.

The Ritva (Avoda Zara 6b) and *Ḥatam Sofer* (*Responsa* 2, *YD* 19) contend that this distinction is due to the existence of a positive obligation (based on the mitzva to distance minors from sin and other similar obligations) to actively prevent Jews from sinning. The *Shakh* argues that one similarly has no obligation to rebuke a *mumar*, a rebellious Jew to whom one has fewer halakhic responsibilities. Others, such as the *Ḥavot Yair* (above) disagree, arguing that one may never aid a Jew in sinning.

This argument seems compelling – how could any halakhic authority permit aiding a Jew to sin? The *Turei Even* (Ḥagiga 13a) suggests that because in these cases, the item used for the sin is easily accessible to the sinner, and the sinner is going to sin regardless, aiding in the sin is meaningless. This does not necessarily mean that one should not offer rebuke or attempt to dissuade the sinner if possible, as rebuke is an independent mitzva by Torah law. It merely means that in a case in which this will not be effective, aiding the sinner is permitted.

The above distinctions between Jews and non-Jews are reasonable according to the Rishonim, like the Rosh (Shabbat 1:1), who characterize this second aspect as a derivative of the obligation to distance Jews from sin. But it should be noted that in some sources, such as *Tosafot Rabbenu Elḥanan,* this rabbinic aspect is referred to as *lifnei iver,* and thus it might apply to both Jews and non-Jews alike (just as the biblical aspect does), as it would not be subject to the differences outlined above.

Several Steps Removed

The classic cases of *lifnei iver* are instances in which one performs an action that directly enables a sinner to violate halakha. By contrast, the kinds of questions raised in the context of social media – such as the responsibility of the social media platforms and/or users for problematic content posted, or for neutral content used for sinful ends – are not nearly that direct. What does halakha say about this?

While the exact details of these laws are complicated, there are several reasons to contend that one is not prohibited to perform an action that can indirectly aid in the performance of a sin.

The first category to examine is *lifnei delifnei* – literally, "before of before." This phrase first appears in the passage of Gemara we have been discussing. As noted, there is a series of prohibitions relating to engaging in business with idol worshippers in the days leading up to their holidays. The Mishna also prohibits selling items normally used for idol worship at any point during the year, unless one has good reason to believe that the items will not be used for such worship. In this context, the Gemara states the following about the prohibition to sell frankincense, which was used for incense:

> The mishna taught that selling **frankincense** to gentiles is prohibited. **Rabbi Yitzḥak says** that **Rabbi Shimon ben Lakish says:** The mishna is referring specifically to **pure frankincense,** which is used as incense for objects of idol worship. A Sage **taught: And with regard to all** of these items whose sale is prohibited, **one may sell to** gentiles a large **bundle** of merchandise, as it is clear that the gentile intends to sell the merchandise rather than sacrifice it to his object of idol worship. **And how much** does such **a bundle** weigh? **Rabbi Yehuda ben Beteira explained:** For the purposes of this halakha, **no bundle is less than** the weight of **three hundred dinars.**
>
> The Gemara raises a difficulty: **But let us be concerned lest** the buyer **go and sell** these items **to another** gentile, **and they sacrifice** them. **Abaye said** in response: This scenario is certainly possible, but **we are commanded** only not **to** "place a stumbling block **before** the blind" (Lev. 19:14), i.e., one may not be the direct cause of a gentile's idol worship. **We are not commanded** not **to** place a stumbling block **before** one who may subsequently place it[12] **before** the blind. (Avoda Zara 14a)

In this passage, the Gemara permits selling frankincense to a non-Jewish businessman even if there is a likelihood that the non-Jew will then sell it to an idol worshipper who will use it in idol worship. The justification is that this is mere *lifnei delifnei.*

Yet, other talmudic passages indicate that even such sales are prohibited. For example, the Gemara (Avoda Zara 65b, Nidda 61a, Pesaḥim 40b) cites a *baraita* that prohibits selling clothing containing *kilayim,* the forbidden mixture of wool and linen, to a non-Jew, out of concern that the non-Jew will then sell the clothing to a Jew:

12. This translation does imply the existence of a physical object, a stumbling block, that is involved. However, one can violate the prohibition without the existence of such an object.

> With regard to **a garment in which diverse kinds,** a prohibited mixture of wool and linen, **has been lost,** i.e., a wool garment into which a linen thread was sewn or vice versa, **one** may **not sell it to a gentile; and one** may **not** even **fashion it** into **a saddlecloth for a donkey.** It is prohibited to do so lest one remove a piece of this garment and sew it onto his own clothing. **However, one** may **fashion it** into **a shroud for a dead body,** as there is no concern that he will remove it from the dead.
>
> The Gemara clarifies this issue: **What is the reason** that one may **not** sell it **to a gentile?** Is it **not due to** the concern **that** the gentile **will resell it to a Jew?** Since the mixture of wool and linen is not visible, it is possible for a Jew to use this cloth unawares. (Pesaḥim 40b)

Why is this prohibited? Isn't the original seller two steps removed from the sin? The Rishonim offer several answers. The *Tosafot Rid* (Avoda Zara 14a, s.v. *amar Abaye*) suggests that it depends on whether the potential sinner would commit the sin intentionally or unwittingly. Were the sinner an intentional sinner, it would be prohibited only to directly enable that person to sin. But in the case of *kilayim,* the concern is that by selling the garment to a non-Jew, a Jew will be *unwittingly* led to sin. In such a case, the *Tosafot Rid* argues, one must do everything possible to avoid causing such an unwitting sin.

R. Baruch Weintraub argues that the reasoning is as follows: One can look at *lifnei iver* as an interpersonal sin or a sin between a person and God. Perhaps when the sinner is an intentional violator, the interpersonal aspect does not apply. After all, he wants to sin. Still, there is a prohibition from the perspective of one's relationship with God, namely that it is wrong to be part of someone else's sin. When the sin is several steps removed from one's actions, it is difficult to claim that one is part of the sin. This eliminates the aspect of the sin that is between a person and God. Nevertheless, one may still be responsible for harming another spiritually. Still, this aspect applies only if the sin is committed unwittingly, and the sinner would consider it a harm to violate the prohibition.[13]

The Ritva (Avoda Zara 14a, s.v. *amar*) suggests that the relevant factor is whether the potential sinner is Jewish or not. One is responsible for preventing other Jews from sinning even if one is several steps removed from the sin. By contrast, one must avoid only directly aiding a non-Jew in sin. R. Weintraub suggests that this is based on the above distinction: a Jew must avoid facilitating a non-Jew's sin only to ensure that one does not violate the former's relationship with God, but among Jews, *lifnei iver* is prohibited also because of the interpersonal aspect, which is more demanding. Alternatively, he suggests, as we did above, that for Jews, in addition to the prohibition of *lifnei iver*, one is obligated to proactively aid other Jews' performance of mitzvot, which entails ensuring that no sin is caused by one's actions even if the result is several steps removed. The opinion of the Ritva is accepted by the *Taz* (*YD* 151:3, *EH* 5:10), as well as other commentaries on *YD* 151 and *EH* 5.[14]

One can only suggest that any action can, in theory, contribute in some way to sin. Thus, there must be some limit as to what is considered *lifnei iver*, and distinguishing between direct and indirect causation is one way of doing this.[15]

Time Delay

Another issue to consider is when there is no intermediary between the facilitator and the sinner, but the aid is offered not at the time of the sin. Commenting on the prohibition for a woman to grind grain with another woman who is suspected of violating *Shemitta* laws, Rashi (Gittin 61a, s.v. *lo*) writes that it is forbidden "to aid her, for it is forbidden to actively aid

13. See: https://tinyurl.com/2p838xxx.

14. It is worth noting that some authorities seem to hold that there is some halakhic value in rebuking non-Jews as well. See discussion in *Responsa Minḥat Yitzḥak* 4:79, based on *Sefer Ḥasidim* 1124.

15. A version of this argument was suggested to me by R. Aryeh Klapper.

sinners at the time of the sin." Rashi thereby indicates that one violates *lifnei iver* only if one helps the sinner at the time of the sin, not before. Yet, as Rabbis David and Avraham Stav note, the Ritva (*Ḥiddushei HaRitva*, Gittin 61a, s.v. *aval*) seems to forbid even such a case as *lifnei iver*.[16]

The most cited source in this context is a responsum by R. Naftali Tzvi Yehuda Berlin, the Netziv. He was asked (*Responsa Meshiv Davar* 2:32) about the permissibility of acting as the matchmaker for a couple in a case in which one knows that the couple will not keep the laws of family purity, *nidda*. The marriage is not sinful; in fact, it is a mitzva (a point we will return to). But by bringing the couple together, on some level one is responsible for their subsequent violation of these laws.

In this context, he notes that the question is subject to a dispute among many Rishonim. He cites R. Yaakov Ettlinger (*Responsa Binyan Tziyon* 15), who argues that according to Tosafot and the Rosh, it depends on whether it is a case of *trei avrei denahara* or *ḥad ever denahar*. If the sinner could not have sinned without help, then it does not matter how long of a time delay there is between the help and the sin – helping violates *lifnei iver*. This is based on the theory developed above, that for a Jew, in addition to the prohibition of aiding others to sin, one must proactively ensure that they observe the mitzvot. This added obligation renders all cases in which one's support is indispensable a full-blown violation of *lifnei iver*. But if the sinner could have committed the sin either way, and there was a time delay between the help and the sin, then it would be permitted, as the rabbinic extensions of *lifnei iver* apply only when the sin occurs immediately.[17]

The Netziv contends that the Ran (in his comments on Avoda Zara 6a–b), like Rashi above, would argue that in all cases one violates *lifnei iver*. But the Netziv argues (*Meshiv Davar* 2:31) that even Rashi would prohibit it only in a case where the aid shortens the time it takes for the sinner to sin, but if there is a time delay between the

16. Rabbis David and Avraham Stav above, 243.
17. It is also possible that this is part of a broader principle that indirect action is not always prohibited with regard to rabbinic prohibitions. This was suggested to me by R. Aryeh Klapper.

aid and the sin, and the sinner could have committed the sin in the same amount of time without help, then even Rashi would permit it. Numerous halakhic authorities discuss this issue, with many accepting the more lenient interpretations, such as *Ketav Sofer* (*Responsa* 83) and Maharsham (*Responsa* 2:184).[18]

Neutral Help

Even halakhic authorities who are not willing to be lenient when there is a time delay note that this prohibition applies only when one's actions can be construed as aiding the sin, but not in cases in which one provides a neutral framework that can be used for good or ill, where one's actions in no way push the potential sinner in either direction.

Maharsham (above), for example, was asked whether it is permitted to rent out a house to those who violate Shabbat, knowing they will desecrate Shabbat in the house. He permits this for several reasons. First, he notes that this is aid not during the time of the sin, which is permitted according to many halakhic authorities, as noted above. Moreover, he notes that this is not really helping one to sin at all. One provides a house for the Shabbat desecrator, but this is not the item used in the sin; the sinner merely sins within the house. R. Eliezer Waldenberg (*Responsa Tzitz Eliezer* 19:33) cites several halakhic authorities who agree with this assessment, and rules accordingly.

R. Moshe Feinstein agrees, and offers a slightly different formulation. He was asked (*Responsa Iggerot Moshe, YD* 1:72) if the owner of a ballroom or hall may rent out the space for a wedding during which there will be prohibited types of dancing. R. Moshe is lenient. He notes that one rents out the hall for neutral purposes: for a wedding or a meal. The fact that the dancing that takes place is problematic does not change the fact that the primary purpose for which it was rented is permitted, thus rendering the entire transaction permitted. One is renting a room for a wedding celebration, not for mixed dancing. Based on this, R.

18. For more, see *Responsa Yabia Omer, OḤ* 2:15; *Responsa Mishneh Halakhot* 7:115; and *Responsa Ateret Paz* 1:1, *OḤ* 13.

Feinstein allows renting out the hall even when there are no other venues available for rent.[19]

In an article by the Bais HaVaad[20] on the culpability of Facebook for harmful posts on its platform, the authors note that in some cases we allow even setting up situations in which people will sin. In the Mishna (Maaser Sheni 5:1), Rabban Shimon ben Gamliel rules that in a non-*Shemitta* year, when it would be theft for someone to take produce from the property of another, the owner of the field does not need to make it known that the produce is forbidden to eat due to *orla*. The Gemara gives the following reason: "*Haliteihu lerasha veyamut* – Feed the evil person and let him die." The Aḥaronim discuss the limits of this principle, but it at least potentially means that there are cases in which we just allow sinners to follow their own path regardless of the permissibility of their actions, taking no responsibility ourselves. The two views that the authors of the Bais HaVaad article cite as relevant are as follows:

> The Chazon Ish (Demai 8:9) writes that the mishna is lenient only where the potential violator would have to steal the item with which he would transgress.
>
> R. Shlomo Zalman Auerbach (Minchas Shlomo, Bava Kama 69a) and other *Acharonim* maintain that so long as one is not participating in the *aveira* actively, he is exempt, so he is not required to intervene.

Cases of Uncertainty

A central avenue for permissibility is cases in which it is not certain whether or not a prohibition will be violated, or when one can plausibly assume that the help being given will be used for permitted purposes. This is based on several *mishnayot* in Shevi'it (5:6–9), which begin with the following ruling:

19. The responsum has several other justifications for leniency in this particular case.
20. https://baishavaad.org/hosting-postings-is-facebook-responsible-for-its-content/.

> These are the implements that a craftsman may not sell in the seventh year: A plow and all its [accompanying] implements, a yoke, a winnowing-fan, and a pickax. But he may sell a sickle used by hand, a scythe, and a cart with all its implements. This is the general principle: [The sale of] any tools designed for work involving a transgression [in the seventh year] is prohibited; but if for a forbidden and a permitted purpose, it may be [sold].

The *Mishna Rishona* (Shevi'it 5:6) notes that the mishna permits lending items that may be used for permitted purposes even though they may also be used for forbidden purposes. For both R. Feinstein and R. Waldenberg (above) this is evidence that whenever the commission of sin is not certain, one does not violate *lifnei iver*.

This seems to be the straightforward understanding of the Gemara in Avoda Zara in its discussion of the list of items that are forbidden to sell to idol worshippers who might use them for sin:

> **Rather, Rav Ashi said: Anywhere that it is** possible **to assign** an innocent motive, **one assigns** such a motive, **and** this applies **even though one is commanded** to allow the item to rest. **And anywhere that it is not** possible **to assign** an innocent motive, **one does not assign** an innocent motive, **even though one is not commanded** to allow the item to rest. (Avoda Zara 15b)

The Ritva (*Ḥiddushim,* Avoda Zara 15b, s.v. *mi dami*) explains that *Ḥazal* permit selling these items when there are potential permitted purposes, because *lifnei iver* by Torah law is violated only when the sin is inevitable. *Ḥazal* forbid giving items to potential sinners where there is a *likelihood* they will be used for sin, but when there is a potential permitted use, the halakha reverts to the lenient standard of the Torah law.

R. Ben Tzion Meir Chai Uziel (*Responsa Mishpetei Uziel, YD* 2:19) argues that this cuts to the heart of *lifnei iver*. One violates this prohibition for tempting or strengthening someone's desire to sin. But one who creates a situation that can be used for permitted purposes does no such thing. The sinner, should he choose to misuse what has been provided, is fully responsible for his choices.

It is worth noting that many (Rambam, *Peirush HaMishnayot,* Shevi'it 5:6; Bartenura, ibid.) rule that it is necessary to justify providing opportunity to sin only if there is reason to believe that the person being helped might actually sin. When there is no such concern, one is permitted to provide help that seems more likely than not to lead to the violation of a prohibition on the presumption that it will not lead to sin.[21]

Darkhei Shalom

Another factor that mitigates the prohibition of *lifnei iver* is concerns for peaceful relations, *darkhei shalom.* This is based on the concluding section of this series of *mishnayot* (5:9), as well as the version found in Gittin (5:9):

> **The wife of a *ḥaver,*** one who is devoted to the meticulous observance of mitzvot, especially the *halakhot* of ritual purity, *teruma,* and tithes, **may lend the wife of an *am ha'aretz,*** one who is not scrupulous in these areas, **a winnow and a sieve, and she may** even **select, grind, and sift with her. But once** the wife of the *am ha'aretz* **pours water** into the flour, thereby rendering it susceptible to ritual impurity, the wife of the *ḥaver* **may not touch** anything **with her, because one may not assist those who commit transgressions. And all of** the allowances mentioned in the mishna **were stated only on account of the ways of peace.**

What is the connection between the leniency of uncertainty of sin and that of *darkhei shalom*? There are several opinions among the Rishonim. Some argue that there are two possible avenues of leniency. Namely, in the cases in Avoda Zara, there will be no loss of peaceful relations if one chooses not to sell the item. Thus, the reason to permit selling the items in question is that they might not be used for prohibited purposes. But in cases where peaceful relations would be put at risk, we can be more lenient in terms of

21. See, for example, *Responsa Yeḥaveh Daat* 3:67 for practical examples.

what we permit for *lifnei iver*. This is the opinion of Rabbenu Tam (*Sefer HaYashar, Ḥelek HaḤiddushim* 121).

Ramban (*Ḥiddushim,* Avoda Zara 15b) and Ritva (ibid.) argue that the real reason to be lenient is the possibility that the item in question will not be used for a prohibition. The relevance of *darkhei shalom* is simply because one might have thought that when it comes to lending an item, where one can always justify not lending it, it would be prohibited even in a case where one can plausibly claim that the item is not being used for prohibited purposes. The Gemara invokes *darkhei shalom* to say that we can rely on the normal standards of assigning motives to provide potential permissible explanations that allow lending the item. This relegates *darkhei shalom* to the role of maintaining the basic law without pursuing stringencies, but does not change the basic law itself.

Tosafot (Gittin 61a, s.v. *mashelet, Rash,* Shevi'it 5:9) offer a third approach. A reasonable justification as to how that help can be used in a permitted manner can always be used to provide aid. But if there are concerns of keeping the peace, one can rely on unlikely justifications to sanction a dispensation to help. Meiri (Avoda Zara 15b) follows this approach, clarifying that under normal circumstances we rely only on "commonly found things" to permit aiding in a case where one's aid could be used for sin. This opinion is adopted by *Magen Avraham* (*OḤ* 347:4; see also *Mishna Berura,* ibid., 9). According to this position, *darkhei shalom* is indeed a mitigating factor, but only in limited circumstances. As *Tosefot Yom Tov* (Shevi'it 5:9) notes, the implication of this opinion is that without a theoretical permissible explanation, *darkhei shalom* alone is not enough to permit the assistance.[22]

22. This opinion is accepted by many authorities, such as R. Natan Gestetner (*Responsa LeHorot Natan* 5:67). For a detailed discussion of the local question concerning *Shemitta,* see *Shabbat HaAretz* (8:7), by R. Avraham Yitzchak Kook.

Preventing Greater Sin

There is another avenue of leniency. Sometimes, enabling a given sin prevents an even greater violation of the Torah. In such a case, several major halakhic authorities rule that it is permitted to facilitate the lesser sin.

R. Shlomo Zalman Auerbach issues this ruling in a well-known case. The Gemara (Ḥullin 107b) forbids giving bread to someone who will not fulfill the mitzva to wash their hands (*netilat yadayim*) before eating. This is accepted as halakha, and is expanded to forbid giving food to someone who will not recite a blessing before eating (see *Shulḥan Arukh, OḤ* 169:1–2). The reason for this is *lifnei iver*. Whoever provides the food is causing the recipient to violate the requirement to bless God before eating.

Yet, R. Shlomo Zalman Auerbach (*Responsa Minḥat Shlomo* 1:35) argues that if the recipient is a non-observant Jew who is positively inclined toward those who keep mitzvot, one *may not* withhold food from such a person. Acting ungraciously will lead this non-observant person to hate those who keep the Torah, and this is a greater violation than eating without a reciting a blessing. Thus, the same principle that in the time of the Gemara forbids giving such a person food now requires it.

As we have seen, this is the kind of thinking that brought Google to work in China in the first place. While they disagreed with China's censorship, they thought that withholding from the Chinese people the tools offered by Google would be an even worse violation of the right of the Chinese people to information. Thus, they initially entered the moral morass of involvement with China. While the calculus eventually changed, we see that this kind of thinking resonates beyond the halakhic system.

Positive Intent

We may posit an even more fundamental argument. R. Asher Weiss notes that *lifnei iver* is a prohibition grounded in one's intent to harm another person, but in any case where one's intent is to help others, there is no prohibition of *lifnei iver*. He uses this to explain why it may not be *lifnei iver* to help someone convert, even if the prospective convert might not keep all the mitzvot, as bringing someone under the wings of the Divine Presence cannot be considered a stumbling block (*Minḥat Asher al HaTorah, Vayikra, Kedoshim, Lifnei Iver*; see his other formulations in *Responsa Minḥat Asher* 2:28–30).

R. Moshe Sternbuch (*Responsa Teshuvot VeHanhagot* 1:358) argues similarly that when one causes potential spiritual harm out of a desire to help the sinner, this cannot be a violation of *lifnei iver*. Thus, he allows inviting one's parents to one's home for Shabbat in an effort to bring them closer to halakhic observance, even if the parents do not observe the halakhot of Shabbat and may violate Shabbat in order to come.

Cost-Benefit Analysis

There is an alternative approach offered by the *Ḥazon Ish* (Shevi'it 12:9; see discussion in *Responsa Minḥat Asher* 2:28). He contends that the reason that it is permitted to lend items to people who might or might not use them for sin is that the Torah does not want *lifnei iver* to become the reason that people refrain from performing acts of kindness. While we do not want to aid sin, being overly zealous in avoiding providing potential sinners with their needs will engender interpersonal hatred and cause other Torah values to suffer. The reason, therefore, that we find leniency when the eventuality of sin is not certain is that it is necessary to balance our desire to avoid sin with the recognition that being too careful comes with its own costs. This position can generate similar conclusions to the models presented above. While there may be subtle differences between these models, we will suffice with this brief treatment, as the practical differences will be limited.

On the Other Hand…

Yet, there are indications that we look to expand, rather than limit, what should be forbidden by *lifnei iver* and its derivatives. Take, for example, the expansion of a law concerning theft in a ruling from R. Yechiel Michel Epstein.

The Mishna (Bava Kama 118b) rules: "Do not buy wool or goat milk from shepherds, nor fruit or wood from orchard watchmen." The majority of halakhic authorities assume that this refers to buying items that may have been stolen. The Rambam (*Hilkhot*

Geneiva 6:1), for example, writes: "It is forbidden to buy anything that has a presumption that it is stolen, and so too we do not buy [an item] if most [merchandise] of that item is stolen." Even though the thief might have been able to sell the item to someone else regardless, buying it is considered participation in the theft. As R. Yehoshua Falk (*Sema, ḤM* 356:1) notes: "Even though the thief could take it to another place, where they do not know he is a thief, still, [if the local people refrain from buying from him] it will not be as common to steal.... Therefore, a person should avoid buying [from him] so that he will not steal regularly."

R. Yechiel Michel Epstein (*Arukh HaShulḥan, ḤM* 356:1, 6; 348:1) understands the *Tur*'s view of this prohibition differently. In several places, he suggests that it may be prohibited to buy *anything* from thieves, as one is not meant to support them in any way, even when not involved in sin.

Chapter 11

Expanding the Discussion: Showing Support for Sin

Related or Derivative Prohibitions

Beyond *lifnei iver* there are several other prohibitions that are either derivatives of these principles or at least related at first glance. These prohibitions will be relevant not only for internet platforms, but for users as well. These relate to cases where one is not enabling or aiding the sin itself, but is encouraging its performance, or is at least perceived to be encouraging it.

Verbal Support of Sin

The central discussion begins with a mishna, which outlines what words of support one may offer to a farmer who is beginning to do fieldwork during *Shemitta,* the Sabbatical year, when Jews are enjoined from performing agricultural work in the Land of Israel:

> We encourage the work of non-Jews in the Sabbatical year, but not that of Jews. And we inquire after their [the non-Jews'] well-being, for the sake of peace. (Mishna Shevi'it 5:9, Sefaria translation)

The Yerushalmi (with slightly different versions in Gittin 5:10, Shevi'it 4:3 and 5:4, and Avoda Zara 4:10) records a dispute as to what "encouragement" the mishna refers to:

> Rabbi Ḥiyya and Rabbi Imi disagree: One says, "Plow it well and I will buy it from you after the Sabbatical year." The other says: "Well done!"
>
> According to the one who says that it means "Plow it well and I will buy it from you after the Sabbatical year," what does it mean to "inquire after their well-being"? [It means saying] "Well done!"
>
> And according to the one who says that it means "Well done!" what does it mean to "inquire after their well-being"? [It means saying] "Peace be upon you."

According to the Yerushalmi, there are two possible ways of understanding this discussion:

1. According to the latter, more straightforward, explanation, it is permitted to say "Well done!" to a non-Jew working his field during *Shemitta*, because the non-Jew is permitted to plow. But one may not indicate support for a Jew who is performing the work, because for the Jew it is prohibited. One can, however, offer this Jew a generic greeting that does not indicate support for the prohibited activity he is engaged in.
2. According to the first explanation, not only may one offer words of support to a non-Jew working his field during *Shemitta*, but one may even commit to buying the produce after *Shemitta* from the non-Jew, despite that fact that for a Jew to engage in that same work would have been forbidden. Variant versions of this text leave it unclear to whom one can say "Well done!" The commentaries are divided on how to interpret this:

a. The *Korban HaEda* (Shevi'it 5:4, s.v. *hakhi garsinan man de'amar ḥarosh*) writes that it is permitted to say "Well done!" only to the non-Jew. To a Jew who is violating halakha one may offer only generic greetings to maintain peaceful relations. The various commentaries on the Yerushalmi offer slight variations on their interpretations of the Yerushalmi, but they all assume that it is forbidden to offer words of support to a Jew who is involved in sinful activity.[1]

b. Tosafot (Gittin 62a, s.v. *asharta*) have a different text of the Yerushalmi that is more similar to a truncated version of the discussion found in the Bavli, which we will discuss below. According to Tosafot, the Yerushalmi is prohibiting offering a greeting that uses the word *shalom* (in the Bavli, it is prohibited only to double a blessing of *shalom*) to a non-Jew, and thus those generic greetings are more problematic than the words of encouragement. This understanding leads to the conclusion that one may say "Well done!" even to a Jew who is plowing his field during *Shemitta*.[2] This conclusion seems to be supported by the ensuing incident in the Yerushalmi:

> Rabbi Ḥanina bar Pappa and Rabbi Shmuel bar Naḥman passed by one who was plowing during the Sabbatical year. Rabbi Shmuel bar Naḥman said to him, "Well done!"
>
> Rabbi Ḥanina bar Pappa said to [Rabbi Shmuel bar Naḥman]: "Didn't Rabbi [Yehuda HaNasi] teach that those who are passing did not say 'The blessing of God is upon you,' for it is forbidden to say 'Well done!' to those who are plowing during the Sabbatical year?"
>
> [Rabbi Ḥanina bar Pappa] responded, "You know how to read, but you do not know how to expound."

1. See *Penei Moshe, Ridbaz,* and *Shayarei Korban* on the various passages.
2. *Maharam Schiff,* Gittin 62a, s.v. *Tosafot asharta,* notes this, though he distinguishes between different expressions of support. For more on this, see the Mesivta edition of the Talmud in the *Yalkut Biurim* section on Gittin 62a.

However, those who prohibit encouraging people currently involved in sin would presumably understand this case as offering encouragement to a sinner *not* while he is actively involved in sin, taking it as a given that offering a support for sin is forbidden.[3]

As Tosafot (above) and the *Pe'at HaShulḥan* (*Beit Yisrael,* Shevi'it 9:23) understand this story, Rabbi Ḥanina believes it is permitted to say "Well done!" to people plowing during *Shemitta,* while Rabbi Shmuel bar Naḥman does not, and the Yerushalmi rules that it is permitted.

According to the explanation of this mishna in the Bavli, the conclusion is that endorsement of sin is indeed prohibited:

> The mishna teaches that **one may assist gentiles** who work the land **during the Sabbatical** Year. The Gemara asks: May **one** really **assist** them? **But didn't Rav Dimi bar Shishna say in the name of Rav: One may not hoe with a gentile during the Sabbatical** Year, **and one may not double the greeting** extended **to a gentile,** saying: *Shalom, shalom*? The Gemara answers: **No,** one may not actually help a gentile in his work, but **it is necessary** to state that one may **merely say to them: Be strong, as in that** incident **where Rav Yehuda said to** gentiles in such a situation: **Be strong,** and **Rav Sheshet said to them: Well done.** Statements of this kind are certainly permitted. (Gittin 62a)

The Bavli rules that it is forbidden to greet non-Jews with the world *shalom* twice (as it is a name of God), but one may encourage them when they work the land during *Shemitta,* either by saying "Well done!" or "Be strong!" By implication, however, this dispensation is limited to non-Jews, who are permitted to work in the fields during *Shemitta,* but according to the Bavli, one may not offer words of encouragement to a Jew who is working the land during *Shemitta* or violating any other

3. See the Artscroll edition of Yerushalmi Shevi'it 5:4, n. 12 based on *Rash Sirilio* on 4:3, s.v. *vesho'alin bisheloman,* and *Ziv HaYam.*

prohibition. The Rambam (*Hilkhot Shemitta VeYovel* 8:8) writes that one may speak this way to the non-Jew because the non-Jew has no prohibition to plow during *Shemitta*, implying that one may not speak similarly to one who does have such a prohibition. The *Magen Avraham* (*OḤ* 347:4) writes this explicitly:

> It is good manners (*derekh eretz*) to say to someone, even a non-Jew, performing work, "Be successful in your task," but it is forbidden to say this to someone performing forbidden work.

The *Mishna Berura* concurs (ad loc. 7), as does the *Kaf HaḤayim* (ad loc. 9). As Rabbis David and Avraham Stav note, if the prohibition is related to *lifnei iver* or *mesaye'a*, then ostensibly, according to the Rishonim who hold that one violates *lifnei iver* by Torah law only by enabling another to perform a sin that could not have otherwise been committed, offering verbal support is likely forbidden only by rabbinic law. For the Rambam, who believes that one violates *lifnei iver* by Torah law even in cases in which the sinner could have violated the prohibition unaided, this verbal endorsement may constitute a violation by Torah law. Either way, it is prohibited. But in addition to *lifnei iver* and its derivatives, verbal support of sin may constitute a violation of another prohibition, which we will now discuss.

Ḥanifa (Flattery)

The Mishna (Sota 7:8) records the following incident:

> **King Agrippa arose, and received** the Torah scroll, **and read** from it while **standing, and the Sages praised him** for this. **And when** Agrippa **arrived at** the verse in the portion read by the king that states: **"You may not appoint a foreigner over you"** (Deut. 17:15), **tears flowed from his eyes,** because he was a descendant of the house of Herod and was not of Jewish origin. The entire nation **said to him: Fear not, Agrippa. You are our brother, you are our brother.** (Sota 41a)

The issue was that Agrippa, a king descended from Herod, was not Jewish, or at least not on both sides (the Rishonim discuss this), which disqualified him from acting as king. Thus, when he reached the verse which forbade a non-Jew from being a king of Israel, he cried. The people comforted him and assured him that he was worthy of being king. While the Mishna does not criticize this, the Gemara does so harshly:

> It is **taught in the name of Rabbi Natan: At that moment the enemies of the Jewish people,** a euphemism for the Jewish people, **were sentenced to destruction for flattering Agrippa.**

"Flattery" here refers to seeing something which is problematic or forbidden, and instead of condemning it, remaining silent or endorsing the sin.[4]

The *Sifrei* (Num. 161) seems to understand this as a prohibition by Torah law derived from a verse: "*Velo taḥanifu et haaretz*" (Num. 35:33). Literally translated, this means something like, "You shall not pollute the land" (JPS translation). The Ramban (ad loc.) explains how the *Sifrei* reaches its homiletic interpretation. The previous two verses forbid taking payment to allow a murderer to avoid the death penalty, or to allow an accidental killer to avoid fleeing to a city of refuge. The Torah then adds that we may not falsely honor sinners to ingratiate ourselves with them, a violation on the same spectrum as the previous prohibitions, which forbid allowing sinners to escape the consequences of their sins. R. Eliezer of Metz, one of the Tosafists, counts this as a mitzva (*Yere'im* 248).

The *Semak* (129) includes it under a different verse: "You shall not render an unfair decision: do not favor the poor or show deference to the rich; judge your kinsman fairly" (Lev. 19:15).

The Gemara (Sota 41b) goes on to decry the flatterer with a series of biting comments, stating that "even fetuses in their mothers' wombs curse him," that he "falls into Gehenna," and that he falls into the hands of the person he flattered, or the hands of

4. It is worth noting that where one is misrepresenting Torah through *ḥanifa*, this may violate yet another prohibition. Maharshal (Bava Kama 4:9) rules that misrepresenting Torah is a cardinal sin and one may not do this even to save one's life. That issue is beyond the scope of our discussion.

the children of the one he flattered. Regarding communities, the Gemara states, "Any congregation in which there is flattery is ultimately exiled." Finally, the Gemara concludes:

> **Rabbi Yirmeya bar Abba says: Four classes** of people **will not greet the Divine Presence: the class of cynics, and the class of flatterers, and the class of liars, and the class of slanderers.** (Sota 42a)[5]

Ḥizuk Yedei Overei Aveira

A similar category to *ḥanifa* is *ḥizuk yedei overei aveira,* supporting the hand of the wicked. The Rishonim equate these categories and derive halakhot about the former from the latter.

As is clear from the above passage, *ḥanifa* may be forbidden even when one has reason to be afraid that criticizing the sinner would bring harm to the rebuker – as was surely the case with King Agrippa. Yet, in a case in which there is a fear of not just harm but death, the Rishonim assume that avoiding such danger allows flattery. The prooftext is the following incident:

> **Ulla, on his ascent to Eretz Yisrael, had two residents of Ḥozai join him.** Because of a brawl between them, **one arose** and **slaughtered the other.** The assailant **said to Ulla: Did I act properly? He said to him: Yes, and open the place of the slaughter,** i.e., cut it more so that he will die faster. **When** Ulla **came before Rabbi Yoḥanan,** Ulla **said to him: Perhaps, Heaven forbid, I strengthened the hands of sinners** by commending him, although I did so merely because I was afraid that he would kill me. **He said to him: You saved yourself** by

5. *Ḥanifa* sometimes refers to other kinds of hypocrisy, pretending to be righteous while secretly being wicked. Clearly these two meanings of the terms are related, but we focus here on the issues as outlined above.

doing so, and it is permitted for one to say words like this in order to save his own life. (Nedarim 22a)

The Meiri (*Beit HaBeḥira,* Nedarim 22a, s.v. *asur*) derives from here that the general prohibition on supporting the wicked is waived when there is a danger to life, specifically noting that this prohibition goes beyond merely prohibiting offering aid and advice, and extends to prohibiting verbal support and praise. Tosafot (Sota 41b, s.v. *kol*) equate this prohibition with *ḥanifa,* and thus provide the same dispensation in the latter case.

Several Rishonim (see opinions of *Ritz* and *Re'em* in *Shita Mekubetzet*) limit this prohibition to supporting Jewish wrongdoers, similar to how the rabbinic extensions of *lifnei iver* were limited above.

In truth, the question of whether fear of retribution allows flattery seems to be the subject of a dispute in the Talmud itself. Commenting on Yaakov's tactic of placating his brother Esav with gifts before meeting him for the first time after having received, in a duplicitous manner, the blessings intended for Esav, the Talmud records the following discussion:

> **Rabbi Yehuda of the West,** Eretz Yisrael, **and some say Rabbi Shimon ben Pazi, taught: It is permitted to flatter wicked people in this world, as it is stated** concerning the future: **"The vile person shall no longer be called generous, nor shall the churl be said to be noble"** (Is. 32:5). **By inference,** this indicates **that in this world it is permitted** to flatter them.
>
> **Rabbi Shimon ben Lakish said** that this can be proven **from here.** Jacob said to Esau: "I have seen your face, **as one sees the face of angels, and you were pleased with me"** (Gen. 33:10). Jacob flattered him by comparing seeing him to seeing a divine vision.
>
> The Gemara notes: **And** Rabbi Shimon ben Lakish, in interpreting Jacob's statement, **disagrees with Rabbi Levi, as Rabbi Levi says:** With regard to the interaction between **Jacob and Esau, to what is this matter comparable? To a person who**

> **invited another** to his home **and** the guest **realized that he wants to kill him.** The guest **said to him: The flavor of this dish that I taste is like a dish that I tasted in the king's house.** The host then **said** to himself: **The king** must **know him.** Therefore, **he was afraid and did not kill him.** Similarly, when Jacob told Esau that his face is like the face of an angel, he intended to let him know that he had seen angels, in order to instill fear in him so that Esau would not seek to harm him. (Sota 41b)

While Tosafot conclude that in cases of real danger such flattery is permitted, Rabbenu Yona (*Shaarei Teshuva* 3:188) concludes that one must put himself in danger to avoid this sin. In addition to the story of Agrippa, which may be read as supporting this opinion, another incident in the Talmud points in this direction as well. The context is a court case against King Yannai. Shimon ben Shetaḥ demanded that Yannai stand during the proceedings. Yannai responded as follows:

> Yannai the king **said to him:** I will **not** stand **when you** alone say this to me, **but according to what your colleagues say,** and if the whole court tells me, I will stand. Shimon ben Shataḥ **turned to his right.** The judges **forced their faces to the ground** out of fear and said nothing. **He turned to his left, and they forced their faces to the ground** and said nothing. **Shimon ben Shataḥ said to them: You are masters of thoughts,** enjoying your private thoughts, and not speaking. **May the Master of thoughts,** God, **come and punish you. Immediately,** the angel **Gabriel came and struck** those judges **to the ground, and they died.** (Sanhedrin 19a–b)

In this case, the judges' lives were clearly in danger. Still, they were punished for not standing up to Yannai.

While for the purposes of our question, this aspect is mostly academic, it highlights how seriously the prohibition of flattery is viewed in halakha. Additionally, even if it is permitted to engage in this flattery in times of danger, it is clear that it is not ideal to be placed in such a situation, as Rabbis David and Avraham Stav note.[6]

More Severe than *Lifnei Iver*

While it is possible that flattery and showing support for sin are derivatives of *lifnei iver*, R. Yitzchak Weiss (*Responsa Minḥat Yitzḥak* 4:79) suggests that these may be independent prohibitions that are in some sense more severe than *lifnei iver*. Specifically, he notes that in cases in which one enables or assists a sinner to commit *a particular forbidden act,* one does not directly cause the sinner to engage in *future illicit activity.* But by offering explicit support and encouragement, one is responsible for creating a framework that will make it more likely that the sinner will make these problematic activities a habit and sin many times in the future.

Silence as Support

The Maharam Schick (*Responsa, OḤ* 303) argues that one violates *ḥanifa* even by remaining silent if that silence is clearly an act of acquiescence. (For more on his sources, see the above discussion in gray about Yannai.) Rabbenu Yona (*Shaarei Teshuva* 3:199) adds that it is forbidden to show honor and respect to sinners, as this will be taken as general support of their activities. This is similar to the opinion of the *Arukh HaShulḥan* that we cited above, that it is forbidden to engage in any commerce with sinners, even when the transaction does not involve the problematic merchandise.

Marit Ayin of Entering Problematic Places

We will discuss the nature of *marit ayin* (the appearance of impropriety) in section 3 of this book. I would like to develop one aspect of this prohibition that is relevant here. As noted, many of the sources in our discussion come from the responsum by Rabbis David and Avraham Stav on participation in a wedding that is against halakha.

Their discussion is obviously relevant to our question of indicating support on social media for weddings, or other activity, not in strict accordance with halakha. In that context, they note

6. For more on the nature of this prohibition and the question of how we rule, see *Responsa Divrei Yatziv, Likutim VeHashmatot* 112.

that cases of *ḥanifa* and of *ḥizuk yedei overei aveira* share certain elements with *marit ayin* – it is forbidden to act in such a way as to give the impression that something that is forbidden is permitted. One of the rationales for the prohibition of *marit ayin* is that if one does an act that appears to be forbidden, it will cause others to think that such an act is permitted. However, the exact nature of all these prohibitions are different.

To explain, they point to several responsa by R. Moshe Feinstein concerning an Orthodox Jew entering a non-Orthodox synagogue.

In one responsum (*Iggerot Moshe, OḤ* 2:40), R. Feinstein forbids praying in a non-Orthodox synagogue that does not have a *meḥitza*, even with a *minyan* in a separate room that has a *meḥitza*. R. Feinstein argues that this is prohibited because whoever participates is *maḥazik yedei overei aveira*. Yet, later in that responsum, he forbids eating kosher food in a non-kosher restaurant only because of *marit ayin*, but does not mention *ḥizuk yedei overei aveira*. Additionally, R. Feinstein ultimately permits entering a non-kosher restaurant under certain circumstances, though he is unwilling to do the same in the case of the synagogue, indicating that *marit ayin* is more easily solved than *ḥizuk yedei overei aveira*.

Why are these distinct? Rabbis David and Avraham Stav suggest that the difference is as follows: a non-kosher restaurant is not trying to become halakhically acceptable. By contrast, the arguments between denominations in Judaism are precisely about halakhic legitimacy. Thus, creating a situation in which one seems to accept the halakhic standards of another denomination lends credibility to their positions in a way that entering a non-kosher restaurant does not. Lending support can also happen by merely attending an event such as a wedding, in a way that is not the case with *marit ayin* (hence the question is primarily about eating in that establishment, not merely walking in).[7]

7. R. Meshulam Roth, *Responsa Kol Mevaser* 2:17, forbids an Orthodox rabbi to teach at a non-Orthodox rabbinical institution based on the passages in Gittin 62a that we addressed above. He negates many arguments in favor of teaching in such an institution. His central argument is that by teaching there, the rabbi is giving his

Based on this, Rabbis David and Avraham Stav move on to their central question – does attendance by an Orthodox Jew at a wedding that is halakhically forbidden indicate support, or is such behavior subject only to potential *marit ayin* concerns? As noted above, the latter would be more easily solved. On the one hand, attending a wedding seems to indicate support and acceptance of the union. On the other hand, in the case of close friends or family, it may be that everyone will understand that one is attending out of respect for the relationship one has with the people getting married, not as a demonstration of approval of the union.

Before providing a ruling, they note another responsum (*Responsa Iggerot Moshe, EH* 2:17) in which R. Feinstein argues that the prohibition against entering a non-Orthodox synagogue applies only to entering for prayer, but attending a halakhically permitted wedding that happens to use space in that building is permitted. Nevertheless, R. Feinstein maintains that a "kosher person should not be there." While a full discussion of the precise contours of his argument are beyond our scope, it is sufficient to note how concerned R. Feinstein was about lending credibility to prohibited institutions and activities.

On the other hand, R. Feinstein (*Responsa Iggerot Moshe, OḤ* 4:91) permits going to synagogues that are fundamentally committed to Orthodox standards of halakha even if there are many halakhot that they do not observe. The difference seems to be that a person lends credibility when entering a place that stands for problematic values, but not by being present in a place where people are merely lax in their observance of various halakhot. No one thinks that the person praying fervently in the corner of a synagogue condones all those standing near him who are talking throughout the repetition of the *Amida* prayer.

stamp of approval, which is the paradigmatic violation of the prohibition in question. R. Aharon Soloveitchik introduced yet another relevant category, arguing that a rabbi who was mitzva observant but affiliated with a non-halakhic movement was disqualified from testifying, as he was part of a *kesher resha'im*, a group of sinners. See *Kiddushin SheNe'erkhu al yedei Rav Konservativi, Techumin* 20, available at: https://www.zomet.org.il/?CategoryID=262&ArticleID=246.

The conclusion of Rabbis David and Avraham Stav is that participation in forbidden weddings is particularly problematic, because by rejoicing with the bride and groom, one indicates that one values the union that is being celebrated. Early in their essay, however, they noted that we could argue that one does not violate *ḥanifa* in cases where it is obvious to all that one does not agree with the union and is there merely to demonstrate that one cares about the celebrants.

Tokhaḥa

Let us consider *tokhaḥa*, the mitzva to rebuke sinners, and why it is usually not relevant on social media.

Until now we have discussed the negative aspects of this question, specifically, what must one avoid so as not to indicate assent to prohibited activity? In addition, one must always remember that there is a mitzva to provide rebuke to those who are sinning. Potentially one could argue that one should write a comment that evinces disapproval of the activity being posted about, but this is usually ill-advised. As Rabbi Elazar ben Azarya says, "I would be shocked if there were someone in this generation who knows how to give rebuke" (Arakhin 16b). Even more importantly, the Gemara issues the following warning:

> **And Rabbi Ile'a said in the name of Rabbi Elazar, son of Rabbi Shimon: Just as it is a mitzva for a person to say that which will be heeded, so is it a mitzva for a person not to say that which will not be heeded.** One should not rebuke those who will be unreceptive to his message. **Rabbi Abba says:** It is **obligatory** for him to refrain from speaking, **as it is stated: "Do not reprove a scorner lest he hate you; reprove a wise man and he will love you"** (Prov. 9:8). (Yevamot 65b)

Giving rebuke when it will be ignored is dangerous. The Rashba (*Responsa* 5:238) even invokes *akirat davar min haTorah*, *Ḥazal*'s ability to temporarily suspend biblical commandments, as a reason for why people should sometimes avoid offering rebuke even when it is called for according to the strict letter of the law. He refers to holding one's tongue in these circumstances as an *aveira lishmah*, a sin for the proper reason.

R. Yehuda Amital (*Resisei Tal*, ch. 37) cites this *teshuva* as part of his broad discussion of the scope of a complex principle in the Talmud, "*Mutav sheyihyu shogegin ve'al yihyu mezidin*," which means that sometimes it is better to allow people to sin unwittingly, rather than inform them of their mistake, knowing they will then violate the Torah intentionally. R. Amital notes that being a leader means recognizing that sometimes we must see beyond the local halakha and understand the communal implications of what we do. Sometimes, as the Rashba says, even when rebuke is in order it is better to remain silent.

He notes that this sensitivity is what drives the opinion we cited earlier from R. Shlomo Zalman Auerbach (*Responsa Minḥat Shlomo* 1:35). Nowadays it is a violation of *lifnei iver* to refrain from giving food to someone who will not recite a blessing before eating, while it was once a violation of *lifnei iver* to give the food. In today's world, potential animosity or real animosity lies beneath the surface in our relationships with people of varying religious commitments, within our community or outside of it. As the Rashba discusses being passive, and R. Shlomo Zalman Aurbach allows one to actively give food to one who will not recite a blessing, the latter reflects a more radical application of the principle.

Returning to the Rashba, R. Amital notes that this does not mean our responsibility to educate disappears. On the contrary, difficult situations demand that we be creative in finding ways to influence and inspire that will not repel people, even sinners, such as *mumarim*, who may not formally deserve our concern.[8]

All these factors are critical when shaping our attitude toward these issues on social media.

8. I wrote about some of these ideas in a blog post here: https://shaashuim.wordpress.com/2014/02/27/balancing-education-rebuke-and-the-fear-of-causing-estrangement/.

Chapter 12

Applying the Principles

Many of the factors discussed above, such as the intent of the potential enabler/aider of sin, the likelihood that a negative result will occur, the cost of not helping, and at what stage in the process the person is involved, are in fact raised by secular thinkers as well. Cass Sunstein,[1] for example, when trying to construct a framework for the responsibility of internet companies for what is posted on their platform suggests four factors that must be considered: 1) state of mind, 2) magnitude of harm, 3) likelihood of harm, and 4) timing of harm. These considerations may parallel those offered through our halakhic analysis, though the precise way in which they are applied will be different. Nevertheless, the fact that the kind of concerns that can be framed by halakha are found in the works of writers aimed at a general audience indicates how thinking seriously about halakha can help us develop tools to contribute to the general societal conversation about these topics.

---

1. See chapter 2 of *Liars*.

To return to our questions that we opened with concerning facilitating sin:

1. Are Facebook, Google, Twitter, and similar companies morally responsible to ensure that their platforms are not misused? To what extent would they be responsible? Would they be required to attempt to limit abuse, to make abuse impossible, or to do nothing at all?
2. If there is moral responsibility, does this extend to the *users* of these platforms – meaning, if we were to conclude that one is accountable for problematic content posted by others, does merely having and using a Facebook account make one a participant in problematic activity?

Now we can cite the sources we have discussed that bear on these issues.

The Responsibility of the Platforms

Assuming that an internet company is not actively posting problematic content, are they responsible to prevent others from misusing their platforms, and if so, to what extent?

Even if they are not actively posting, is it fair to frame them as passive? Would creating algorithms that prioritize some content over other content be considered active involvement in what is posted? A growing consensus has seen precisely such actions as reasons to hold them responsible.

It seems clear from the perspectives raised above that in any case where they do not review or cull the material, they are providing only a neutral tool that can plausibly be used for neutral or positive purposes. They are in no way directly involved with the sin, thus negating *lifnei iver* and its possible rabbinic derivatives. Through their passivity, they do not encourage or show approval for problematic material that is posted, thus negating the *meḥazek yedei overei aveira* or *ḥanifa* concerns. Thus, it seems most reasonable that they are not responsible for the material in this sense.

Furthermore, even though the companies know that some people will likely misuse their platforms, several halakhic authorities assume that if the intention of those providing the item that can be misused had positive intentions (which in the case of Google, they explicitly claimed), then the culpability for misuse is further vitiated.[2]

Additionally, culpability is reduced when the item or platform being provided is not immediately misused, which in the case of internet platforms, is arguably the case, as the platform is provided before it is misused. On the other hand, the constant upkeep of the platforms and ongoing hosting of the material may more directly implicate the platforms in what is posted.

At any rate, the more lenient conclusion is not warranted in all cases, or depending on whom one asks, in most cases. If they in some way elicit the problematic content, then they would seem to encroach upon *lifnei iver* concerns by participating in the posting, or at the very least be seen as approving of the material, parallel to or worse than the *ḥizuk* and *ḥanifa* issues. In many ways, it seems that many of the algorithms used do exactly this, especially as the most problematic material is often that which goes viral and brings people to or keeps people engaged on social media. One expert in the field who reviewed this chapter went further and rejected the claim that most platforms should be considered neutral, considering how much they "read, parse, and utilize all content."[3] The more this is true, the more culpability would be shifted to the platforms, even if they are not the creators of the material posted.

Additionally, as we discuss in later chapters, social media companies use the data culled from all that is posted on their platforms. The more data that is posted, the more material they can use to advertise or sell to advertisers. Therefore, even without actually writing that which is posted, they are closer to creators, or at least to enablers.

Let us turn to some history of how American law has treated these issues to illustrate how these issues might manifest. American law distinguishes, broadly speaking, between providers (neutral platforms) and publishers/speakers. In the latter case, one is responsible for the content

2. One might wonder, however, if the same will apply when one can be nearly certain about the "misuse" of the platform, such as cases in which public shaming and the like specifically drive the traffic they need for business.
3. Thank you to Galina Dastkovsky Moerdler for her invaluable insights on this chapter.

one provides. However, in most cases, they are not held responsible when they function merely as a platform and the problematic content is provided from others. What happens if the platform *elicits* that content? This was the question posed to the US Court of Appeals for the Ninth Circuit in the case of "Fair Housing Council of San Fernando Valley v. Roommates.com, LLC." In this case, Roommates.com had asked a series of questions to those using the platform to help determine which roommates to pair them with. Some of those questions would have been illegal for a realtor or the like to ask, due to concerns of discrimination. The question posed to the court was whether Roommates.com was responsible when other people provide that information. The court ruled in that case that there was a distinction between answers that were elicited by the targeted questions and those that were written in the "additional comments" section. Concerning the answers elicited directly by the platform, since Roommates.com was responsible for causing the potentially discriminatory information to be posted, they could not claim immunity simply because they themselves did not post it. By contrast, the court ruled that providing space for additional comments was not enough to make them responsible for content included in that section. Recently there have been several legal cases and bills that have challenged and changed this presumption, and this will likely continue in coming years.

From a halakhic perspective, explicitly asking for information to be posted that likely will be problematic might indeed be prohibited. But it may depend on how likely the content is to be problematic, dependent on the issues raised above concerning cases in which one is unsure if the sin will be committed and whether we can explain the potential use in others ways.

An article by the Bais HaVaad discussed this point and presented the following, specifically with regard to Facebook, though their arguments will apply to YouTube, Instagram, or any other similar platform. Their conclusions are as follows:

> If you establish a communications platform and you publish rules that ban forbidden speech, you are not required to intervene against violators (unless someone is endangered). Nevertheless, it is an act of piety to do so.

They reach their conclusion (adapted from the writings of R. Ariel Ovadia) as follows:

1. They argue that Facebook's responsibility for what is posted on its platform is similar to the responsibility of the owner of a bulletin board. Is that owner required to monitor the material placed on the board?

As noted above, this equivalency is questionable, as it becomes clearer that the social media companies are much more heavily involved, at least through algorithms, in what gets posted, or at least seen, most.

2. They rule that enabling sin is forbidden by Torah law, while assisting a sin (*mesaye'a*) is forbidden only by rabbinic law, and reject the position that assisting is entirely permitted. As we have noted, according to the Rambam, this may even be prohibited by Torah law. They reject the leniency of the *Shakh* that *mesaye'a* does not apply to *mumarim*, perpetual sinners, or that of the *Dagul MeRevuva*, that one does not need to stop intentional sinners.
3. Nevertheless, they argue that Facebook has no responsibility, either by Torah law or by rabbinic law, for what is posted on its platform. They argue that Facebook is similar to the ballroom or hall discussed by R. Feinstein (or, we can add, the house discussed by the Maharsham). A platform is fundamentally neutral. The fact that some people use it for ill does not make the creation of that platform problematic. As they note, it is specifically Facebook's attempt to monitor the problematic content that raises the question at all. Had they treated their platform as a tool that they allow others to use without concern as to the way in which it is used, people would have intuitively equated Facebook with the ballroom. Indeed, they note that other providers of communication technology do just that, namely telecommunications companies, which make no attempt to curtail problematic conversations.

They write:

> Arguably, the company's troubles are largely self-inflicted. Along with other social media companies, it chose not to be a passive forum where users publish what they will. Instead, it actively polices its platform, banning and promoting viewpoints according to its own values and politics.
>
> By contrast, there are other services that provide a forum for communication but do not concern themselves with its content. Phone companies take no interest in what is said on their lines, so it occurs to no one to punish them for the activities of prank callers or telemarketers or terrorists planning attacks. Ditto for email providers and the postal service. Because these entities claim no jurisdiction over the content they transmit, they are not held accountable for it.

At this point, they fall into exactly the concern that prompted Section 230. According to their logic, were the company to not moderate at all, no matter how bad the material posted was, they would be guilt free, but if they try to imperfectly moderate, they become halakhically liable. This seems paradoxical. Assuming they have no intention of controlling every piece of content that is posted, and simply intervene when egregious cases are brought to their intention, they can be considered better than neutral and face fewer concerns. As we have seen, positive intent makes *lifnei iver* less severe, not more severe.

Yet, the reason that legislation seems to be moving in the direction of making them responsible is because it is clear that they are not passive, nor do they get involved only to remove problematic material. Rather, they collect data and use algorithms to prioritize posts that benefit themselves and their advertisers. The more this is true, the larger their share of the blame. For example, they may not be responsible for someone posting a misleading, rage-inducing news article. But if their algorithms prioritize such posts to increase traffic, they are arguably eliciting the material and should be considered active and not passive. This would significantly increase their culpability for how their platforms are used.

4. Within their understanding of the topic of *haliteihu lerasha*, they note a potential reason to be strict.

According to the Chazon Ish, because the service enables forbidden conduct, it is the provider's responsibility to prevent it. To R. Shlomo Zalman, however, because the sinner is helping himself, as it were, one does not need to intervene. It would seem that even the Chazon Ish would agree if the platform's rules forbade the behavior in question.

This seems to depend on whether they actually expect people to keep those rules or encourage their violation.

5. As we have noted, in addition to *lifnei iver,* there are potential concerns of *arvut,* of being responsible to actively encourage proper behavior, assuming of course that the owners and users of a social media platform are Jewish.

   Nevertheless, the authors of the Bais HaVaad article claim this does not impose the obligation to prevent problematic content from being posted, for two reasons. First, they argue based on R. Yerucham Fishel Perlow's comments on Rabbenu Saadia Gaon's *Sefer HaMitzvot* (57) that one is not responsible for preventing the sins of another who is involved in multiple sins in any event. Second, they cite R. Yitzchak Elchanan Spektor as saying that even *arvut* does not apply when it is not certain that there will be a sin. I find this argument surprising, since, as we have seen, several halakhic authorities think that even in cases when it is not certain that there will be a sin, one violates *lifnei iver* or *mesaye'a.*

Constructing a Permissive View

In addition to the above, one could argue the following to generate the permissive view.

1. Social media platforms provide neutral spaces. Thus, even if one is inclined to accept the stricter interpretations on the enabling versus aiding question, this neutrality alone might eliminate the halakhic concerns.
2. They are removed from the commission of sins by several steps, and as we have seen, whether one is several stages removed from

the sin or simply assists the potential sinner not at the time of sin, many of the *lifnei iver* issues no longer apply.

3. Providing community rules and attempting to enforce them might count as some form of rebuke and encouragement to act properly. While the halakhot of protesting someone sinning are too broad to fully address here, there are limits to the extent to which one must protest. Providing community rules may not solve the *lifnei iver* problem, but it cannot possibly make it severe, contrary to the implications of the Bais HaVaad article, as noted above.
4. As we have noted in the story of Google in China, whether or not the executives of the company always succeed, one of their goals is to bring about positive change. As we have seen, many halakhic authorities are willing to accept enabling sinful activity if it is necessary to achieve greater goals. Assuming that one believes that these companies are in business not only to make money, but also to make the world a better, more connected place, which the creators of both Facebook and Google explicitly claim, the fact that their platforms may also be used for negative purposes would be viewed as less problematic from the perspective of halakha.

The Pious Person

Despite the above arguments, the authors of the Bais HaVaad article argue that it is proper for Facebook and similar companies to attempt to stop their platforms from being used for problematic content.

They point to the Mishna in Maaser Sheni (5:1):

> With regard to **a vineyard in its fourth year, they would demarcate it with clods of earth** placed around it on the ground, to alert people that they may not eat or derive any benefit from its grapes without redeeming them. **And** a grapevine **of *orla*** is demarcated **with potsherds** placed around it, to alert people that its grapes may not be eaten nor may any benefit be derived from them at all. **And** an area **of graves** is demarcated **with lime,** to notify people that the demarcated area is ritually impure and will impart impurity to those who pass over it. **Rabban Shimon ben Gamliel said: In what** case **is this statement,** that vineyards of

> the fourth year and of *orla* require demarcation, **said? During the Sabbatical** Year. **But the pious ones would set aside** some **coins and say: Anything that was picked from this** vine by passersby **shall be desacralized onto these coins. But during the other years of** the Sabbatical **cycle,** when anyone who takes the grapes of another is guilty of theft, there is no requirement to demarcate these vineyards. This is in accordance with the adage: **Feed it to the wicked man and let him die.** That is, one is not required to take precautions to protect the wicked from the consequences of their own sins. Here too, there is no obligation to warn a thief that the grapes he is stealing are prohibited. (Translation taken from Koren, Bava Kama 69a)

For all new trees and grapevines, the produce of the first three years is forbidden as *orla,* while the produce of the fourth year (*kerem reva'i* in a vineyard) must be taken to Yerushalayim and consumed there in a state of purity. For those who do not want to bring the actual produce, it is permitted to redeem the produce and use that money to buy food in Yerushalayim. Then, the original produce is desacralized and becomes permitted to eat. Rabban Shimon ben Gamliel's qualification means that the owner does not need to indicate the status of the produce in the first six years of the Sabbatical cycle, as one does not have to prevent potential thieves from violating other prohibitions. But in the Sabbatical year, when all are permitted to take produce from any field, the owner must demarcate what is forbidden. Nevertheless, righteous people redeem the produce of the fourth year, so that any thief will not violate eating it in a forbidden manner.

Based on this, the authors of the Bais HaVaad article argue that while it is not obligatory, it is correct for social media platforms to try to prevent people from misusing their platforms.

Pushing Back

As mentioned at several points, much of this is not sufficient to account for the facts on the ground. Social media companies collect data and benefit from the additional data that is shared on their platforms. To this end, they encourage posting, and more evidence has arisen that through algorithms they actively promote some material over other material. In some cases it may be to contribute to a particular agenda, and in some cases it may be to encourage the most viral material to be shared, despite that material being the most problematic.

As this does seem to be the reality on the ground, the platforms should be responsible. The growing communal and legal consensus reflects exactly this point. Many of these issues are in flux and have changed while this book was being written and edited, and therefore a full discussion of these laws is beyond our scope. For now, we must suffice with saying that the halakhic sources we have seen can provide language to explain why culpability increases as involvement increases.

In addition, I think that there is another reason for social media companies to attempt to mitigate harm on their platforms. It does not relate to *lifnei iver*, but to the mitzva of *lo taamod*, the proactive obligation to protect others, as we will discuss below. Before we do so, we must outline how the principles we have established relate to the users.

Chapter 13

The Potential Problems for Users, Rather than Platforms of Social Media

For users, I think the most relevant categories are that of *ḥizuk yedei overei aveira* and *ḥanifa* (indicating support for improper behavior), as Liao noted from a secular perspective. As noted above, he pointed to the ethical questions raised by liking and sharing posts. This is where users have to be careful. Every "like" can be a tacit acceptance of the activity portrayed by a post, and in halakha, offering support for illicit activity, even verbally, may be prohibited.

Let us take a few potential examples: If someone sees a post announcing an interfaith wedding (or any other forbidden union), are they allowed to "like" or share the post? May one offer *mazal tov* or congratulations? The same question may be raised regarding commenting on the post of a friend who attended a party on Shabbat that entails violation of its laws, eating non-kosher food, or violating any other prohibition.

To reiterate, the question is not whether or not one may be friends with people who are less observant, whether or not we think they are good people, or whether or not we judge them or leave that to God. The question, rather, is very local: May we show our support for specific actions they engage in that are problematic according to halakha? It is to this question that we now turn our attention.

The Broader Question

Let us once again cite Dr. S. Matthew Liao's op-ed in *The New York Times*:

> Among Twitter users, a common refrain is "retweets are not endorsements." In a similar manner, one might also think that "sharing" or "reacting to" are not "endorsements." This is a mistake. By sharing or reacting to a post, even if one explicitly criticizes the post, one is amplifying the message of that post and signaling that the post warrants further attention.[1]

As noted, halakha recognizes this concept, as we have seen:

1. It is forbidden to encourage people who are sinning, either based on *ḥizuk yedei overei aveira* or *ḥanifa*.
2. These standards can be quite demanding. As R. Yitzchak Weiss noted, flattery and showing support for sin may be independent prohibitions that are in some sense more severe than *lifnei iver*. Specifically, he notes that in cases in which one enables or assists a sinner to commit *a particular forbidden act,* one does not directly cause the sinner to engage in *future illicit activity.* By contrast, by offering explicit support and encouragement, one is responsible for creating a framework that will make it more likely that the sinner will make these prohibited activities a habit and sin many times in the future.
3. Even silence can be perceived as forbidden support.
4. People also have an active obligation to rebuke wrongdoers.

---

1. Available at: https://www.nytimes.com/2018/11/24/opinion/sunday/facebook-immoral.html.

This general framework creates serious halakhic demands on users of social media to ensure that the way they share, "like," and tweet does not send a wrong message to the world about their values.

Practical Conclusions

I think it is safe to say that offering criticism on social media concerning a forbidden marriage, violation of Shabbat, or any other sin is counter-productive. While there is a mitzva of rebuke, social media is usually not the forum for it. The echo chamber of social media will make any comment of this sort a catalyst for animosity, as many or most of the friends of those violating halakha probably think there is nothing wrong with these activities. I think this is a clear case to apply the principle: "Just as it is a mitzva for a person to say that which will be heeded, so is it a mitzva for a person not to say that which will not be heeded."

On the other hand, it does not seem that halakha would share Liao's conclusion, that sharing problematic content to condemn it is participating in the moral problem. In cases in which drawing attention to a problematic (racist, anti-Semitic, violent) tweet would be for the greater good, someone who highlights this accomplishes a value of rebuke. Even if it will not make the person change, it may be beneficial to protect others, or to set the moral tone in society. It is worth pointing to several positions we will discuss in our chapter on judging favorably.

Maharil Diskin, at the very end of his responsa (*Pesakim, Dan LeKhaf Zekhut*), writes that it is important for people to believe they live among good people. When they do not believe this, they will hold themselves to a lesser standard. People generally feel the need to be only a bit better than those around them. If they believe that the people around them are terrible, they will strive to be only bad. But if they think everyone is good, they will try to be great.

Meiri (*Ḥibur HaTeshuva* 1:4, 84–85) writes similarly that the reason one who suspects a good person of evil is punished is that this will make it hard for the one doing the suspecting to accept rebuke. A similar opinion is presented by R. Nissim Karelitz in the name of the *Ḥazon Ish* (*Ḥut Shani, Shemirat HaLashon*, ch. 2). Based on this, R. Daniel Feldman notes[2]

2. *The Right and the Good* (Yashar Books, 2005), ch. 8.

that in cases in which one knows that someone is evil, he may not bend over backward to defend the person's ostensibly evil actions, as this would lead to the same phenomenon. If known evil is tolerated, it will encourage society to become worse. This, he notes, is an opinion cited by R. Moshe Sternbuch (*Responsa Mo'adim UZemanim* 7:192) in the name of R. Yoel Teitlebaum, the Satmar Rebbe.

One can argue that condemning certain statements or actions on social media makes it clear what is considered acceptable in society, whereas deafening silence implies that the problematic statement is widely accepted. According to Maharam Schick, silence can also cause one to violate *ḥizuk yedei overei aveira* and *ḥanifa*.

On some level, wishing a public *mazal tov* on Facebook is not as bad as actually attending a forbidden wedding. On the other hand, explicitly congratulating a couple on their interfaith wedding might not have the potential leniency that Rabbis David and Avraham Stav suggest. While people might interpret parents' attendance at their child's interfaith wedding as an attempt to avoid severing ties with their child, rather than as an expression of support for the marriage,[3] publicly writing a gushing *mazal tov* on their Facebook wall or sharing all the beautiful wedding shots may easily be interpreted as condoning or celebrating the union itself. Thus, both attending forbidden weddings and expressing congratulations are problematic for different reasons, and each has aspects that indicate approval for sinful activity in differing severe ways.

Yet, there is another reason why we need to think more carefully about the pictures and posts we share, comment on, or "like." In my experience, while people understand that there are potential halakhic issues with attending a wedding that is not in accordance with halakha, such as an interfaith wedding, and often ask for halakhic guidance when there might be a need to attend such a wedding, they do not have the same compunctions about offering their congratulations to the new

3. R. Aryeh Lebowitz cites R. Hershel Schachter as ruling that a parent may attend the intermarriage of a child for this reason, while friends may not attend such a wedding, as a friend's participation will be viewed as approval of the union. See https://www.yutorah.org/lectures/lecture.cfm/914845/rabbi-aryeh-lebowitz/from-the-rabbi-s-desk-attending-a-parent-s-forbidden-wedding/.

couple.[4] Even if they feel uneasy offering their blessings in person, the disinhibiting effects of the internet and the ease of "liking" a post on their smartphones make them feel that doing so could not possibly be a violation of halakha.

In truth, in many ways, it is worse. While one can offer congratulations to the newly married couple in private, perhaps avoiding outsiders' perception that one is sanguine or even joyful about the forbidden relationship, one cannot keep this private on social media. All one's friends and followers on social media can and will see that "like" and share. Retweets, all protestations to the contrary, are often viewed as endorsements.

Similarly, if a friend posts a picture from the party they attended on Friday night, a "like" or comment as innocuous as "looks like fun" or "I hope you enjoyed it" implies that one does not view the Shabbat violation as sufficiently problematic. The same can be said about any post of forbidden activities.

As R. Feinstein noted, there are cases in which the sinful activity is incidental. For example, if a friend posts an album of pictures from their halakhically permitted wedding, but some of the pictures are of dancing that may be a halakhic concern, it seems that it would still be permitted to offer a *mazal tov* on the wedding and "like" the album as a whole. Few people would interpret that *mazal tov* as an endorsement of all that happened at the wedding. Even commenting "beautiful pictures!" is unlikely to be interpreted as "I agree with everything you did at the wedding that is captured in this album." In the same way that no one thinks the Orthodox relative eating his airplane meal at a wedding with non-kosher food endorses eating non-kosher, everyone understands that one may be happy about a marriage without approving of every way the couple chooses to celebrate their wedding.

There are surely borderline cases, but the principles seem clear. In any case in which one's "liking," sharing, commenting, or retweeting may

4. I have observed a similar phenomenon concerning holiday greetings. While many people understand that there are potential halakhic issues with attending a Christmas party, they do not realize that wishing "Merry Christmas" or "Happy Holidays" also carries serious halakhic issues.

be interpreted as support of forbidden activity, one potentially violates derivatives of *lifnei iver, mesaye'a, ḥizuk yedei overei aveira,* and *ḥanifa.* In cases in which it is clear that one may be happy about the core positive content of a post without signing on to every problematic aspect that it entails, reacting in a positive manner to such a post would be permitted.

Positives

As noted above, I think that a social media platform is rarely the place to give rebuke for a particular sin. (We will see exceptional cases later in the book in the context of using social media to shame *get* withholders.) Yet, in the spirit of R. Amital's comments above, this does not mean we should ignore the potential educative role of social media.

Posting Torah thoughts, questions, links to *shiurim,* anecdotes of impressive acts of *ḥesed,* and sometimes even constructive criticism concerning social issues can all have a powerful impact. "Liking" and sharing the comments of others express our support for such posts. Social media enables us to reach many more people than we can in person, and we can create an online presence that helps others in a positive way. Similarly, when people post about loved ones who have passed away, a brief "*Barukh Dayan ha'emet*" or "Sorry for your loss" indicates that one cares. Just as saying *mazal tov* or "liking" a wedding announcement or picture can indicate support for prohibited marriages, under other circumstances, a *mazal tov* or "like" can demonstrate that one shares in the joy of others. In brief, the halakhot we discussed that indicate the potential negative power of a thoughtless reaction on social media should remind us that the same tools can be used just as easily in positive ways.

While this covers the responsibilities derived from *lifnei iver* and its related categories, we must now turn to another category that may demand intervention by platforms and users alike to prevent harm: *lo taamod al dam re'ekha.*

Chapter 14

Another Angle for Responsibility: Protecting Victims

Lo Taamod

Recently, social media platforms have put more effort into protecting their users. For example, many either banned or flagged information that might be misleading concerning Covid-19, or that discouraged people from vaccinating. Take, for example, these guidelines from Facebook's "Advertising Policies Related to Coronavirus (COVID-19)":

> In response to the coronavirus (COVID-19) pandemic, we've been working to support global health officials and keep people informed, safe and connected. As we continue to monitor the situation, we may make adjustments to our Advertising Policies to help protect people from exploitative tactics in ads related to COVID-19.[1]

1. https://www.facebook.com/business/help/1123969894625935?id=434838534925385.

In many of the cases where they are doing this, they are working under the assumption that the original material is problematic. Thus, they would be removing material to protect people, but part of the reason they are removing it is that they feel it is problematic to begin with, returning us to our discussions above.

I want to highlight one case in which the original material was completely innocuous, and nevertheless, YouTube moved to deal with misuse of the material to protect innocent victims. This will isolate the value of *lo taamod* from *lifnei iver* and its derivatives.

YouTube would never allow child pornography on its platform (this is indeed one example of something not protected by Section 230). However, it was recently uncovered that child pornographers who are excited by videos of children in bathing suits and the like make comments on innocuous videos of children to help others who are similarly perverted to use these videos for their fetishes and predatory behavior. YouTube has been attempting to fight this phenomenon, an initiative that is clearly commendable.[2]

This is despite that fact that the moral (and legal) culpability in that case is less than it would be if Alphabet (YouTube's parent company) allowed problematic content to be uploaded, rather than failing to successfully stop perverted people from misusing innocuous material. In this case, YouTube is removing comments to prevent the expansion of misuse.

Based on all we saw concerning *lifnei iver,* neither that prohibition nor its derivatives are helpful to explain why YouTube's actions are intuitively correct. Even if we accept that it is problematic to allow unethical material to be uploaded to one's platform, how can there be a moral obligation to ensure that non-problematic material is not misused? As we have seen, time delay, uncertainty as to whether there will be a sin, and possible positive use all serve as mitigating factors. But is there a way to ground the admirable actions of YouTube here in actual halakha?

The answer, it seems, is the obligation of *lo taamod al dam re'ekha,* protecting victims. It is written in the Torah, "Do not stand idly by the

2. See https://www.theverge.com/2019/2/19/18229938/youtube-child-exploitation-recommendation-algorithm-predators.

blood of your friend" (Lev. 19:16). The Gemara frames the obligation that emerges from that verse as follows:

> **The Sages taught** in a *baraita*: **From where** is it derived **that with regard to one who pursues another** in order **to kill him,** the pursued party **may be saved at** the cost of the pursuer's **life? The verse states: "You shall not stand idly by the blood of another"** (Lev. 19:16); rather, you must save him from death. The Gemara asks: **But does this** verse really **come to** teach us **this? This** verse **is required for that which is taught** in a *baraita* : **From where** is it derived **that one who sees another drowning in a river, or being dragged away by** a wild **animal, or being attacked by bandits, is obligated to save him? The Torah states: "You shall not stand idly by the blood of another."** The Gemara answers: **Yes,** it **is indeed so** that this verse relates to the obligation to save one whose life is in danger. (Sanhedrin 73a)

The Gemara continues to note that this obligation requires not only personal effort, but hiring others and spending money to help if necessary:

> Concerning **the** matter **itself,** it is taught in a *baraita*: **From where** is it derived **that one who sees another drowning in a river, or being dragged away by** a wild **animal, or being attacked by bandits, is obligated to save him? The verse states: "You shall not stand idly by the blood of another"** (Lev. 19:16). The Gemara asks about this derivation: **But is this** really **derived from here?** It is **derived from there,** i.e., from a different verse, as it is taught: The Torah teaches that one must return lost property to its rightful owner. But **from where** is it derived that one must help his neighbor who may suffer **the loss of his body** or his health? **The verse states: "And you shall restore it** [*vahashevato*] **to him** [*lo*]" (Deut. 22:2), which can also be read as: And you shall restore him [*vehashevato*] to him, i.e., saving his body. Consequently, there should be no need for the additional verse: "You shall not stand idly by the blood of another."

> The Gemara answers: **If** this *halakha* were derived only **from there, I would say** that **this matter** applies only **to** saving the person in danger **by himself**, i.e., that he himself must come to his neighbor's rescue if he can, as is the *halakha* with regard to returning a lost item. **But to trouble himself and hire workers** for this purpose, one might **say** that he is **not** obligated, just as he is not obligated to hire workers to recover another's lost item. Therefore, the verse "Do not stand by the blood of another" **teaches us** that he must even hire workers, and he transgresses a prohibition if he does not do so. (Ibid.)

While the most extreme examples of this mitzva refer to actually saving a life, nevertheless, as we saw in our discussion of *lashon hara* for constructive purposes, halakhic authorities assume, especially based on the connection the Gemara above makes to *hashavat aveida*, that even protecting people from other harms, even monetary harm, falls under this obligation. A central source for this is the comment of the *Sifra* in grounding the prohibition against withholding testimony that one knows can benefit someone else:

> And from where is it derived that if you can testify on someone's behalf, you are not permitted to remain silent? From "You shall not stand idly by the blood of your neighbor." (*Sifra, Kedoshim* 2:4:8)

R. Efraim Fischel Weinberger (*Responsa Yad Efrayim* 1) offers a detailed analysis of this passage. He notes that the scope of *lo taamod* depends on whether the testimony in question here relates to capital issues, specifically evidence that would exonerate a defendant, in which case we could limit *lo taamod* to actually saving lives, or even to monetary cases, in which case *lo taamod* extends to saving others from monetary harm. He outlines three opinions:

1. Rambam (*Sefer HaMitzvot, Lo Taaseh* 297) understands the testimony in question as monetary in nature, thus making *lo taamod* extend to protecting others from monetary harm:

> And they already said that one who represses [his] testimony is also included in this prohibition. For he sees the money of his fellow destroyed and he is able to return it to him by saying the truth. And also already appearing about this is "if he does not tell, he shall bear his iniquity" (Lev. 5:1). And the language of the *Sifra* (*Sifra, Kedoshim,* Chapter 4:8) is "From where [do we know] that if you know testimony for someone, you are not permitted to remain silent? [Hence] we learn to say, 'you shall not stand idly by the blood of your neighbor.'" (Sefaria/Nataf translation)

This opinion is also found in the *Sefer HaḤinnukh* (237):

> And our Rabbis, may their memory be blessed, also included in this warning (negative commandment) not to suppress testimony so that his fellow not lose money. (Sefaria/Nataf translation)

As noted by Netziv (*Haamek She'ala* 69), this is also the opinion of R. Aḥai Gaon in the *She'iltot* (*She'ilta* 69). This opinion is adopted by *Mishkenot Yaakov* (*ḤM* 12) and *Shaar Mishpat* (*ḤM* 28), who both derive from this that the obligation to testify to save someone from monetary loss applies even without being asked to testify. These opinions are recorded by *Pitḥei Teshuva* of R. Avraham Hirsch Eisenstadt (*ḤM* 28:4). They argue that the separate punishment recorded for those who deny having testimony to offer is necessary only to teach that the punishment and atonement for this is to sacrifice an offering, but not to teach the essential obligation to testify.

The *Ḥafetz Ḥayim* also writes that *lo taamod* applies to monetary issues as well.[3] I have heard suggested that the source for this concept may be that *dam,* while it can mean "blood," is also related to the word *damim,* money. Thus, one could read the verse as saying "*lo taamod al dam re'ekha* – do not stand idly by while your friend's money is in danger."

2. Several Rishonim (*Semag Lo Taaseh* 165; *Yere'im* 43) have a version of the *Sifra* in which the line about withholding testimony

3. We will explore the exact position of the *Ḥafetz Ḥayim* later in the book.

is not present. The *Ḥafetz Ḥayim* argues that this may be the opinion of the Rambam in *Mishneh Torah,* unlike the *Sefer HaMitzvot,* as he formulates the mitzva as follows:

> Anyone who can save and does not save transgresses "do not stand idly by the blood of your neighbor." So too one who sees his friend drowning in the sea, bandits attacking him or a bad animal attacking him and he is able himself to save him or he could hire others to save him but he does not; one who hears idol worshippers or informers plotting harm for him or laying a trap for him and he doesn't tell his friend and inform him; or if he knows that an idol worshipper or a thug are on their way to his friend and he could appease them on behalf of his friend to change their intention and he doesn't appease him; and so too any similar case; one who does any of these transgresses "do not stand idly by your neighbor's blood." (*Hilkhot Rotze'aḥ* 1:14, Sefaria translation)

R. Weinberger takes this opinion to be more authoritative, as the *Mishneh Torah* is more authoritative than *Sefer HaMitzvot.* This would remove the obligation to testify from the category of *lo taamod.* Yet, one can accept that *lo taamod* applies in principle to saving others from monetary loss and offers technical reasons to explain why the Rambam did not cite the *Sifra* in the *Mishneh Torah.* For example, the *Minḥat Ḥinnukh* (237:3) argues that since only two witnesses can testify, a single witness who knows information that can be helpful cannot violate *lo taamod,* as without a partner, he cannot offer effective testimony. The *Ḥafetz Ḥayim* (*Hilkhot Rekhilut* 9:1) writes similarly, arguing that it is obvious that *lo taamod* does apply to monetary issues.

3. R. Meir Simcha of Dvinsk (*Meshekh Ḥokhma,* Lev. 19:16) argues that one violates *lo taamod* only for withholding life-saving testimony, but not monetary testimony. According to this, presumably, *lo taamod* does not apply to protecting people from monetary harm.

R. Yosef Shaul Nathanson (*Responsa Sho'el UMeshiv* 2:3:110) also argues that *lo taamod*, especially with its demanding details, such as the requirement to spend money to protect others, does not apply to protecting others from monetary harm. Thus, in the case of testimony, for example, one is obligated to testify only if the litigant requests it. (He has technical reasons for this as well.) He notes that this is why many commentaries ground the obligation to testify in monetary cases on the generic obligation of *ḥesed*, kindness.

Even according to this opinion, R. Weinberger assumes that one would be obligated to protect others from physical harm, even if it is not life threatening, due to *lo taamod*.

In general, it seems to me that the halakhic authorities have accepted the more expansive definition of *lo taamod*, that one is obligated to protect others not only from death but all kinds of harm. As noted, the *Ḥafetz Ḥayim* takes this is as obvious. Despite the change of the Rambam from *Sefer HaMitzvot* to *Mishneh Torah*, R. Ovadia Yosef (*Responsa Yeḥaveh Daat* 4:60) cites the former and takes it as a given that preventing monetary harm is included in *lo taamod*. R. Yaakov Breisch (*Responsa Ḥelkat Yaakov*, *EH* 79) extends this beyond monetary harm to emotional pain. He argues that one is obligated to tell a woman that her potential husband has a terminal disease, because *lo taamod* mandates that one save her from the pain of young widowhood. R. Eliezer Waldenberg (*Responsa Tzitz Eliezer* 16:4) rules that one must reveal problems of infertility to save people from the physical and spiritual pain it causes, also based on *lo taamod*. Many of these examples can be derived from the examples provided by the *Ḥafetz Ḥayim* at the end of chapter 9 of *Hilkhot Rekhilut*, which he bases on *lo taamod*, in which he permits revealing many kinds of physical or spiritual flaws to protect potential spouses.

Even those who do not accept this expansion often suggest a functional equivalent. As seen from the Gemara in Sanhedrin, the mitzva to return lost objects is invoked by the Gemara as another potential source for the obligation to save someone's life, as if one must return someone's property, they must surely "return his life." Yet, as the *Ḥafetz Ḥayim* notes in his introduction to *Ahavat Ḥesed* (*Petiḥa* 3 and note 5), the comparison teaches that *hashavat aveida* is not only to return an object after it is lost, but to prevent someone from losing property. Thus, even if one were to reject the source from *lo taamod*, it is clear that one is obligated to prevent others from all forms of harm if possible.

This is the basis for the opinion of R. Yisrael Isserlein (*Pitḥei Teshuva* on *Oraḥ Ḥayim* 156, by a different author than that on *Ḥoshen Mishpat* cited above) concerning speaking *lashon hara* about someone when it is necessary to protect someone, which we will return to in our discussion of *lashon hara*:

> I have seen [it fitting] to mention here something about that which all the ethical writings have made so much noise in the world, about the sin of *lashon hara*. I will make noise in the world about the opposite, a sin much greater than this, and more common. Specifically, [I am referring to] the holding back from speaking when it is needed to save the oppressed from an oppressor. By way of parable: Concerning one who saw a person who was ambushing one's friend deceitfully on the way in the desert to kill him, or saw him tunneling into his house or store at night, is it possible that [the onlooker] should refrain from letting his friend know that he should be careful because [he was worried about violating] *lashon hara*?! His sin would be too great to bear, for he violates "and you shall not stand idly by your friend's blood!" *The same is true about money, which is included in the obligation of returning lost objects....* As long as one's entire intention is not to harm [the potential assailant] but for the benefit of the second person and the betterment of society and to protect them, then he fulfills through this a great deed, which is invaluable! (*Pitḥei Teshuva, OḤ* 156)

While he clearly relegates monetary issues to the category of *hashavat aveida* rather than *lo taamod*, the two mitzvot function in parallel ways, and thus generate the same obligation to protect potential victims even when it is necessary to speak negatively about a potential perpetrator. This is also the opinion of R. Shlomo Kook (father of R. Avraham Yitzchak Kook, recorded in the latter's *Mitzvat Re'iya*, 104). *Maadanei Yom Tov* (Rosh, Nidda 61b, note 6) further argues that offering such protection, and the scope of this obligation, are most simply derived from the mitzva of *ve'ahavta lere'akha kamokha*, to love others as one loves oneself. Thus, the existence of such an obligation is agreed upon, even if the exact source is unclear. We will return to all these positions in our discussion of *lashon hara.*

While there is much discussion in the halakhic authorities as to the extent one must go to fulfill the mitzva of *lo taamod,* how much one must sacrifice,[4] and the like, the point for our purposes is clear. The Torah demands that if we can protect others from harm, we must. Accordingly, even if based on *lifnei iver* and its derivatives, an internet company cannot be held responsible for the posting of information that is false, slanderous, leads to bullying or violence or any other problem; if they can step in to protect victims, they should.

As we have seen, YouTube is specifically trying to close a loophole that allows child pornographers to use innocuous videos of children to satisfy their fetishes. I think their intuition is correct. I do not think allowing people to post innocuous material that might be misused could possibly be a violation of *lifnei iver*. In this case, the platform is neutral, the material is several steps removed from the sin, and here one could invoke the principle of "*haliteihu lerasha veyamut.*" If a sinner wants to dive into the mire of sin, we do not need to stop him or her from doing so.

However, what drives YouTube to act in this case is that there are victims. If, therefore, a social media company can act to protect children from being harmed, they must. This is not because they are responsible for the material being uploaded in the first place, or even for how it is being used. It is because they are in a position to shelter potential victims from harm. The same argument applies to the attempts to shut down hate speech and cyberbullying. Even if on *lifnei iver* grounds there is no difference between allowing people to post promiscuous photos of themselves if they so choose and allowing them to post pictures that

4. In *Ahavat Ḥesed* (*Petiḥa,* note 5), the *Ḥafetz Ḥayim* argues that in principle, just like one must hire workers and spend money to save someone's life, the same is true to save property. However, in this case, one may recoup one's expenses, and may refrain from saving the property if he is not assured that he will be repaid. For the *Ḥafetz Ḥayim,* the two kinds of *lo taamod* are halakhically similar, and distinguished by a technicality, namely that a person has the right to prioritize his own money over that of others. R. Yair Bacharach (*Responsa Ḥavot Yair* 165), however, rules that even in principle, the higher-level obligation, to spend money to fulfill the mitzva of *lo taamod,* does not apply to saving the property of another. See also *Gilyonei HaShas* on Sanhedrin 73a.

will be used to fetishize children, on the grounds of *lo taamod* there is a world of difference.

There must be limits to this argument as well, and one could construct a version of it that would obligate Facebook and YouTube to remove every article that contains any bit of false information because it harms people by exposing them to untruths that shape their political views, and so on. But the fact that this argument could be expanded because its contours are not fully clear does not mean that it does not have merit. Even if these companies cannot possibly remove everything, it is important that they take more responsibility to address content that endangers people who may be harmed.

Of course, this analysis is in many ways theoretical. As we have seen, many of the classic sources that expand *lo taamod* relate to cases of *lashon hara*. In halakha, victims of gossip must be protected even when the information is true (in cases where the revelation is not needed to protect others). This kind of information, and even most false information, will not be removed from the internet. In fact, many of the landmark rulings concerning Section 230 specifically shield internet platforms from being held liable for lawsuits, even in cases where libel was published and resulted in harassment of the victims, or worse. This was true in the cases of "Zeran v. AOL" (Zeran was falsely presented as a supporter of the Oklahoma City bombing), "Blumenthal v. Drudge" (Blumenthal was falsely accused of spousal abuse), and "Batzel v. Smith" (Batzel was falsely accused of holding on to artwork stolen by the Nazis), for example.

It may be that the current pushback against Section 230 is a recognition that it is worth limiting the absolute freedom and immunity of internet companies because the cost has grown too high for victims. Ultimately, halakha will almost definitely have a higher demand for protection of victims than American law. And ultimately, we are dealing with corporations whose status as people in halakha is limited, and in most cases, the owners are either not Jewish or not committed to halakha, so this analysis is not practical. Nevertheless, *lo taamod* provides a language for why internet companies should be encouraged, however imperfectly, to protect victims, and perhaps advocate for systems that are more proactive (as is currently being done in the United States). Even Jeff Koseff, who wrote an entire book defending the broad protections of Section 230, acknowledges that there is a limit, as he describes in his chapter "Exceptional Exceptions."[5] Halakha should inform the way we think about what we expect from internet companies, even when we know that they will not, or perhaps need/should not, follow the exact guidelines that an individual Jew would be obligated to follow.

The User

If even the platforms may defend themselves against claims of *lifnei iver* because the sin is too far removed, because the commission of sin is uncertain, or because the platform is neutral, this is even more true for the average user. The fact that a platform has users makes it more likely that people will post problematic content, but this does not seem to make users responsible for the misuse of a platform. If I use Facebook only to share Torah sources, the fact that others may post false information in an attempt to sway opinions should not make me guilty of violating *lifnei iver*.

On the other hand, just as the platforms bear responsibility to protect victims who are being attacked, so do users, often more so. Preventing, countering, and reporting cyberbullying, for example, presumably does fall under the category of *lo taamod*. As noted above, this mitzva requires all those who can influence the situation to step in. While users may have less control, if they have a way to protect potential victims, it seems obvious that they must.

Conclusion

In this chapter, we have explored many halakhic principles that indicate how all involved with the internet are responsible, at various levels, for what is posted and how it is shared. As general society continues to grapple with these questions, on both the moral and legal level, we hope the rich framework provided by halakha can provide some direction.

5. Chapter 14 of *Twenty-Six Words*.

Section 3

Issues of Perception in the Digital Age

Chapter 15

Judging (Strangers) Favorably

As everything we do is increasingly accessible to the world, we are constantly judging and being judged by others. As halakha dictates both how we are to judge, as well as how we are to present ourselves, it is critical to explore the unique challenges we face in the digital age. This is even after we have dealt with the issues of confidentiality and privacy in the previous sections.

To illustrate how these issues can manifest, I want to begin with a story about something that happened when I worked in Toronto. Several students, as well as a teacher in a local high school, had traveled to New York City for an NCSY Shabbaton. After Shabbat, while walking through Central Park, the students ran into Conan O'Brien. As they had not yet returned home to retrieve their phones, Conan took a selfie on his phone. He posted the picture, noting that they did not have their phones due to Shabbat. R. Gil Student mistakenly thought the picture had been taken on Shabbat and published an article about the prohibition of taking selfies on Shabbat.[1] The teacher with the students then reached out to him to correct the mistake. R. Student subsequently published a retraction and apology. However, he then wrote an article explaining why he thought halakha had not required him to judge these students favorably under the circumstances.[2]

The following morning, the principal of the school, R. Seth Grauer, used this as an opportunity to teach the students a lesson. He noted that in the world of social media, a small mistake, even a slight one, can instantly be publicized across the world and remain online forever. These can have effects on the jobs one gets, the schools one is admitted to, and the person one marries. Thus, he warned the students to exercise extreme caution to act in such ways as to maintain a positive image.

This story highlights two complementary areas of halakha that have been affected by our current communication technology, both of which relate to perception. The first relates to the viewers of ambiguous material: how has the obligation to judge favorably changed when we are no longer in contact only with those near us (with whom we may have some familiarity), but rather with complete strangers from all over the world?

The second is our obligation as those being viewed. Halakha has a series of laws that obligate us to ensure that people do not suspect us of sin, even if we are not actually guilty, such as avoiding *marit ayin* (the appearance [of impropriety]) and *ḥashad* (suspicion). How has this obligation been altered by the extreme difficulty in protecting our image? When we no longer know who is watching, how much must we go out of our way to make sure that no one, anywhere on earth, will see a picture on Facebook or Instagram and suspect us of wrongdoing?

Judging Favorably – How Favorably?

The Mishna in Avot (1:6) introduces the obligation to judge favorably (*lekhaf zekhut* – literally, toward the pan of merit [as if balanced on a scale]) as follows:

---

1. Available at: https://www.torahmusings.com/2017/11/celebrity-selfies-shabbos/.
2. Available at: https://www.torahmusings.com/2017/11/judging-a-stranger/. I would like to thank R. Student for reviewing this chapter and for his helpful contributions.

> Yehoshua ben Peraḥya says: Make for yourself a teacher, acquire for yourself a friend, and judge every person favorably.

The Gemara in Shabbat (127b) records several stories that seem to demand that we bend over backward, almost to the point of incredibility, rather than judge someone negatively, even if that is what his or her actions seem to demand. We will cite two of those stories at length, as the combined effect of these anecdotes underscores the issues:

> **The Sages taught** in a *baraita*: **One who judges another favorably is himself judged favorably. And there was an incident** involving **a certain person who descended from the Upper Galilee and was hired** to work **for a certain homeowner in the South** for **three years. On the eve of the Day of Atonement, he said to** the homeowner: **Give me my wages, and I will go and feed my wife and children.** The homeowner **said to him: I have no money. He said to him:** In that case, **give me** my wages in the form of **produce. He said to him: I have none.** The worker said to him: **Give me** my wages in the form of **land.** The homeowner said to him: **I have none.** The worker said to him: **Give me** my wages in the form of **animals. He said to him: I have none.** The worker said to him: **Give me cushions and blankets.** He said to him: **I have none.** The worker **slung his tools** over his shoulder **behind him and went to his home in anguish.**
>
> **After the festival** of *Sukkot,* **the homeowner took** the worker's **wages in his hand, along with a burden** that required **three donkeys, one** laden **with food, one** laden **with drink, and one** laden **with types of sweets, and went to the** worker's **home. After they ate and drank,** the homeowner **gave him his wages.**
>
> The homeowner **said to him: When you said to me: Give me my wages, and I said: I have no money, of what did you suspect me?** Why did you not suspect me of trying to avoid paying you? The worker answered, **I said: Perhaps the opportunity to purchase merchandise** [*perakmatya*] **inexpensively presented itself, and you purchased** it **with** the money that you owed me, and therefore you had no money available. The homeowner

asked: **And when you said to me: Give me animals, and I said: I have no animals, of what did you suspect me?** The worker answered: **I said: Perhaps** the animals **are hired to others.** The homeowner asked: **When you said to me: Give me land, and I said: I have no land, of what did you suspect me?** The worker answered: **I said: Perhaps** the land **is leased to others,** and you cannot take the land from the lessees. The homeowner asked: **And when** you said to me: Give me produce, and **I said: I have no produce, of what did you suspect me?** The worker answered: **I said: Perhaps they are not tithed,** and that was why you could not give them to me. The homeowner asked: **And when I said: I have no cushions or blankets, of what did you suspect me?** The worker answered: **I said: Perhaps he consecrated all his property to Heaven** and therefore has nothing available at present.

The homeowner **said to him:** I swear by **the** Temple **service** that **it was so.** I had no money available at the time because I **vowed** and consecrated **all my property on account of Hyrcanus, my son, who did not engage in Torah** study. The homeowner sought to avoid leaving an inheritance for his son. **And when I came to my fellow** residents **in the South,** the Sages of that generation, **they dissolved all my vows.** At that point, the homeowner had immediately gone to pay his worker. Now the homeowner said: **And you, just as you judged favorably,** so **may God judge you favorably.**

On a similar note, the Gemara relates that **the Sages taught** in a *baraita*: There was **an incident involving a certain pious man who redeemed a young Jewish woman** from captivity. When they arrived **at the inn he had her lie beneath his feet. The next day, he descended, and immersed** in a ritual bath to purify himself before Torah study and prayer, **and taught his students.** This conduct could arouse suspicion that the pious man kept the maiden for himself, as immersion in the morning is customary for men who have experienced a seminal emission by engaging in sexual relations.

And the pious man **said to** his students: **When I had her lie beneath my feet, of what did you suspect me?** They said

> to him: **We said: Perhaps there is a student among us whose** conduct **is not established** before **the rabbi,** and he wanted to make certain that this student would not inappropriately accost the young woman. Therefore, the rabbi kept the woman close by.
>
> He said to them: **When I descended and immersed, of what did you suspect me?** They answered: **Perhaps due to the exertion of travel,** a seminal **emission befell the rabbi. He said to them:** I swear **by the** Temple **service** that **it was so. And you, just as you judged** me **favorably,** so **may God judge you favorably.** (Shabbat 127b)

In both of these stories, the evidence seemed damning, yet the expectation seems to be that the viewers were supposed to deny what their eyes saw and judge favorably against all odds. Is this what the Talmud expects? Is this a righteous thing to do or an absolute obligation?

In the *She'iltot* (40), the worker is Rabbi Akiva, indicating perhaps that granting this level of benefit of the doubt is reserved for the most pious. This is what the Rambam implies by listing this as the practice of *talmidei ḥakhamim,* Torah scholars (*Hilkhot De'ot* 5:7).

However, while this might ease the expectations of the average person, the implications are still scary. How are we expected to root out evil and corruption if we don't see it? Furthermore, the Rambam in *Sefer Hamitzvot* (*Aseh* 177) seems to think this is a formal obligation, which only compounds the problem.

Whom Do We Have to Judge Favorably?

This problem is partially solved by answering another question: Whom do we have to judge favorably? Does it apply to people who have been known in the past to be righteous? Does it apply to people known to be evil? What about people who are average, or people about whom we know nothing – such as those we have never met, but only seen in pictures on social media?

The Rambam (*Commentary on the Mishna,* Avot 1:6) sets out the following guidelines: If someone has been known to be righteous, and the perceived offense is out of character, one must try very hard to explain it in a positive way. If someone is average, or one knows nothing about him or her, ambiguous things should be judged favorably, but there is no need to explain away activity that strongly seems negative. When someone has been known to be evil in the past, even those actions which seem positive should be suspect.

Rabbenu Yona (*Shaarei Teshuva* 3:218) argues similarly. He notes that the reason one bends over backward to explain away the indiscretions of righteous people is that doing so is logical – when something does not fit with what we know about them, it makes sense that there is another explanation. This may not mean that we don't have to keep our eyes open for further indiscretions which might demonstrate a pattern, but as long as an act remains anomalous, there is reason to explain it away.[3] As for evil people, he goes further than the Rambam, arguing we should actively assume it is actually insidious. The *Ḥafetz Ḥayim* (*Hilkhot Lashon HaRa* 3:3, 3:7) takes this general approach as well. However, he rules that judging a righteous person favorably is an obligation, but expending extreme mental energy to exonerate an average person is a pious thing to do, not obligatory.[4]

Based on the above, R. Student argued that while it would have been meritorious to judge these unknown students, with no presumption of exceptional piety, he was not technically obligated to do so. However, he also noted that in an age of superficiality, generated by modes of communication such as social media, there is good reason to take the extra step. This was his conclusion:

> Obviously, I cannot be objective about my own behavior. Based on what I wrote above, it seems that on seeing a picture of people I don't know in a situation that could be interpreted positively (taken after Shabbos) or negatively (taken on Shabbos), I was not obligated to judge favorably. However, as a pious or proper practice, I should have judged favorably anyway. While I am

---

3. I note this with caution, as the assumption that rabbis are righteous has been what has enabled too many cases of abuse. It is clear to me that we cannot allow people to hide their predatory nature behind the obligation to judge favorably.
4. As for the exact definition for each of the three categories, see R. Gil Student's article here: http://www.aishdas.org/student/zechus.pdf.

> neither a Torah scholar nor a pious man, in these types of matters we should all act strictly. The world needs stringencies on interpersonal commandments.
>
> In truth, it never occurred to me that there was a positive way to judge this case. I jumped to the negative conclusion without considering alternatives. I say this not as a justification but as a confession. Whenever we see something, we need to think carefully before we react. Superficiality is the great sin of our TL;DR world, a trait that blinds us to our own faults. Like mockery, superficiality prevents us from hearing others and therefore from accepting rebuke.[5]

While I may not disagree with his technical conclusions, I think there is a more expansive discussion to be had.

Why Do We Have to Judge Favorably?

To fully understand our obligations in the age of social media, we must understand why we must judge favorably in the first place. R. Eliyahu Dessler (*Mikhtav Me'Eliyahu,* vol. 5, 431) argues that the obligation stems from the mitzva to love others. When we see someone we love doing something wrong, we do our best to explain it away. To the extent that we are meant to love all Jews, the same tendency should be extended to all Jews. The *Sefer HaḤinnukh* (235), on the other hand, argues that this is necessary to create peace. If we are constantly suspecting others of wrongdoing, society will not function properly. R. Shlomo Luria (*Responsa Maharshal* 64) writes similarly that this generates peace.

Maharil Diskin, however, suggests a radically different possibility. At the very end of his responsa (*Pesakim, Dan Lekhaf Zekhut*),[6] he writes that it is important for people to believe they live among good people. When they do not, they will hold themselves to a lesser standard. People generally only feel the need to be a bit better than those around them. If they believe that the people around them are terrible, they will strive to be only bad. If, however, they think everyone is good, they will try to be great.

5. See above, note 2.
6. See also his comments on the Torah, *Parashat Vayikra.*

Meiri (*Ḥibur HaTeshuva* 1:4, 84–85) writes similarly that the reason one who suspects a good person of evil is punished is because this will make it hard for him to accept rebuke. A similar position is presented by R. Nissim Karelitz in the name of the *Ḥazon Ish* (*Ḥut Shani, Shemirat HaLashon*, ch. 2).[7] Based on this, R. Daniel Feldman[8] notes that in cases in which one knows that someone is evil, he cannot defend it, as this would create the same phenomenon. If known evil is tolerated, it will encourage society to become worse. This, he notes, is a position cited by R. Moshe Sternbuch (*Responsa Mo'adim UZemanim* 7:192) in the name of the Satmar Rebbe.

The *Yismaḥ Moshe* (Avot 1:6) suggests yet another reason: assuming there is less sin in the world minimizes desecration of God's name (*ḥillul Hashem*).

There are many technical differences between these suggestions, but we will focus on a few that touch on our issue. In *LeRe'akha Kamokha* (vol. 8, *Kuntres HaBiurim* 2), R. David Ariav notes that if this is an interpersonal mitzva, then it may be waived when there is practical benefit (based on *Kovetz He'arot* 70). He uses this to explain why the court is allowed to "suspect" the *Kohen Gadol* of wanting to diverge from the accepted practices on Yom Kippur. As there was a real concern that the Sadducees had infiltrated the *Beit HaMikdash*, they had to adjure the *kohen* to follow the halakha according to the rabbinate, even if he had given them no reason to suspect him (Yoma 18b). Based on this, he suggests that when there is an educational or societal reason to judge unfavorably, this is warranted.

Implications

If one judges favorably only to keep the peace locally, then perhaps R. Student is correct. Judging a complete stranger unfavorably won't do much to a non-existent friendship. However, if judging favorably is about

7. He writes that if people think that others are violating Shabbat, they are more likely to violate it themselves, and the more cars they saw being driven on Shabbat, the more likely they were to feel this way. Hence, he thinks that people should tell themselves that all the cars they see being driven on Shabbat are the same ones over and over, simply to minimize the perception of Shabbat violation.
8. R. Daniel Feldman, *The Right and the Good*, ch. 8.

promoting a perception about the world that will encourage holding oneself to higher standards, being consistently critical of every person seen doing something questionable on Facebook and Instagram is arguably worse, as it lowers one's expectation of the whole world. Similarly, if the issue is *ḥillul Hashem*, constantly assuming the worst about strangers does create the feeling that God's Torah is not being kept anywhere.

However, there are times when it is specifically important to be critical. If a particular sin is rampant, judging favorably the pictures and stories one sees on social media creates a perception that the sin is condoned. This can be dangerous, and we will return to these issues later.

This has been at the heart of the #MeToo movement: the belief that if we always judge the suspected abusers favorably, no one will believe that the behavior is really wrong. Thus, while we cannot jump to conclusions about any specific accused abuser, if we don't judge society a bit more critically, we will never change.

However, without judging any individual in the court of public opinion, judging society as a whole less favorably is what might be needed to fix it. As *LeRe'akha Kamokha* notes, one may specifically not judge favorably if it will be beneficial. When being critical is what is needed to fix society, then that is what should be done.

Of course, some of the detractors of the movement warn that creating a society that is too quick to judge will harm all men, as people who should have been in a neutral state and given the benefit of the doubt will be assumed to be offenders. Whoever is correct, what is critical is that we recognize the resources that halakhic and philosophical texts from Torah sources provide to help us navigate the complex issues that have come to the fore in our age of social media.

In this chapter, we dealt with our responsibility to judge others favorably. In the next chapter, we will deal with the reality that we are always being judged.

Chapter 16

Marit Ayin, Ḥashad, and Social Media

While we may hope that others judge us fairly, we must be aware that they may not – and we must accordingly. How does the reality that someone may always be watching us affect how we must conduct ourselves? Knowing that a picture may be taken out of context, and that there will be likely no opportunity to clarify what the picture actually shows, how careful must we be to make sure that no one, anywhere, will have reason to doubt our integrity and piety?

To return to our example above, the high school students who innocently took a selfie after Shabbat with Conan O'Brien had no idea how that picture would be understood. When Conan wrote that he needed to take the picture on his phone because the students did not have theirs due to Shabbat, they did not realize that would be interpreted to mean that they had taken the picture on Shabbat itself. Did they have to be concerned about this? While their principal used this as an educational moment to teach them about how easily their reputations could be ruined in the world of social media, were they halakhically bound to be worried about such eventualities?[1]

This is especially poignant when so many politicians and celebrities have destroyed their careers and reputations because of a single post on Facebook or Twitter. In many of those cases, the people were actually guilty of the indiscretion, but this phenomenon still highlights the power of social media to destroy one's public image. There are as many cases of people whose reputations were destroyed due to a mistake over those same media, as discussed in earlier chapters. Here we turn to our obligation to protect our own images, even when we have done nothing that deserves suspicion.

The Difficulty of Maintaining a Righteous Image

First, we need to establish that we care about perceptions at all. If we are doing nothing wrong, why should we care what other people think?

Ḥazal insist many times that we do need to be concerned. When Moshe instructs the tribes of Reuven and Gad that they must fight as the vanguard for the Jews in the Land of Israel in order to be allowed to inherit on the east bank of the Jordan, he tells them, "*Vihyitem nekiyim meHashem umiYisrael,*" "And you shall be clean before God and Israel" (Num. 32:22).

From here (and from a similar verse in Proverbs 3:4), the Mishna derives an obligation to not only avoid sin, but to avoid the perception that one has sinned – to remain innocent in the eyes of people, not just God. The Mishna states this in the context of the extent to which the treasurer of the *Beit HaMikdash* must go to ensure that no one suspects that he is stealing funds. The Mishna assumes that people will always suspect him of pilfering the property of the Temple: If he becomes rich, they will assume he stole; if he becomes poor, they will assume he stole and was being punished by God for having stolen. No matter his financial situation, people will look for reasons to accuse him of dishonesty. The solution, according to the Mishna, is for him to avoid wearing anything in which he could hide money:

1. For many of these sources, see: http://olamot.net/ on *Marit Ayin.*

> The one who made the appropriation did not enter the chamber wearing a bordered cloak, or shoes, or sandals, or tefillin, or an amulet, lest he become poor and [people] say that he became poor because of a sin committed in the chamber, or lest he become rich and [people] say that he became rich from the appropriation in the chamber. For one must be free of blame before others as he must be free of blame before God, as it is said: "And you shall be guiltless before the Lord and before Israel" (Num. 32:22), and it says: "And you will find favor and good understanding in the eyes of God and man" (Prov. 3:4). (Mishna, Shekalim 3:2, translation from Sefaria.org)

The Yerushalmi (Shekalim 3:2) offers several other sources for this obligation, from Torah, *Nevi'im,* and *Ketuvim.*

The *Ḥatam Sofer* bemoans the difficulty of this expectation:

> [K]now that my whole life I have been troubled by the verse, "And you shall be clean before God and Israel," and these two obligations we have: to be clean before God and clean before Israel His nation. These are two paired riders on our backs.
>
> However, it is much easier to fulfill the first obligation, meaning, in the eyes of God, than it is the second, to fulfill one's obligation to people. For they think strange thoughts and the weavers speak of it by moonlight. Its punishment is quite severe, to no end, more than one who does not fulfill his obligation to Heaven, God forbid. This emerges from the Talmud at the end of the chapter *Yom HaKippurim* (Yoma, ch. 8) regarding desecrating God's name, which has no atonement, such as when a rabbi purchases meat but does not pay right away.
>
> In our great iniquity, people commonly talk about how this studious person did such and such. It is fluent in their mouths, even if it is just a suspicion. And in this case, even if the studious person acted properly in the eyes of God as much as possible, but not carefully enough, such that some drunkards made a mistake about him and wrote mocking songs about him, he has been caught in their trap. Over this, all sufferers shall

> grieve, and the verse screams out: "You have let them ride over us" (Ps. 66:12).
>
> And I have wondered many times if it is even possible that a person in the history of the world has fully fulfilled this verse. Perhaps this idea is included in what King Shlomo said, "There is no righteous person in the world who does only good and no wrong" (Eccl. 7:20) – which means to say that even if his deeds were all good [in the eyes of God], it is impossible to not sin in the second way, fulfilling the obligation [in the eyes of] people. (*Responsa Ḥatam Sofer*, vol. 6, *Likutim*, 59)

If the *Ḥatam Sofer* wrote this in his time, how much truer is it in the age of social media. All that needs to happen is for someone to snap a picture that might be perceived as compromising, post it on Facebook or Instagram, tweet it, send it to a few friends, and countless strangers will doubt the integrity of an innocent person. If halakha demands that we avoid being suspect even in such cases, how could anyone claim to have fulfilled his obligation to keep his reputation clean in the eyes of humanity!

Marit Ayin

Based on the ethos of this value, the Talmud in many places presents a rabbinic prohibition of *marit ayin*, avoiding circumstances in which someone seems to violate a prohibition, even if in fact that individual is doing no such thing.[2] *Encyclopedia Talmudit* (*Ḥashad*) notes that the cases in the Talmud seem to indicate that it is prohibited to cause people to think that one is currently violating a sin, that one has violated a sin in the past, or that one is going to violate a sin in the future.

Thus, the Gemara in *Keritot* (21b) forbids eating collected fish blood, even though fish blood is not forbidden, as it looks like one is eating forbidden animal blood, i.e., violating a prohibition in the present. The Mishna in Shabbat (146b with Gemara) forbids one whose clothes are wet after falling into water from hanging his wet clothes on

2. See *Shabbat* 64a–65a, 146a; Avoda Zara 12a; and elsewhere.

Shabbat in front of people, lest they think he has washed his clothes on Shabbat, meaning that he has violated in the past. The Mishna in Beitza (9a with Gemara) cites Beit Shammai, who forbid moving a ladder from dovecote to dovecote on Yom Tov, out of the concern that the person may be suspected of going to fix his roof in the future – meaning later in the day on Yom Tov.

Some Rishonim further forbid performing permitted acts which other people mistakenly believe are forbidden.[3] However, some Rishonim suggest that this is a more lenient kind of *marit ayin,* permitted in private.[4]

In the Bavli, Rav (Shabbat 146b) is cited as saying that these prohibitions are forbidden even in private. However, in the Yerushalmi (Kilayim 9:1), this seems to be presented as a dispute. While this Yerushalmi is cited by some Rishonim, the majority position, as recorded in *Shulḥan Arukh* (*OḤ* 301:45), is in accordance with Rav. This, however, may be limited to *marit ayin* of biblical, not rabbinic, prohibitions.[5]

Why would prohibitions done in private be prohibited out of concern for what people might say? There is no one there to misinterpret them! *Encyclopedia Talmudit*[6] summarizes the three possibilities that emerge:

1. We are concerned that someone may indeed see these actions even in private.
2. We are concerned that if someone gets used to doing something in private, that person may do so in public where someone will see him.
3. We apply the principle of *lo pelug:* once something is prohibited rabbinically, we forbid it across the board.

---

3. See Ritva, Eiruvin 88b, s.v. *ita,* and other sources cited in *Encyclopedia Talmudit,* note 207.
4. Meiri, Beitza 9a, s.v. *inyan.* See *Encyclopedia Talmudit,* notes 292–293.
5. See *Naḥalat Tzvi, YD* 87:3, cited in *Pitḥei Teshuva, YD* 87:10, to explain the view of the Rema. This is based on Tosafot, Ketubot 60a, s.v. *memaakhan.* See *Shulḥan Arukh, OḤ* 301:45, with *Mishna Berura* 165 and *Be'ur Halakha* ad loc.
6. Notes 262, 308–309. See Ran, Beitza 9a, and *Maḥatzit HaShekel, OḤ* 640:8.

Some *posekim*, such as the *Peri Ḥadash*, argue that only those things which *Ḥazal* explicitly prohibited because of *marit ayin* are prohibited. Anything else is permitted.[7] Others, however, argue that this is not the case.[8]

However, the *Peri To'ar* notes that even if we are lenient following the *Peri Ḥadash*, as the Torah clearly cares about presenting ourselves in a way that does not cause others to believe we are sinners, it is worth being stringent unless there is a compelling reason to be lenient.[9]

Ḥashad

Sometimes, a prohibition that seems related to *marit ayin* is referred to as *ḥashad* – it will cause one to be suspect. R. Moshe Feinstein (*Responsa Iggerot Moshe, OḤ* 2:40, 4:82) suggests that these are distinct categories.

He writes that *marit ayin* refers to cases where *Ḥazal* wanted to avoid having a person do something that might cause others to violate prohibitions, by mimicking the activity in cases that were more problematic. This is rabbinic in nature.

Ḥashad, on the other hand, refers to cases in which an observer may assume that the actor is violating a prohibition – and this is the biblical prohibition based on being clean in the eyes of man, which we saw above. This is true even though people should really give the "violator" the benefit of the doubt. However, as the Torah knows that this will not always happen, it forbids people from engaging in such suspicious activities. (Note that many believe that all these prohibitions are rabbinic.[10])

Responsa Ḥesed LeAvraham 1:21 cites *Ḥavot Daat,* suggesting that *ḥashad* applies even when the actions can be interpreted equally as permitted or forbidden. The formal prohibitions of *marit ayin* are only introduced for things that seem more likely to be prohibited.

Ḥashad has positive obligations attached to it. For example, Shabbat 23a obligates one who has two entrances to his courtyard to

7. See *Peri Ḥadash, YD* 87:7.
8. *Magen Avraham, OḤ* 463:3.
9. *Peri To'ar, YD* 87:3.
10. See *Responsa Penei Yehoshua* 2:2 and *Minḥat Asher,* vol. 4, *Bamidbar, siman* 96, p. 777–785.

light Hanukka candles at both entrances, so no one will suspect him of being derelict in his mitzva.

In a separate piece (*Iggerot Moshe, OḤ* 1:96), R. Feinstein suggests that there are limits to this. In cases in which one is doing something that doesn't even look prohibited, but someone else might think that it is prohibited due to a mistake, one does not have to be concerned. Thus, he feels it is permitted for a man to drive to *shul* after lighting candles but before Shabbat has started, even though women might think that it was prohibited, as women generally do not perform *melakha* after lighting candles. However, highlighting the sensitivity the Torah has for maintaining one's reputation, R. Feinstein committed not to do this after someone criticized him for it.

When Things Become Accepted

The Mishna (Kilayim 9:2) prohibits wearing wool garments that are mixed with silk. This is because wearing *shaatnez,* a mixture of wool and linen is biblically forbidden, and many people cannot distinguish silk from linen. The Rema (*YD* 398:2), however, writes that it is permitted nowadays, as silk is common and people are aware that what seems to be linen is probably silk and therefore permitted.

Baḥ (ibid.) and *Shakh* (ibid., 2) note that this is even true when the average person cannot distinguish based on looking at the material; it is sufficient that silk is common and that there is a ready explanation as to why the person is not violating *shaatnez.* R. Asher Weiss states that the simple understanding of this is that we even waive those prohibitions of *marit ayin* instituted by *Ḥazal* when the situation becomes such that there is no longer any concern. While he notes that some disagree, this is the accepted position.[11]

Responsa Ḥeishev HaEifod (1:20) uses this to permit eating margarine on bread with meat, because margarine is as common as butter, so there is no reason for someone to suspect the person is using the prohibited dairy one rather than the *pareve* one. R. Ovadia Yosef (*Responsa Yabia Omer, YD* 6:8) uses the same argument to permit having *pareve* milk at meat meals. Some, however, are less confident and require putting

11. See *Minḥat Asher* as cited above.

a visible sign on the table to indicate that the milk is not dairy,[12] and are hesitant about using margarine.[13]

This argument is used by R. Moshe Feinstein (*Responsa Iggerot Moshe, EH* 2:12) to permit women to cover their hair with wigs, even when it is hard to distinguish from their real hair. He says this even though he knows that there are many women who don't cover their hair, thus creating a real concern. Thus, R. Feinstein seems to think that *marit ayin* is waived when there is a reasonable explanation for one's seemingly prohibited activity, even when the concern is not dispelled. (He does add the possibility that we limit the prohibition of *marit ayin* to those things that were already instituted as another reason to be lenient.)

In the Age of Social Media

What are the implications in the age of social media? Without getting into all the details, the position of the *Peri To'ar* is particularly relevant. Even if one could make an argument for why any specific act might be permitted, the thrust of the halakha is that one should try, even when not formally obligated, to avoid situations that may be interpreted as questionable.

For some, the reason *Ḥazal* forbid actions even in private due to *marit ayin* is that there may actually be someone watching. While this concern may have once been farfetched, it no longer is. One may see no camera, but so many scandals have happened because someone was there to catch a picture on his or her phone. That incriminating photo, whether it captures a real crime or not, can and often will be spread across the world. One may never be able to delete it or erase it from the internet or from people's memory.

This is the reality of our world: being concerned about *marit ayin* in *ḥadrei ḥadarim* (chambers within chambers, i.e., innermost rooms) is not just the halakha, it is good advice. The same goes for what we say, which can and often is taken out of context by people too lazy to read everything we have said or written, or by those who are intentionally trying to "catch us" in indiscretion. Similarly, knowing that whatever

12. See summary in *Sefer HaKashrut* 10:41.
13. See R. Shimshon Frankel in *Tel Talpiyot*, vol. 67, 153.

we write does not have our tone of voice accompanying it, we must be careful about what we write, so that it will never be understood in an offensive manner, when that is not what was intended. We all know how many fights, personal or political, have been caused by misunderstood tweets or Facebook posts.

As mentioned, this is important because we need to maintain our image as the good people that we strive to be. More than that, however, as we have seen, some commentaries think these laws are meant to protect others from committing sins as well. When people think we are violating sins, they are more likely to mimic those sins, or similar ones.

As we saw earlier, the Maharil Diskin and others believe that the obligation to judge people favorably stems from a desire to ensure that society holds itself to high standards. As people often strive to be as good as, or only slightly better than, the person next door, the perception that people are sinning weakens the communal resolve to be good. The categories of *marit ayin* and *ḥashad* obligate us to avoid (as much as possible) damaging the communal self-perception of righteousness. If we are not careful, and our images are used to make people think that certain sins are commonplace, we have contributed to the collective lowering of expectations.

Many *posekim*, however, have noted that we are more lenient in cases of compelling need. There is admittedly a limit to what we can do to avoid becoming suspect. Try as we may, we can never fully avoid the possibility that what we do may be misconstrued. While it is critical that we do our best, we cannot cause ourselves psychological stress trying to ensure that no one, anywhere, will understand our innocuous words and actions in a negative light. The fact that *posekim* are willing to use this type of argument in cases where the potential for misunderstanding is great lends credence to the intuition that there must be a limit as to when we are required to be concerned about others' potential perception of our actions.

Similarly, once there exists a plausible counter-explanation, not based on the assumption that we are sinning, many *posekim* are willing to be lenient. As we saw, R. Feinstein is willing to be lenient in allowing married women to wear wigs, even though he knows that many married women do not cover their hair, and thus there is a real concern that people would suspect the women in question are not covering their hair. A similar argument can be made for many things in life. We are all aware of countless cases in which people's lives have been destroyed by a misunderstood post on social media. We can expect a certain level of understanding by others of this reality. We should, therefore, be able to engage in normal activities, whenever the positive interpretation is not just possible, but the most plausible.

Nevertheless, the extent to which *Ḥazal* go to force us to protect our own image is striking. This standard, combined with all the tragic cases of destroyed lives arising from misunderstandings on social media, should encourage us to exert extra caution in everything we do. As the principal told his students, they may not have imagined what that selfie would cause, but such a situation is not anomalous. We must expect that eventuality and do our best to avoid it. The near impossibility of escaping any possible misunderstanding does not absolve us of our responsibility to do our best.

Chapter 17

The Hashkafic and Psychological Downsides of Curiosity in the Age of Social Media

Introduction

In our previous chapters, we discussed the potential halakhic issues that arise in violating the privacy of others for curiosity's sake. Those prohibitions are primarily relevant when the person whose information is being accessed would object to this violation of privacy. However, even when people *want* their profiles to be accessed, there are several Torah values that may suggest that one should limit taking advantage of this information. Several of these issues are more philosophical than legal, but they are worth exploring to complete our perspective.

Psychology

In 2012, Hui-Tzu Grace Chou and Nicholas Edge published an article whose title summarizes one of the central problems created by Facebook and other social networks: "'They Are Happier and Having Better Lives Than I Am': The Impact of Using Facebook on Perceptions of Others'

Lives."[1] They note that while jealousy may be normal, it is particularly insidious in the world of Facebook, where people craft their own profiles and therefore can generate the perception that their lives are perfect, or at least better than the lives of others. When people consume this information, they inevitably judge their own lives as less successful than those of their friends. Their conclusion is as follows:

> The results of this research support the argument that using Facebook affects people's perceptions of others. For those that have used Facebook longer, it is easier to remember positive messages and happy pictures posted on Facebook; these readily available examples give users an impression that others are happier....
>
> [T]he results show that the longer people have used Facebook, the stronger was their belief that others were happier than themselves, and the less they agreed that life is fair. Furthermore... this research found that the more "friends" people included on their Facebook whom they did not know personally, the stronger they believed that others had better lives than themselves. In other words, looking at happy pictures of others on Facebook gives people an impression that others are "always" happy and having good lives, as evident from these pictures of happy moments. In contrast to their own experiences of life events, which are not always positive, people are very likely to conclude that others have better lives than themselves and that life is not fair. The correspondence bias is more likely to occur when people make inferences about people whom they do not know well. They tend to perceive that others are constantly happy, while paying little attention to the circumstances that affect others' behavior. One could argue that frequent Facebook users shall know the tricks others use to manage the impression; therefore, experienced Facebook users could avoid the potential distorted perception. However, the results of the research suggest that frequent Facebook users tend to perceive that others are happier. In other words, they are more likely to be affected by the

1. *Cyberpsychology, Behavior, and Social Networking*, vol. 15, no. 2, 2012.

> easily recalled content and tend to have the correspondence bias, whether consciously or unconsciously. The problems of relying on an availability heuristic and having correspondence bias can be alleviated by having more balanced information, which can be gained through deeper interactions with others. The results of this research found that the more time people spent going out with their friends, the less they agreed that others have better lives and are happier. In other words, when people have more off-line interactions with their friends, knowing more stories about others' lives, both positive and negative, they are less persuaded that others are happier than themselves. In this way, they can avoid correspondence bias. Since becoming "Facebook friends" usually starts with two people knowing each other in person, it follows that those with more friends on their Facebook tend to have a more balanced view of others because they know more people in person. Therefore, they are more likely to agree that life is fair, and less likely to agree that others are happier, as the results of this research indicated.

Thus, the nature of Facebook, as opposed to real friendships, exacerbates the problems of jealousy, including the problem of inaccurate perceptions of people's lives.

Happiness in Judaism

Some have noted that the Torah's perspective on happiness militates against defining happiness based on that of others, perceived or real. For example, R. Dr. Motti Klein has noted that while Festinger's Social Comparison Theory indicates that people usually judge their self-worth based on the perception of others, the Torah advocates for a radically different perspective.[2]

Ben Zoma in the Mishna in Avot (4:1) suggests the following definition of wealth:

2. Available at: https://www.yutorah.org/lectures/lecture.cfm/901425/rabbi-dr-motti-klein/torahpsych-8-facebook-self-worth-social-comparison/.

> Who is the rich one? He who is happy with his lot, as it says, "When you eat [from] the work of your hands, you will be happy, and it will be well with you" (Ps. 128:2).

The commentaries focus on several related points. If one is happy with the portion granted him, it prevents him from stealing or committing other crimes to illicitly increase his wealth.[3] More fundamentally, the identifying quality of someone who is impoverished is that he is lacking to the point that he constantly desires and is seeking more. Someone who has vast material wealth but is never happy will similarly be overcome by cravings and devote himself to expanding his property, rather than enjoying the wealth he has amassed. Thus, he is essentially in the same category as a poor person. On the flipside, by being happy with one's lot, one can enjoy what he does have, which is the identifying quality of living an affluent lifestyle.[4]

As true as these sentiments are when one compares himself to the reality of what others have, it is even more striking when comparing oneself to the intentionally positively spun lives of those around him. This is true even in cases in which there is no invasion of privacy. In fact, people put these versions of themselves on social networks specifically for others to see their lives. Nevertheless, the effect of obsessing over the lives of others drives people away from the Torah ideal of happiness.

Beyond the hashkafic element, however, there is a potential legal one as well: the prohibition of "*Lo taḥmod*," "You shall not covet."

Lo Taḥmod

"Lo taḥmod" appears in the two versions of the *Aseret HaDibberot,* Ten Commandments, in Exodus 20:14 and Deuteronomy 5:18. In the latter source, the Torah adds, *"velo titaveh,"* "and do not desire." Ibn Ezra explains the following:

> The Hebrew word ḥ-m-d has two different meanings. One meaning is robbery, oppression, taking from others through force or

3. See Rashi.
4. See Rashi, Rabbenu Yona, and R. Matitya HaYitzhari.

> compulsion (as in, "no man will attack your land" [*Exodus* 34:24] – for if the verb denotes jealousy, then a verse intending to extol the land instead deprecates it!). The other meaning is jealousy that does *not* express itself in overt action. (Ibn Ezra, Deut. 5:18, translation by Jay F. Shachter)

As my teacher R. Michael Rosensweig has pointed out, it is these two understandings that drive the main interpretations as to the nature of the prohibition.[5] Namely, is this prohibition fundamentally a problem of thoughts and desires, or one of illicit actions?

The *Mekhilta* (*Yitro* 8) argues that one does not violate the prohibition until one performs an action, though it does not specify what action that is. At the other extreme, the *Moshav Zekenim* (Ex. 20:14) cites a position that one violates *lo titaveh* as soon as he covets and violates *lo taḥmod* as soon as he *verbalizes* his desire, even if he does nothing to actualize it.

What action might be required? R. Naftali Tzvi Yehuda Berlin (*Birkat Netziv,* ibid.) argues that it is the *attempt* to actualize desire that causes one to violate the prohibition. R. Rosensweig argues that according to both the *Moshav Zekenim* and Netziv, the prohibition is essentially emotional. The requirement to verbalize the desire or attempt to achieve it is simply a measurement of the degree of desire that one must have in order to violate the prohibition – not mere "wanting," but an overpowering longing that spills over into words or actions.

Rambam (*Hilkhot Gezeila* 1:9) and many other Rishonim argue that one does not violate the prohibition unless he *successfully gains the object of his desire.* At first glance, this would indicate that these Rishonim understand that the prohibition is *action-oriented* rather than *emotion-oriented.* However, Rambam writes that one does not receive lashes for this crime, despite that being the normal punishment for violating a biblical prohibition, because *lo taḥmod* is a *lav she'ein bo maaseh,* a prohibition that does not entail an action. Raavad is dismayed by this position; if, after all, one does not violate the prohibition until

5. *"BeInyan Lo Taḥmod," Beit Yitzḥak* 19. Available at: https://tinyurl.com/3uycwzn5. Most of the analysis that follows comes from this article.

he successfully takes the object, it should be defined as a *lav sheyesh bo maaseh,* a prohibition that entails an action! R. Rosensweig suggests that Rambam's position lies on the same continuum as the positions above: the prohibition is emotion-oriented, but the degree of emotion that is prohibited is only that which ends with successfully taking the object.[6] This seems to be the way the *Semak* (19) understands the view of the *Mekhilta* mentioned above.

Other Rishonim, however, clearly believe that this prohibition is one of criminal actions. Tosafot in some places argue that the prohibition is identical to theft, and its relevance is that it causes one who takes something without paying (due to desire?) to violate two prohibitions.[7]

In other places, Tosafot[8] follow the position of Raavad, namely arguing that *ḥemda* refers to cases where one pressures someone into selling his property.[9] Formally, this is obviously not theft, as he is paying for the property. However, Raavad may still think that this a prohibition related to theft, as evidenced by the requirement that he cites for one to return property that he pressured someone into selling.[10]

Formal Violations in Viewing Social Media

According to the above, does one violate this prohibition by becoming envious of someone else's life or property, a common occurrence when constantly viewing the lives of others on social media, whether it be Facebook, Instagram, or anything else?

According to the *Moshav Zekenim,* if one's envy leads him to verbalize his jealousy, he has already violated the prohibition. However, according to most of the positions above, *lo taḥmod* is not mere desire; rather, it is the attempt, successful or not, to take someone else's property

6. This seems to be how *Maggid Mishneh* understands Rambam.
7. Tosafot Bava Metzia, 5b, s.v. *belo dami;* Sanhedrin 25b, s.v. *mei'ikkara.*
8. See above, as well as Bava Kama 62a, s.v. *ma, ḥamsan.*
9. The Gemara in Bava Metzia 5b notes that people do not understand that one can violate this prohibition even when he pays for the property. Thus, while it is prohibited to do so, those who violate the prohibition remain valid witnesses, though violating biblical prohibitions under many circumstances invalidate people's status as witnesses.
10. See R. Rosensweig's article for a full discussion of these positions.

by theft or pressure them into selling it. Just viewing the lives of others and wanting what they have does not entail a violation of *lo taḥmod*. This is especially the case as *lo taḥmod* seems to prohibit an attempt to take *someone else's actual property*. Deciding to buy the same car one's friend has, just to be like him, may not reveal control of one's passions, but it is not a formal violation of *lo taḥmod*.

It is also interesting to wonder whether one would violate *lo taḥmod* for desiring someone else's life, when the life they desire is not real, but a construction intended to deceive. According to the positions that tie this to theft and the like, it may be that one cannot violate the prohibition when the object of desire is imaginary. If the sin is in the emotion itself, it would seem that one would violate the prohibition even in these cases. However, this is speculation.

The Ethic of the Law[11]

While, as we have noted, one probably does not violate the technical prohibition of *lo taḥmod* by becoming overcome with envy due to viewing the lives of others, whether in person or through social media, the philosophy behind the mitzva can shed light on the potential problems involved, beyond those outlined based on the value of true wealth introduced above.

The first point emerges from *Sefer HaḤinnukh*, which notes that many people are surprised that the Torah issues commands directed at thoughts and desires at all. They assume that they cannot control these facets of their personalities. However, this commandment proves that God cares about what people think and feel, and more importantly, that people have the ability to control their inner lives:

> And do not wonder to say: How is it in the hand of a man to prevent his heart from desiring the storehouse of every delightful vessel that he sees in the hand of his fellow, whereas he is totally empty of them; and how does the Torah forbid that which is

11. R. Elchanan Samet has a thorough summary of many of the possible rationales for this mitzva, at: https://www.etzion.org.il/en/tenth-commandment-you-shall-not-covet. Several others are mentioned in R. Rosensweig's article.

> impossible for a man to avoid? This is not the case, and only silly evildoers and those who sin with their souls say it.
>
> Truly, it is in the hand of a man to dissuade himself and his thoughts and his desires from anything that he wants; and [it is] within his control and his cognizance to distance or to bring close his want for all things according to his will. His heart is given into his hand; to anything that he wants can he incline it. God – who sees all that is hidden – "searches all the rooms of the belly, sees the kidney and the heart." Not one of man's thoughts – little or big, good or bad – is concealed from Him; nor is it covered from His eyes. [Hence] He will bring vengeance upon those who transgress His will in their hearts, while "He safeguards kindness for the thousands [of generations] for those who love Him," who dedicate their thoughts to His service. There is nothing as good for a man as positive and pure thought, as it is the beginning of all actions, and their end. This is apparently the matter of the "good heart" which the Sages praise in Tractate Avot 2:9. (*Sefer HaḤinnukh* 416)

Rabbenu Yona (Ex. 20:14) writes that desire causes one to lose fear of God. Presumably this is because constant desire causes the fulfillment of one's passion to become the more important goal in one's life, no matter the expense. *Sefer HaḤinnukh* (38) adds that the desires can lead one to violations, as those desires may eventually know no bounds. Rambam (*Hilkhot Gezeila* 1:11) notes that in some cases in Tanakh, such as the story of Aḥav and Navot, it even leads to murder (I Kings, ch. 21). Rabbenu Baḥya (Ex. 20:14) contends that this mitzva comes at the end of the *Aseret HaDibberot* because envy can cause one to violate any and all of the Ten Commandments! Even when one's desire may not reach the technical level of *lo taḥmod,* as psychologists have noted, this can be the result of the nature of jealousy that social media enables: constantly seeing the "perfect" lives of others can overtake a person, driving all positive thoughts from his mind.

Ibn Ezra (Ex. 20:14) sees the key to this mitzva in fear of God, but in the opposite way from Rabbenu Yona. He provides a parable to explain how the Torah could command one to feel a certain way. If a commoner sees a beautiful princess, he will not (usually) realistically desire to be with her, as he knows this is impossible (*Aladdin* notwithstanding). Similarly, he argues, one who truly fears God and believes that all he needs in life, God has provided and will provide for him, will not desire that which belongs to others. God gives each what he needs. Thus, the problem for Ibn Ezra is not that *lo taḥmod* drives out fear of God, but that it indicates a lack of that fear and belief.[12] R. Yaakov Mecklenburg (*HaKetav VeHaKabbala,* Ex. 20:14) makes the same argument, though for love of God, rather than fear. Again, while one who spends his days envying the illusions of perfection he views in the lives of others on Facebook may not violate the letter of the law, the spirit of the law will have been lost.

In his comments on Deuteronomy, ibn Ezra adds, in line with the view of *Sefer HaḤinnukh* above, that while it may be hard to control these emotions, this is the purpose of the Torah. It is specifically the difficulty that causes the Torah to mandate this behavior.

Umberto Cassuto argues in his book *Exodus* (p. 166) that the victim is not God, but rather the person whose life and property is being desired. The Torah is teaching that even when one does not actually steal, the very act of desiring and obsessing over that which belongs to someone else is a kind of trespass. Many people, I would think, would indeed feel violated if they knew that others were constantly viewing their profile, wishing that they could live their lives. Many other commentaries, including the Midrash, note that *lo taḥmod* seems to be the antithesis of *ve'ahavta lere'akha kamokha.*[13]

However, as the psychologists above note, in many ways it is the person overcome by desire who is the real victim; he forfeits the true wealth that the Mishna in Avot advocates for. R. Elchanan Samet summarizes the view of Philo of Alexandria, who sees this as the key to *lo taḥmod* as well:

12. See the similar comments made by Rambam in the context of the prohibition against revenge in *Hilkhot De'ot* 7:7.
13. See Leviticus Rabba 24.

> The introverted nature of the prohibition against coveting – the limitation that it places on a person's internal, emotional world – gives rise to another possible explanation: this prohibition is meant to educate the coveter himself, and to bring him to a level of spiritual purity, free of forbidden desires. It is not the "neighbor" that the Torah means to protect here – for what harm is there in someone else's covetous thoughts (especially since there are people who actually wish to arouse the envy of their neighbors)? Rather, it is the coveter himself that the commandment comes to protect, for "Jealousy and desire and honor remove a person from this world" (Avot 4:21).[14]

Beit HaLevi (Ex. 20:14) suggests a solution. He observes that no matter what passion one may be overtaken by, if one is overcome by fear, that passion will be extinguished. Thus, if one manages to inculcate fear of God, he will manage to subdue his passions. The same can be said for love of God, based on R. Mecklenburg's words above. Alternatively, if one manages to understand how self-destructive these emotions can be, self-preservation can help him overcome it.

Conclusion

While obsessing over the lives of others through their Facebook profiles or what they post on Instagram may not be prohibited, there are many hashkafic and psychological reasons to avoid it. It shares many of the negative qualities of *lo taḥmod,* and leads to depression, damaging our relationship with others, God, and ourselves. We must recognize that the lives we see are not as perfect as they seem; even if they were, our lives do not have to be identical to theirs to be meaningful and positive. This seems to the most healthy and spiritually proper direction to take.

---

14. See above.

Section 4

Privacy, Confidentiality, Gossip: The Dangers and Benefits of Spreading Information

Chapter 18

Privacy: The Halakhic Background

Introduction

When people think about violating the privacy of others, they usually think about publicizing secrets, neutral or negative, to third parties. As we will see, halakha seems to prohibit the breaking of confidences; moreover, conveying negative information, secret or not, falls under the prohibitions of *rekhilut* and *lashon hara,* gossip. These sins are relatively well known.

Before we discuss these, however, we must focus on the lesser-known and seemingly less egregious problem of violating the privacy or intimacy of others for mere curiosity. Why is that wrong, and what counts as private?

In our age of digital communication, there will be new applications to this question. Can one read someone else's email? What about reading an email sent to a listserv that one is not a member of? Is that considered secret? After all, it was sent to many people. How about using someone else's Facebook account to access the profile of a third person? Should we assume that because that third party has not "friended" the viewer that all information found therein should be considered private, or does the knowledge that a profile can be easily accessed in this way create a presumption that the content is not truly private? Perhaps the issue is not knowledge that the profile could be accessed but the preferences of the person posting. If someone has an anonymous Twitter account, is it wrong to try to unmask the owner, or is the owner's anonymity something that deserves to be shattered?

We will try to lay out the potential halakhic issues, focusing on cases where there is no intent to spread the information to others first, then moving to cases of breaching confidentiality and spreading information.

Philosophical Background

Before we explore the halakhic and ethical issues, it is worth outlining the importance of privacy in Torah thought. R. Dr. Norman Lamm[1] notes that shame was the first feeling that humanity had after eating from the Tree of Knowledge, after understanding that nakedness was inappropriate. The story of Noaḥ cursing Canaan for Ḥam "seeing his nakedness" and blessing Shem and Yefet for covering Noaḥ also revolves around a primal understanding of the value of privacy. Thus, from the beginning, the Torah emphasizes the importance of privacy.

R. Lamm grounds the theological value of privacy in the notion that human beings are created in the image of God. A full understanding of God, as described throughout the Torah and expanded upon in most philosophical and mystical material, is beyond humanity's comprehension. God's essence always remains unknowable, as "My face cannot be seen" (Ex. 33:23). In Moshe's first interactions with God, Moshe hides his face rather than gaze upon divinity (Ex. 3:6). Thus, R. Lamm argues, to respect the divinity in people is to respect their right to have some things remain unknown, at least to those other than oneself.[2] R. Lamm further argues that the prohibition to seek to understand God's essence (Ḥagiga 2:1) is a function of respecting God's dignity, "His exclusive divine privacy.... Dignity (*kavod*) is thus a correlative of privacy." To respect man, he contends, one must similarly respect that there are things

1. Norman Lamm, *Faith and Doubt, Studies in Traditional Jewish Thought,* "Chapter 9: Privacy: Law and Theology" (KTAV, 2006), 285–304.
2. Ibid., 302–303.

that should not be known about others. Thus, he grounds the value of privacy in that of human dignity. He wrote these words as the modern challenges to privacy were first coming to the fore, and their urgency is only compounded as the digital world continues to make privacy more difficult. Halakha has many models in place to grant people the right to privacy, and it is to these models that we now turn.

Potential Halakhic Issues

There are several central halakhic issues that we will explore.

The first is *lashon hara* or *rekhilut*. While these terms generally refer to gossip, we will see that accessing information may be similarly prohibited under this general category.

The second issue is *hezeik* (damage). Many *posekim* have wondered whether a category known as *hezeik re'iya* (damage by vision), which prohibits people from looking into the property of others in such a way that problematically invades their privacy and limits the use they will be willing to make of their space, may be expanded to information.

A third issue is that of *gilui sod,* the prohibition of breaching confidence, though we will return to this more below.

The fourth issue is the *ḥerem* (excommunication) of those who read the correspondence of others. This is classified as a *ḥerem* of Rabbenu Gershom, a point we will return to. Is this a third issue, or simply a halakhic mechanism used to enforce a different prohibition? There are also a series of overarching halakhic values that are raised by the *posekim* to ground the *ḥerem.*

The Case of the Security for a Loan

R. Norman Lamm adds that a cognate case that expresses the value of privacy is the prohibition for a lender to enter the debtor's home to collect his security. Rather, the Torah demands that "when you make a loan of any sort to your countryman, you must not enter his house to seize his pledge. You must remain outside, while the man to whom you made the loan brings the pledge out to you" (Deut. 24:10–11). The Talmud disputes whether these limitations apply to the representative of the court as well, or only the private individual (see Bava

Metzia 113a–b). While this discussion highlights the value of privacy, as R. Lamm notes, the primary halakhic issues are found elsewhere, as we discuss below.[3]

It is also worth noting that many commentators understand the purpose of this law to be unrelated to privacy, but rather to the various principles of kindness that the Torah demands of a lender toward his debtor. Furthermore, the Talmud assumes that the prohibition extends to approaching the debtor in the street, seemingly indicating that the issue at hand is not privacy per se.[4] Nevertheless, several classical commentaries share R. Lamm's assessment that at least one of the rationales for this commandment is maintaining the privacy of the debtor, preventing the lender from being privy to his private affairs, financial or otherwise. This is cited by R. Yosef Bekhor Shor (*Bekhor Shor,* Deut. 24:10),[5] Ḥizkuni (ibid.), and R. Beḥaye (ibid.).[6] The latter argues that respecting the privacy of the debtor is itself motivated by compassion, a value among others that may ground the halakhic value of privacy.

Other Cases

There are several other potential sources for this value. R. Aryeh Klapper[7] suggests as another source the laws of *ba bamaḥteret* (Ex. 21:34–22:3), which allow a person to use lethal force against those who break into one's property at night. Several commentaries ground this not only in the potential threat to life, but specifically in the right of a person to stand his ground in his property, and that generates the cycle that leads to potential violence.[8]

---

3. Ibid., 293–294.
4. See, for example, *Ḥinnukh* 585, who claims that this prevents powerful creditors from taking advantage of debtors.
5. Bekhor Shor contends that we are also worried that the lender will be alone with the wife of the debtor, raising suspicion and leading to fights.
6. R. Beḥaye also mentions the concern that this will lead to a fight.
7. R. Klapper's comments were made in conversation with this author, and in a series of lectures given at the Summer Beit Midrash of the Center for Modern Torah Leadership.
8. See *Yad Rama* on Sanhedrin 72a; R. Shlomo Zalman Auerbach, *Responsa Minḥat Shlomo* 1:7.

Rekhilut

The Torah prohibits gossip: "Do not go as a talebearer (*rakhil*) among your people" (Lev. 19:16). Colloquially, this verse is known to prohibit *lashon hara,* which usually refers to conveying negative information to third parties. However, several authorities have argued that this also prohibits the initial gathering, and subsequent sharing, of private information, whether or not it is negative.

Rashi ad loc. notes that the word *rakhil* is related to the term for spying. Based on this etymology, R. Yaakov Hagiz argues that the target audience does not matter. R. Dr. Asher Meir accepts the position of R. Hagiz, summarizing the implications as follows:

> R. Yaakov Hagiz, in his well-known responsum of the seventeenth century, writes that this would be a transgression of *rechilut.* "What difference does it make if he goes about as a spy to reveal something to someone else or to himself?" (*Hilchot Ketanot* 1:276). R. Hagiz's ruling relates to the outcome of the act: becoming cognizant of someone's private information. According to R. Hagiz, it is *rechilut,* as there is no difference between revealing something to others and revealing something to oneself.[9]

Intuitively, this makes sense. One can "spy" on others to gather information to use against them or to provide to interested outsiders, or for voyeuristic reasons. All of these aims may be problematic.

R. Hagiz himself, in a responsum about the *ḥerem* against reading the mail of others, summarizes the problem similarly: "Perhaps the sender doesn't want his affairs to be known" (ibid., 1:59). As much as one doesn't want his private life spread to many people, he doesn't want it invaded by individuals.

R. Eliezer Shenkolvsky argues that the Rambam would accept a similar argument, that listening in to the secrets of others is *avak rekhilut,* the dust of gossip, though he seems to propound this category with no precedent.[10]

---

9. https://jewishaction.com/religion/jewish-law/internet-privacy-halachah/.
10. See his article "*Haazanat Seter*" in *HaMaayan,* vol. 37.

Hezeik Re'iya

Another potential issue is that violating one's privacy is damage, prohibited under tort law. The basis for this emerges from a category introduced in the first chapter of Bava Batra, *hezeik re'iya,* damage by sight. The opening pages of the tractate discuss the circumstances under which partners who share a courtyard or garden are required to divide their properties with a wall. The Mishna and Gemara discuss the size and material of said wall. The Gemara (2b) wonders: Is the context of the Mishna when the parties agree to build a wall, but in a case where they did not want to, there would be no need; or is the Mishna ruling that as long as they want to divide the property, they are forced to build a wall? (Of course, if the parties want to continue to own the property jointly, they are entitled to do so.)

The Gemara suggests that this depends on whether or not we are concerned about *hezeik re'iya.* If we are, then once the parties agree to divide the property, we must build a wall to prevent them from seeing each other (easily) in their newly divided plots of land. If not, then we can allow them to divide the land, even though they will be granted no privacy.

At first glance, it seems as if the Gemara is debating whether we give value to privacy at all. However, the Gemara then argues that there is only a dispute in a courtyard and the like. Everyone agrees that extreme breaches in privacy must be stopped; in such cases, *hezeik re'iya* is considered actionable damage. Thus, the Gemara argues, one must be prevented from seeing into his neighbor's house. As Rashi (2b, s.v. *hezeika devayit*) explains, in a home, people are engaged in acts that require privacy. By creating a situation where people can always see in, the inhabitants of the house are in effect losing the rightful usage of their house.

Thus, in the final assessment, the Gemara clearly rules that there are cases in which the very ability to invade the privacy of others is considered damaging and may be prevented by the courts, as would any case of physical damage. Several reasons are given for this. The Ramban (Bava Batra 59a) summarizes three of them:

1. By seeing what others are doing, one creates an *ayin hara,* an evil eye. The exact definition of this phrase is debated. Some believe

that people actually create metaphysically damaging rays from their eyes that must be avoided.[11] Others explain that the jealousy that is caused by seeing the other person brings God to scrutinize their actions, leading to potential damage. Alternatively, people are punished for doing things that cause others to feel jealousy. One could take a more rationalist approach and argue that jealousy often brings negative consequences, whether or not directly ordained by Heaven.[12]

2. It causes *lashon hara*, gossip and related issues.[13] R. Avraham ben Haim contends that Ramban believes that the damage is not the *lashon hara* per se, but the feeling of discomfort caused to the person who now must live in fear that his private affairs will be revealed to the world.
3. It is a violation of *tzeniut*, modesty.

Perhaps related to the third value is a fourth – unwanted gaze prevents people from engaging in normal home activities without their violation of these norms. This may be the intention of Ramban, or this may be related to a different model which focuses solely on the problem of diminishing the usage one will be willing to make of his property.

Whatever the rationale, the prohibitions that emerge are prohibited in standard codes of Jewish law.[14]

These explanations break down into two kinds of answers. The first two seem to understand *hezeik re'iya* as actual damage. According to the final answer, the word damage is being used loosely. The real intent is that one is preventing his neighbor from fully utilizing his property.[15]

11. See, for example, Maharal in *Netivot Olam, Netiv Ayin 1. Levush, ḤM* 157, even argues that it is a direct damage, "like his arrow."
12. For discussions of many of these possibilities, see *Ayin HaRa Be'Ein HaYahadut.* For a brief summary, see: http://olamot.net/shiur on *Ayin Hara.*
13. See *"Petiḥat Ḥalon Mul Ḥalon VePetaḥ Mul Petaḥ," MeKavtziel* 33 (5768): 432.
14. See *Shulḥan Arukh, ḤM* 154, 155, 159, 160.
15. Seemingly, this prevention of use is indirect damage, and therefore should not be considered damage according to the normal principles of Jewish law. See *Even HaAzel, Hilkhot Shekhenim* 2, who deals with this problem. See also *Kehillat Yaakov,* Bava Batra 5. R. Klapper argued to this author that it is specifically the issue of prevention of use that is the most direct damage, and the others use this term more loosely.

It is worth noting that whether or not *hezeik re'iya* refers to breaching modesty, *Ḥazal* see maintaining this value as definitional to the Jewish people and being enshrined in law as well. The Mishna and Gemara later in Bava Batra (60a) forbid building houses that have windows or openings that open directly into the house of a neighbor, as this is a breach of modesty. The Gemara then expounds on this, arguing that it is the insistence of Jews to avoid this practice that causes Bilam to exclaim (Num. 24:5): "How great are your tents, Yaakov, your dwellings, Yisrael!"

> The Gemara asks: **From where are these matters,** i.e., that one may not open an entrance opposite another entrance, or a window opposite another window, derived? **Rabbi Yoḥanan says that** the **verse states: "And Balaam lifted up his eyes, and he saw Israel dwelling tribe by tribe;** and the spirit of God came upon him" (Num. 24:2). The Gemara explains: **What** was it that Balaam **saw** that so inspired him? He **saw that the entrances of their tents were not aligned with each other,** ensuring that each family enjoyed a measure of privacy. And he **said:** If this is the case, **these people are worthy of having the Divine Presence rest on them.** (Bava Batra 60a)

Rashba (*Responsa* 2:268) does equate this value with *hezeik re'iya,* and argues that any violations of these laws cause the Divine Presence to leave the Jewish people.[16] *Yad Rama* (Bava Batra 60a) contends that in cases such as this, of gazing into the houses of others, the tort law is supplemented by ritual law. Thus, one has never waived his rights to maintain his privacy, even if by the normal laws of torts one would have given up these rights. *Ḥazon Ish* (Bava Batra 12:4) assumes that this means that we cannot conclude that he has given up these rights. However, R. Avraham ben Haim understands that fundamentally, the value of privacy and the prohibition against violating it makes it that waiving the right to privacy is legally meaningless in this case.[17]

---

16. See also *Shulḥan Arukh HaRav, ḤM, Hilkhot Nizkei Mammon* 12.
17. Cited in n.7, p. 435. See there at length regarding the potential differences between privacy breaches through windows and doors.

Elsewhere, the Talmud records that it is forbidden for one to stand near the field of another when he can see his friend's ripe produce. Based on this, the Talmud says that it is beneficial to have one's fields near a city only in a case where one has a wall to block others from seeing his produce. The Talmud justifies this principle as a way to avoid the "evil eye."

> **Rav Yehuda said to Ravin bar Rav Naḥman: Ravin my brother, do not buy land that is near a town, as Rabbi Abbahu says** that **Rav Huna says** that **Rav says:** It is **prohibited for a person to stand by another's field when its ripe grain is standing,** i.e., when its produce is ready for harvest, as he might harm the produce with the evil eye. Similarly, land near a town may be harmed by the people of the town watching it. The Gemara asks: **Is that so? But when Rabbi Abba encountered Rav's students** he **said to them: What does Rav say with regard to** the meaning of **these verses** of blessing: **"Blessed shall you be in the city, and blessed shall you be in the field"** (Deut. 28:3) ... : **"Blessed shall you be in the field"** means **that your property should be near the city**.... In any case, it is evident that Rav approves of one whose property is located near a city. How does this accord with his statement that there is concern for the evil eye when one's field is viewed by people? The Gemara answers: This is **not difficult. This** statement is referring to **a wall and** an additional **partition** [*ritka*] **that surround** the plot and prevent it from being harmed by the evil eye. **That** statement is referring to a case **where a wall and** an additional **partition do not surround it.** (Bava Metzia 107a–b)

Arukh HaShulkhan (*ḤM* 378:1) equates this with classic *hezek re'iya.* Presumably, this is why he argues that preventing the "evil eye" is the motivation for the all the principles of visual damage (*ḤM* 154:6). (It is worth noting, however, that he further adds that in addition to *ayin hara,* one must contend with the fact that a lack of privacy will prevent people from fully using their own property.) However, many others distinguish between the cases. Rambam, in a responsum to the sages of Lunel (*Responsa Rambam* [Blau 395] cited in *Migdal Oz, Hilkhot*

Shekhenim 2:16) writes that *hezek re'iya* refers to the greater violations of privacy that occur when one can gaze at someone else's *person.* In the case of the field, however, one is only seeing *property,* which is not nearly as invasive. Rambam therefore argues that the latter violation is not really prohibited, but it is a *middat ḥasidut,* a pious approach, to refrain from it. *Sema* (*ḤM* 378:5) accepts this distinction. R. Yosef David Sinzheim, the head of Napoleon's Sanhedrin, suggests that the damage that can be caused by the "evil eye" is rare, and thus refraining from activities that might cause such damage is merely pious (*Yad David,* Bava Metzia 107a, s.v. *asur*).[18]

What emerges is that the principles of visual damage actually represent several related values, some of which are enforceable under tort law and others that represent halakhic morals. All of them, in some way or another, support the value of privacy. As R. Lamm notes, on some level, it is the moral law that is more significant than the monetary law, and even for those who rule that these cases are actionable in court, it may be that it is the moral imperative that drives the monetary consequences.[19]

Hezeik Shemia

If we are dealing with accessing private pictures, perhaps the above categories will be relevant, and we will return to that later. However, if we are dealing with merely accessing information, we must deal with the question raised by other authorities – namely, does the above prohibition apply to "hearing"? If one manages to hear others, is that considered damage (*hezeik shemia*), in whatever way seeing is?

The Meiri (Bava Batra 2a, s.v. *uma*) writes that we are not worried about *hezeik shemia* at all because most people are careful about how they talk, and therefore being too close to someone's property should not limit their activities – they will know how to be sufficiently quiet. R. Eliyahu Mizrachi (*Responsa Re'em* 8) writes more categorically: "We have not found in the entire Talmud [a mention of] damage of this sort."

18. See *Kehillat Yaakov,* Bava Metzia 45:1, as to whether this proves that damage caused by metaphysical forces is not considered damage for the purpose of tort law.
19. See Lamm, 295–297, noting his comparison to the various interpretations of the Fourth Amendment that conform to the various views of privacy outlined above.

While one could have argued that the Meiri and R. Mizrachi agree, many have seen them as presenting opposite opinions. R. Ben Tziyon Nesher (*Responsa Even Pina* 167), for example, argues that according to the latter, merely hearing others' information cannot be considered damage. For the Meiri, however, this is only the case if the person could have prevented the eavesdropping. People should not scream near their windows if they don't want the neighbors to hear. However, if one would use a secret recorder which would prevent people from speaking freely in the privacy of their own home, that would be prohibited and considered damage. In such a case, the Meiri's argument, that people know to avoid such things, does not apply.

R. Nesher further argues that these two formulations depend on the above discussion regarding *hezeik re'iya*. If *hezeik re'iya* is considered damage, then hearing someone's secret, which has no explicit source defining it as damage, should not be included. If, however, the real issue is that violations of privacy prevent people from safely using their own space, eavesdropping is no less effective than peering into someone's home, if it violates their property.

This argument is also advanced by R. Eliezer Shenkolvsky.[20] However, he is hesitant to accept the implications of the Meiri's view, as he finds no other Rishon or Aḥaron who explicitly articulates such a position. R. Norman Lamm, on the other hand, accepts the implication from Meiri and takes it as a given that this would prohibit "bugging."[21] R. Yitzchak Zilberstein writes similarly (*Ḥashukei Ḥemed,* Bava Batra 4a). R. Dr. Asher Meir argues that this extension of the prohibition of *hezeik re'iya* is natural and should be accepted. As he writes:

> A protracted discussion in the first chapter of tractate Bava Batra concludes that *hezek reiah* – defined as being in a position to scrutinize the private activities of a neighbor – is considered a kind of damage or tort, which the offending neighbor must take steps to prevent. The *gemara* (Bava Batra 6b) objects that an offending neighbor could claim that passersby are ultimately

20. See his article cited above.

21. See above, pp. 295–296.

> able to see the same kind of activities that he is required to take steps to avoid seeing. The *gemara* answers with the justification of the protected neighbor, among them: "Passersby see me only if they look carefully; you see me in any case." On this basis, the halachic authorities draw a distinction between casual seeing – which is not considered harmful – and scrutinizing or actively looking.

For example, the Rema (*ḤM* 144) writes explicitly that one must take precautions not to look (*lehistakel*) into his neighbor's house; it is understood that occasionally he will see what goes on there. The *hezeik re'iya* approach focuses on the process – snooping around in someone's private domain – irrespective of the outcome.

Later we will return to the implications that R. Meir draws from this analysis.

Ḥerem

The third area of halakha that forbids violating the privacy of others is the *ḥerem* against reading others' mail. This *ḥerem* is first mentioned in the responsa of R. Meir (Maharam) of Rothenburg, writing in the thirteenth century (*Responsa* 1022). It is part of a list of early decrees from Ashkenazic scholars, including the tenth–eleventh-century scholar, Rabbenu Gershom ben Yehuda, or Rabbenu Gershom *Me'or HaGola*, the Light of the Exile. Other decrees there include the prohibition against polygamy.

Most scholars assume that the decree against reading others' mail is also by Rabbenu Gershom. However, R. Yehuda Herzl Henkin (*Responsa Benei Vanim* 3:17) has argued that a close reading of the above responsum does not indicate that this is true; rather, it is an unattributed early decree. Either way, we are dealing with an early Ashkenazic decree.

A *ḥerem* carries many different social and economic punishments. In some cases, these punishments must be instituted by a court. In other cases, they are automatic. Which punishments take effect when one reads someone else's letter without permission and how they take effect are discussed at length by R. Henkin in the above responsum, but they are not relevant to our discussion.

A more central question is whether the *ḥerem* was creating a new prohibition or enforcing an existing one. In the case of prohibiting polygamy, for example, it is clear that the *ḥerem* was introducing a new prohibition. On a biblical level, it is permitted for a man to marry multiple wives. However, when it comes to this *ḥerem,* many Aḥaronim believe that Rabbenu Gershom only instituted the *sanctions,* but the *prohibition is biblical.* The *ḥerem* was protecting the prohibition with added levels of stricture.

This may be related to another issue: Does the *ḥerem* expire? Maharik (*Responsa* 101) is cited by the *Beit Yosef* (*EH* 1) as saying that technically, the *ḥerem* against polygamy was only until the end of the fifth millennium, meaning the Hebrew year 5000. Additionally, many assume that the decree was not accepted by all communities; perhaps it was never formally accepted by any communities but the Ashkenazic ones. (This is despite the fact that all Jewish communities now accept it, regardless of whom and when it was originally limited to.[22])

However, that limitation may only make sense for a *ḥerem* that was introducing a new prohibition, not one that was protecting a biblical one. Thus, similar limitations may not apply to the *ḥerem* against reading others' mail.[23]

Which prohibition is being violated? As we have already seen, R. Hagiz argues that it is a violation of *rekhilut,* of going as a talebearer. R. Haim Shabbetai (*Responsa Torat Ḥayim* 33) argues that as the person is usually accessing the information to use it in some way, and the information is owned by the writer and receiver of the letter, reading the letter is a form of theft – specifically borrowing without permission, which is a subsection of theft. (Based on this, he argues that it is prohibited to read someone's letter even for a mitzva purpose.)

R. Haim Palagi (*Responsa Ḥikekei Lev, YD* 49) similarly argues that it is like a guardian who violates his stewardship, which is another subcategory of theft. R. Palagi also offers several more generic prohibitions. First, he suggests that it is a violation of loving one's fellow as oneself (Lev. 19:18). As Hillel famously formulates it, "Don't do to your

22. See *Pitḥei Teshuva, EH* 1:19, at length.

23. See discussion in the footnotes in the *Tur Yerushalayim,* note 18.

friend what you would not want done to you" (Shabbat 31a). As most people don't want their private communications accessed by outsiders, one should not do it to others. He also suggests that it is *geneivat daat,* which usually refers to deceit, but literally means to steal that which is known (knowable/information).[24]

Some *posekim*[25] assume that this *ḥerem* is violated even if the letter is opened without reading the text. This would seem to indicate that while aspects of the *ḥerem* might be covered by other prohibitions, the *ḥerem* expanded them.

However, the possibility that the *ḥerem* enforces pre-existing prohibitions opens the possibility that the severity of the *ḥerem* would be limited to very specific circumstances. R. Shenkolvsky, for example, argues that while all the above prohibitions might apply to eavesdropping on a secret, the *ḥerem* would be limited to reading written material, as that is all that is explicitly covered in all versions of the *ḥerem.*

Many *posekim*[26] suggest, for example, that if the *ḥerem* protects the obligation to love others, that would be limited to reading the letters of Jews, as only they are "your fellow." If, however, the prohibition is *geneivat daat,* it might apply to the letters of non-Jews as well, as it is prohibited to deceive any people (Ḥullin 94a). If it is theft, it would similarly be universally prohibited.

However, R. Yitzchak Zilberstein cites R. Yosef Shalom Elyashiv's view that this may not be the case. Even if reading someone's letter is a kind of theft, it may not be equivalent to theft in all respects. Thus, it may be that this heightened sensitivity would be limited to Jews.

The *posekim* also debate whether this prohibition may be waived for the purpose of a mitzva. However, we will return to these discussions later when we deal with spreading the information gathered. We are limiting ourselves here to the violation of gathering information per se.

---

24. These answers are summarized in the *Encyclopedia Talmudit, Ḥerem DeRabbenu Gershom,* as well as by R. Henkin, above.
25. *Responsa Beit David,* YD 158, cited in *Encyclopedia Talmudit.*
26. See *Ḥikekei Lev* above, as well as the summary in R. Shenkolvsky's article and the entry in *Encyclopedia Talmudit.*

Before moving to modern applications, we must explore some of the exceptions to the *ḥerem,* which will shed light on cases when privacy is not assumed.

Once the Letter Has Been Thrown Out

The *Be'er HaGola* (*ḤM* 334) writes that once a letter has been thrown out, anyone is permitted to read the letter. The assumption is that once a letter has been thrown out, the receiver of the letter no longer considers it private. In *Encyclopedia Talmudit* ("*Ḥerem DeRabbenu Gershom,*" n. 894), they present this as the law without qualification.

However, as R. Shammai Gross (*Responsa Shevet HaKehati* 1:315) and R. Yehuda Herzl Henkin (*Responsa Benei Vanim* 3:17) note, this probably does not apply nowadays. Most people assume that there are not people rummaging through their garbage. Thus, when they throw out a letter, they assume that it will never be seen again. (Material that is particularly sensitive is sometimes shredded, but that is to prevent particularly unscrupulous people from stealing financial information and the like.) This is indeed the position of the US Courts in "State v. Hempele" (1990). Thus, if throwing out a letter uproots the prohibition to read it, based on the assumption that the receiver no longer considers the correspondence private, this assumption would no longer hold true. In each circumstance, rather, we would have to gauge what indicates a lack of desire for confidentiality.

R. Hayim David HaLevi (*Responsa Aseh Lekha Rav* 5:108) writes that in a case when a letter has been placed in *geniza,* it is obvious that the desire is that it should remain private. He also notes that people must quell their natural curiosity in order to respect the privacy of others.

Permission from the Receiver

As the above case indicates, the assumption of the *posekim* seems to be that the primary person who determines the confidential status of correspondence is the receiver of the letter. Hence, the receiver's throwing it out lifts the *ḥerem* against reading it. This is true despite the fact that the sender has no say in when the letter is thrown out. R. Yaakov Kanievsky, the author of *Kehillat Yaakov,* is cited (*Halikhot VeHanhagot,* 18) as drawing this conclusion: permission from the receiver allows a third party to read the letter. R. Gross (above) agrees with this position, though he notes that this would only be in the case when reading the letter would cause no damage to the sender. If it would cause damage, one must assume that the material is meant to stay confidential.

However, some *posekim* disagree. R. Palagi, basing himself on the general prohibition to share information until one has been told that it is not confidential (Yoma 4b), writes as follows (*Responsa Ḥikekei Lev, YD* 49):

> If one sends a letter to someone else, the one who receives the letter is prohibited from showing it to another, even if there is nothing hurtful or incriminating in the letter, just as if you were told something you aren't allowed to repeat it without permission to do so.[27]

Furthermore, R. Hagiz (*Responsa Halakhot Ketanot* 1:59) writes that if a note is put on the letter stating that it is "protected" by the *ḥerem derabbenu Gershom,* then there is certainly an assumption that the sender wants the letter to remain private. Thus, it would seem that one cannot uniformly assume that the receiver of correspondence can waive the potential prohibitions involved with reading it. In order for the correspondence to be permissible for public consumption, it must be a case in which there is no indication or reason to believe that the sender would consider it a violation of his privacy.

R. Gross notes that in a case where the sender explicitly indicates that it is prohibited to share the information, it would be unequivocally prohibited to do so, based on the prohibition to breach confidentiality mentioned above by R. Palagi.

Postcards

The *Arukh HaShulḥan* (*YD* 334:21) raises a question concerning postcards: Is there an assumption of confidentiality when the letter is written in such a way that it is always open? R. Henkin assumes that it is permitted to disseminate the information. He derives this from the language many *posekim* use to describe the *ḥerem,* applying it to one who "opens

27. Translation by R. Josh Strulowitz.

a letter." The assumption seems to be that it is the sealing of a letter that indicates that the sender wants it private. When it is left open, because the sender knows how easy it is to read it, there is no problem.

R. Gross, on the other hand, assumes that when it comes to postcards, the material is probably not sensitive; thus, the sender does not mind if the (anonymous) postman reads it. This in no way indicates that he would want people he knows, other than the intended recipient, to read it.

There seems to be a dispute between these two *posekim* as to whether it is the assumption of privacy that creates the imperative to respect that privacy, or whether all material is off-limits until one is granted personal permission to read it. Alternatively, this turns on the question of the point at which an expectation of privacy or intimacy is meaningless, which we return to below.

To'elet

As we will see, many laws of *lashon hara* are waived when there is a need (*to'elet*) for the information. While one might assume that the same dispensations would apply to issues of confidentiality, the *posekim* actually debate this point. The Rashba assumes that such a dispensation does apply, specifically applying it to the *ḥerem* against reading the mail of others.

The Rashba seems to permit precisely these cases, focusing on the *ḥerem derabbenu Gershom* against reading others' mail, which we will return to soon (*Responsa Rashba* 1:557):

> Rabbenu Gershom did not make his decrees so that people might violate biblical or rabbinic halakha because of them. Just the opposite, they were instituted only to ensure compliance with our Torah and to ensure that Jewish people act in a correct and modest manner.

Therefore, if a court, parents, or educators objectively determine that in a certain situation they can only ensure compliance with our Torah by "violating the privacy" of an individual by reading their mail or diary, or by listening in on their telephone conversations, there is no doubt that Rabbenu Gershom would agree that it would be a mitzva to do so.

Other *posekim* disagree. For example, R. Nissim Karelitz (*Ḥut Shani, Hilkhot Lashon HaRa* 5:1:1) argues that only in cases of danger is one permitted to divulge secrets. However, in cases where there is simply a benefit, he argues that the same dispensations due to *to'elet* do not apply. He cites the view of the *Ḥazon Ish,* who refused to share the reasons behind a person's divorce with a potential future spouse, claiming it was a violation of the professionalism mandated by the above laws. He argues that the same would apply to a doctor. This, as we have mentioned above, is a questionable assumption. I also wonder whether the *Ḥazon Ish* would limit his claim to a judge in court, the paradigmatic case of the Gemara which many think would be the strictest category of revealing secrets.

(R. Yaakov Epstein, in *Responsa Ḥevel Naḥalato* 1:83, seems to lean in this direction, as such behavior will cause a lack of trust, but he does not rule as clearly as R. Karelitz does.)

However, these *posekim* are primarily dealing with cases in which the information will be used or spread. Thus, we will return to the parameters of *to'elet* when we deal with the issue of breaching confidentiality by relaying information to others, as well as *lashon hara* in the classic sense of gossip.

Chapter 19

Modern Applications

Moving from the theoretical to the practical, we must ask the following: How do the prohibitions and exceptions outlined in the previous unit and the first half of this unit apply to the numerous new ways of communicating that the age of social media has introduced?

As we have seen, the potential issues are:

1. *Rekhilut*
2. *Hezeik re'iya/hezeik shemia*
3. *Ḥerem derabbenu Gershom* against reading mail, which itself may be based on other prohibitions such as:
   a. Loving one's neighbor as oneself and avoiding actions that one would not want done to oneself
   b. *Geneivat daat* – deception or stealing information

The exceptions to these prohibitions are:

1. Cases where it is clear that no privacy was intended originally.

2. Cases where it has been made clear that privacy is no longer demanded.
   This was derived from the case of the thrown-out letter.
   (As noted, what qualifies in the modern era is unclear.)
3. Cases in which the receiver waives privacy.
   This is disputed, as well as conditional on the sender's not making clear an expectation that privacy be maintained.
4. *To'elet*
   The exact definition of benefit and its applications will be discussed below.

All of these prohibitions apply regardless of whether the information is being passed on. These cases may include various prohibitions that we have mentioned, but not expanded upon.

Emails, Texts, WhatsApps

It seems obvious that reading an email not addressed to you is prohibited and covered by the *ḥerem derabbenu Gershom* and all prohibitions implied by it. This is especially the case if the text of the email indicates that it is confidential. For example, some emails will include a disclaimer that the email is meant only for the recipient, and if it has been received by mistake, the sender should be made aware of the error. In such a case, all *posekim* would agree that it is prohibited to read someone else's email.

If the intended recipient wants to share an email, it would depend on the dispute above. For an innocuous email, the above discussion would determine whether the recipient has the right to share the email. If it is damaging, or there is an explicit indication that it is meant for the recipient only, it should not be shared. These restrictions would apply to forwarding emails, texts, or WhatsApp messages.

What about a listserv? In most cases, it would seem that one may not read an email from a listserv of which one is not a member, as the very notion of membership seems to indicate that the material is presumed to be private and reserved only for the members. Thus, even though some *posekim* give the recipients of letters the right to share the information, they all agree that this is not the case when there is reason to believe that the senders did not have this expectation.[1] This also violates the prohibition of breaching confidentiality, to which we will return.

Snapchats

Snapchat differs from other forms of messaging in one crucial respect. You can talk to someone off the record, just like you could do in person. Texts sent in Chat are automatically deleted (though you also have the option to save them with a single tap, or a screenshot).

With this being the case, it would seem to be problematic to look at a Snapchat intended for someone else. Since the default procedure is that the message will be deleted, this seems to imply a desire for secrecy on behalf of the sender. This would seem to exacerbate the problem of saving a Snapchat to show.

Cyberspying

R. Dr. Asher Meir takes several of the sources, specifically the position of R. Hagiz, that *rekhilut* applies even when one merely accesses private information but does not share it, plus an expanded understanding of *hezeik re'iya,* and forbids what he refers to as "cyberspying." Under this category, he subsumes such actions as attempting to uncover the author of an anonymous blog. He argues that many other attempts to access the identity or information of others may be similarly prohibited. However, he argues that the use of casual technology is permitted and not considered spying, as opposed to methods that require effort and expertise. Here is how he formulates the problem:

> The case discussed by R. Hagiz is essentially identical to that of reading someone's diary, so clearly he would view it as forbidden. I think it is obvious that scrutinizing someone's diary would likewise cross the line from casual "seeing" to "looking." What about

1. One reader suggested to me that this should not be the case if the expectation is unreasonable. From my experience, while not often the case, there are those who indeed try to maintain the implied confidentiality of listservs.

> the cyberspying example...? According to R. Hagiz, it is clear that the outcome is revealing a person's private information and would therefore be forbidden.
>
> What about the process? I think it makes sense to distinguish between a routine Google search or visit to a person's Facebook page and a determined, sophisticated use of powerful online tools which cross the line from casual "seeing" to "looking" online and would therefore be forbidden.
>
> The example I used is an extreme one of utilizing seemingly public information and powerful online tools to disclose the identity of a blogger who has taken pains to maintain his privacy. But my belief is that there are many lesser examples where legitimate curiosity can easily cross the line into unwitting cyber-transgression.

R. Dr. Meir is particularly harsh in his formulation, as he considers these violations of halakhic tort law. However, as we have seen, there are many *posekim* who did not accept the notion of *hezeik shemia*. If one takes a limited approach to *hezeik re'iya,* limiting it only to the kind of visual violation of privacy mentioned in the Talmud, accessing information might similarly be excluded from this category. Thus, it may be prohibited under *rekhilut,* but not considered damage.

However, one could argue that using these methods to access pictures would be more similar to *hezeik re'iya.* Just as it is prohibited to peer into another's property and prevent the owners from using their property privately, it could be that knowing that people are accessing pictures they should not limits the kinds of activities the subjects of the pictures engage in, or at least those activities they memorialize with pictures. On the other hand, it seems that this is much less direct than the classic cases of *hezeik re'iya.*

Thus, it seems to this author that those *posekim* who do not accept *hezeik shemia* would probably reject the application of the laws of damages to such cases.

Facebook

The use of Facebook raises several possible applications of the above discussion. For example, creating a fake account to trick others into acceping friendship in order to view their profiles would seem to be prohibited under many of the above prohibitions. This is especially the case when the information might be used to the detriment of the persons being spied on. Thus, an employer or potenital employer using this method to determine who deserves to keep or get a job, or a school administrator doing so to determine whom to punish at school, would violate this. However, as noted above, a full discussion of this issue requires the exploration of *to'elet,* which we will return to in later sections.

What about using a mutual friend's account to "spy"? On the one hand, one could argue that the fact that Facebook offers a variety of privacy settings (which allow one to share certain information with friends, certain information with friends of friends, and certain information with the public) would indicate that people want to hide information only from those not in the proper category.

On the other hand, there may not really be such an expectation. It is somewhat common for people to casually view the profile of others using the account of a mutual friend. In some cases, it is to be expected. For example, I imagine that most people are aware that spouses or siblings of their friends may casually use their account. In other cases, when one actively looks for a mutual aquaintance to gain information, it may be less expected.

Another factor, which we will return to in our discussion of *lashon hara,* is the possibility that information that is considered public may no longer have any limitations on whom it can be shared with, and *a fortiori* who may access it. This is based on an engimatic line in the Gemara, which rules that "anything which is said in front of three people is not subject to [the prohibition of] evil speech" (Arakhin 16a). For some *posekim,* as we will see, this means that not only is *lashon hara* no longer a concern, but confidentiality and the like may also be waived once the information is considered public enough.

However, as we will see, this may be true only in cases in which the speaker, having stated the original information in a public group, presumes that it will be spread. In cases in which the situation is different, such as ten lawyers at a practice who are internally sharing confidential information about a client, there is no such permission.

When it comes to Facebook, an unofficial poll at a *shiur* on the topic yielded a variety of opinions. Some people felt that anything they post on Facebook is assumed to be for public consumption. Others, however, felt differently, especially when they imagined specific people whom they would not want to access their profiles (e.g., when school principals view pictures of their students.)

Regarding closed and secret groups, it would seem that there is a strong assumption of privacy. The fact that the group is intentionally closed, or in some cases only visible to a select group of people, makes this case more similar to the case of the law firm above. Although it is a relatively large group, confidentiality is still to be assumed.

The Complexity

At a *shiur* in Toronto, one attendee noted that the amount of signficance given in this area regarding what people expect seems to run afoul of the tedency in halakha toward uniformity. However, what emerges from the sources is that these kinds of laws do not lend themselves to uniformity. The central principle often comes down to what people's expectations and assumptions are, and these may change over time, based on demographic factors and a host of other considerations. As we saw above, for example, the dispute as to whether the *ḥerem* applies to postcards rests mostly on whether people care about privacy in messages conveyed via postcard. Thus, the best we can do is to outline the general princples.

Metaprinciples

Another attendee of that *shiur* in Toronto noted that much of this discussion assumes the more formal approaches to these laws. However, if, as some *posekim* argue, the *ḥerem derabbenu Gershom* is merely protecting some vague rules derived from the biblical directive of *"Ve'ahavta lere'akha kamocha,"* these laws would be further-reaching and harder to define. General princples like "Don't do to others what you would not want done to yourself" are, on the one hand, applicable in almost every area of life. For our purposes, that might prohibit one from accessing information about others even when a technical problem is difficult to pinpoint.[2] On the other hand, as seen above, such overarching principles are almost impossible to quantify and define.

While we cannot know exactly what the future holds, we know that as technologies advance, the importance of maintaining privacy, and the difficulty in doing so, will only increase. We must continue to respect the values of human dignity and turn to the various halakhic principles to guide us.

Taking a Picture Without Permission

Before we move to issues of sharing information, it is worth noting that there is one more halakhic issue that some *posekim* raise that touches on invasion of privacy per se, though it has several unique halakhic elements as well: May one take a picture of someone without permission?

There are many *posekim* who forbid taking photographs of people.[3] Some prohibit this for halakhic reasons based on issues related to *avoda zara* (idolatry), and many others think there are mystical reasons to be concerned about such activity.

Let us assume that we accept the majority halakhic position that there is no such prohibition. If someone does not want his picture taken, can he prevent others from taking it? This question is posed to R. Yosef Chaim Sonnenfeld (*Responsa Salmat Ḥayim* 2:19). The questioner suggests that a person should be allowed to stop others from taking his picture for these reasons. Additionally, he notes that we rule that we must listen to someone when he requests that he not be eulogized (*YD* 344:10). From this, he extrapolates that it is forbidden to use that person's picture or any other representation of him without permission.

R. Sonnenfeld rejects this, arguing that as we do not accept these positions, there can be no prohibition in taking a picture. R. Betzalel Stern (*Responsa BeTzel HaḤokhma* 4:85) clarifies that while a person may own himself, that does not imply that he owns all replications of his image.[4]

---

2. See R. Eliyahu Bakshi Doron, "*Ḥokrim Perati'im BeHalakha UVaMisphat HaKelali,*" who briefly mentions several prohibitions including *rekhilut, lashon hara, ve'ahavta lere'akha kamokha,* and *gilui sod.*
3. For several sources, see *Gan Na'ul* of R. Yaakov Levi, vol. 3, ch. 13, n. 128.
4. The question of whether people own themselves has become a central part of modern debates about informed consent in medical contexts. See R. S. Y. Zevin in *Mishpat*

On the other extreme, R. Menasheh Klein (*Responsa Mishneh Halakhot* 7:114) disagrees. He contends that:

1. People have the right to be stringent even if the accepted view is to be lenient. Others must respect their wishes and refrain from taking pictures.
2. Even those who do not have a halakhic issue with having their picture taken may object to others taking their picture, and this is for two reasons.
   a. It may be a form of damage.
   b. It may be a form of theft, taking someone's image without permission.

R. Shlomo Aviner (*Piskei Shlomo*, vol. 3, 146–148) takes issue with R. Klein's ruling, arguing that one's image is not "real enough" to be stolen, and this cannot be considered damage. In his parenthetical comments, R. Aviner cites the discussions of several rabbis asking whether people could take or even sell pictures of others without permission.

R. Aviner's conclusion, however, should guide much halakhic discussion in this area. He notes that while there may not be any of the formal prohibitions above, the universal obligation to love others as we love ourselves requires us to respect people's desire to not be photographed. After all, all people would want the same. In the words of Hillel to the convert who wanted the summary of the entire Torah while standing on one foot (Shabbat 31a): "That which is hateful to you do not do to another; that is the entire Torah, and the rest is its interpretation. Go study."

As R. Gil Student notes, before we outline the more specific prohibition that may be violated by posting or sharing information without

---

Shylock LeOr HaHalakha (Tel Aviv: Zioni Publishing, 1957), 318–335; R. Shaul Yisraeli, "*Takrit Kibya LeOr HaHalakha*," *HaTorah VeHaMedina* 5–6 (1953–1954); R. Dr. Avraham Steinberg, "Informed Consent: Ethical and Halakhic Considerations," *The Jewish Law Annual*, vol. XII, 137; and R. Avraham Steinberg, *Encyclopedia of Jewish Medical Ethics*, 555.

permission, this basic obligation must remain in the background of all discussions of the legal issues:

> This applies with even greater force to posting someone else's picture online. Do not do to others what you would not want them to do to you. And if you have a uniquely free spirit and want every unguarded moment of yours memorialized in eternal online images, you must still act considerately to others.[5]

Even in cases in which the technical prohibitions may not apply, one must approach these issues with a broad sensitivity as well. As all of our private information is similarly in danger of becoming public, we should strive to respect others as we would want to be respected.

5. Available at: https://www.torahmusings.com/2014/11/instagram-and-jewish-law/, and in greater detail in R. Student's book, *Search Engine: Finding Meaning in Jewish Texts, Volume 1: Jewish Life* (Kodesh Press, 2018), 284–287. I thank R. Student for his help in finding these sources and for making his book available to me.

Chapter 20

Confidentiality in the Digital Age

Introduction

The issue of sharing data in the digital age, and specifically in the context of social media, is one of the most hotly debated topics in recent years. This came to the fore during the 2016 US presidential campaign. Public debates arose after it was revealed that the campaign of Donald Trump had used the company Cambridge Analytica to gather information from Facebook and to target specific kinds of political ads to individuals or demographic groups to influence them.[1] To understand the halakhic issues, we must examine perspectives on confidentiality, and then move from there to the laws of *lashon hara*, gossip. It is worth noting that the assumption of all *posekim* is that these laws are equally prohibited whether one communicates in person or through synchronous communication technologies, as there is no fundamental difference between breaching confidentiality or gossiping in person or over the phone, except that technology has made it easier to violate this prohibition. The same can be said for asynchronous communications

1. A simplified summary of what happened can be found here: https://www.vox.com/policy-and-politics/2018/3/23/17151916/facebook-cambridge-analytica-trump-diagram.

technologies, though there are some unique issues that arise that we must explore. Since in the previous chapter we dealt with the invasion of privacy per se, we now move to the additional halakhic issues that are raised when that information is shared.

The Prohibition to Reveal Secrets

Proverbs criticizes a person who reveals secrets. "A gossiper reveals secrets, but a trustworthy person hides things," or "a trustworthy person keeps a confidence" (11:13; see also 20:19). The Talmud specifically states that there is a presumption of confidence whenever someone is told something. One can only spread information after being given explicit permission:

> The verse says: **"And He called unto Moses, and** the Lord **spoke** unto him from within the Tent of Meeting, saying" (Lev. 1:1). **Why** does the verse mention **calling before speaking,** and God did not speak to him at the outset? **The Torah is teaching etiquette: A person** should **not say anything to another unless he calls him** first. This **supports** the opinion of **Rabbi Ḥanina, as Rabbi Ḥanina said: A person should not say anything to another unless he calls him** first. With regard to the term concluding the verse: **"Saying," Rabbi Musya, grandson of Rabbi Masya, said in the name of Rabbi Musya the Great: From where** is it derived with regard **to one who tells another** some **matter, that** it is incumbent upon the latter **not** to **say it** to others **until** the former explicitly **says to him: Go and tell others? As it is stated: "And the Lord spoke to him from** within **the Tent of Meeting, saying [*lemor*]."** *Lemor* is a contraction of *lo emor,* meaning: Do not say. One must be given permission before transmitting information. (Yoma 4b)

The context of this passage is that God, when speaking to Moshe, explicitly tells him that he is supposed to convey the message to the Jewish people. Had God not done so, Moshe would have assumed it was prohibited. This is striking, as there is presumably nothing negative or embarrassing about the prophecies Moshe receives. After all, it is

God telling him His commandments. Nevertheless, secrecy is assumed until Moshe is told otherwise. From this, the Gemara derives that one must always assume that anything he or she is told is meant to be in confidence, unless they are told that this is not the case. (See *Ḥafetz Ḥayim, Hilkhot Lashon HaRa* 2:13:27; see below for further discussion of his position.)

The Gemara records a similar prohibition in the context of a court, forbidding a judge from exposing which judge has ruled in favor or against a particular defendant. When someone is found to have violated this norm, the Talmud is quite harsh toward him:

> The mishna teaches: **And from where** is it derived that **when** the judge **leaves** the courtroom, he should not say: I deemed you exempt and my colleagues deemed you liable, but what can I do, as my colleagues outnumbered me and consequently you were deemed liable? About this it is stated: "You shall not go as a talebearer among your people" (Lev. 19:16), and it says: "One who goes about as a talebearer reveals secrets, but one who is of a faithful spirit conceals a matter" (Prov. 11:13). **The Sages taught** in a *baraita*: **From where** is it derived that **when** the judge **leaves he should not say: I deemed** you **exempt and my colleagues deemed** you **liable, but what can I do, as my colleagues outnumbered me** and consequently you were deemed liable? **The verse states: "You shall not go as a talebearer among your people"** (Lev. 19:16), **and it says: "One who goes about as a talebearer reveals secrets"** (Prov. 11:13).
>
> The Gemara relates: There was **a certain student, about whom a rumor emerged that he revealed a statement that was stated in the study hall** and should have been kept secret, and the rumor emerged **twenty-two years after** the time the statement was revealed. **Rav Ami removed him from the study hall** as a punishment. Rav Ami **said: This is a revealer of secrets** and he cannot be trusted. (Sanhedrin 31a)

This last source, however, as Rambam suggests in his *Commentary on the Mishna,* may be limited to courts, as there is particular value in ensuring that people continue to have a good relationship with the judicial system.

What is the nature of this prohibition? Is it biblical, rabbinic, or simply an ethical thing to do? Meiri (Yoma 4b, s.v. *mima*) writes that it is *derekh eretz,* the right thing to do. Indeed, this halakha is not found in *Shulḥan Arukh,* which may indicate that this is not formal law. Nevertheless, it seems that no one would dispute that violating a confidence would be a violation of *ve'ahavta lere'akha kamokha.* Additionally, the *posekim* who do identify specific prohibitions will accept that this underlying issue is always a potential concern. R. Azarya Ariel uses this as his introduction to this topic.[2]

Many Rishonim and Aḥaronim, unlike the above authorities, do take this as a specific biblical law.[3] *Magen Avraham* (*OḤ* 156) includes this in his list of laws that are not mentioned in *Shulḥan Arukh.* Many Rishonim, in fact, think that when the Gemara discusses *lishna bisha* or *lashon hara,* this does not refer to gossip, as is commonly assumed (based on Rambam and *Ḥafetz Ḥayim*), but rather to the prohibition of betraying confidence. R. Aḥai Gaon (*She'iltot* 28) seems to think that *lashon hara* refers exclusively to this violation, while Ritva (*Ḥiddushei HaRitva,* Bava Batra 29b, s.v. *lit ba*) thinks that it equally refers to gossip and revealing secrets.[4] The definition of revealing secrets seems to be explicitly used by the Talmud, as noted in *Sedei Ḥemed.*[5] Rambam seems to take this position (*Hilkhot De'ot* 7:2), as does Meiri (*Ḥiddushei HaMeiri,* Shabbat 31a).

Rabbenu Yona (*Shaarei Teshuva* 3:225), on the other hand, distinguishes between the two categories, though he still understands this as

2. Available at: https://www.yeshiva.org.il/ask/104573.
3. It is worth noting that the *Ḥafetz Ḥayim* contradicts himself on this point, ruling in two places that this involves a formal prohibition (*Hilkhot Lashon HaRa* 9:6 and *Hilkhot Rekhilut* 8:5), and elsewhere that avoiding such behavior is just *midda tova,* a good character trait (*Hilkhot Lashon HaRa* 2:13:27).
4. See also *Sefer Hashlama* on Bava Batra 39b, *Semag* 9.
5. See *Shabbat* 33a–b, Rashi 33b, s.v. *peh gomer* (first), as pointed out in *Sedei Ḥemed, Lashon HaRa,* as well as Rashi, Arakhin 15b, s.v. *lishna.* See also *Ḥayei Adam* 143. See, however, Sota 42a, which distinguishes between the sinners who speak *lashon hara* and those who lie, indicating that *lashon hara* refers primarily to true gossip rather than false slander. This is used by the *Ḥafetz Ḥayim* to support his terminology.

an obligation. Thus, he writes that it is forbidden to reveal secrets even if the information does not constitute *rekhilut.*

A particularly harsh assessment of this prohibition is found in the ethical work *Pele Yo'etz* by R. Eliezer Papo. He contends that one who reveals secrets is like an idol worshipper![6]

Why is it prohibited or unethical to reveal secrets? Rabbenu Yona offers two explanations. The first is that revealing secrets can cause real damage to the person whose information is exposed. The second is that it is a breach of *tzeniut,* propriety, to divulge things said privately. He further notes that even if a given piece of information is not negative gossip, the kind of person who does not respect privacy on neutral matters will end up spreading negative information as well. R. Yaakov Epstein (*Responsa Ḥevel Naḥalato* 1:83) adds that breaching confidence prevents necessary information from being told in the future. People often convey things to those they trust when they deem it necessary and they are confident that the information will not be spread without their permission. Without that confidence, people will be reticent to tell things to other people, even when it is critical to do so.

The potential damage that this kind of activity can cause is illustrated by the Talmud's record of why Rabbi Shimon bar Yoḥai ends up in hiding for over a decade: due to Rabbi Yehuda ben Gerim (son of converts), who relays a conversation that put Rabbi Shimon bar Yoḥai in danger.

> In this *baraita* Rabbi Yehuda is described as head of the speakers in every place. The Gemara asks: **And why did they call him head of the speakers in every place?** The Gemara relates that this resulted due to an incident that took place **when Rabbi Yehuda and Rabbi Yosei and Rabbi Shimon were sitting, and Yehuda, son of converts, sat beside them. Rabbi Yehuda opened and said: How pleasant are the actions of this nation,** the Romans, as **they established marketplaces, established bridges,** and **established bathhouses. Rabbi Yosei was silent.**

6. *Pele Yo'etz,* s.v. *hamegaleh.*

> **Rabbi Shimon ben Yoḥai responded and said: Everything that they established, they established only for their own purposes. They established marketplaces to place prostitutes in them; bathhouses to pamper themselves;** and **bridges to collect taxes from** all who pass over **them. Yehuda, son of converts, went and related their statements** to his household, **and** those statements continued to spread until **they were heard by the monarchy. They** ruled and **said: Yehuda, who elevated** the Roman regime, **shall be elevated** and appointed as head of the Sages, the head of the speakers in every place. **Yosei, who remained silent, shall be exiled** from his home in Judea as punishment, and sent **to** the city of **Tzippori** in the Galilee. **And Shimon, who denounced** the government, **shall be killed.** Rabbi Shimon bar Yoḥai **and his son,** Rabbi Elazar, **went** and **hid in the study hall.** (Shabbat 33b)

This anecdote also illustrates the fine line between violating confidence and spreading gossip, further supporting the Rishonim who combine the two. As *Sedei Ḥemed* notes, Rashi on this passage seems to agree with this assessment.[7]

In *Shu"t LeḤafetz Ḥayim* (8), the author suggests that the *Ḥafetz Ḥayim* believes that simply revealing secrets is not a good character trait, revealing somewhat negative information is prohibited by dint of the verse in Proverbs, and revealing damaging information is included under the biblical prohibition of *rekhilut,* as the line between the two is non-existent.

Rabbi Yitzchak Zilberstein (*Ḥashukei Ḥemed,* Bava Metzia 29b, Bava Batra 4a) suggests that one also violates the prohibition of *geneivat daat,* deception, which is detailed in the Talmud (Ḥullin 94). Presumably, this is because when someone says something in confidence, the implied assumption is that his privacy will be kept.

There are many midrashic sources that emphasize the severity of the prohibition, but we will suffice with these for now.

---

7. See above.

It Was Not Secret, but It Shouldn't Be Spread

R. Betzalel Stern (*Responsa BeTzel HaḤokhma*) suggests that there are instances in which spreading secrets constitutes a formal violation of the law, and cases where it is merely a violation of *derekh eretz*. As we will explore, the prohibition does not apply when the information was never intended to be secret. According to many opinions, there are circumstances in which the information can be spread freely even when the person who originally conveyed it would not want it spread, simply because it is assumed to be public. R. Stern argues that in cases such as these, maintaining confidentiality is merely a righteous thing to do. However, in cases where the information is clearly intended to be private, violating that confidence would constitute a formal violation. Maharsha (*Ḥiddushei Aggadot,* Yoma 4b, s.v. *shehu beval yomar*) develops a similar theory based on an analysis of the context of the verses used by the Talmud to ground this prohibition.

The *Ḥafetz Ḥayim* (*Hilkhot Lashon HaRa* 2:13:27) makes a slightly different distinction. As noted before, the *Ḥafetz Ḥayim* proves that the problem of divulging secrets includes cases that could cause no damage, as God could not be hurt or embarrassed by Moshe teaching His Torah. However, the *Ḥafetz Ḥayim* contends that in such cases, breaching confidentiality is merely a *midda tova,* an expression of good character traits. However, when not respecting privacy will harm the person whose information is being shared, the spreading of that information would constitute *lashon hara,* forbidden gossip.

Assumed and Non-Assumed Confidentiality

As noted above, the Talmud propounds that any information that is shared with an individual must, barring other considerations, be assumed to be private. In other cases, however, confidentiality is *not assumed,* either because there is reason to presume that the original speaker did not intend for the information to remain secret, or because privacy has already been breached. Obviously, the implications for social media will be vast.

In order to understand the central talmudic passages that provide the groundwork for this discussion, we must briefly review a bit of terminology.

Lishna bisha in Aramaic is the literal rendering of *lashon hara* in Hebrew, evil speech or evil tongue. The *Ḥafetz Ḥayim,* throughout his work, accepts the definitions outlined by Rambam in the seventh chapter of *Hilkhot De'ot.* Rambam writes that *lashon hara* (or *lishna bisha*) refers to gossip, negative information which is true. This is distinct from *hotzaat shem ra,* which refers to defamation or slander; and from *rekhilut,* which implicates speakers in *lashon hara* such that animosity is caused.

However, many Rishonim believed that *lishna bisha* refers either exclusively or additionally to the prohibition of breaching confidentiality. The sources for this contention are the passages we will explore.

Anything Said Before Three People

In two places, the Talmud states the following:

> **Rabba bar Rav Huna says: Any matter that is said in the presence of three** people **is not subject to** the prohibition of *lishna bisha.* (Bava Batra 39a–b, Arakhin 15b)

In Bava Batra, the context of this statement is in a wider discussion of *meḥaa,* legal protest. The topic of much of the third chapter is squatters' rights. One who squats on land for three years is assumed to be the owner of the property. To prevent the squatter from being able to claim ownership by dint of his physical presence on the land, the original owner must issue a formal protest, which breaks the contiguity of the three years needed by the squatter. The Talmud presents a dispute as to how many people must witness the protest:

> The Gemara relates: **Rabbi Yosei, son of Rabbi Ḥanina, encountered** the **students of Rabbi Yoḥanan** and **said to them: Did Rabbi Yoḥanan say in** the presence of **how many** people a **protest** must be lodged? **Rabbi Ḥiyya bar Abba says** that **Rabbi Yoḥanan** says: **A protest** must be lodged **in the presence of two** people. **Rabbi Abbahu said** that **Rabbi Yoḥanan** said: **A protest** must be lodged **in the presence of three** people. (Bava Batra 39a)

The Talmud then suggests that this dispute hangs on whether or not one accepts the statement of Rabba bar Rav Huna in the context of *lishna bisha*. The simplest explanation of this suggestion is that the common denominator between these two laws is that they both depend on publicity. The protest, if public, can be assumed to have reached the ears of the squatter such that he will take pains to defend his legal rights, if he has any. *Lishna bisha,* for some reason, is not a problem once the information in question is public. At this stage, the Talmud assumes that Rabbi Ḥiyya bar Abba would argue that both the protest and the *lishna bisha* can be presumed public once two people have heard the information.

> The Gemara elaborates on the suggestion that the dispute hinges upon this point: **The one who says** that a protest can be lodged **in the presence of two** people **is not of** the opinion that the ruling is in accordance with the opinion **of Rabba bar Rav Huna** and holds that even if only two people hear of a matter it will become a matter of public knowledge. Therefore, it is sufficient to protest in the presence of two witnesses. **And the one who says** that a protest must be lodged **in the presence of three** people **is of** the opinion that the ruling is in accordance with the opinion **of Rabba bar Rav Huna.**

The Gemara then launches into several possibilities that do not depend on this equation. The assumption that three people (or two) will ensure that the squatter hears about the protest even without being present is based on a statement earlier on that page:

> **We** are **not** going to **tell him personally,** but **we are** going to **tell others.** In that case, word of the protest will reach the possessor, since **your friend has a friend** whom he tells about the protest, **and your friend's friend has a friend** whom he tells about the protest; therefore, it is a valid protest.

In other words, we rely on the grapevine to ensure that the squatter is given ample opportunity to defend himself or herself.[8]

---

8. This principle is also introduced in Ketubot 109a–110a and Bava Batra 28a–b.

This statement also appears in Arakhin 15b, in the middle of longer discussions of *lashon hara*: It is permitted to say *lishna bisha* said in front of three people because your friend has a friend and your friend's friend has a friend. It is also preceded by a dispute as to whether *lishna bisha* said in front of the object of the information is prohibited.

Lishna Bisha

In the passage in Arakhin, the simplest understanding of the phrase *lishna bisha* is gossip, based on the broader context. However, based on the context in Bava Batra, many Rishonim feel otherwise. Noting that *meḥaa,* the protest against a squatter, is not gossip, at least at first glance,[9] the issue at hand seems to be simply about the presumption of whether information can and will remain secret or will travel. Thus, they understand the phrase *lishna bisha* as revealing secrets. Ritva (*Ḥiddushei HaRitva,* Bava Batra 39b, s.v. *lit ba*), for example, notes the opposite implications in the two passages and argues that the phrase *lishna bisha* can refer both to the breaching of confidentiality and to forbidden gossip.

It is obvious that under certain circumstances, the fact that information has been shared publicly negates any obligation to respect confidentiality. However, the exact implications the authorities draw vary. Their answers shed light on two different questions:

1. When may one assume the original speaker did not assume secrecy?
2. In what cases may one be permitted to spread information even when the original speaker would be opposed to such an act?

Rav Aḥai: Presumed Permission

R. Aḥai (*She'iltot* 28) equates *lashon hara* with the prohibition of breaching confidentiality from Yoma 4b. He understands the issue of "in front of three" as follows:

9. We will return to the positions according to which, in both cases, the phrase can be understood as gossip or the equivalent. The Rashbam cites and rejects a position that defines *meḥaa* as gossip, and *Yad Rama* (Bava Batra 2:101) accepts this argument as correct.

> [Do we say that] since [the Talmud ruled that one cannot share information] until he tells him "Go and say," this applies to three people as well – since he did not tell them [explicitly] "Go and say," they cannot? Or, perhaps, that which we require him to say "Go and say" is only where he did not say it in front of three, but said it in private. However, when he said it in front of three, it is like it is public and it is as if he said, "Go and say." Let us prove it: "Rabba bar Rav Huna says: Any matter that is said in the presence of three [people] is not subject to [the prohibition of] *lishna bisha*."

In other words, the Gemara's question is whether confidentiality is assumed under all circumstances – even those in which the original context was not totally private. For R. Aḥai, the conclusion is that whenever the context implies that the information being shared is not private, in this case because it is said in public, there is presumed consent to share what has been said.

R. Aḥai thus rules that one does not need explicit permission to share information; contextually implied permission is sufficient. However, he does not deal with cases in which:

1. Saying something in front of multiple people does not necessarily imply that the information is public; or
2. The original speaker speaks to three people but explicitly stipulates that the information must remain confidential.

However, his words imply that in both these cases, one would have to maintain confidentiality. The central issue for him seems to be whether or not the original speaker granted (or may be presumed to have granted) permission to share the information.

The general understanding is accepted in the *Sefer Hashlama* (Bava Batra 39b).

Several Rishonim seem to take this position as well, though it not absolutely clear whether they are referring to the prohibition of breaching confidentiality or gossip. Both Rashi and Rabbenu Gershom in Arakhin, for example, write that once the speaker has divulged the information in front of three people, it is permitted to repeat it, for the original speaker knows that it will be spread. While this sounds like the position of R. Aḥai, it is hard to prove it, as these Rishonim are not as explicit as R. Aḥai is in *She'iltot*. However, as we have previously noted concerning the view of the *Sedei Ḥemed,* Rashi seems to accept the position of R. Aḥai as to the definition of *lishna bisha,* thus indicating that he would agree with the above presentation. This is further bolstered by the fact that for Rashi, it is critical that the information be said by the primary subject, indicating that the issue at hand is secrecy, not gossip.[10]

It Is Already Public

Many Rishonim, while not as explicit as R. Aḥai, seem to take a different direction, one that may hold true for either definition of *lishna bisha,* breaking confidentiality or gossip (what is more colloquially known as *lashon hara*). They understand that both of these prohibitions are aimed at preventing the speaker from damaging someone using speech. However, once information is public, they are of the opinion that it does not matter whether it is repeated.

It is quoted in the name of R. Zalman Nechemia Goldberg that the logic is as follows:[11] When information is conveyed in front of one or two people, those people will keep it secret. They do not want the original speaker to know that they are responsible for sharing the information. However, once information is shared in front of three people, the potential guilt can always be deflected. Once that is the case, it is inevitable that the information will not remain private. Thus, the original

10. This seems to be a more accurate understanding of the view of Rashi than the one presented in *Din Davar HaNe'emar Bifnei Shelosha Ein Bo Mishum Lashon HaRa?!* by Neria Rut and Chaggai Mizaki, available here: https://asif.co.il/wpfb-file/1-2-pdf-3/. They assume that Rashi interprets *lashon hara* as gossip; therefore, he is providing a very limited dispensation for when gossip can be shared, meaning only when someone badmouths himself or herself in public. However, it is more reasonable to assume that Rashi understands the issue at hand to be secrecy. This does not require that someone speak badly about himself or herself. Rather, Rashi meant that when someone shares neutral or positive information about himself or herself in a somewhat public matter, the speaker waives any rights to privacy, either because of implied permission or because expecting confidentiality would be unreasonable.
11. See citation here: https://daf-yomi.com/DYItemDetails.aspx?itemId=31820.

speaker will give up, even if unwittingly, on privacy being maintained. He bases this on a law in the Gemara which says that when an object is lost in front of three people, a finder can keep it, but not if it falls in front of two. The Gemara explains this as follows:

> **Rav Naḥman says:** If one **saw a** ***sela*** coin **that fell from** one of **two** people, he is **obligated to return** it. **What is the reason? The** person **from whom** the *sela* **fell does not despair** of recovering it. **He says: After all, no other person was with me, only this** one who was with me, as he is unaware that the *sela* was found by a third party. He therefore thinks: **I will seize him and say to him:** It **is you who took it.**
>
> **In** a case where the coin fell from one of **three** people, the finder **is not obligated to return** it. **What is the reason? The** person **from whom** the *sela* **fell certainly despairs** of recovering it. **He says: After all, two** other people **were with me. If I seize this** one, he will **say: I did not take it. And if I seize that** one, he will **say: I did not take it.** Since he cannot make a definitive claim, he despairs of recovering his coin. (Bava Metzia 26a–b)

A more straightforward formulation is to say that once information is public, it is public. As Meiri writes, once the information has been divulged in front of three people, "it is as if he said it in front of the entire world."

The *Ḥafetz Ḥayim* (*Hilkhot Lashon HaRa* 2:3:4) notes that this seems to be the understanding of the Rashbam in the discussion in Bava Batra. The *Ḥafetz Ḥayim* provides an argument for this position from the *pesukim*. As we have noted before, the prohibition of gossip and/or violating confidentiality comes from the *pasuk* that warns a person not to be a *rokhel*. Literally, this means a peddler. The metaphor is used because a gossiper/sharer of secrets takes information that would not have been available to others and brings it to them. The metaphorical *rokhel* does the same with information. However, if this is so, the *Ḥafetz Ḥayim* contends that once the information is known, the one who spreads it is not comparable to a peddler. He is not needed for his "wares."

The *Ḥafetz Ḥayim* equates the position of the Rashbam and the Rambam, though the Rambam, as he notes, puts an important limitation on this dispensation.

Spreading Further

While the Rambam (within the understanding that *lashon hara* refers to gossip) accepts a form of the argument above, he limits it as follows:

> If such evil be spoken in the presence of three persons, the matter is thereby considered public. Thus, if one of the three who heard it repeats it to others no sin of an evil tongue is found therein, provided that in re-telling it he had no intention to spread the rumor and advertise it still more. (*Hilkhot De'ot* 7:5, Glazer translation)

This means that in the case of gossip, the Rambam believes that it is permitted to spread information to audiences who already know it, as no damage is being added. However, if one is introducing the gossip to a new audience, it would be prohibited.

While the Rambam does not say this regarding breaching confidentiality, one could make an identical argument under that understanding of *lashon hara.*

It Is Universally Known

Some authorities, however, argue that there are various levels of publicity, and while there may be some limitations placed on spreading secrets and/or gossip even when it has reached a lower level of publicity, there comes a point at which the information has become universally known, and prohibiting sharing that information would be pointless.

R. Azriel Ariel[12] argues as follows: the dispensation of "in front of three" provides certain permission simply because the information *will eventually get out.* However, he does not believe (unlike Meiri above) that we consider something said in front of three to be *already publicly known.*

---

12. *Lashon HaRa BeMaarekhet Tzibburit Demokratit* (2), available at: https://asif.co.il/wpfb-file/zhr-6-3-pdf/. He notes that Ari Shvat raises this point as well in *Yeisha Yemino,* vol. 45, 39–41. See R. Ariel, n. 9.

If this is the case, then we must be more permissive when the information is indeed *universally known*. His example is gossip (or a secret) that has been publicized by mass media. Discussing what is on the news rarely introduces people to information they have not already heard.

R. Shlomo Aviner[13] suggests that the Rambam's limitation might not be relevant in these cases. Meaning, while something said in front of three people may be repeated only with no intent to spread it further, something already known globally may be repeated freely. R. Ariel notes that even the *Ḥafetz Ḥayim*, who in the end rejects the above understanding of "in front of three," accepts the notion that there is no prohibition in sharing information that is known to all (*Hilkhot Lashon HaRa* 4:10:41).

However, R. Ariel notes that just because something is at one point so well known that further sharing it is meaningless, this may not always be the case. He cites R. Avraham Shapira as suggesting that once something has fallen out of the news cycle, the information becomes subject to the more limited dispensations seen above. He notes that this is particularly relevant in the modern era when people are over-inundated with information, and thus they quickly forget about the news from a few weeks earlier. Mentioning news from last month may really be introducing something "novel."

He further cites R. Dov Lior, who notes that *Ḥazal* write that people forget things after twelve months (Bava Metzia 24a). Thus, news from a year ago, as public as it may have been, can no longer be considered "known to all."[14] On a practical note, R. Lior's argument does not always seem true. Certain scandals become so well known that one can safely assume that they are still publicly known even decades later (Watergate, for example).

I would add that R. Betzalel Stern's argument mentioned above – that even in cases where the technical prohibition against violating confidentiality does not apply, there is an ethical imperative to remain silent – may not apply in cases such as these. On the other hand, one might argue that from an ethical standpoint, repeating something that should have been secret is not ethical, even if the effect is minimal.

---

13. *Itturei Kohanim*, vol. 82, 16. Cited by R. Ariel, n. 9.
14. See note 11.

When Public Is Not Public

The *Ḥafetz Ḥayim* (*Hilkhot Lashon HaRa* 2:5) notes that there may be cases where saying something in front of a group of people does not automatically indicate that it is public. For example, if one shares something in front of a group of his loved ones, family, or friends, there may still be an assumption that the information is meant to stay in that group, even if it is larger than three people. The *Ḥafetz Ḥayim* goes further, arguing that if something is said in front of three people, but one person in the audience is known as God-fearing to the point that no one expects him to share it, there are no longer three people who would share it, so it is as if it was said in front of only two, and the allowances do not apply. Even if one does not accept this application, the general point that something said in front of three people does not always grant a *carte blanche* is compelling.

R. Shlomo Rosner (*Ali Be'er* on *Ḥafetz Ḥayim, Hilkhot Lashon HaRa,* 2:28) suggests that the Gemara limits its dispensation to information said "*in front of* three." However, when information is said "*among*" people, it is *still presumed private.* Thus, a law firm, doctor's office, or school that has an internal meeting about clients, patients, and students can demand privacy, even if there are more than three people present at the meeting. *The context makes it clear that secrecy is expected and reasonable.* This point seems irrefutable, based on the mishna we have seen regarding courts. The mishna, based on the verse about *rekhilut/lashon hara,* forbids sharing the internal discussions of a court after a verdict is issued:

> After the judges **finish the matter** and reach a decision, **they bring in** the litigants. **The greatest of the judges says: So-and-so, you are exempt** from paying; or: **So-and-so, you are liable** to pay.
>
> **And from where** is it derived that **when** the judge **leaves** the courtroom **he may not say: I deemed** you **exempt and my colleagues deemed** you **liable, but what can I do, as my colleagues outnumbered me** and consequently you were deemed liable? **About this it is stated: "You shall not go as a talebearer among your people"** (Lev. 19:16), **and it says: "One who goes about as a talebearer reveals secrets,** but one who is of a faithful spirit conceals a matter" (Prov. 11:13). (Mishna Sanhedrin 3:6–7, Sanhedrin 29a)

In such a case, there are at least three judges, but divulging what happened behind closed doors is forbidden. This is true even in court cases that have more than three judges. The reason seems to be that information which is said *within a professional group* is considered private.

Summary of the Halakhic Models for the Potential Allowance to Share Secrets That Are Already Public

The following models emerged from our analysis above:

1. R. Aḥai understands *lishna bisha* to be the prohibition against breaching confidentiality. He argues that when something is said in front of three people, there is presumed consent by the original speaker for the information to be spread.
   a. We understood that according to R. Aḥai, in cases where such consent cannot be assumed or is explicitly denied, it would be forbidden to spread the information.
2. The *Ḥafetz Ḥayim* proposes that according to the Rashbam, once information is said in front of three people, it is permitted to repeat it, as it is assumed to be public.
   a. R. Zalman Nechemia Goldberg agrees, though he bases the permission on the assumption that people have given up hope that their information will remain private once it has been said in such a way that anyone who shares the secret would have plausible deniability.
3. Based on the Rambam's presentation of this dispensation in the context of forbidden gossip, it can be argued that it is only permitted to spread the information if one does not have the intent to spread it further than it has already spread.
4. R. Azriel Ariel and R. Shlomo Aviner argue that information that is universally known will be permitted to be spread no matter what, without the limitation mentioned by the Rambam.
   a. R. Avraham Shapira and R. Dov Lior argue that this is only true while the information is universally known. Once people begin to forget, it becomes prohibited again.
5. R. Betzalel Stern notes that there can be cases where it is technically permitted to share a secret, but it remains unethical to do so.

We wondered whether the same ethical imperative would exist in cases where the information is not just public, but universally known.

6. Information that is shared within a closed group, whether of family, friends, or colleagues, is not assumed to be public just because it has been shared with a large group. Information shared within a closed group is not the same as information shared with a group of outsiders. In such cases, all the people can be expected, legally and realistically, to maintain the secret; thus, sharing it further is forbidden.

How does this apply in the case of social media?

Facebook Post

A publicly sharable Facebook post is obviously permitted. It is already public, and by making it sharable, one is explicitly allowing it to be shared beyond one's friends. The same is evidently the case for a Twitter post.

What about a post shared only with friends? For R. Aḥai, it could be that the fact that one has limited access to the post to friends indicates that despite the inherent publicity of the post, there is no implied permission to share it more widely. However, based on R. Zalman Nechemia Goldberg's argument – once something is public, the possibility of every person involved to deny being responsible for spreading it further causes the original speaker to give up on maintaining any semblance of privacy – a Facebook post would surely fall into this category. For the Rambam, who forbids spreading the information further, it might be prohibited. However, based on the point that R. Ariel develops, this may apply only to things that are not universally known. A Facebook post to thousands of friends may be so public that its further dissemination is no longer meaningful enough to be prohibited. One may wonder, however, based on the position formulated by R. Stern, whether it would be ethically appropriate to share such a post further.

In a case where everyone understands that there is a specific person with whom the post was not meant to be shared, it would seem that it would be prohibited to do so. For example, sharing pictures of a student with his or her principal or parent would likely be prohibited, even if that student does not mind the picture being shared with peers, even those who are not officially among his or her Facebook friends. We will return to the question of when it would be permitted to share this information for educational purposes or some other pressing need.

In a Closed Facebook Group

What about a post in a private group? According to R. Aḥai, it would seem to be prohibited to share this, as there is an indication that the original speaker wants the information to remain private, despite his or her sharing it somewhat widely.

Perhaps one could take this further. R. Nissim Karelitz stakes out a very strong position on this issue (*Ḥut Shani, Hilkhot Lashon HaRa* 5:1:2). He argues that if one has *committed* to keeping something private and then hears the information from another source (meaning that it is already somewhat public), it is still prohibited to spread it. This position is briefly mentioned by *Semag* (9) and *Hagahot Maimoniyot* (*Hilkhot De'ot* 7:7). It seems that what is relevant is the explicit (or perhaps implicit) commitment one makes by discovering information in a non-public forum. Entering into a closed group may bind one, by virtue of his or her commitment, to try to keep the information as private as possible, even when one knows it is impossible. R. Stern's argument, that ethically one should be bound to keep things private even when not legally required, would certainly apply in this kind of case.

R. Gil Student notes that in cases in which one explicitly commits to keeping the secret, it may be that breaking the promise also entails *ḥillul Hashem,* desecrating God's name. Thus, he suggests that while, as we will see, there are cases of need that permit the breaching of confidentiality, the bar for what counts may be raised in these cases:

> If you verbally promise (even without an oath) not to release the recording, then you are further bound to maintain the confidentiality even if there is a public need because of the Chillul Hashem. According to some, you may tell the person in advance, thereby

removing the Chillul Hashem, and then release the recording. But if the need becomes great, there may be more room for leniency.[15]

Based on the view of the Rambam, this would clearly be forbidden, as sharing the information beyond the closed group would be spreading it beyond the original public audience. If the information has not yet become universally known, the dispensation developed by R. Ariel would not apply either.

Arguably, this case would also be subject to the distinction between sharing information *in front of people* and *sharing among them.* In a closed group, this may be similar to sharing among family, friends, or colleagues. The *Ḥafetz Ḥayim,* who believes that in any case where one can plausibly expect secrecy it becomes obligatory to maintain it, would likely rule that this case fits that paradigm.

Texts, WhatsApps, Emails, and Listservs

Showing or forwarding a private text, WhatsApp message, or email is clearly prohibited due to these prohibitions, as duly noted by R. Ariel.[16] If, however, a message has been shared in a WhatsApp *group,* R. Ariel, based on the position of R. Aḥai, argues that it is permitted to share it further. However, if the original writer makes it clear that he or she does not want it to be spread further, then R. Ariel notes that it would be prohibited. This would be the ruling of the Rambam and the *Ḥafetz Ḥayim,* and we have argued that R. Aḥai would concur.

A closed listserv, while aimed at a large group, is presumed to be private. In cases where the rules are explicitly outlined and demand that the emails are to remain private, it would be prohibited to forward them, and the same is true where context indicates that this is the case. While we could make the argument that when one publicizes material on a listserv one waives the prohibition (perhaps based on arguments such as that of R. Goldberg above), this position does not seem to be compelling. As we have argued regarding the closed Facebook group, a

15. *Search Engine,* 298–299.

16. Available at: https://www.yeshiva.org.il/ask/104573.

listserv is about sharing information among people, rather than *in front of them*, and thus secrecy may be expected and demanded.

Torah: Is It an Exception?

One might have thought that if the content under discussion is connected to the study of Torah, these prohibitions would not apply, a position taken by R. Goren. R. Gil Student summarizes how this topic comes to be debated as follows:

> Teaching and learning Torah are obligations. There is room to say that teaching a unique Torah insight, especially a practical conclusion, constitutes a public need. If so, we may be allowed to record and release a Torah lecture without permission of the speaker.
>
> A related incident occurred 30 years ago. When the Israeli army invaded Lebanon the first time in 1982, with God's help it proceeded quickly through the country and laid siege on Beirut. R. Shlomo Goren argued in an article that the Israeli army was halakhically obligated to leave one side of the city open so residents can flee (see *Mishneh Torah, Hilkhos Melakhim* 6:7). R. Shaul Yisraeli sent a private letter disagreeing. He distinguished between a mandatory war (*milkhemes mitzvah*) and an optional war (*milkhemes reshus*). We are only limited to a partial siege in the latter type of war, while the war in Lebanon was of the former type.
>
> To R. Yisraeli's surprise, his private letter was soon published in the newspaper. R. Goren wrote to R. Yisraeli an apology for the confusion but added that he did not really need permission to publish R. Yisraeli's Torah insights (note that R. Goren published a critique of his views by R. Yisraeli; this entire letter and R. Yisraeli's response are published in *Techumin*, vol. 4). R. Goren points out that the Tosefta (Bava Kama 7:3) states that someone who overhears ("steals") another's Torah insights may repeat them to others (giving proper attribution to the source, of course). Based on this, the *Shakh* (*Choshen Mishpat* 292:35) rules that you may copy a Torah text from

> someone else's scroll even if he does not allow it. According to R. Goren, teaching Torah is sufficient reason to set aside the prohibition against revealing confidential information (i.e. private teachings).

However, this position is not accepted by R. Shaul Yisraeli, nor by R. Ariel, his student. Thus, he argues that even if the group under discussion is focused around Torah the same general prohibition about sharing information applies.

R. Yisraeli (*Ḥavot Binyamin* 2:75) argues that a Torah scholar may insist that his Torah remain private, especially when damage might be caused by publicizing his position. This is bolstered by the fact that the original obligation to maintain confidentiality is derived from a case in which *God relays laws to Moshe.* It is specifically from this case that the Talmud (Yoma 4b) extrapolates that one needs permission to share something told in private. Thus, a response offered on a *Shu"t* SMS or *Shu"t* WhatsApp or any other Torah group, whenever it has been made clear that privacy was intended, must remain among the intended audience. R. Yisraeli argues that the sources marshaled by R. Goren only apply to Torah taught originally in public, in which case privacy cannot be assumed.

R. Yitzchak Zilberstein (*Ḥashukei Ḥemed,* Bava Metzia 29b) agrees, noting that the same logic that prohibits disclosing information in general, whether it is based on the obligation of *ve'ahavta lere'akha kamokha* or the prohibition of *geneivat daat* (as he proposes), applies equally to *talmud Torah.* However, as in the above cases, if the context indicates that the rabbi in question would not mind being recorded or having his positions shared, it would be permitted. In cases where he would mind, it would be prohibited. Thus, he notes that people who secretly record and share recordings of private *shiurim* or discussions with rabbis are violating the halakha.

R. Moshe Feinstein (*Responsa Iggerot Moshe, OḤ* 4:40:19) similarly forbids recording *shiurim* without permission, especially when the lecturer explicitly objects. He argues that while it is not theft, it is *geneivat daat,* especially when the lecturer sells recordings of his *shiurim.*

More relevant for our discussion is a second concern he raises. Namely, he argues that rabbis may feel uncomfortable being recorded (or, we may add, having their lectures or positions spread), as they may be unsure that what they have said is correct. While one would hope that rabbis would attempt to only issue proper rulings always, especially in public settings, they, like all human beings, can make mistakes. They may want to retract, and they may want their rulings to remain within the group that will see their corrections or retractions. Disseminating their positions beyond the group makes that impossible. Thus, the limitations that apply to general information should apply to Torah material as well. We should note that R. Moshe disagrees with R. Yisraeli, who feels that all public lectures may be publicized freely.

R. Menasheh Klein (*Responsa Mishneh Halakhot* 7:273) notes that the same rules apply to Torah material as to general material. Thus, he forbids recording a private conversation with a scholar, and even more so, to disseminate it. In a case in which the dissemination may damage the scholar's reputation, this is even truer. However, at a public *shiur*, under most circumstances, one may assume that the lecturer does not mind if the content becomes public, and thus it may be recorded and spread.

However, he then raises a concern similar to those expressed by R. Dov Lior and R. Avraham Shapira: Even if something is public now, it may be forgotten in time. Thus, even if a lecture has been *given* publicly, this does not mean that the lecturer would want the *shiur* to be *recorded* and spread in such a way that it will be preserved for an unknown period of time. Therefore, while there may be reasons to argue that even this would be permitted, he advises refraining from this.

What emerges from the rulings of these *posekim* is that the same principles that guide the obligation to maintain confidentiality concerning general material apply to Torah material as well. While there may be some practical differences as to under what circumstances information may be assumed to be public, the rules that govern the sharing of Torah material would be similar to those that govern the sharing of general material.

Snapchat

Originally, Snapchat did not allow sending messages to groups of people, presumably as part of its attempt at enabling secrecy. However, in the last several years, it has allowed sending messages to groups.[17] As with a normal Snapchat, the default assumption is that messages will be deleted after a certain amount of time. Concerning this feature, it would seem even more obvious than with regular texts or WhatsApps that confidentiality should be assumed, even if the message is sent to a group of people.

Spying

Creating fake IDs or hacking into private Facebook or Instagram accounts is prohibited for a host of reasons. Spreading the information would violate even more prohibitions, no matter how many followers or friends the person may have on his or her account.

Time Limit

There does not seem to be any time limit after which the assumption of secrecy is waived. This point is made in the following talmudic passage:

> The Gemara relates: There was **a certain student, about whom a rumor emerged that he revealed a statement that was stated in the study hall** and should have been kept secret, and the rumor emerged **twenty-two years after** the time the statement was revealed. **Rav Ami removed him from the study hall** as a punishment. Rav Ami **said: This is a revealer of secrets** and he cannot be trusted. (Sanhedrin 31a)

Thus, mere passage of time will not solve the issue, and in fact, it may make things worse as information that was once well known may become unknown again.

Until now we have dealt with the problems of invasion of privacy and breaching of confidentiality when the information in question is neutral. However, when the information is negative, we must deal with many other halakhic issues, as we explore in our coming sections.

---

17. See here: https://www.cnet.com/news/snapchat-groups-mass-send-selfies-up-to-16-snaps/.

Chapter 21

Lashon HaRa on the Internet: A Fundamental Change?

Our discussions above focused on the issues that arise from invading the privacy of others and breaching confidentiality with "neutral" information. However, when the information being shared is negative and damaging, we must also deal with the prohibition against gossip, colloquially known as *lashon hara.*

In many respects, the conceptual questions that are raised for *lashon hara* in the various media we have explored are straightforward. Synchronous and asynchronous communication technology have provided new and wider audiences to target, but they have not radically changed the parameters of the discussion. Destroying someone's reputation in front of a global audience is obviously a more egregious violation of *lashon hara,* but again, the classical sources already develop the notion that public *lashon hara* is worse than private gossip, even if they could never have imagined the ease with which a modern person can make something known to people all over the globe.

Cass Sunstein wrote an entire book on the topic, entitled *On Rumors: How Falsehoods Spread, Why We Believe Them, and What Can Be Done.*[1] He opens the book, in the chapter entitled "The Problem," as follows:

> Rumors are nearly as old as human history, but with the rise of the Internet, they have become ubiquitous. In fact we are now awash in them. False rumors are especially troublesome; they impose real damage on individuals and institutions, and they often resist correction. They can threaten careers, relationships, policies, public officials, democracy, and sometimes even peace itself.

In an article on the same topic, he summarizes the reality that must be addressed:

> False rumors are pervasive on the Internet, and otherwise sensible people believe them. Self-interested and altruistic propagators spread rumors about prominent people and institutions. Such rumors cast doubt on their subject's honesty, decency, fairness, patriotism, and sometimes even sanity; often they portray public figures as fundamentally corrupt. Those who are not in the public sphere are similarly vulnerable. In a matter of seconds, it is easy to portray almost anyone as some kind of wrongdoer, and in that sense to injure their reputation, if only because of the easy availability of information on the Internet. The Internet, then, has two important effects. It allows information to be provided to the world, in an instant, and it allows easy discovery, by anyone, of that information, also in an instant.[2]

---

1. Princeton University Press, 2014.
2. Cass R. Sunstein, 'She Said What?' 'He Did That?' Believing False Rumors (November 21, 2008). Harvard Public Law Working Paper No. 08–56, available at: https://papers.ssrn.com/sol3/papers.cfm?abstract_id=1304268.

As he notes, although rumors existed before the internet, it seems to have made them more pervasive, easier to spread, and easier to find. However, none of those, at first glance, imply a qualitative change.

On the other hand, there are a few issues that are not merely quantitative, but require rethinking of categories. One of these is the topic that we discussed regarding confidentiality. Can we reach a point where information is sufficiently public that it is not problematic to further discuss it? This must be examined from the standpoint of *lashon hara,* just as we did from the standpoint of the prohibition against breaching privacy. We must also explore the implications for putting information out in the world that can almost never be retracted. Therefore, after we have set up the basic framework, we will return to the category of "in front of three" and the interpretations that relate to gossip rather than revealing secrets.

There is also some discussion in early halakhic sources of unique problems that may be caused when gossip is shared anonymously. This problem has been exacerbated by the internet, and much psychological research has been published illustrating the disastrous effects that internet anonymity has caused by generating "disinhibition." Again, while the basic issues that drive this problem are similar to those found in classical sources, the applications are different.

Finally, we will explore the potential cases of societal benefit that override or allow breaching confidentiality and spreading negative information.

Note that as the *Ḥafetz Ḥayim* (*Lashon HaRa* 1:8, with n. 12) notes, it seems obvious that the prohibition of *lashon hara* applies in writing as much as in speaking, and we will assume as much. As he notes, in a paradigmatic case of *lashon hara,* the Talmud specifically discusses a case of writing (Sanhedrin 30a). As R. Asher Weiss (*Minḥat Asher,* Lev. 41) notes, considering that central to that prohibition is the damage that can be caused, writing is obviously equivalent to speaking as it can also cause damage. For other understandings of *lashon hara* discussed below, there does not seem to be any reason to distinguish between speaking, writing, or other forms of communication. For example, the *Ḥafetz Ḥayim* (ibid.) assumes that it is obvious that hinting or implying *lashon hara* is also forbidden.

Defining Terms: What Is *Lashon HaRa/Lishna Bisha*?

The Torah states as follows: "Do not go as a talebearer (*rakhil*) among your people; do not stand [idly] by the blood of your friend, I am the Lord" (Lev. 19:16). This is the source for the prohibition against *lashon hara* (Hebrew) or *lishna bisha* (Aramaic), evil speech. As we have noted, many early commentaries, Geonim and Rishonim, understood this as the source for the prohibition to breach confidentiality. However, the understanding accepted by most modern authorities is that outlined by the Rambam and recorded by the *Ḥafetz Ḥayim* – namely, that it refers to gossip. In this model, gossip, broadly speaking, consists of three different sins.

1. *Rekhilut* is a term used by the Rambam (*Hilkhot De'ot* 7:2) to refer to reporting what others have said. For example, informing person A that person B spoke badly about him is *rekhilut*.
2. *Lashon hara* (not the general category but the specific prohibition) refers to conveying accurate negative information about others (*Hilkhot De'ot* 7:3).
3. *Hotzaat shem ra* refers to the spreading of false negative rumors, or slander.
4. In addition to the three biblical prohibitions, there are the rabbinic prohibitions called collectively *avak lashon hara,* the dust of gossip. These prohibitions include hinting about the existence of negative information by conspicuously refraining from talking about person X, as well as praising someone in front of his or her enemies, knowing that the praise will encourage insults (*Hilkhot De'ot* 7:4).

Some Rishonim agree that *lashon hara* refers to gossip but do not use the same terminological distinctions of the Rambam. For example, the *Sefer Ḥasidim* (Margolies edition, 44), the twelfth-century German pietistic work, defines *hotzaat shem ra* the way the Rambam defines *lashon hara,* as truthful gossip, and the term *lashon hara* the way the Rambam defines *rekhilut.* As we have noted before, the Talmud itself seems to use *lashon hara* to refer to slander in at least one place, as detailed by the *Sedei Ḥemed.*[3]

3. See *Shabbat* 33a–b and Rashi 33b, s.v. *peh gomer* (first), as pointed out by the *Sedei Ḥemed, Lashon HaRa.* See also *Ḥayei Adam* 143. See, however, Sota 42a, which

We will primarily use the terms as they are used colloquially in accordance with the definitions provided by the Rambam and adopted by the *Ḥafetz Ḥayim,* though we must be aware that the widespread acceptance of these terms is relatively recent in halakhic literature. This does not speak to the legal implications, but simply to the categorization and terminology.[4]

There is another explanation we will return to, that of R. Eliezer of Metz, in *Sefer Yere'im* (191). He claims that the prohibition of *lishna bisha* relates to being two-faced: speaking negatively of someone in a way the speaker never would in the subject's presence. We will see the implications of this when we return to our discussion of "in front of three."

Lashon HaRa: How Bad Is It?

The Talmud uses harsh rhetoric to highlight the gravity of this sin. The Talmud (Arakhin 15b) remarks that *lashon hara* is as evil as the three cardinal sins – murder, sexual immorality, and idol worship – combined. God is said to declare that He cannot dwell in the same world as the consistent speaker of *lashon hara*. God, as it were, joins forces with the angelic overseer of purgatory to punish those who commit this sin. The Gemara describes *lashon hara* as killing three people: the speaker, the listener, and the subject. While these statements are likely meant as exaggeration, they are still meaningful. Hyperbole highlights the gravity of the sin and the importance of avoiding it.[5] Thus, the disposition of the Talmud toward *lashon hara* is crystal clear.

The Rambam (*Hilkhot De'ot* 7:1) succinctly indicates how damaging gossip can be and how it can literally lead to murder by connecting it to a tragic story from Tanakh, that of Do'eg the Edomite. When David flees from Shaul, he stops in the priestly city of Nov. Believing

---

distinguishes between the sinners who speak *lashon hara* and those who lie, indicating that *lashon hara* refers primarily to gossip rather than slander. This is used by the *Ḥafetz Ḥayim* to support his terminology.

4. In many modern works, misconceptions about this terminology lead to mistakes in the understanding of classical texts.

5. See *Responsa Rivash* 171 and *Responsa Penei Yehoshua, EH* 44. See, however, the *Taz* on *Shulḥan Arukh, YD* 242:1, who argues that the comparisons should be taken literally.

David to still be in the good graces of the king, as he is both his trusted servant and son-in law, the people of Nov provide him with food, as well as with the sword of Golyat. The ensuing disaster is described in I Samuel, chapter 22:

> And Doeg the Edomite, who was standing by Sha'ul's servants, answered. "I saw the son of Yishai – he came to Nov, to Aḥimelekh son of Aḥtuv," he said, "who made an inquiry of the Lord for him and gave him provisions – he even gave him the sword of Golyat the Philistine."
>
> So the king summoned the priest Aḥimelekh son of Aḥituv and all the priests of his father's house, who were in Nov; and they all came to the king. Sha'ul said, "Now listen, son of Aḥituv."
>
> "Here I am, my lord," he said.
>
> "Why did you conspire against me, you and the son of Yishai," Sha'ul said to him, "by giving him bread and a sword, and making an inquiry of God for him – that he may rise up against me in ambush this very day?"
>
> "But out of all your servants, who is as faithful as David?" Aḥimelekh answered the king. "The king's son in law and captain of your bodyguard, so honored in your house? Have I begun to make inquiries of God for him? Absolutely not! Let the king not accuse his servant or any of my father's house of anything, for your servant knew absolutely nothing of all this – not the slightest hint."
>
> But the king said, "You will surely die, Aḥimelekh – you and all your father's house."
>
> And the king said to the couriers attending him, "Go around and kill the priests of the Lord, for they, too, side with David – they knew that he was fleeing, but they did not let me know." But the servants of the king were not willing to raise their hands to strike the priests of the Lord.
>
> So the king said to Doeg, "You go around and strike down the priests." And Doeg the Edomite went around and struck down the priests himself; that same day he slaughtered eighty five men who were clad in the linen ephod.

While the information shared was mostly true, the spin put on it by Do'eg, combined with Shaul's explosive temper and paranoia, leads to a massacre. Hence, this story stands as the paradigm of *lashon hara* that can actually kill.

Is *Lashon HaRa* Really Subject to Law?

Before the *Ḥafetz Ḥayim,* there is relatively little halakhic literature about *lashon hara.* While the Rambam devotes several laws to it, neither the *Tur* or *Shulḥan Arukh* discuss it. The *Magen Avraham* (*OḤ* 156) includes it in his extensive list of laws that are left out of *Shulḥan Arukh.*

Despite this, most modern authorities accept the basic framework of the *Ḥafetz Ḥayim* and treat it as law. However, Professor Benjamin Brown has argued that the absence of any similar material in early authorities may indicate that the project of the *Ḥafetz Ḥayim* was more novel than he realized or admitted. He argues that most authorities prior to the *Ḥafetz Ḥayim* understood *lashon hara* to belong to the world of ethical principles rather than formal law, and thus actively chose not to subject it to classic legal analysis. The *Ḥafetz Ḥayim,* on the other hand, was generally convinced that when at all possible, ethical principles should be translated into hard and fast rules. Brown describes this process as follows:

> ...the traditional rule-centered genre in Jewish tradition is halakha, while the principle-centered one is known as musar. The Hafetz Hayim's literary enterprise in this branch should therefore be considered as the halakhization of musar, or, if we allow ourselves a less accurate term, a legalization of ethics.[6]

While I believe that Brown's claim is too radical, and we will generally proceed on the assumption that *lashon hara* is subject to formal legal

6. *Benjamin Brown,* "From Principles to Rules and from Musar to Halakhah: The Hafetz Hayim's Rulings on Libel and Gossip," *Dinei Yisrael* 25 (2008): 174–175. See also R. Asher Weiss (*Minḥat Asher,* Lev. 41), who takes up the question of whether *lashon hara* is properly defined as law or a *midda tova,* good character trait.

analysis, as most modern authorities do, his claim has merit and is worth considering. While both ethics and laws are critical to develop a complete Torah perspective on a topic, they are understood and applied differently. Thus, if we treat *lashon hara* as law, if Brown is correct, the analysis will be overly formal and will not capture the issues with complete accuracy. This is also the approach taken by R. Daniel Feldman in his masterful book about *lashon hara* in the modern era, *False Facts and True Rumors: Lashon HaRa in Contemporary Culture.*[7]

Is *Lashon HaRa* Really "True"?

Even if we accept the taxonomy of the Rambam and the *Ḥafetz Ḥayim,* it may be too simplistic to refer to gossip as "true." R. Daniel Feldman notes that modern psychology sheds light on why *lashon hara,* even when it consists of technically true information, may be prohibited, in part because even facts can be false.

Specifically, he notes that gossip, even if true, is almost definitionally only part of the picture. Partial information, even if technically accurate, can paint a dangerously misleading picture of the person being spoken about. Psychologists such as David Kahneman and Amos Tversky have argued that while we believe that we are in control of how we think, the majority of what we think and do is not the product of our conscious mind. Rather, it is instead due to our instinctual reactions that happen beneath the surface. (The research Kahneman and Tversky did on these issues earned Kahneman the Nobel Prize in economic sciences in 2002, though Tversky had passed away by that point.)

Kahneman summarized the central insights of their research in his ground-breaking *Thinking Fast and Slow*.[8] He divides the functioning of the human mind into System 1 and System 2, metaphorical descriptions of the two ways in which human beings assess the world around them. The first is quick, emotional, and instinctual; the second is slow, logical, and deliberate. People assume they are

7. YU Press/Maggid, 2015.
8. Farrar, Straus and Giroux, 2011.

influenced primarily by System 2, but in truth most of our perceptions are products of System 1.

Among those instincts are a series of heuristics, or psychological shortcuts, that we use to judge the truthfulness and integrity of people. The "halo effect" and "devil effect" (also described as the "horn effect"), for example, refer to our inclination to view people in light of our first impressions of them. If our first encounter is positive, we tend to view even their questionable behavior as meritorious (following our confirmation bias). If our first encounter is negative, even their seemingly good intentions will be questioned. This is despite there being no rational reason to think this way. Rather, Kahneman argues that these tendencies are a form of "exaggerated emotional coherence."

Cass Sunstein formulates a similar concern: "This phenomenon comes with an unlovely label: biased assimilation. The simple idea is that people process information in a way that fits with their own predilections."

Another relevant heuristic is what Kahneman dubs the "What you see is all there is" effect (WYSIATI) While logically, human beings should not form opinions of others until they have enough information, people usually do not wait for all the data to come in to form such opinions. Rather, our desire for coherence and clarity drives us to shape perceptions based on the information available to us, regardless of how partial it may be.

Nicholas DiFonzo, a leading scholar of rumors, argues that there are two factors that make rumors as powerful as they are: human beings' social tendencies, and as outlined above, our desire to make sense of the world:

> Why are rumors such a regular part of people's experience? What is it about being human that sets the stage for rumor activity? The answers can be found in two fundamental features of human nature. First, people are social and relational entities. There is something especially "we" about our encounter with existence, even for the solitary loners among us. John Donne's memorable poetic phrase "No man is an island" suggests this sentiment.

> Like most creatures, we seem to be designed for social interaction. We talk together, eat together, work together, we trade, barter, and bicker. A large part of what it means to be human is to communicate with one another. We also view ourselves in relation to other persons – a man may be a father, a friend, or a follower. As psychologist Susan T. Fiske put it, we are fundamentally social beings.
>
> Second, humans have a deeply rooted motivation to make sense of the world. From ancient times men and women have been conceived as rational embodied entities; flesh-and-blood creatures in which reside the faculties of sensing, perceiving, thinking, deciding, believing and choosing. In other words, we are sensemaking beings. To make sense is to give meaning to our sensations, to put a context around them so that they gain significance and fit into an understanding that coheres. It means looking at the picture side rather than the tangled underside of a woven tapestry. To make sense is to put our experiences into perspective so that they can be understood, known about, navigated and predicted. Without the ability to make sense, our world would be "blooming, buzzing confusion," as William James put it. Making sense of the world makes sense.
>
> So, we are fundamentally social beings and we possess an irrepressible instinct to make sense of the world. Put these ideas together and we get shared sensemaking: we make sense of life together. Rumor is perhaps the quintessential shared sensemaking activity. It may indeed be the predominant means by which we make sense of the world together.[9]

R. Feldman argues that the laws of *lashon hara* can be better understood in light of these (and many other) insights from modern psychology. If, through negative gossip, we impart bias toward a person our listener has never met or formed an opinion of, the listener will now, subconsciously, cast everything the unfortunate subject of the gossip does in a

9. Nicholas DiFonzo, *The Watercooler Effect* (Avery, 2008).

negative light, even when there is no reason to do so. Furthermore, the listener will construct an entire narrative about the subject that conforms to the minimal information, now negative, that the listener has about the subject. Thus, even if the subject is guilty of some wrongdoing, the resulting picture created in the mind of the listener is *unfairly and untruthfully negative*. Similarly, as both psychologists and ethicists (Jewish and non-Jewish) have pointed out, when we do something questionable, we provide justification for our actions, as we know the backstory. We do not do the same for others. Thus, even if the information we convey is technically true, knowing that the listener is unlikely to search for context to explain what happened, we are leading the listener to believe something that is more negative than the unembellished facts would indicate.

Also, as noted above by the Talmud, rumors kill not only the subject, but the speaker and listener as well. As DiFonzo notes, part of what makes gossip so powerful is the social component. Perhaps this is why *Ḥazal* see it as so harmful – it unites people in unfair crimes against others in favor of social binding and coherence-making.

These insights are particularly relevant in the age of social media, in which a compromising picture may be shared widely and irreversibly. Even when such a picture captures an actual event, the number of people it reaches almost guarantees that it will shape the first impressions of many future acquaintances, employers, or school admission boards, biasing them in ways that are unfair to the subject's overall character.

As we have already noted, the Gemara in several places presents the possibility that *lishna bisha* said in front of three people (*be'apei telata*) may be repeated. According to several authorities, such as R. Aḥai Gaon, this is the source for interpreting *lishna bisha* as the prohibition against breaching confidentiality. The argument is that once something is public, either there is presumed permission to spread it further, or it is automatically permitted, as further spreading the information is meaningless. We began discussing some explanations that apply to the understanding of *lishna bisha/lashon hara* as gossip, and we will flesh those out, as well as introduce several others.

Rambam

As we noted, the Rambam understands this dispensation as follows:

> If such evil be spoken in the presence of three persons, the matter is thereby considered public. Thus, if one of the three who heard it repeats it to others no sin of an evil tongue is found therein, provided that in re-telling it he had no intention to spread the rumor and advertise it still more. (*Hilkhot De'ot* 7:5, Glazer translation)

This means that the dispensation is limited to repeating gossip to audiences who may already be presumed to have heard it. However, if one intends to increase the size of the audience, it is prohibited. We noted that this basic understanding is accepted by the *Ḥafetz Ḥayim*.

Furthermore, several modern authorities develop the notion that even the Rambam might agree that information which is not only public but universally known might not carry this limitation.

It is worth noting that the very fact that the written word (and even more so, that which is published on the internet) lasts may mean that according to the Rambam it will rarely be permitted to spread something simply because it has been published already.

R. Menasheh Klein (*Responsa Mishneh Halakhot* 9:353), for example, states that it is obvious that *lashon hara* applies to writing (see *Ḥafetz Ḥayim, Hilkhot Lashon HaRa* 1:8), but even more so, written gossip may be worse because it lasts longer. Thus, as the Rambam notes, the intent to spread information further negates the dispensation of "in front of three," so writing gossip would be permitted in far fewer circumstances, as the intent in writing is often to ensure that the gossip will have staying power beyond what it would have had were it only said publicly.

In *Responsa BeMareh HaBazak* (6:96) the authors invoke this argument for digital media as well. While the authors are willing to argue that even such information may be shared if it is not only "in front of three" but universally known, one could argue, as we saw some authorities do, that when it comes to digital media, the staying power of the internet may (as it were) make things which are universally known even more universally known, by keeping them in people's minds after they might have forgotten it. Still, as the authors of the above responsum note, it may be that such considerations are irrelevant and information that is known by all has no limitations at all upon it.[10]

A Psychological Aside: Cascades

While Rambam believes the issue at hand is merely spreading the information farther, it may be that the very act of spreading information increases its ability to convince people. This is more than a mere numeric issue of how many people have heard it. This is due to the power of informational cascades. Cass Sunstein sees this as a particularly pernicious power of rumors:

> Rumors frequently spread through informational cascades. The basic dynamic behind such cascades is simple: once a certain number of people appear to believe a rumor, others will believe it too, unless they have good reason to believe that it is false. Most rumors involve topics on which people lack direct or personal knowledge, and so most of us defer to the crowd. As more people defer, thus making the crowd grow, there is a real risk that large groups of people will believe rumors even though they are entirely false. Imagine a group of people who are deciding whether Senator Jones has done something scandalous. Each member of the group is announcing his view in sequence. Andrew is the first to speak; perhaps he is the propagator of the rumor. Andrew states that Senator Jones has indeed done something

10. It is worth noting that some have dissented from the view of the above *posekim*. R. Gil Student, for example, has argued that the dispensation of "in front of three" is only due to presumed consent, and it is limited to cases in which the sinner acts in public, which implicitly grants consent for his or her actions to be made known. As he writes:

> I suggest that the leniency of publicized information (*nisparsem ha-davar*) only applies to an act committed in front of others. By sinning in public, the actor is declaring that he does not care whether other people know of his infractions. He does not consider discussion of his actions insulting. He gives permission, thereby removing the prohibition of *lashon ha-ra*. However, when information about a private act is publicized, the prohibition still applies, albeit under the category of *apei telasa*.

See https://www.torahmusings.com/2012/04/lashon-ha-ra-and-political-campaigns/.

> scandalous. Barbara now knows Andrew's judgment. Exercising her own independent judgment on the basis of what she knows of the senator, she might agree with Andrew. If she has no knowledge at all about Senator Jones, she might also agree with Andrew; perhaps she accepts Andrew's claim that he knows what he is talking about. Or suppose that her independent judgment is that Senator Jones probably did not engage in the scandalous conduct. She still might believe the rumor. If she trusts Andrew no more and no less than she trusts herself, she might not know what to think or do; she might simply flip a coin. Now consider a third person, Carl. Suppose that both Andrew and Barbara suggest that they believe the rumor, but that Carl's own information, though far from conclusive, indicates that their belief is wrong. Even in that event, Carl might well ignore what he knows and follow Andrew and Barbara. It is likely, after all, that both Andrew and Barbara had reasons for reaching their conclusion, and unless Carl thinks that his own information is better than theirs, he may follow their lead. If he does, Carl is in a cascade.

This process can continue and contribute to the rapid spread of rumors.

Based on this, one could offer a modern psychological interpretation of why spreading information further is so terrible.

Rabbi Eliezer of Metz

The passage in Arakhin presents the discussion about *lishna bisha* as follows:

> The Gemara asks: **What is considered malicious speech?** In other words, how is malicious speech defined and what are the limits of the prohibition? **Rava said: For example, if one says: There is** always **fire at so-and-so's home,** indicating that they are always cooking food there. **Abaye said to** Rava: **What did** this person **do** wrong by saying that there is always fire in that home? His statement **is merely revealing** the true **facts,** and is not malicious speech. **Rather,** it is considered malicious speech if he **expressed** this **in a slanderous** manner. For example, **if he**

> **says: Where** else can one **find fire except at so-and-so's home,** because they are always cooking food there.
>
> **Rabba says: Any statement that is said in the presence of its master,** i.e., if the subject of the statement was there, **does not have** any prohibition **due to malicious speech.** Abaye **said to him: All the more so** it is proscribed speech, as it is both **impudence and malicious speech.** Rabba **said to** Abaye: **I hold in accordance with** the opinion of **Rabbi Yosei, as Rabbi Yosei says: In all my days I never said something and then turned around** to see if the person I was speaking about was standing behind me listening, as I would say it even to the person involved. He **says,** i.e., **Rabba bar Rav Huna** says: **Any matter that was said in the presence of three** people **does not have** the status **of malicious speech** if one subsequently repeats it. **What is the reason?** The reason is that **your friend has a friend, and your friend's friend has a friend.** (Arakhin 15b–16a)

This passage is quite enigmatic. Several questions immediately emerge:

1. Why would it ever be prohibited to talk about there being a fire in someone's house? Most Rishonim understood that to mean that the people in the house are always cooking, or perhaps that they are hospitable.
2. Even if this is *lashon hara,* why would this be the paradigmatic case of *lashon hara*?
3. Why is it not *lashon hara* if one would not be afraid to say it in front of the subject of the gossip?
4. Is there a connection between the position of Rabbi Yosei that one does not violate *lashon hara* if the speaker would be willing to say it in front of the subject and the exception of "in front of three"?

R. Eliezer of Metz (*Yere'im* 191) suggests the following resolution: *Lashon hara* is really a prohibition against being hypocritical or two-faced. By simply gossiping, one may violate other prohibitions, such as the general prohibition of *onaat devarim,* harming people through words. However, *lashon hara* is only gossip that one says while pretending to like someone and not wishing to hurt someone. Thus, if one is willing to say something to the subject's face, or is willing to say it publicly such that the information will surely get back to the subject, this is not *lashon hara.*

The *Shita Mekubetzet* (Arakhin 15b) offers another text of the Gemara which may support this view. His version does not read "in front of three," "*be'apei telata,*" but rather "*in front of the subject,*" "*be'apei mara.*"

According to the *Yere'im,* there is no reason to allow the spreading of information already said by someone else in front of three people. However, his position is relevant when we discuss the question of whether in cases in which it is permitted to spread gossip, one is allowed to do so anonymously. In fact, his position most accurately is a prohibition against anonymous sourcing or gossiping anonymously or pseudonymously.

Textually, the *Yere'im* diverges from the explanations that we have seen until now. Most commentaries understand that information said by the *subject* in front of three people, or perhaps by a *third party,* might be permitted. If the issue is the subject, that is because he or she clearly waives the expectation of privacy. If we are dealing with a third party, the principle at play is that information already public can be further spread. The *Yere'im* argues that saying lashon hara in front of three people is permitted.

Tosafot in Arakhin

Tosafot (Arakhin 16a, s.v. *kol milta*) accept the linguistic understanding of the *Yere'im,* according to which the issue at hand is that there are cases in which it is permitted to say *lashon hara* in front of three people. However, they maintain that the issue is gossip, not hypocrisy.

This seems to emerge from the first two questions that we raised above. Tosafot reject the notion that this case is the paradigm. Rather, they argue that unambiguously negative gossip is always prohibited, whether it is said in front of three or not. The issue at hand is an ambiguous statement. That there is a fire in someone's house could mean that a given family is hospitable and is always hosting, or something positive like that. On the other hand, it could indicate something negative, such as that the family is rich and gluttonous and is always cooking.

Tosafot argue that in such a case, the barometer of whether the intent is hurtful or complimentary/neutral is whether the speaker is willing to say it to the subject's face. If the speaker is, the statement must not be intended as gossip. Hence, if the speaker does not bother turning around to check if the subject is present, or if the speaker would say it publicly knowing the information would reach the subject, it is permitted to spread the statement further.[11]

Rabbenu Yona

Rabbenu Yona discusses this passage in two places (*Aliyot DeRabbenu Yona,* Bava Batra 39b, s.v. *kol; Shaarei Teshuva* 3:228). Like Tosafot, he assumes that the content of the information being spread is not gossip per se. However, unlike Tosafot, he does not think we are dealing with ambiguous gossip. Rather, in this case, there is negative data which is being shared for a constructive purpose, and therefore it is permitted to do so. (When and why a constructive purpose permits gossip will be discussed below.)

He derives this from the passage in Bava Batra, where a landowner is issuing a challenge to the rights of a resident to prevent the latter from gaining squatters' rights. The need for publicity is to prevent the *appearance of ill intent.* When the landowner issues his challenge in front of three people, he makes it clear that he wants what he says to reach the ears of the subject. This makes it clear that his intent is constructive and permitted. However, were he to issue the challenge in front of one or two people, while he may still have constructive intent, rendering what he says permitted, the secret manner in which he acts *makes it seem as if he is merely gossiping.*

In a second argument, reminiscent of the view of the *Yere'im,* Rabbenu Yona argues that if one does not speak in a public manner, it *seems as if he or she is trying to hypocritically ingratiate himself or herself with the subject.* While the *Yere'im* writes that the prohibition of *lashon hara* is to be two-faced, Rabbenu Yona argues that it is the appearance of hypocrisy that is the issue in this case, though the prohibition remains that of gossip per se. However, since for Rabbenu Yona the issue is merely

11. The *Ḥatam Sofer* (*Ḥiddushei Ḥatam Sofer,* Bava Batra 39b, s.v. *kol*) argues that Tosafot's position may hang on the order of the statements in the Talmud, of which there are different versions.

one of perception, he permits speaking negatively about someone in private, when the intent is constructive, if the speaker has a legitimate reason to be afraid of the subject.

Rabbenu Yona offers yet another argument. When one is sharing necessary information, secrecy makes the publicizing less effective. What is critical in order for listeners to take the information seriously is that they trust the source. Were the speaker to be anonymous, listeners would be less likely to believe the information and take the necessary actions, thus negating the justification for sharing the information in the first place. The statement must be public, thus putting the speaker's reputation on the line and granting authority to what the speaker says. Even if the listeners don't immediately believe the speaker, they will hopefully at least take the warning seriously enough to investigate it.

Finally, Rabbenu Yona raises the possibility that the *lashon hara* under discussion should not be classified as spreading gossip but rather as breaching confidentiality, in which case the very fact that the information is public may permit spreading it further, whether or not one's intent is constructive, a position we have developed previously.

The *Sefat Emet* (Arakhin 15b, s.v. *kol milta*) takes a similar position as to the meaning of Rabbi Yosei's statement. If something is said in front of the subject, it is probably intended as rebuke, which is a biblical commandment. However, if the speaker is unwilling to say it to the subject, it is likely false (or, one might suggest, pointless gossip, even if true), and thus prohibited.

Tosafot in Bava Batra

Tosafot in Bava Batra (39b, s.v. *kol*) simply say that it is permitted to say *lishna bisha* in front of three people. The *Ḥafetz Ḥayim* (*Hilkhot Lashon HaRa* 2:1:1) notes that some people understand this passage as offering a carte blanche; it is only prohibited to gossip in private. R. Elchanan Wasserman (*Kovetz Shiurim,* Bava Batra 166–167) seems to take this as the simplest understanding of the view of Tosafot. Thus, he throws up his hands and references the *Ḥafetz Ḥayim* for the rejection of this position. The *Ḥafetz Ḥayim* strongly rejects this possibility, noting that it makes no sense. If the Torah doesn't want us to hurt people through words, then publicly shaming someone is surely worse, rather than better. He proves this from the general prohibition against causing pain through words, *onaat devarim,* as well as the uniquely harsh statements found in the Gemara about those who embarrass others publicly. Furthermore, the Gemara (Arakhin 16a) specifically notes that the *me'il,* the robe of the high priest, secures atonement for *lashon hara* said in public, thus implying that such action is indeed prohibited.

It could be, therefore, that Tosafot in Bava Batra mean the same thing as Tosafot in Arakhin, or perhaps they accept positions such as that of Rabbenu Yona or the *Yere'im*. However one understands it, it is indeed difficult to accept that they would simply permit publicly gossiping.

Rashbam

The Rashbam (Bava Batra 39b), at least as interpreted by the *Ḥafetz Ḥayim* (*Hilkhot Lashon HaRa* 2:1:1), understands that the dispensation offered in this gemara is for what the Rambam understands as *rekhilut*: namely, if A speaks about B publicly, then C may inform B of this. While this is normally *rekhilut,* when A knows that it might get back to B, it is permitted. *Rekhilut,* as understood here, is somewhere between a breach of confidence and gossip. Thus, the Rashbam seems to be assuming that if the speaker does not care whether the fact that he or she has gossiped is kept private, the listener may share the information, even though it may harm the relationship between A and B. Rabbenu Yona briefly alludes to this possibility at the end of his comments in Bava Batra.

Gossip vs. Confidentiality

What emerges from these positions, especially those of Tosafot in Arakhin and Rabbenu Yona, is that while *posekim* are relatively ready to accept that there may be no prohibition against sharing information that is already public, they are more reluctant to permit actual gossip. The Rashbam, though talking about *rekhilut* which is in between, seems to support this general tendency as well. This may be due to their conviction that even if the damage is done, there is an ethical problem with badmouthing others.

Alternatively, as we noted based on R. Feldman's position, facts may often be untrue in the sense that the effect they have on the listeners is beyond what is deserved. Perhaps these Rishonim understand that the more people hear a specific piece of gossip, the more it will affect their opinion of the subject. Reinforcing what is likely a one-sided perspective of the subject can actually cause more harm, making it harder for the listeners to form positive or unbiased opinions of the subject's later actions.

Finally, as suggested by the *Ḥafetz Ḥayim,* they may see *lashon hara* from the perspective of other verbal prohibitions such as *onaat devarim.* Even when a subject knows that gossip about him or her is swirling around, it may still hurt every time it is repeated.

These Rishonim are willing to accept that whether someone is willing to say something in public may shed light on whether information that is ambiguous in its intent is positive or negative.

Rambam, as we have already seen, is never willing to allow further publicizing of harmful information, though he does permit sharing information within circles that have likely already heard it. Perhaps he understands the primary problem of *lashon hara* as being the damage to the subject, without accepting our suggestions for Tosafot and Rabbenu Yona above.

The *Ḥafetz Ḥayim* (*Hilkhot Lashon HaRa,* ch. 2) combines many of these sentiments to issue a very strict ruling. First, as mentioned above, he notes that forbidden *lashon hara* said in public is surely worse than that said in private (2:1). For the most part, he accepts the stringent view of Tosafot and Rabbenu Yona, limiting the dispensation to cases where the information is not clearly negative, and the very act of saying it publicly indicates that the speaker has positive intent.

Then, he accepts the added limitation of the Rambam, namely that even in cases when information might be public, it can never be permitted to intentionally spread it further (2:3), though as we noted, his position is less clear regarding information that is universally known (2:4). He further notes that even these dispensations might apply only when the three people who hear the information are not righteous, but if they are (or are otherwise motivated to not share the gossip, perhaps because they are friends or relatives of the subject), the information cannot be presumed to be known, and thus it cannot be spread according to anyone (2:5). The three people must also hear the gossip at the same time (2:8). He also suggests that even when gossip is public in a given place, no assumption can be made about other cities. There, one must assume the information is not known, unless one finds out otherwise (2:6).

Furthermore, he notes that even in cases in which it is permitted to share *lashon hara,* this does not necessarily imply that the listeners may believe the information. They must do their due diligence and investigate what is being said (2:4).

He further says that if a speaker specifically forbids anyone from sharing what was said, the prohibition against breaching confidentiality would prevent one from sharing information, even if it is already known (2:7–8).

Even if all these conditions are met, the *Ḥafetz Ḥayim* notes that this at most would allow one to share the information exactly as it was stated. However, to add or spin the information would be a qualitative addition, and that would be prohibited (2:9). Furthermore, if the speaker knows the listener will spin it or exaggerate it, the speaker must not share it (2:10).

He notes that these principles are particularly important when dealing with communal institutions sharing private information that is neutral or negative (2:11).

However, when it comes to confidentiality, the *Ḥafetz Ḥayim* accepts the more lenient positions, arguing that at least when a subject has shared secrets publicly, further sharing of that information is permitted (2:13).

Applications

As we have seen, while *posekim* are relatively more lenient about sharing information that is already known as long as the only issue at hand is privacy, they are more reluctant when it comes to gossip. In the age of social media, the reasons are obvious. Even if information has already spread, every new share on Facebook opens up a new circle of friends to the information (prohibited according to the Rambam). Even if it does not, sharing may hurt the subject in unimaginable ways each time a new person affirms knowing or caring enough to share the information (*lashon hara* and *onaat devarim* for Tosafot and *Ḥafetz Ḥayim*). Even when things are universally known, the more something is put online, the harder it is to erase it from the Web, the more likely it is to appear on Google searches, etc. Thus, according to *posekim* such as R. Avraham Shapira and R. Dov Lior, the act of emphasizing this information may be problematic even if we assume that it is almost always permissible to pass on universally known information. While earlier *posekim* raise these issues, the problems are incalculably more severe in our world of social media. Thus, care should be taken to not misuse this tool, which too easily becomes a weapon.

Furthermore, as we have discussed, even in cases when there are technical dispensations available, the overriding principle of *ve'ahavta lere'akha kamokha* should enjoin us to be careful about how we treat the reputations of others.

For those who are not convinced about the damage that can be done and how long it can last, a particularly chilling article by Helen Andrews records several anecdotes that illustrate how the digital age has magnified the problems we have discussed, and we will return to them in our discussions about shaming.[12] However, we must first explore cases in which the sharing of such information is permitted. It is this that we turn to in our next section.

12. Available at: https://www.firstthings.com/article/2019/01/shame-storm. See also David French's reaction to this article: https://www.nationalreview.com/2018/12/kyler-murray-helen-andrews-shame-mob-america-intolerance/amp/?__twitter_impression=true&fbclid=IwAR2CuoqEHfGs5xXuv3GR8JEe9-yCsFNz1bofgFEqdKMvOw8_NIALG3mHQdg.

Chapter 22

When It Is Permitted to Share *Lashon HaRa* or Secrets

As we have noted, sharing confidential information or spreading potentially harmful information may be permitted on the grounds that it is already public. One perspective we explored was that these prohibitions are intended to prevent damage to the subjects. Once the information in question has become public, perhaps universally so, no further damage can be done, thus permitting its further proliferation. However, there are cases in which there is a need to share information even when it *will damage the subject.* Specifically, revealing information about a subject in cases in which withholding the said information will damage *other people* may be allowed even though it entails hurting the original subject. The assumption in halakha is that there are cases in which it is nevertheless permitted to share such information. What is the nature of this dispensation and what are its parameters?

The Given: It Is Permitted

The fact that there are circumstances in which one is allowed to share secrets or what would be gossip in order to protect people is a given in halakhic discourse. The *Ḥafetz Ḥayim* (*Hilkhot Lashon HaRa,* ch. 10; *Hilkhot Rekhilut,* ch. 9) mentions several of the proofs (see the footnotes throughout the chapters). For example, the laws of giving testimony prove that there are at least some cases in which it is permitted to share negative information. After all, it is a mitzva for witnesses to an attempted crime to warn the potential criminal, and if the criminal fails to heed their warning, to later testify about the crime. If their testimony is accepted by the court, the criminal can potentially be subjected to punishment. Were it not for the category of *eidut,* legally admissible testimony, that same information would be forbidden gossip. This is clear from the following passage in the Talmud:

> **The Holy One, Blessed be He, hates three** people: **One who says one** statement **with his mouth and** means **another in his heart,** i.e., a hypocrite; **one who knows testimony about another** person **and does not testify on his behalf; and one who observes a licentious matter** performed **by another** person **and testifies against him alone.** His testimony is meaningless, as he is the only witness; consequently, he merely gives the individual a bad reputation.
>
> The Gemara comments: This is **like** that incident **where Tuveya sinned** with immorality, **and Zigud came alone to testify about him before Rav Pappa.** Rav Pappa instructed that **Zigud be lashed.** Zigud **said to him: Tuveya sinned and Zigud is lashed,** an objection that became a popular saying. **He said to him: Yes, as it is written: "One witness shall not rise up against a man"** (Deut. 19:15), **and you testified against him alone. You have merely given him a bad reputation.** (Pesaḥim 113b)

In this passage, Zigud is lashed for attempting to offer testimony when it could not be accepted, as Torah law requires at least two witnesses. As he testifies alone, what he says is not admissible. Rav Pappa feels that without Zigud's statement counting as testimony, it is mere gossip, as he is relating something criminal, and therefore negative, about Tuveya. The implication, however, is that despite the fact that the content of testimony may be identical to that of forbidden gossip, the context can make it permitted or even obligatory.

Secondly, as we have explored above, a central passage about the parameters of the laws of *lashon hara* is from the Talmud's discussion about *meḥaa* (Bava Batra 39a–b), a protest issued to prevent an illegal squatter from gaining squatters' rights. As many Rishonim note, were it not for the fact that the owner has a legitimate reason to issue a complaint and challenge, it would have been forbidden to make such allegations against the current resident of the property. However, the Talmud takes it as a given that the owner has the right to defend himself or herself from being cheated out of his or her own property, even if it entails accusing the squatter of wrongdoing. Despite the fact that similar statements in other contexts might be deemed *lashon hara,* in this case it is permitted.

This is true not only here, but in all cases in which a plaintiff takes a defendant to court. By making claims against the defendant, the plaintiff is often accusing the defendant of a crime, or perhaps negligence, something which reflects negatively on the defendant. Nevertheless, to stand up for one's rights is obviously permitted.

Additionally, there are many instances throughout the Talmud in which it is simply assumed that negative information has been shared. For example, the Talmud states the following about a scholar who was dogged by rumors of impropriety:

> **There was a certain Torah scholar who gained a bad reputation** due to rumors about his conduct. **Rav Yehuda said: What should be done? To excommunicate him** is not an option. **The Sages need him,** as he is a great Torah authority. **Not to excommunicate him** is also not an option, as then **the name of Heaven would be desecrated.**
>
> Rav Yehuda **said to Rabba bar bar Ḥana:** Have **you heard anything with regard to this** issue? **He said to him: Rabbi Yoḥanan said as follows: What is** the meaning of that **which is**

> **written: "For the priest's lips should keep knowledge, and they should seek Torah at his mouth; for he is a messenger** [*malakh*] **of the Lord of hosts"** (Mal. 2:7)? This verse teaches: **If the teacher is similar to an angel** [*malakh*] **of the Lord,** then **seek Torah from his mouth,** but if he is **not** pure and upright, then **do not seek Torah from his mouth;** even if he is knowledgeable about Torah, do not learn from him. Based on this statement, **Rav Yehuda ostracized** that Torah scholar. (Moed Katan 17a)

In the passage, the existence of rumors is a given. While one could argue that the Gemara is not condoning such rumors, but simply recording the proper reaction to them, this would seem odd. The Gemara seems to take these rumors as a legitimate source of information, to the extent that Rav Yehuda acts on this basis to excommunicate the subject. The fact that the Gemara gives credence to these persistent rumors is more easily understood if it is legitimate to spread them to begin with.

It Is Permitted to Listen to Such Information

In two anecdotes, the Gemara entitles and obligates people to listen and take precautions in light of what should ostensibly be defined as *lashon hara.* The first part of the passage is framed around the story of the leader of the Jews after the destruction of the First Temple.[1] The Babylonians appoint a governor, Gedalya ben Achikam. Gedalya is warned by some of his men that the rebels led by Yishmael ben Netanya are planning to assassinate him. Gedalya disregards the warnings and is indeed assassinated and his men killed. Commenting on this passage, the Talmud states as follows:

> It is **taught: That** pit that they found is **the pit that Ishmael, son of Nethaniah, filled with corpses, as it is written: "Now the pit where Ishmael cast all the dead bodies of the men whom he had slain by the side of Gedaliah** was that which Asa the king had made for fear of Baasa king of Israel; the same Ishmael, son of Nethaniah, filled with them that were slain" (Jer. 41:9).

1. See Jeremiah, chs. 40–41.

> The Gemara analyzes that verse: **And did Gedaliah kill them? But didn't Ishmael kill them?** Gedaliah was one of those killed by Ishmael and his men (see Jer. 41:2). The Gemara answers: **Rather, since** Gedaliah **should have been concerned** and cautious based **on the advice of Johanan, son of Kareah,** who warned him that Ishmael was conspiring to kill him and even offered to go and kill Ishmael in a preemptive strike (see Jer. 40:13–16), **but** Gedaliah **was not concerned** and he refused to listen to Johanan's advice, saying that he did not want to listen to malicious speech, **the verse ascribes him** blame **as though he** himself **killed them.** (Nidda 61b)

The Talmud chastises Gedalya for failing to at least take precautions, even if he was correct in not blindly accepting the reports.

The Talmud presents a second story to the same effect.

> In relation to the above comment that Gedaliah was killed after not heeding the warning of Johanan, the Gemara clarifies what is permitted when receiving such a warning. **Rava said:** With regard to **this** prohibition against listening to **malicious speech, even though one should not accept** the malicious speech as true, **one is** nevertheless **required to be concerned** about the harm that might result from ignoring it.
>
> The Gemara cites examples of people who were concerned about malicious speech. There were **these people of the Galilee about whom a rumor emerged that they had killed someone. They came before Rabbi Tarfon** and **said to him: Will the Master hide us?** Rabbi Tarfon **said to them: What should we do? If I do not hide you,** your pursuers **will see you** and kill you. If **I do hide you,** this too is problematic, as **didn't the Rabbis say:** With regard to **this** prohibition against listening to **malicious speech, even though one should not accept** the malicious speech as true, **one is required to be concerned** about the harm that might result from ignoring it? Therefore, **you** must **go** and **hide yourselves.** (Nidda 61b)

What emerges from the above is that there must be limits to the prohibition against *lashon hara,* however it is understood. The question we now turn to is why these limits exist, what their parameters are, and what justifies them.

It seems that there are two central models.[2] While these two models may often overlap in their practical applications, there seem to be potential differences between them. Furthermore, the very act of framing shapes the directions *posekim* take when they make halakhic decisions.

The "Permitted Gossip" Model

The *Ḥafetz Ḥayim* devotes two chapters to outlining when it is permitted to share such information. His approach is best characterized as the "permitted gossip" model. He refers to cases where is it permitted to spread negative information as *lashon hara leto'elet,* beneficial evil speech. It may be permitted, but it is still framed as gossip. It is fundamentally a *dispensation to engage in forbidden activity*. This framing seems to lead to the strict parameters he establishes to qualify *lashon hara* as *leto'elet.* In general, the *Ḥafetz Ḥayim* is very demanding about the conditions that must be met.

I would propose that this is driven by his framing. By referring to these cases as *lashon hara,* albeit of a permitted variety, he assumes that the given is that such information should be forbidden. Thus, he needs to justify it, to carve out space within a broader forbidden category. The tendency of such an approach is to err on the side of "caution," to avoid saying anything which may fail to fulfill all the necessary conditions to permit the *lashon hara.*

For the moment, I will assume that whatever the *Ḥafetz Ḥayim* writes about gossip (his understanding of *lashon hara*) would be true for breaching confidentiality, though there are some who dispute that. R. Elchanan Wasserman (*Kovetz He'arot* 70) argues that this permission for *to'elet* holds true for all interpersonal prohibitions, further making it logical to extend it to the prohibition against sharing secrets.

2. R. Daniel Feldman notes these two models in his book, *False Facts and True Rumors: Lashon Hara in Contemporary Culture* (YU Press/Maggid, 2015). We will take a different approach.

The Mitzva Approach

However, many other halakhic authorities seem to frame the issue differently. They assume that any time one is required to speak *lashon hara* to protect someone, it is an obligation deriving from "*Lo taamod al dam re'ekha*," the prohibition to stand idly by when one's fellow's blood is being spilled. They present the two options not as forbidden *lashon hara* or an exception, but as *lashon hara* or an obligation. This framing prevents there being a safe option. If one chooses to speak, this may be a violation of *lashon hara*. If one chooses not to speak, this may be a dereliction of responsibility toward a potential victim. This approach, I believe, leads *posekim* to be more likely to rule that one should share negative information when potential harm can be averted. As noted above, in many if not most cases, this approach may generate the same conclusion as that of the *Ḥafetz Ḥayim*. However, as we will see, this is not always the case.

The source most often quoted by *posekim* who seems to endorse this framing is *Pitḥei Teshuva* of R. Yisrael Isserlein.[3] He writes as follows:

> I have seen [it fitting] to address what all the ethical writings have made so much noise about in the world, about the sin of *lashon hara*. I will make noise in the world about the opposite – a much greater and more common sin. Specifically, [I am referring to] holding back from speaking when it is needed to save the oppressed from his oppressor.
>
> By way of parable: One who sees a highwayman about to ambush his friend in the desert to kill him, or one who sees an intruder breaking into his friend's house or store at night, is it possible that the observer would refrain from letting his friend know to be careful because [he was worried about violating the prohibition of] *lashon hara*?! His sin would be too great to bear, for he violates "*Lo taamod al dam re'ekha*"! The same is true about money, which is included in the obligation of returning lost objects....

3. This is not to be confused with the commentary by the same name that appears in the other sections of *Shulḥan Arukh*, written by R. Avraham Eisenstadt.

> As long as all of his intention is not to harm the subject but for the benefit of his friend, for the betterment of the group and to protect them, then he fulfills through this a great deed which is invaluable! (*Pitḥei Teshuva, OḤ* 156)

This perspective is endorsed by many, such as the *Sefer Ḥaredim* (24), R. Eliezer Waldenberg (*Responsa Tzitz Eliezer* 15:3 and 16:4), R. Ovadia Yosef (*Responsa Yeḥaveh Daat* 4:60), and others. While many of these *posekim* do assume that this perspective is identical to that of the *Ḥafetz Ḥayim,* I believe that there are significant differences between the positions, in addition to the subtler differences that emerge simply by dint of the framing.

Indeed, this framing seems to emerge from the *pasuk* itself. The verse (Lev. 19:16) which prohibits *lashon hara* is the same one that sets out the prohibition of standing idly by when one sees another in danger. Many commentaries (*Haamek Davar, Or HaḤayim,* and others) suggest that the juxtaposition is meant to ensure that people don't refrain from helping others in danger out of a concern that they may violate *rekhilut.* Rather, in the same breath as it prohibits gossip, the Torah makes it clear that not everything that is negative is *lashon hara.* The *Or HaḤayim* even notes that it is this implication that is lost on Gedalya, whom, as noted above, the Talmud holds responsible for the death of his men for his refusal to consider seriously critical "gossip."

The Definitional Approach

In many ways, an even more radical version of this is presented by R. Asher Weiss (*Minḥat Asher* 41:3). He argues that by definition, the prohibition is to gossip for the purpose of harming. Thus, if one is relaying negative information for a positive purpose, it is permitted by definition.

An alternative thesis which may overlap, though not for reasons of virtue, is presented by R. Elchanan Wasserman (*Kovetz He'arot* 70) for all interpersonal commandments. He argues that the Torah does not forbid hitting others, for example, but rather attacking them. For our purposes, the latter two formulations are similar in that they do not view this as *lashon hara* at all.

Presumably this approach can work in tandem with the mitzva approach, arguing that it is not *lashon hara* by definition, and when necessary, it is obligatory to share the information which will protect others. Thus, we will combine these two approaches in our analysis.

The Application for Breaching Confidentiality

The latter framing, at the very least, should carry over to the prohibition against breaching confidentiality, especially as many *posekim* derive both prohibitions from the same verse, which as we noted, may be the source for this concept. This is indeed the majority position expressed by most *posekim*. As we noted above, this position is explicitly taken by the Rashba (*Responsa Rashba* 1:557) in his discussion of the *ḥerem* against reading others' mail.

> Rabbenu Gershom did not make his decrees so that people might violate biblical or rabbinic halakha because of them. Just the opposite, they were instituted only to ensure compliance with our Torah and to ensure that Jewish people act in a correct and modest manner.

While we noted that not all *posekim* accept this in all cases, when it comes to actual danger, this seems to be the consensus view of virtually all *posekim*.

R. Dovid Lichtenstein summarizes some of these positions, and then outlines the way in which modern communication technology has introduced new applications for this principle:

> Accordingly, R. Moshe Sternbuch (*Teshuvos Ve'hanhagos,* 1:869) ruled that if a doctor determined that his patient is physically unfit to drive – such as in the case of an ophthalmologist who diagnoses his patient with a visual impairment that compromises his ability to drive safely – he can and must inform the relevant government authorities. Although medical information is confidential, the doctor must break his trust of confidentiality for the sake of public safety. R. Ovadia Yosef (*Yechaveh Da'as,* 4:60) issued a similar ruling concerning a

patient with epilepsy. If the doctor determines that this condition makes it unsafe for the patient to drive, he must notify the authorities.

Another fascinating – albeit tragic – modern-day application of this ruling is the controversy that arose in the wake of the devastating shooting attack at the Inland Regional Center in San Bernardino, California in December, 2015. The perpetrators – Syed Farook and Tashfeen Malik –were found and killed by police in a shootout that same day, and two months later, on February 9th, the FBI announced that it had recovered Syed's iPhone, but was unable to unlock the device in order to find clues of the shooter's possible accomplices and other important contacts. This information, the FBI claimed, was vital to the Bureau's ongoing investigation into the terrorists' motives and modes of operation. The FBI asked that Apple disable the phone's security system to enable them to access Mr. Farook's information, but the company refused, arguing that it needed to strictly uphold its commitments not to compromise its customers' security. The FBI then appealed to a federal judge, and a court order was issued ordering Apple to comply with the FBI's demands by February 26th. The brief legal battle came to an anticlimactic end on March 28th, when the Department of Justice announced that it succeeded in unlocking the device.

It stands to reason that given the international threat of Islamic terrorism, and the vital importance of intelligence information in identifying and capturing potential attackers and their accomplices, accessing the information on a terrorist's device would certainly appear to fall under the category of public safety, which, as noted, overrides the prohibition against invading privacy.[4]

4. Available at: https://www.yutorah.org/lectures/lecture.cfm/906213/mr-dovid-lichtenstein/facebook-cambridge-analytica-and-the-right-to-privacy-a-halachic-overview/.

Whether one agrees with these precise conclusions, the potential relevance of the values addressed by halakha should be clear.

Similar dynamics would permit sharing with the authorities inflammatory remarks which either explicitly or implicitly threaten violence, or telling parents or school authorities that a child seems to be suffering from depression or to be involved in illegal or self-destructive activity. However, most of these applications seem to belong to the more classic definition of *lashon hara*. Benign information would probably not be permitted based on this leniency, as by definition, it is benign. At the margins, perhaps we could find some cases that are necessary to share for dating or employment that are not negative, just relevant.

At any rate, what is clear is that most *posekim* assume that when actual danger is involved, it is obvious that information must be shared due to "*Lo taamod.*" However, cases which do not rise to that level are a bit trickier, though as we have seen, *lo taamod* may expand beyond cases of danger. For this reason, we must return to the detailed conditions presented by the *Ḥafetz Ḥayim* which must be met to permit *lashon hara leto'elet.*

To summarize, there are two models for understanding when it is permitted to share negative information. One is to conceive of a category of *lashon hara leto'elet,* beneficial gossip. The implication of this framing is that the prohibition is in effect, just suspended. Thus, there are many qualifications that must be met to justify this suspension. The other is to recognize that there are countervalues that override the concern of *lashon hara* and actually transform what could have been forbidden gossip into a positive fulfillment of the commandment to protect others.

The former approach, adopted by the *Ḥafetz Ḥayim,* not surprisingly will require high standards to permit sharing information, and he indeed outlines such demands, to which we now turn.

The Seven Conditions of the *Ḥafetz Ḥayim*

The *Ḥafetz Ḥayim* outlines seven conditions that must be met to define negative information as *lashon hara leto'elet* and thereby make its transmission permitted/obligatory.

1. The speaker of the information must have first-hand knowledge of the event being discussed. This entails either seeing it oneself, or, if the speaker originally heard it from a third party, the speaker must verify the authenticity of the information before further sharing it.
2. The speaker must reflect on the "crime" under discussion to determine that it is actually a violation of halakha.
3. Before resorting to *lashon hara,* the speaker should attempt to solve the problem by privately rebuking the sinner. If the sinner can be convinced to repent, the speaker will not have to resort to gossip. It is only if this approach does not work that the speaker may use the strategy of publicizing the information.
4. The speaker can only relate the information accurately, without exaggeration or any other distortion.
5. The speaker must have pure intentions, namely sharing the information to protect the potential victims, not to enjoy harming the subject of the *lashon hara.*
6. Related to condition number 3, the speaker should only solve the problem using *lashon hara* if there is no other way to accomplish the goal. If, however, the goal can be achieved by using another method, that method should be used. (I am unsure as to whether all other methods would be preferable to *lashon hara.* Presumably, the *Ḥafetz Ḥayim* intends to limit this rule to cases in which the alternative would be preferable to *lashon hara.*)
7. The *lashon hara* should not cause damage to the subject which would be unwarranted based on Jewish law. If the consequences would be greater than those dictated by halakha, the *lashon hara leto'elet* should not be shared.

What is clear from this perspective is the following:

1. The *Ḥafetz Ḥayim* views *lashon hara leto'elet* as fundamentally forbidden with a dispensation. Hence, the requirements to carve out this allowance are quite demanding.
2. The *Ḥafetz Ḥayim* seems wary of the notion that sharing negative information can be a positive thing. While he admits that this

> situation is tenable, his tendency is to avoid sharing negative information as much as possible.

The Countervalue Perspective

As we have noted, there are *posekim* who frame this category differently, namely by holding that sometimes there is a mitzva, not just begrudging permission, to share negative information. Let us recall the conclusion of the *Pitḥei Teshuva* (*OḤ* 156):

> As long as all of his intention is not to harm him but for the benefit of the second person and the betterment of the group and to protect them, then he fulfills through this a great deed which is invaluable!

A similar perspective may emerge from the following passage in the Talmud:

> One exposes the hypocrites due to the desecration of [God's] name, as it is stated: "When a righteous man turns from his righteousness and commits iniquity, I will lay a stumbling block before him" (Ezek. 3:20). (Yoma 86b)

In this passage, the Gemara seems to capture a sentiment articulated by US Supreme Court Justice Louis Brandeis in a celebrated statement:

> Publicity is justly commended as a remedy for social and industrial diseases. Sunlight is said to be the best of disinfectants; electric light the most efficient policeman.[5]

While the *Ḥafetz Ḥayim* does not explicitly reject this, one would find it hard to imagine that the *Ḥafetz Ḥayim* would articulate the positive

5. Louis D. Brandeis, *Other People's Money and How the Bankers Use It* (New York: Frederick A. Stokes Company, 1914), 92. Originally published in *Harper's Weekly*. Also available at: https://louisville.edu/law/library/special-collections/the-louis-d.-brandeis-collection/other-peoples-money-by-louis-d.-brandeis.

value of spreading negative information, though the passage from Yoma could indeed be construed as a celebration of the power of transparency. The *Ḥafetz Ḥayim,* however, subsumes it under the category of *to'elet.* Benjamin Brown summarizes it thusly:

> With regard to permission given to publicly disclose hypocrites, the Hafetz Hayim stipulates that the permit is only given to prevent damage. Therefore, it cannot be done if the damage has already occurred. Thus, for example, a person is allowed to warn his friend against entering a business relationship with a particular person under the following conditions: "They only said (Yoma 86b) that it is a commandment to publicly disclose the hypocrites in order to warn another person not to get involved with him a priori so as not to suffer loss, or even if he is already involved with him, and he knows the nature of the person that he is telling about, only so he will consider his words and protect himself, but not to cause him actual damage." Similarly, the Hafetz Hayim stipulates that the permit applies only to a hypocrite who is known to habitually cheat, but not to one who might have done so only once.[6]

Thus, the *Ḥafetz Ḥayim* sees this as simply another instance of *to'elet.*

Others, however, see this as a more expansive statement. For example, the anonymous work of *musar* (Jewish ethics) entitled *Orḥot Tzaddikim* (2) explains this line as follows:

> Therefore, those who are modest in their dress and speak gently and conduct themselves as pious and just in order that others should believe them and depend upon their works, and flatter those who should not be flattered, and make secret schemes and do not worry about fulfilling the commandments except when they are in the public eye and not when they are alone, and thus deceive the people – these are profaners of God,

6. Benjamin Brown, "From Principles to Rules and from Musar to Halakhah: The Hafetz Hayim's Rulings on Libel and Gossip," *Dinei Yisrael* 25 (2008).

> Blessed be He, more than all others – for they cause people to disbelieve the good teachers and prophets, for these latter are then suspected by people who say, "Perhaps these men are like those who deceived us." When anyone recognizes a false and lying prophet, he should spread this abroad and let everyone know, as our Sages said: "We must publicly expose those who are flatterers" (Yoma 86b).[7]

Implications of the Two Perspectives

To illustrate the practical implications that emerge from these two perspectives, we will present a couple of examples:

1. Spreading information when one is unsure of the truth of the statement
The first condition of the *Ḥafetz Ḥayim* is that one must either have first-hand knowledge of the information or verify it. Thus, even if there is a potential victim who could be protected by sharing doubtful information, a straightforward application of the *Ḥafetz Ḥayim*'s rules would forbid sharing this information.

However, as several Aḥaronim have noted, this seems to be in tension with an explicit position of the Gemara. As noted above, one of the classic sources for the idea of *to'elet* is the Gemara (Nidda 61b) that holds Gedalya responsible for the death of his men due to not taking seriously enough the rumors that there was an assassination plot. The straightforward explanation of this passage is that to protect oneself, one is allowed to take unverified rumors seriously, a conclusion which the *Ḥafetz Ḥayim* accepts (*Hilkhot Lashon HaRa* 6:2, 10). The *Ḥafetz Ḥayim*'s rules would imply that one should not share similarly dubious information to protect others, due to the prohibition of *lashon hara;* but as the Gemara blames Gedalya for the death of his men, it would seem that it would be permitted to share such *lashon hara* even though its veracity is in doubt. The *Maadanei Yom Tov,* for example, concludes in accordance with this implication, explaining the logic as follows:

7. Translation from: https://www.sefaria.org.il/Yoma.86b.17?lang=bi&p2=Orchot_Tzadikim.2.42&lang2=bi&w2=all&lang3=en.

> Implicitly, it would seem that just as one must take precautions if damage might come to him, the same applies if damage might come to others, for why would it be different? Certainly, a person must be concerned for the damage to others just as he is concerned about damage to himself, and the great rule in the Torah is "Love your fellow as yourself!" (*Maadanei Yom Tov,* Rosh, Nidda 61b, n. 6)

One could have argued that an exception may be carved out for actual cases of *pikuaḥ nefesh,* protection of life, as that overrides all mitzvot in the Torah with the exception of the three cardinal sins: murder, idolatry, and forbidden sexual relationships (see, for example, Sanhedrin 74a–b and *YD* 157).

However, R. Shlomo Zalman Kook, father of the famed R. Avraham Yitzchak HaKohen Kook, criticizes the simple application of the *Ḥafetz Ḥayim*'s rules even in cases where the potential harm is only monetary.

> In my humble opinion, the opposite approach is the reasonable one. Since there is logic to explain why it should be permitted *a priori,* of course he is obligated to tell him, as this is included in the obligation of returning lost objects (*hashavat aveida*)![8]

In other words, he follows a *Pitḥei Teshuva*-like perspective, according to which we don't start with the assumption that all negative information is prohibited as *lashon hara.* Rather, we recognize that sometimes spreading information is the best way to fulfill a mitzva, and thus we must do so even if we cannot check all the boxes of the *Ḥafetz Ḥayim.*

While most modern Aḥaronim are not as explicit as R. Shlomo Kook or the *Maadanei Yom Tov,* many of their halakhic rulings tacitly accept this approach. For example, in a responsum by R. Moshe Sternbuch (*Responsa Teshuvot VeHanhagot* 1:869), when he is asked whether someone is permitted to remain silent if he knows of potential danger to others, he argues that it is forbidden to be silent and refrains

---

8. This passage is recorded in R. Avraham Kook's *Mitzvat Re'iya,* 104.

from even mentioning the prohibition of *lashon hara* as a consideration. While in other responsa, R. Sternbuch does quote the *Ḥafetz Ḥayim*'s rules, it may be that he uses the term *toelet* for simplicity – or he may generally agree that they are accurate guidelines, even he does not feel bound to their strict application.

The *Ḥafetz Ḥayim* does attempt to reinterpret this passage to negate the above challenge. He argues, for example, that while one may pass on information of this sort, the speaker must be sure that the listener will not accept the information, but will rather take precautions in light of it. As this is the minimal violation of *lashon hara* that is necessary, this is all that is permitted.[9] He also finds several creative ways to minimize the circumstances in which people are allowed to keep their ears open for this kind of information, allowing it only when the listener ensures that the speaker has proper intent.[10] When these conditions are not met, the *Ḥafetz Ḥayim* explains that he is willing to risk the safety of the potential victim rather than allow the violation of *lashon hara,* arguing that the alleged perpetrator's right to not be suspected outweighs those of the potential victim.[11]

To justify this claim, he adduces the argument used by the Talmud for why murder is one of the cardinal sins (Sanhedrin 74a). When faced with the choice of murdering or being murdered, the Talmud argues, "Who says your blood is redder than his?" Therefore, one has no right to take an innocent life to save one's own.

The *Ḥafetz Ḥayim* strikingly adopts this same line of reasoning here: Who says that the potential victim's safety is more important than the right of the potential aggressor not to be subject to *lashon hara* or perhaps even *hotzaat shem ra*? R. Shlomo Rosner, in his *Ali Be'er,* points

9. See the notes on 6:10, especially *Be'er Mayim Ḥayim* 30. See, however, the notes of *Ali Be'er* of R. Shlomo Rosner.
10. *Hilkhot Lashon HaRa* 6:2.
11. However, the *Ḥafetz Ḥayim* seems to have no exception to his principle. See also R. Meir Menachem Maggid in *Kol Torah* 55 (Tishrei 5664), 55–57, who analyzes and endorses this assumption of the *Ḥafetz Ḥayim,* showing that the *Ḥafetz Ḥayim* has an expansive understanding of what one is permitted to do when the potential harm may come to that individual, highlighting the novelty of his forbidding one to allow others to avail themselves of similar information.

out that this argument fails if the alleged damage to the potential victim far surpasses the possible damage caused by putting the alleged perpetrator under suspicion. As we have outlined above, this is an outgrowth of the *Ḥafetz Ḥayim*'s approach to this law, which is not fully accepted by other authorities.

It is possible to read the *Ḥafetz Ḥayim* in a more limited way. He may mean that in a case in which the potential response is as great as the potential harm, as one does not know that the suspected perpetrator actually intends on harming the possible victim, one cannot be party to encouraging a preemptive strike on the suspect. However, it seems to this author that while in this case many authorities might rule not to share the information (as one now has an obligation to protect the suspect from undeserved harm), the *Ḥafetz Ḥayim* is not limited to this case. This is because he specifically argues that one is protecting the suspect from potential damage *or embarrassment,* even in a case in which protecting the victim rises to the level of *lo taamod.* Furthermore, rather than frame this case as competing claims of *lo taamod,* the *Ḥafetz Ḥayim* writes that the issue is that this fails the *to'elet* test, returning us to the laws of *rekhilut* and *lashon hara.* This framing makes it clear that the issue is the primacy of the laws of *lashon hara,* even at the expense of *lo taamod.*

2. *Pure intentions*

A straightforward application of the *Ḥafetz Ḥayim*'s fifth rule, that one must only engage in *lashon hara leto'elet* for the proper reasons, would dictate that if someone is in danger, but the speaker of *lashon hara* holds a grudge against the potential aggressor and would enjoy saving the victim at the expense of the would-be criminal, it would be prohibited to share the information.

The *Ḥafetz Ḥayim* notes that whether this is true depends on a dispute among the *posekim* in a similar case. *Shulḥan Arukh, ḤM* 421:13, rules that one may use force to protect a victim who is being physically assaulted. *Sefer Me'irot Einayim* (ibid., 28) rules that the protector must be the type of person who would normally save others; the victim may not be saved out of a vendetta toward the attacker. *Taz* (ibid.) argues that this is irrelevant; the rescuer has a responsibility to protect the victim, regardless of whether his intentions are impure. The *Ḥafetz Ḥayim* (note on *Hilkhot Rekhilut* 9:10) rules in principle like *Sefer Me'irot Einayim,* but being unable to accept the implications, he rules that one must simply force oneself to act with pure intentions.

However, if one actually accepts this argument and takes it to its logical conclusion, this solution falls short, as in a case where the protector is unable to do so, he would seem to be required to stand by and watch the victim being brutalized.[12] It is worth mentioning that Jewish law affirms that people may be expected to control their emotions. *Sefer HaḤinnukh* (416), commenting on the prohibition to desire or covet, points out that this indicates that God expects people to be able to control their emotions. Still, this ideal is not always reached, and relying on people to change their natural inclinations may have dangerous consequences.

It is obvious that such an eventuality does not exist from the perspective of the *Pitḥei Teshuva.* If one frames his approach to *lashon hara* in these cases with the many obligations that demand, rather than merely allow, sharing information, there would be no need to defend why it is permitted and mandatory to protect the potential victim in the above case.

R. Asher Weiss (*Minḥat Asher* 41:3) also draws the above implications from the *Ḥafetz Ḥayim,* and rejects him accordingly, relying on the understanding that *lashon hara* is about bad character traits, and when one is intending to help (even with some other intentions mixed in), the information is not defined as *lashon hara.*

Expanding *To'elet*

Several modern rabbis have attempted to offer expanded understandings of *to'elet* to provide a space for allowing the flow of information for more long-term goals, such as providing the openness necessary for a healthy democratic society. R. Yuval Cherlow, for example, argues for such a model.[13] R. Azriel Ariel[14] tries to use the model of testimony to justify enlightening the public as to sins of public

12. See *Ali Be'er* on *Hilkhot Rekhilut* 9:3.
13. *Bein Ish VeIshto: Dinei Lashon HaRa, Techumin* 27.
14. Available here: http://www.yeshiva.org.il/midrash/shiur.asp?id=1200.

officials that would shed light on whether they are worthy of being in public office. While their arguments may have merit (though I have doubts concerning the arguments they make), they are unlikely to fit the model of *to'elet* as strictly presented by the *Ḥafetz Ḥayim*. Benjamin Brown notes:

> Even if each of these is a "benefit," they relate to long-term outcomes on the general societal level. In contrast, the considerations of the Hafetz Hayim were short-term concerns relating to the level of the individual (except for issues relating to the denunciation of heretics and evil people). Consider the fact that the Hafetz Hayim, in raising the possibility of permitting libel in the case of one who stole from or damaged another in the hope that it would pressure him to give back the stolen object or compensate the damage, rejects this possibility on the basis of his own reasoning, contending that this hope is "very distant,"[15] particularly in comparison to the more immediate damage that might be caused by the libel. If this "benefit" is considered "very distant" in his eyes, then how much more so would he find the "benefits" contained in the above rationales, which are less imminent and more general, to be distant.[16]

Implications

While in many (if not most) cases, the two models would be in agreement, there are differences. For an average question about whether or not one should gossip about his or her friend, I assume most *posekim* would take the principles of the *Ḥafetz Ḥayim* as good guidelines, if not strict halakha.

However, some of the more complicated cases which are unique to the age of social media may depend on the posture one takes to the above framings. For example, the kinds of goals that the #MeToo movement are trying to accomplish probably do not fall within the parameters of *to'elet* as understood by the *Ḥafetz Ḥayim*. Furthermore, the nature of the movement is that it often shares information (even if

15. *Raḥok* in this context probably means "unlikely," rather than "distant." This would at least somewhat undermine Brown's claim.
16. See Brown above.

not about specific people) without verifying it, often when no attempt has been made to accomplish the same goals through other methods, such as approaching the accused perpetrators and trying to get them to repent. This notion sounds absurd and anathema to the ethos of the movement.

Even within the more expansive model, one must weigh the concerns of the *Ḥafetz Ḥayim* to avoid false accusations or unwarranted damage. However, within this model, there is at least more room to talk about the greater communal benefits that are being sought. I am not qualified to weigh in on these, but it is clear that the above framing question will be critical to shaping a halakhic perspective on the issue.

An issue that has recently been hotly debated among the *posekim*, which we will turn to below, is the question of social-media shaming as a way of dealing with recalcitrant husbands who refuse to grant *gittin* (bills of divorce) to their wives, leaving the latter as modern-day *agunot* (chained women).[17] The way the *posekim* have approached this issue, especially in light of a recent ruling by an Israeli rabbinical court encouraging this method as a legitimate means to force a husband to follow his duty, sheds light on the way the *posekim* are thinking about these questions in the digital age.

There is much more to discuss about *to'elet,* but for now we have sufficed with the general principles to highlight the questions they raise when social media is brought into the mix.

---

17. While the term *aguna* originally referred to a woman whose husband was missing, often in modern times it refers to a woman whose husband refuses to grant her a divorce (*me'ukevet get*). As in halakha, a husband must give a *get* to his wife of his own free will, its withholding can be used as a weapon – out of spite, as a last-ditch attempt to keep the marriage from ending, or as a bargaining chip in divorce settlements or child custody. One of the tools that has been used to encourage a recalcitrant husband (*sarvan get*) to grant a *get,* once a *beit din* (Jewish court) has determined that he is obligated to do so, is shaming. Social media has been added to the toolbox of methods that can be used to shame the husband, including in some contemporary celebrated cases, as noted here: http://www.timesofisrael.com/new-technology-may-be-key-to-set-chained-women-free/?fb_comment_id=237114606451224_774713.

Other Issues to Discuss

After we have discussed the contemporary issue, we will return to the severity of the prohibition to embarrass people publicly. If, at the end of the day, we determine that specific gossip is not legitimate, the publicity of social media exacerbates the gravity of wrongly humiliating the subject of the *lashon hara,* especially considering the harshness with which the *posekim* have treated public embarrassment in the era before it was truly global.

Furthermore, we will have to discuss the ways in which these principles apply when information, secret or negative, is being used against people, but without human beings becoming privy to any of it. In many cases, the information is being shared by computers and smartphones directly into computer programs that utilize it to make decisions about targeted advertising or other goals. Our challenge will be to explore whether the principles we have developed can speak to these contemporary applications, which are not discussed in classic halakhic sources for obvious reasons.

Chapter 23

The Unique Challenges of the Digital Age: Transfer of Information, but No Audience

The Problem

In the above chapters, we have explored various potential prohibitions that relate to the transfer of information, from breaching confidentiality to gossip to public humiliation, et cetera. In classic halakhic literature, all these cases assume an audience, admittedly of various sizes, and for good reason. It would be meaningless to gossip to, or share a secret with, no one. However, the digital age has introduced a new problem – the sharing of information, with real-world consequences, but with no audience.

Companies like Facebook and Google acquire information, though no person may ever see it. Information gathered from people's searches and posts enables advertisers to provide targeted content, a fact that most people know, and many are okay with or even happy about. However, as the Cambridge Analytica case revealed, much more is at stake.

The information that is harvested may affect the political ads that are directed at people, shaping the contours of political debate and affecting the results of elections, as evidenced in the election of Donald Trump in the United States and the decision of the United Kingdom to leave the EU (Brexit). In some countries, with less strict data-privacy laws, the information gathered from texts and emails can be used to determine who is eligible for a loan.[1]

As a friend involved in data protection noted, the classic halakhic literature does not address these cases. In most of the above cases, there is no person who knows the information being transferred. Rather, the data is fed into computer systems and algorithms determine how the information is used. Sometimes, actual people will interact with the data, though all of the identifying markers have been stripped out. The results deeply affect the lives of all of us. What language does halakha have for "gossip" or secrets revealed only to a computer or anonymously? Alternatively, as Professor Nachum Rackover presents the question in his book *HaHagana al Tzinat HaPerat* (Protecting the Privacy of the Individual), does halakha recognize a right of privacy? If we could establish that it does, then violations of privacy, even in the ways outlined above, would presumably be prohibited.

For our purposes, we will avoid the issues of legality. Obviously, in a country where the collection of certain data is forbidden by law, one must contend with the halakhic principle of "*Dina demalkhuta dina*," "The law of the land is binding." Much of the debate has been about what *should* be legal, and in some cases, whether data has been collected illegally. Our goal is to explore what values halakha may add to the conversation which is currently at the crux of legal and ethical debates worldwide.

We will have to relate to the question of consent as well. In many cases, legal issues may be avoided by apps requesting consent before download. However, while this may solve the legal problems, it may not always be sufficient legally or halakhically, if it is clear that those consenting do not have a full grasp of the extent to which they are permitting their data to be used. Thus, we must ask whether a formal acceptance

1. From my private conversation with a friend who deals with issues of data security.

would be sufficient, assuming that without consent the collection of data would be prohibited.

Speech Ethics

If the issues of *lashon hara* and the like are about speech ethics, it would seem that these categories would have little relevance for our conversation. Take, for example, the mystical comments presented by R. Yisrael Meir Kagan, the *Ḥafetz Ḥayim*:

> It is written (*Mishlei* 21:23), "One who keeps an eye on his mouth and tongue protects his life from troubles."
>
> It is known that every man has 248 physical organs and 365 physical sinews, as it is written (*Iyov* 10:11): "With skin and flesh did You clothe me and with bones and sinews did You cover me...." Now, every organ of the soul is clothed from above with a bodily organ which corresponds to that organ as a garment to the body.
>
> Corresponding to this, the Holy One Blessed be He gave us 248 positive commandments and 365 negative commandments, which are also distributed among the organs; for there is a mitzva depending on the hand and a mitzva depending on the foot. The same is true of all the other organs, as stated in *Sefer Charedim*.
>
> Now, when a man fulfills a mitzva in this world with a certain organ, in the World to Come, the light of the Lord reposes on that organ, and it is that light which vivifies that organ; and so, with each and every mitzva. It emerges, then, that when a man fulfills the 248 positive commandments, then he is the "complete man," who is sanctified to the Lord with all of his organs....
>
> [This holds true] especially in the area of guarding one's tongue. For if he permits, God forbid, his soul to be in the category of speakers of *lashon ha-ra* in this world, and, as a matter of course, does not prevent his ears, too, from always hearing *lashon ha-ra* and *rekhilut* and accepting it...then he will have damaged his faculties of speech and hearing, and will certainly be punished

> in his soul, correspondingly, in the World to Come, in these two faculties themselves, speech and hearing....
>
> For in the prohibition of speaking *lashon ha-ra* and *rekhilut* that he speaks with his mouth, he transgresses "You shall not go talebearing among your people," most of which inheres in the mouth. Similarly, in hearing *lashon ha-ra* and accepting it, he infringes on the transgression of (*Shemot* 23:1): "You shall not bear a false report...."
>
> Now, it is known that these [speaking and hearing] are the major faculties of the "form" of man and of his perfection, even in this world. (*Sefer Shemirat HaLashon,* Introduction[2])

While the *Ḥafetz Ḥayim* discusses different rationales for the prohibitions elsewhere, this aspect clearly does not speak to the unique modern reality. The ethics of speaking and listening are almost irrelevant when dealing with nameless data sharing.

Ḥerem DeRabbenu Gershom

Without reiterating our full discussion about this decree, I would assume that it does not apply in a case when no human being actually sees the information. The focus of the decree seems to be upon actually reading someone's mail, which does not happen when the data is utilized by machines; even if it is accessed by people, it is without identifying markers. However, as we noted above, the decree may have been instituted to protect one from violating other prohibitions, which may indeed be relevant for our discussion.

"VeAhavta LeRe'akha Kamokha"

As we noted many times in previous chapters, in addition to any specific violations that may be involved in sharing information, an overarching concern that must guide our behavior is the general obligation to love others as ourselves and treat them as we would want to be treated. This general perspective, while it may not

2. Translation modified from Sefaria Community Translation, *Shmirath Halashon* by R. Shraga Silverstein.

provide pointed prescriptions in any given circumstance, obviously must remain in the background of our discussions. The same may be true for those who understand the prohibition against breaching confidentiality as an expansive ethical mandate. Our focus here will be on whether there are specific prohibitions that are violated in these cases.

Hezeik Re'iya and Hezeik Shemia

We explored the debate about the parameters of *hezeik re'iya* and whether it could be expanded to *hezeik shemia.* Several authorities contend that in any case in which eavesdropping or the like would prevent people from living their normal lives, it would be prohibited to access their information as an extension of this category.

This kind of expansion can be relevant in this context. For many people, the knowledge that their information is being used to create targeted advertisements for them does not in any way hinder their use of Google, Facebook, or the like. In fact, for many people, they would prefer that they only get targeted ads. Hence, Facebook asks its users which advertisements they do not want to see in order to better provide advertisements which they do want to see.

On the other hand, many people, if they knew that their information was being used to sway whom they would vote for in a political election, would probably be more careful. While much of the outrage around the Cambridge Analytica case hangs on whether they gathered the information legitimately, part of it is because people are genuinely upset about how their data was being used. If people knew that the messages they send could determine what loans they may be approved for, I would assume it would limit the way they use their computers and smartphones. If so, a potential way of framing the halakhic perspective based on an expanded notion of *hezeik re'iya* would be the following: If the data collection means that the subjects, had they known that such data was being collected, would have limited the way they lived their lives and used their technological devices, such collection may be a violation of Jewish law. We will return to the question of whether consent may obviate this concern.

***Lashon HaRa* and Revealing Secrets**

Is there any way to argue that someone who transfers data without an audience might be considered to have gossiped or revealed a secret? As noted above, if the focus of these prohibitions is ethical speech, then we would assume that this is not the case.

However, as many commentaries note, the primary reason *lashon hara* is prohibited may be the damage it causes. They derive this from the prohibition that is juxtaposed to the prohibition of *lashon hara* in Leviticus 19:16, namely, "Do not stand idly by as your fellow's blood is spilled." If this rationale for the mitzva indicates its nature (without focusing on the question of *darshinan tama dekra,* whether the philosophical rationale for a mitzva can affect its juridical application), then perhaps any transfer of information that may cause damage should be prohibited, whether there is an audience or not. For example, Rambam begins his discussion of *lashon hara* with a focus on the potential harm it might cause:

> He who bears tales against his fellow violates a prohibitive commandment, saying: "You shall not go talebearing among your people" (Lev. 19:16); and although the punishment of flogging is not inflicted for violating this charge, it is a gross iniquity. Moreover, a great deal of blood has been shed as a result of this sin, as indicated by the verse's conclusion, "Do not stand idly by as your fellow's blood is spilled." Now, go and learn of that which happened due to Do'eg the Edomite. (*Hilkhot De'ot* 7:1)

However, there is an even more striking possibility that hangs on a more literal interpretation of the verse. The Torah refers to the prohibition of *lashon hara,* whether that refers to gossip and its related prohibitions or to the prohibition against breaching confidentiality, as "You shall not go talebearing (*rakhil*)." What is *rakhil*? In the nominative form, a *rokhel* is a peddler. Why is one who is a gossipmonger referred to as a peddler?

The Yerushalmi in Pe'ah (1:1) explains that the metaphor is as follows: A peddler buys merchandise and circulates around until finding someone to buy it. The same is true of a gossipmonger, who collects information and looks around for someone who will listen to it. In the parable, information is referred to as a commodity.

Rashi (Lev. 19:16) expands on this as follows:

> Similarly, the peddler is one who goes around and searches for (spies out) all kinds of merchandise, and so also the seller of perfumes which women use to make themselves pleasant; because he constantly goes about in the villages, he is called *rokhel*, which has the same meaning as *rogel* (spy)....
>
> [Based on the comments of Targum:] It seems to me that people had the custom to eat a little snack in the house of him who listened to their slanderous words, and this served as the final confirmation that his (the slanderer's) statements were well founded and that he would maintain the truth of them....
>
> [I]t is the manner of all who go about slandering to wink with their eyes and to suggest their slanderous statements by innuendos in order that others who happen to hear them should not understand them.

Rashi understands that the gossipmonger acts like a peddler. The focus is not on what the speaker says, but the way the speaker peddles information. Many other commentaries accept the position of the Yerushalmi.

The modern world seems to open the possibility of a return toward the literal understanding of the metaphor. Now data is literally a commodity, *even when no audience hears or sees it*! Indeed, the companies that sell the information are literally peddlers of information, of data.

The *Or HaḤayim* (ad loc.) seems to take this literal understanding as the most straightforward application of the halakha as well:

> I believe the plain meaning of the Torah is a warning to each individual not to become a vehicle for potential defamatory information about others. How does one prevent this? By not revealing any information, even innocent information, in the hearing of anyone who might use this information or part of it and turn it

> into something defamatory. If that were to happen then the person who merely related the original, harmless-sounding story would share part of the guilt. The Torah purposely writes, "among your people," referring to people close to one who are indiscreet and blabber about any confidence they have heard or overheard. God adds: "I am the Lord," i.e. I am going to track down whence the defamatory remarks originated.[3]

A recent popular article explains how the techniques used by companies like Google and Facebook are essentially a return to this literal peddling of information:

> It is the strangely conspiratorial truth of the surveillance society we inhabit that there are unknown entities gathering our data for unknown purposes.
>
> Companies and governments dip into the data streams of our lives in increasingly innovative ways, tracking what we do, who we know and where we go. The methods and purposes of data collection keep expanding, with seemingly no end or limit in sight.
>
> These range from irritating infringements, including WhatsApp sharing your name and phone number with Facebook so businesses can advertise to you, or a startup that uses your phone's battery status as a "fingerprint" to track you online, to major intrusions such as Baltimore police secretly using aerial surveillance systems to continuously watch and record the city. Or like the data brokers that create massive personalized profiles about each of us, which are then sold and used to circumvent consumer protections meant to limit predatory and discriminatory practices.
>
> These instances of data harvesting are connected by a shared compulsion – a data imperative – that drives many corporations and governments. This imperative demands the extraction of all data, from all sources, in whatever ways possible. It has

3. Translation modified from Sefaria.

> created an arms race for data, fueling the impulse to create surveillance technologies that infiltrate all aspects of life and society. *And the reason for creating these massive reserves of data is the value it can or might generate....*
>
> German tech firm Siemens echoes this capitalist sentiment: "We need to understand that data is everywhere, and it is generated every second of the day. *We need to understand data as an asset – and turn it into a value.*"[4]

Thus, if we accept this return toward *peshat* (the simple meaning of the verse), perhaps such sharing of information would be *lashon hara* or *rekhilut,* understood either as damaging gossip or breaching confidentiality.

Of course, as this is not how halakha has classically understood this prohibition, this approach does assume that we are able to derive new applications of halakhot based on how we understand the words of the Torah and the ways they are understood by *Ḥazal.* This is not quite deriving new laws straight from the Torah, which is subject to an extensive debate among the *posekim,* but it is clearly a radically new application.[5]

R. Shimshon Raphael Hirsch (Lev. 19:16) seems to entertain this possibility most explicitly:

> A *rokhel* is a "news peddler" who goes from person to person and from house to house, prying into the affairs of one person and telling of them to another. Of such a person, the Torah says: "You shall not go talebearing among your people." Do not tell things about your brother that are unknown unless you know he is comfortable with it....

4. Available at: https://www.theguardian.com/technology/2016/aug/31/personal-data-corporate-use-google-amazon. (Emphasis added.)
5. For more on this, see my *shiur*: https://www.yutorah.org/sidebar/lecture.cfm/848986/rabbi-jonathan-ziring/are-we-rabbinic-or-biblical-jews-do-we-still-derive-new-laws-from-pesukim-/.

> This prohibition perceives national society as "peoples" – as closed circles, as households and as families. Family members discuss their affairs within the boundaries determined by natural training, and things will not pass on their own "from people to people," from group to group. The people of one group give their trust to each other, and on the basis of this they speak and act. Therefore, one who passes this information to another group is going as a *rokhel* among his or her people. We are commanded to protect the dignity of every person and to respect his or her private affairs. It is our obligation to be careful in our words, when we speak about others. One cannot know how far reaching the results of *rekhilut* about the private affairs of someone can else be.

This, in many ways, captures the modern reality.

Sho'el SheLo MiDaat

A position that combines several of the above notions, both that of *hezeik re'iya* and treating information as a commodity, is that of the *Torat Ḥayim*. According to this position, using someone's information without permission is theft under the category of *she'eila shelo midaat,* borrowing without permission. R. Dovid Lichtenstein presents how this would apply to personal data as follows:

> Another possible basis for such a prohibition is the notion that a person "owns" his private information. According to many halachic authorities, *halacha* recognizes the concept of legal ownership over one's intellectual property. Perhaps one is similarly considered the legal owner of his private information. As such, peering into a person's home, viewing medical records, or reading his personal correspondence would be forbidden on the grounds of *sho'el she-lo mi-da'at* – "borrowing" someone's property without his permission, which *halacha* equates with theft.

This theory is advanced by R. Haim Shabbetai of Salonika (Maharchash), the *Torat Ḥayim* (3:47), in reference to reading someone else's personal correspondence. He writes that reading someone's letter without his consent is *she'eila shelo midaat,* as the writer has legal ownership over the letter, stipulating that it be read by a particular individual. Some have suggested applying the approach of the *Torat Ḥayim* to all situations of accessing private information, claiming that a person has legal ownership over all of one's private information and therefore, obtaining such information without the "owner's" consent would constitute theft.

The concept that violating someone's privacy constitutes theft may be reflected in the *Siaḥ Yitzḥak* commentary on the siddur, which asserts that when we confess "*Gazalnu,*" "We have stolen," in the *Vidui* prayer, this includes "*Ḥatanu behezeik re'iya,*" "We have sinned by damaging others by looking at their personal property." Classifying privacy violations under the category of theft might mean that this prohibition stems from the unauthorized "use" of a person's "property."[6]

R. Lichtenstein notes that while this argument was put forth by R. Avraham Sherman in a decision of the Tel Aviv Rabbinical Court, both Professor Nachum Rackover[7] and R. J. David Bleich[8] reject this implication. They argue that the focus of the Maharchash is on the use of the letter, not the information contained within. Thus, these sources are insufficient to establish a right to privacy that would obtain even when there is no audience for the breach of secrecy.

Geneivat Daat

R. Chaim Palagi (*Responsa Ḥikekei Levi, YD* 1:49) argues that breaching confidentiality is forbidden because it is *geneivat daat,* which normally refers to deception. However, R. Palagi notes that in this case, "he steals that which is hidden in his heart." This formulation also points in the direction of understanding information as a commodity that can be sold, as well as illicitly taken and transferred.

6. *Headlines: Halachic Debates of Current Events,* vol. 2 (OU Press, 2017).
7. *HaHagana al Tzinat HaPerat,* 114–115.
8. *Bioethical Dilemmas,* vol. 1, 176.

Stealing Information

In addition to those authorities who entertain the possibility that using information without permission may be a form of stealing – either due to an expanded understanding of *geneivat daat,* which usually refers to deception, but literally means the stealing of knowledge, or under the rubric of *she'eila shelo midaat* – there is another possible kind of "stealing" that can be relevant. Specifically, there are *posekim* who entertain this model when the question at hand is the stealing of trade secrets. Professor Nachum Rackover (*HaHagana al Tzinat HaPerat,* ch. 5) notes that that the *Kesef Kedoshim* (*ḤM* 183:4) refers to this as theft, as does R. Shmuel Wosner (*Responsa Shevet HaLevi* 4:220). It is unclear to me whether this classification entails an acceptance of the notion of intellectual property in halakha as real property, or they are using theft in the sense of *geneivat daat* or loosely. What is clear is that when information is taken in such a way that it causes real monetary damage, these *posekim* either fully or nearly equate the illicit use of it with theft.

However, it seems to me that even the use of information which would prevent people from being approved for loans would rise to this level. These *posekim* seem to be motivated by their conviction that trade secrets have positive monetary value, not just that sharing them causes monetary harm.

Consent

One potential argument for why this discussion is irrelevant is that in most cases, the people whose information is being taken have given consent. In a case in which the information is obtained without consent (or perhaps, as in the Cambridge Analytica case, information was gathered from the Facebook friends of people who took a survey), then all the potential prohibitions discussed would apply. However, in a case in which users know that the price of accessing Google or Facebook is that their information will be used, shouldn't that implied consent be enough to negate any potential prohibitions? This is even more true for applications that require one to provide consent that one's information be shared before downloading the application.

The problem, already noted in secular literature, is that this consent is usually not given with a full understanding of the consequences. Take, for example, this lengthy quote from an article in *The Guardian*. In it, the author highlights several issues we have discussed: that the information being gathered has real monetary value and has been commoditized; that the gathering of this information has not been treated as theft, but re-evaluating that assessment may be critical in developing proper ways of controlling it; and that while consent is often given, that consent may not be meaningful for a host of reasons:

> Contrary to the oft-repeated rhetoric, data does not exist independently in the world, nor is it generated spontaneously. Data is constructed by people, from people. As digital studies scholar Karen Gregory puts it: "Big data, like Soylent Green, is made of people." Wringing the value from data requires more than just collecting it. Gathering it requires expertise in creating, extracting, refining and using it. This often goes hand-in-hand with increasingly invasive systems for probing, monitoring and tracking people.
>
> Now here's the rub: if corporations and governments are going to up the ante by treating data as an asset, then we – the targets of this data imperative – should respond in kind. Many common practices of data collection should actually be treated as a form of theft that I call data appropriation – which means capturing data from people without consent and compensation.
>
> People often do not even know how their data is taken and used, let alone how to give meaningful consent. Data brokers, for instance, aim to provide their services from the shadows, while amassing billions and trillions of data points about people worldwide.
>
> Data-driven policing technologies are shielded by trade secrets, which prevent the public from knowing what data the analytics crunch and how it influences police activity.
>
> When companies do seek consent, it is typically through terms of service agreements – overly long contracts are full of dense legal language that users are expected to "agree" to without

understanding. It is a remarkable victory for the data appropriators that acquiescence has become the standard model for obtaining "consent."

Data appropriation is a form of exploitation because companies use data to create value without providing people with comparable compensation. While some might argue that Google and Facebook pay us for our data with "free" services, this still does not account for the multitude of data appropriators that have no intention to provide some kind of mutual benefit to those whose data they possess.

The data as an asset paradigm has helped create a lucrative market for data – the data broker industry alone generates around $200bn in annual revenue – which cuts out the people that data is about.

In short, rampant practices of data appropriation allow corporations and governments to build their wealth and power, without the headache of obtaining consent and providing compensation for the resource they desire.

Data appropriation is surely an ethical issue. But by framing it as theft, we can lay the groundwork for policies that also make it a legal issue. We need new models of data ownership and protection that reflect the role information has in society.

In the Gilded Age 2.0, a laissez-faire attitude toward data has encouraged a new class of robber barons to arise. Rather than allow them to unscrupulously take, trade and hoard our data, we must reclaim their ill-gotten gains and rein in the data imperative.[9]

What does halakha have to say about this? There are many relevant sources on this issue, but we will explore a few, starting with the question

9. "Companies are making money from our personal data – but at what cost?" by Jathan Sadowski, available at: https://www.theguardian.com/technology/2016/aug/31/personal-data-corporate-use-google-amazon.

of whether explicit agreement to terms one may or may not understand is acceptable in halakha.

In general, the assumption is that one is bound by whatever one agrees to when signing a contract, regardless of understanding what is at stake. For example, *Shulḥan Arukh* (*ḤM* 45:3) states explicitly that even if one does not understand what one signs, one is bound by the contract.

Similarly, the Rema (*EH* 66:13) rules that a husband is bound by the terms of a *ketuba,* and he cannot avoid paying by claiming he was ignorant when he signed the *ketuba* and did not understand its implications.

The Rashba (*Responsa* 1:629) cites two opinions on the topic. His argument, accepted by the *Beit Yosef* (*EH* 66), is that we must not accept such arguments as then all ignorant people could avoid any obligations by claiming that they didn't understand the details of the contracts they signed. (See also *Responsa Rashba* 5:228.)

R. Ovadia Yosef assumes that this is the majority position (*Responsa Yabia Omer, EH* 3:13). The Rashba in that responsum seems not to rule in line with this position, but R. Yosef assumes that this is only out of deference to R. Meir (whose view we will discuss below), whom he cites as having already ruled otherwise.

In many of these sources, the assumption is that we simply do not believe the person claiming ignorance. However, the *Sema* (*ḤM* 45:5) cites a different passage from the Rashba (*Responsa Meyuḥasot LeRamban* 77), arguing that the reason is more fundamental: when people sign a document, they rely on and trust the scribe. Thus, even if we know that they didn't understand the terms, they are bound by them. The *Shakh* (*ḤM* 45:5) rules similarly.

One could have simply understood this as saying that people are responsible for understanding what they are signing; and if they don't, it is their fault. However, *Responsa Mahariaz Ansel* 49, cited in *Divrei Geonim* 102:20, argues that it is the trust in the scribe that is critical.

Rav Avraham Sherman (*Techumin* 8:163–165) contends that according to this formulation, only a contract reviewed by a trusted outsider would have this status, not a contract written by the opposing side (in his case, a bank was obligating someone based on a clause in the contract they had given him).

However, as noted above, there are those who contest this. The Rashba (*Responsa* 1:629) cites the view of R. Meir, who argues that one may indeed claim not to have understood the implications of a contract one has signed and thereby be exempted from the obligations dictated therein. While the Rashba does not reverse the decision, most authorities assume that he disagrees.

However, certain authorities present a more nuanced position. For example, the *Knesset HaGedola* (commenting on *Beit Yosef, ḤM* 147:8) suggests that either 1) the Rashba would accept the argument that one did not understand a *detail* in a contract, but not that one did not understand the basic obligations one committed to; or 2) the Rashba would accept an argument for exemption if this was a case of *anan sahadei,* a general acknowledgment that one did not understand. R. Ovadia Yosef notes that some authorities, like R. Betzalel Ashkenazi (*Responsa Rav Betzalel Ashkenazi* 24), cited by the *Knesset HaGedola* (*Beit Yosef, EH* 66), argue that one can only put forth such an argument when one has witnesses sign the contract. However, after signing a document oneself, one cannot make such an argument.

The relevance of these positions is clear when one does not read all the details in a contract made with a bank or the like. For many *posekim,* this is never an excuse. Others, however, argue that if there is strong circumstantial evidence that one did not understand what one was agreeing to, or did not sign oneself and thus cannot be assumed to have understood everything, we would accept such a claim.[10]

The upshot of these positions is as follows: According to most *posekim,* one cannot claim not to have understood the implications of a contract one signed. Others maintain that this is a legitimate claim. Some will accept this only when there is strong circumstantial evidence that one did not understand the contract or had someone else sign.

10. See here for a summary of these issues: https://shulchanaruchharav.com/halacha/is-a-signed-document-legally-binding-if-one-was-unaware-of-its-content/.

Finally, based on the view of the *Knesset HaGedola,* there may be room to exempt someone from a detail found in the fine print, though not from the main obligations outlined in a contract.

So does the fact that one accepts that one's data will be used affect whether it can be used? An argument may be made that it does; after all, one is responsible for reading the fine print. Either we assume that one should have read it, or we assume one actually did read it and understand it. On the other hand, when it is common knowledge that no one reads the full contract (and could not understand every detail in any case), an argument may be made that this cannot constitute full consent.

All these issues came to the fore when Mark Zuckerberg was questioned by the US Congress about the way Facebook uses data and gets consent. Take, for example, this summary of that meeting from CNBC:[11]

> Republican Senator John Kennedy of Louisiana confronted Facebook CEO Mark Zuckerberg about the transparency of the social media company's policies during a joint hearing of the Senate Judiciary and Commerce committees on Tuesday.
>
> "Here's what everyone's been trying to tell you today – and I say it gently – your user agreement sucks," Kennedy said. "The purpose of a user agreement is to cover Facebook's rear end, not inform users of their rights."
>
> Zuckerberg appeared momentarily amused, but the comment hits at an issue central to Facebook's data scandal: transparency. Critics argue Facebook users aren't well informed about Facebook's plans for their data. Kennedy believed this partly because those plans are laid out in a long and complicated user agreement. Even Zuckerberg later admitted most users probably don't read it.

11. https://www.cnbc.com/2018/04/10/senator-to-zuckerberg-your-user-agreement-sucks.html.

> "I would imagine probably most people do not read the whole thing," Zuckerberg said. "But everyone has the opportunity to and consents to it."
>
> Just in case Zuckerberg wasn't entirely clear on Kennedy's point, the senator left him with some colorful advice.
>
> "I'm going to suggest you go home and rewrite it, and tell your 1,200-dollar-an-hour lawyer...you want it written in English, not Swahili, so the average American user can understand," Kennedy said.

Zuckerberg presented the argument that all users have the opportunity to read the details, and if they don't, that is their problem. Indeed, as Senator Kennedy noted, that might be enough to cover them legally, as it might be in halakha too. However, the point of the potential regulation, according to Kennedy, would be, in halakhic language, to accommodate the *Knesset HaGedola.* People need to actually understand the agreement, including the fine details.

Practically, this approach might lead us to distinguish between the data collection which people know about and have tacitly accepted, such as for targeted advertisements (which some people not only accept but prefer), on the one hand; and on the other hand, data collected for political purposes or (to use our example from above) to determine who is approved for loans, which people do not realize and do not really accept.

However, this will be enough to cover only Facebook and other applications that require consent. When it comes to Google, for example, to whose terms no one ever explicitly consents, it may be that the information may be used with even less permission.

Consent in *Hezeik Re'iya*

When dealing with Google, we are dealing not with explicit permission, but implicit permission. Perhaps we can gain insight as to the implications of this distinction if we return to our model of *hezeik re'iya.*

Concerning *hezeik re'iya,* the Gemara records a dispute as to whether one can acquire a *ḥazaka* to allow engaging in what would otherwise be *hezeik re'iya.* For example, if one has a window facing a neighbor in such a way that it violates the neighbor's property rights and the neighbor does not protest, does that allow the person to continue having that window when the neighbor does protest?

> **The Sages taught** in a *baraita*: There was **an incident involving a person who opened his windows into a courtyard belonging to partners and came before Rabbi Yishmael bar Rabbi Yosei,** who **said to him: You have established an acquired privilege, my son; you have established an acquired privilege,** and you may not be prevented from using the windows. **And he came before Rabbi Ḥiyya,** who **said** to him: **You toiled and opened** the windows; you must **toil and seal** them, as the partners have the right to prevent you from using these windows. (Bava Batra 59b)

The Rishonim disagree as to whether this passage indicates that there is never a *ḥazaka* with regard to *hezeik re'iya,* and the neighbor may always claim that such a situation is harmful and force the homeowner to stop, or whether this case is unique. The Ri Migash (Bava Batra 2b) notes that the Rif rules that this passage indicates that there is never a *ḥazaka* in such a case, while the Ri Migash himself disagrees, arguing that one can establish a *ḥazaka.* However, in the above case, there is no *ḥazaka* for two reasons:

1. When neighbors are damaging each other, they can claim that their previous silence was not due to a lack of opposition, but due to the mutuality of the damage.
2. When neighbors damage each other in this way, it is not considered an action, as the windows have already been opened.

However, if someone does something active and no opposition is elicited, that would create a *ḥazaka.* The Rosh adds another distinction – a *ḥazaka* can be created by low-level *hezeik re'iya.* However, concerning open windows, a situation in which privacy may be utterly destroyed, one may always claim that this level of "damage" is unbearable.

Some Rishonim (Rashbam, Rabbenu Gershom, Meiri on Bava Batra 59b) argue that even in the case of windows, the Gemara only means that there is no immediate *ḥazaka,* but after a requisite amount of time, there would be a *ḥazaka.*

The Ramban (*Ḥiddushei Ramban* 59b) explains the rationale for rejecting *ḥazaka* in cases of *hezeik re'iya.* The Gemara assumes earlier (23a) that for certain intensely harmful damage, one cannot develop a *ḥazaka,* as in such situations, not just property but people are harmed. *Hezeik re'iya* harms the people themselves because it causes *ayin hara,* it enables *lishna bisha/lashon hara,* and it breaches *tzeniut,* privacy.

The majority position is to accept that a *ḥazaka* can be created as long as the potential damage was done in an active way that should have elicited a response (*Shulḥan Arukh, ḤM* 154:7–8). However, the Rema notes (ibid., 7), based on the Rashba (*Responsa HaRashba* 3:180, cited by *Beit Yosef* ad loc.) that even if such a *ḥazaka* may be established to leave a window open, a homeowner cannot violate a neighbor's privacy by actually staring into the neighbor's property.

Let us apply this principle to our case. Assuming that the use and sale of data (even stripped of identity markers) constitutes a potential violation of *hezeik re'iya,* as people learn about new implications to the use of their data, does the fact that they have not protested until now prevent them from protesting at the present time?

On the one hand, once people learn about what Google can utilize their data for and they continue to use the service, one might argue that this is a new act of consent. What about the previously collected data? May companies like Google simply assume they have consent because they have not received pushback? (Granted, the objections have been growing recently.) Does the fact that there exist alternatives like DuckDuckGo, which do not track data, indicate that those who use Google accept its conditions?

According to the Ramban, one may argue that this type of invasion of privacy is so great that people can always demand that their data not be used, even the parts of it that have already been collected. According to the Ri Migash, the situation is more complicated. One might argue that the fact that people don't actually realize what is going on makes this case similar to the case of the jointly owned courtyard, where the passivity with which people are damaged makes a lack of response not dispositive.

More importantly, according to the Rema, even if a *ḥazaka* can be established, this only allows leaving the window in place, parallel to allowing Google to collect data. However, to use the data in such a way that is considered a breach of privacy remains prohibited always.

I am unsure of the exact conclusions to derive from this, but I think the nuances raised by the *posekim* in the context of *hezeik re'iya* may help us shape a language for determining *what* assumptions may be made about the type of data which it is legitimate to collect and utilize.

To'elet

It should be obvious that in cases of *pikuaḥ nefesh,* in which data is used to prevent terrorist attacks or other dangerous criminal activity, it would be legitimate for the authorities to access information. However, when it comes to lower-level *to'elet,* we have previously discussed the possible differences between *lashon hara* and breaching confidentiality. How we conceptualize the accessing of data may generate different conclusions. A friend pointed out to me that, theoretically, a bank could claim that there is *to'elet* in its knowing whom to lend to. While this may justify accessing this type of information if the only problem is *lashon hara,* as we have noted, there are many other prohibitions in play which complicate the matter.

Conclusion

This section has convinced me, more than most of the topics explored in this book, that:

1. The challenges that we face in the digital age are in many ways unique.
2. Some of these challenges have not been dealt with by the *posekim* at all.

I have tried to present my thoughts, though I must note that they are tentative and meant to begin the discussion. My hope is that the *posekim* will begin to grapple with these questions in serious ways and push the conversation forward.

Chapter 24

Shaming in Halakha: A General Overview

Introduction

In the past several chapters, we have discussed the prohibitions involved in invading and sharing information, and the unique ways this is manifested in the digital age. We also explored the factors that permit spreading *lashon hara* or revealing secrets. Beyond the issues of *to'elet* and "*Lo taamod al dam re'ekha*" (the prohibition against standing idly by while one's fellow's blood is shed), there are many other data points that must be taken into account when discussing when halakha allows or even mandates weaponizing information to accomplish a goal. Many of these must recognize that while in many ways, the digital age has merely increased the reach of gossip and shaming, in certain ways, these quantitative shifts have brought about fundamental changes in reality and with it, the halakhic implications.

These changes manifest both on the negative side, but also on the positive. Specifically, the unique ways in which this is manifested in the world of social media (and mass communication more generally) have come to the fore as social-media shaming has become a key method used to force recalcitrant husbands to grant their wives *gittin* (halakhic bills of divorce). We will explore both sides of the equation.

As part of this, we must explore the prohibition of embarrassing people publicly. While we will focus on cases in which it is legitimate not only to share what would be *lashon hara,* but to do so publicly, we must keep in mind what is at stake. Embarrassing anyone, especially publicly, is considered a grave sin in halakha. Many *posekim* even think it is a cardinal sin! Even more so, as we will see, the staying power and reach of social-media shaming, and the subsequent damage it can inflict on the subject of the shaming, are beyond what could have been imagined before the advent of social media.

Again, while we have explored the question of when it is legitimate to spread negative information, and will continue exploring those principles, it must be kept in mind that if one decides incorrectly and uses these tools when they are not legitimate, the costs are significant.[1]

Weaponizing Information

Tsuriel Rashi and Hananel Rosenberg outline several instances in which halakha legitimates weaponizing information:

1. Excommunication (*Ḥerem*)

There are various stages of excommunication imposed by the Jewish court to punish certain kinds of infractions, many outlined in the third chapter of Moed Katan. *Shulḥan Arukh,* for example, provides the following case of a person who refuses to appear before a Jewish court after being summoned numerous times:

> In which manner is a defendant summoned to appear in court? The [members of the] court send their messenger to him in order that he may come on the appointed day to court. [If] he does not appear [on the appointed day], they summon him a second time; [if] he does not appear [after the second summons], they summon him a third time; [if] he [still] does not appear, they wait

1. Most of the analysis that we will present on this topic comes from the excellent article, "Shaming in Judaism: Past, Present, Future," by Tsuriel Rashi and Hananel Rosenberg, published in *Journal of Religion & Society,* vol. 19 (2017).

> for him all day, and if he does not appear, they place him under sentence of separation on the morrow. (*ḤM* 11:1)

What does excommunication consist of? The Rambam summarizes the terms of *niddui* (separation) as follows:

> What regulations should one under sentence of separation follow himself, and how should others act toward him? One under sentence of separation is forbidden to shave and wash, as one in mourning, all the days of his separation. He must not be counted in among three to bless God after meals, or among ten in any religious service which requires ten adults, and no one is permitted to sit within four cubits of him. Nevertheless, he may give instruction to others and others may instruct him, and others may hire him and he may hire others. If his demise occurs while under sentence of separation, the tribunal has a stone sent which is deposited on his coffin, as if saying that he is being stoned because he had to be separated from the community. Needless to say that no mourning is permitted for him, and that his hearse is not followed. (*Hilkhot Talmud Torah* 7:4)

In general, *ḥerem* was used as rarely as possible. When it was used, however, it was declared publicly, often in synagogue with the Torah scrolls. Rashi and Rosenberg refer to this as "shaming as communal pressure."

A lower level of excommunication was introduced by Rabbenu Tam (*Sefer HaYashar* 24) to be used against *get* refusers. The reason that a lower level must be used is that, as we noted above, a Jewish divorce cannot be coerced. The husband must give the *get* of his own free will.

R. Michoel Zylberman, the associate director of the Beth Din of America, summarizes the basic halakhic approaches to the use of this method. (I have emphasized a particularly striking line.)

> The package of communal measures that a *beit din* may impose is referred to as *harchakot d'Rabbenu Tam,* literally the distancing methods of Rabbenu Tam (1100–1171). Rabbenu Tam, in his work *Sefer Hayashar* (24), writes that in a situation where a

husband refused to comply with the ruling of a *beit din* to give his wife a *get,* the members of his community were proscribed from speaking with him, doing business with him, hosting him, providing him with food and drink, escorting him and visiting him when he is sick. [*Rema* (*Even Haezer* 154:21) adds to this list not burying the individual and not performing *brit mila* for his son.]

Rabbenu Tam reasons that such social pressures are permissible because they fall short of physical or financial coercion; these methods serve to not provide benefits that the husband is not objectively entitled to rather than remove something that he already has (either money or physical health) (see Responsa Binyamin Zev 88 – 16th century). Another version reasons that the husband could always move to a different community or a different country where he would not necessarily be subject to the same sanctions (R' Joseph Colon ben Solomon Trabott, 1420–1480, Mahari"k 135, citing Rabbenu Tam). *Arguably, this reason may apply in fewer situations in our more mobile, contemporary society with enhanced communication abilities.*

While some authorities opposed applying *harchakot d'Rabbenu Tam* absent a *beit din* ruling allowing for coercive measures (see for example *Chazon Ish Even Haezer* 108:12), both R. Ovadia Yosef (*Yabia Omer* 7 *Even Haezer* 23) and R. Eliezer Waldenberg (*Tzitz Eliezer* 17:51) advocated withholding communal honors from a husband who refused to comply with the ruling of a *beit din* to give his wife a *get.* In the particular case referenced in R. Yosef's responsum, the *Beit Din Hagadol* (Supreme Court of Appeals) declared that the synagogues in the husband's neighborhood should not allow him to enter or give him an *aliya,* and that his neighbors should not inquire as to his welfare until he complies with the *beit din*'s directive.[2]

2. https://www.jewishlinknj.com/index.php?option=com_content&view=article&id=9230:communal-pressure-in-the-get-process-harchakot-drabbenu-tam&catid=156:features&Itemid=585.

As we will see, R. Zylberman expresses some hesitation because the purpose of this mechanism, namely to pressure the husband without formally coercing him, may not apply in the modern world. If what defines this mechanism as not (fully) coercive is the ability of the husband to escape to another place, in an era of mass communication, the husband may not be able to escape, making this mechanism harder to justify.

R. Zylberman notes that in Israel, the courts have allowed for several punishments that are in the spirit of these *harḥakot:*

> The State of Israel, in a law emended in 1996, provides for removing some privileges from a recalcitrant party when instructed to do so by a *beit din*. This law allows for preventing the non-compliant spouse from leaving the country, receiving an Israeli passport, receiving or renewing a driver's license, and opening or withdrawing funds from a bank account. This law has engendered discussion in the rabbinic literature as to whether it is more sweeping than what would be allowed as part of *harchakot d'Rabbenu Tam* (see, for example, R. Yosef Goldberg, *Get Meuseh*, appendix 5–6). If an Israeli *beit din* ruled that actual coercion is appropriate, the recalcitrant party may be jailed for not complying with a *beit din*'s ruling. In a 2008 ruling, the *Beit Din Hagadol* ruled that a husband incarcerated for refusing to comply with a *beit din* ruling to give his wife a *get* (in which the *beit din* ruled that he could be forced to do so) could be denied *mehadrin* food, in the spirit of *harchakot d'Rabbenu Tam.*

R. Zylberman closes his piece by noting that while *batei din* outside of Israel are not granted these coercive powers, they will often use some form of shaming to pressure the husband to grant the *get.*

An Important Note

It is worth noting that all these methods are last resorts. Many mechanisms exist to minimize or prevent such cases. For example, the Beth Din of America has its halakhic prenuptial agreement.[3]

3. Basic information can be found here: https://theprenup.org/.

In Israel, the version used is called the *heskem lekavod hadadi,* agreement of mutual respect.[4]

Dr. Rachel Levmore describes why this was deemed necessary despite the coercive powers available to the secular courts and *batei din* in Israel in her article, "Get-Refusal and the Agreement for Mutual Respect: Israel Today," *Hakira* 9 (2010).[5]

In places like New York and Canada, there are certain *get* laws in place that are supposed to minimize the number of cases of *get* refusal. While they may reduce the prevalence of the phenomenon, they have not eliminated it. R. Mordechai Ochs of the Toronto Beit Din, for example, estimates that the law decreased the number of cases of *get* refusal by 85 percent, which, while impressive, does still leave some cases unresolved.[6]

Thus, despite all the worthwhile and necessary attempts to minimize *get* refusal, it still happens. In such cases, or in cases in which none of the above mechanisms have been used or are relevant, *batei din* turn to the possibility of using the various forms of shaming to pressure the husband to free his wife.[7]

2. Public Shaming

There are many records of Jewish communities using public shaming as a way of punishing sinners and warning members of the community to avoid following similar sinful paths. As Rashi and Rosenberg write:

> Jewish communities in the Middle Ages also made use of shaming as a punishment for criminals and sinners. So, for example, those who departed from the straight and narrow of communal norms and were caught in the sin of adultery, drunkenness, theft,

4. Basic information can be found here: https://web.archive.org/web/20230203001822/https:/iyim.org.il/prenup/.
5. Available at: https://hakirah.org/Vol%209%20Levmore.pdf.
6. See John Syrtash, "Celebrating the Success of Canada's 'Get' Legislation and Its Possible Impact on Israel," paper delivered at the *Conference on Resolving Get Refusal in Civil Laws and the Corresponding Halachic Approaches* (Bar Ilan University, September 13, 2005).
7. For a summary of these different methods and the opposition that has been raised to some of them, see: https://www.yutorah.org/lectures/lecture.cfm/913304/rabbi-mordechai-torczyner/prenuptial-agreements-the-rca-edition-and-the-agreement-for-mutual-respect/.

> or contempt of the communal court were publicly chastised. We find such an instance in the writings of R. Moshe Mintz, the son of R. Isaac HaLevi Mintz (1415–1485), one of the most important rabbis in the Rhineland, who obliged his community to denounce one of its members who had reneged on a monetary undertaking to a fellow Jew in the synagogue toward the end of the prayer service (Responsa Maharam Mintz 101). The objective of public criticism of the sinner is both to punish him and to warn the public that he is not trustworthy. Similar practices were effected through placing the names of members of the community who had sinned on the synagogue notice board.

Rashi and Rosenberg refer to this category as "shaming as punishment."

3. *Ikuv Tefilla* (Delaying Prayer)

A custom that existed in the medieval and modern period in Europe was the delaying of prayer or the Torah reading. A person who felt he or she had been wronged had the right, at certain parts of the prayer service, to demand that his or her claim be heard before the prayers would continue. In *Shulḥan Arukh, OḤ* 54:3, R. Yosef Karo states the fundamental law about interrupting between *Yishtabaḥ*, the final blessing of the Songs of Praise, and *Yotzer* (*Or*), the initial blessing before the recitation of *Shema.*

> One who speaks between *Yishtabaḥ* and *Yotzer,* it is a sin in his hand, and he would be required to return from the battlefield [due to fear that his sin may lead to his death] (see Deut. 20:9, Sota 44b). However, there are those who say that it is permitted to interrupt at that point for communal needs or to bestow charity upon those who come to seek alms.

The Rema adds his gloss:

> From this stems the custom in many places to say a blessing for the sick *or for a claimant to ask for judgment between Yishtabaḥ*

> *and Yotzer*, because these are instances of [interruptions for] the purpose of a mitzva.

Rashi and Rosenberg refer to this as "shaming as a tool for the individual to correct an injustice."

4. *Pashkevilim*

Anyone who has walked through Me'ah She'arim in Jerusalem has seen countless signs decrying immoral or anti-halakhic activities. These posters are referred to as *pashkevilim*. Rashi and Rosenberg explain the etymology as follows:

> The Yiddish word "*pashkevil*" derives from the name of a citizen of Rome by the name of Pasquino, who used to hang satires and critical comments about the pope on the pedestal of a headless statue. His name was eventually given to the statue and then to the square where the statue stood (Piazza Pasquinate); the initiative taken by one individual evolved into a common practice whereby citizens hung anonymous vilifying signs around the city. The phenomenon spread throughout Western Europe during the sixteenth century as this channel began to accompany religious and social struggles.

This phenomenon of "shaming as exposure and public criticism," they argue, derives from the talmudic passage we will develop later as a possible source for a halakhic value of transparency, "*Mefarsemin et haḥanifim mipenei ḥillul Hashem,*" "We publicize the hypocrites [to prevent] the desecration of [God's name]" (Yoma 86a, see chapter 21). However, they assume, it is used primarily when leaders do not want to impose the harsher kinds of humiliation such as excommunication.

In the Spirit of the *Pitḥei Teshuva*

While we might be able to defend each of these mechanisms from the perspective of the *Ḥafetz Ḥayim*'s model of *lashon hara leto'elet,* I think the prevalence of public shaming as a tool in the Jewish community points to an implicit acceptance of either the expanded model of *to'elet* we alluded to above, or, more likely, the alternate model we presented from the *Pitḥei Teshuva*. If one conceptualizes *lashon hara* and the prohibitions against embarrassing people as halakhot and values that must be weighed against obligations such as rebuking sinners and protecting the innocent, one is more likely to utilize the above methods. From this perspective, some of the modern movements of using social-media shaming to solve social ills may find precedent in these methods.

Of course, that does not mean at all that one has free license to humiliate someone on the assumption that shaming is always the best course of action. Rashi and Rosenberg write in the epilogue to their article:

> Throughout history, shaming has been considered a legitimate tool to publicly criticize someone who deserves it. To strike a balance between slander and damage to a person's good name and the need to publicly rebuke those who are guilty, the public has followed the religious leadership that has defined the limits of action.

Challenges Remaining to Be Addressed

Rashi and Rosenberg's epilogue notes one of the unique challenges that *posekim* face when applying these principles in the age of social media. Namely, while the above methods were used by rabbinical courts, or at least rabbinic authorities, social-media shaming is in the hands of the laity. Even when the court sanctions this activity, controlling its extent is difficult.

Furthermore, as we will discuss, while in traditional cases, the court could end the excommunication when the person listened to the court, it is very hard to erase records of shaming carried out through any form of mass or social media, making it more dangerous to use these methods.

Finally, as R. Zylberman notes, the fact that the shamed person may not be able to escape from his humiliation may affect the way halakha views the legitimacy of such methods.

These and other points will be discussed as we explore the specific arguments presented in Israel after a rabbinic court officially endorsed the use of social-media shaming to pressure a husband into granting his wife a *get.*

Reconstituting Community

As we outlined above, the Jewish community has used many kinds of shaming throughout history to punish sinners and pressure them to repent. One factor that enabled these methods to be effective was the closeness of the community. Jews usually lived in tight-knit communities, sometimes by choice, often not. Before the modern period, people had to live in a religious community, and the only way out was to convert. In that context, shaming and social pressure were quite effective.

However, in the modern period, this is no longer the case. People may live wherever they want and need not identify with any community. Thus, methods like excommunication became weak, as people pressured by methods like it can simply leave the community.

We noted in our discussions of the nature of *mara de'atra* that globalization has basically eviscerated geographic models of halakhic authority. However, we further noted that modern methods of communication also have enabled the recreation of community along ideological lines. Similar dynamics are at play here.

When dealing with issues of public shaming, a similar phenomenon has happened. Social media has made it nearly impossible to escape a concerted effort to follow someone. Helen Andrews, a Robert Novak Journalism fellow, recently described her decades-long attempt to escape a viral video of an ex-boyfriend accusing her of being a sadist and the effects it had on her life:

> Moving to the other side of the world did not diminish the video's place in my life as much as I thought it would. It was still the first result when you Googled my name, which presumably is one reason I couldn't find a job for the first eighteen months.... When I moved back to Washington, D.C., and started meeting some of the younger writers in town, it took them less than a week to

> find the clip and ask me about it. Most of them had been in high school when it happened.[8]

Cass Sunstein generalizes the issue:

> In the era of the Internet, it has become easy to spread false or misleading rumors about almost anyone. A high school student, a salesperson, a professor, a banker, an employer, an insurance broker, a real estate agent – each of these is vulnerable to an allegation that can have a painful, damaging, or even devastating effect. If an allegation of misconduct appears on the Internet, those who Google the relevant name will immediately learn about it. The allegation will help to define the person. (It might even end up on Wikipedia, at least for a time.)[9]

Thus, the interconnected world has recreated a world in which social shaming can be effective, in which information can be weaponized. A superficial understanding might have suggested that we can take advantage of this reality to invoke *ḥerem*-like punishments (or *harḥakot* of Rabbenu Tam, or other similar mechanism) in cases where a *beit din* would have invoked these methods. However, there are several salient differences that may affect how this should be applied in this global community:

1. Social-media shaming is effective because it goes viral. This requires handing the tools over to the laity, rather than leaving it in the hands of judges.
2. The lasting power of the internet is basically eternal. While in the past, public pressure was rolled back after the sinner had repented, it is nearly impossible to counter social-media shaming once it has begun.
3. As we saw in the words of R. Michoel Zylberman, certain leniencies related to *harḥakot* of Rabbenu Tam derive from the fact that

8. https://www.firstthings.com/article/2019/01/shame-storm.
9. *On Rumors.*

> they are, in theory, escapable. The fact that the recalcitrant husband can leave the community means that the pressure exerted is not defined as coercion from a halakhic perspective. Thus, the *get* can be considered to have been given of the husband's free will. If, as Andrews indicates, this is not the reality of social-media shaming, this might require an assessment of whether social-media versions of *harḥakot* of Rabbenu Tam would share the leniencies of the originals.

Posekim are also concerned about the conditions the *Ḥafetz Ḥayim* propounds for justifying *lashon hara.* Especially considering the potential damage that social-media shaming can cause, exploring other options first becomes critical. More importantly, if one accepts the *Ḥafetz Ḥayim*'s claim that one must not engage in *lashon hara leto'elet* (which the above cases are at least related to) if the resulting harm would be greater than that which halakha would formally apply to the sinner, it would be forbidden to do so. Considering the lasting harm that a campaign of shaming can cause, this is something that must be considered. This framing will help us understand the debate that arose after a recent ruling of a *beit din* in Israel.

Harḥakot of Rabbenu Tam on Social Media

As we noted above, there have been several celebrated cases in America where social-media shaming was used to pressure a recalcitrant husband to grant a *get.*[10]

In Israel, a public discussion arose after a *beit din* officially endorsed it. There was a physics lecturer living in Israel, Dr. Oded Guez, who refused to grant his wife a *get* for years. He had been called to several hearings in *batei din,* all of which were unsuccessful. In 2016, one of the courts of the Chief Rabbinate formally endorsed invoking social-media shaming as part of a version of *harḥakot* of Rabbenu Tam. The sources for this court ruling and the subsequent rabbinic responses are taken from "Shaming in Judaism: Past, Present, Future," by Tsuriel Rashi and Hananel Rosenberg.

10. For a thorough analysis of these, see Machtinger below.

> It is incumbent on every Jewish man and woman and everyone associated with them not to have any dealings with him, whether in business or monetary matters, not to provide him hospitality, feed him or give him to drink, not to visit him when he is sick, and not to seat him in the synagogue, and all the more so not to call him up to the Torah, and not to let him say *kaddish* [prayer for the departed], and all the more so not to lead the prayer service, not to ask how he is, not to give him any form of respect or honor until such time as he relents from being stiff necked and listens to the words of the teachers, and grants a divorce in Jewish law to his wife, and to free her from her marital chains.

As Rashi and Rosenberg record:

> The rabbinical court did not limit itself to this declaration; it further supported the application of his spouse to publicize his photograph together with the rabbinical court ruling on social media, thereby contravening the original prohibition regarding publicizing Guez's name and picture.

They quote Pinchas Tannenbaum, spokesman for the chief rabbi:

> The decision was taken with much pain, but there was no other choice. The rabbinical court does not publish advertisements and does not know the word "shaming"; however, in this case the rabbinical judges felt that publicity on social media would be a more effective tool. The wife claimed that from her acquaintance with her husband this was the right tool, and who should know better than her.

Further, they note:

> It transpires that this was not the first time that the rabbinical court was aware of the great power of social media. The director of the *Yad La'Isha* organization that assists "chained women," clarified that this was a "phenomenon that started in the rabbinical

> courts in the last year or two," and she recounted another case of a well-known businessman who fled abroad and left his wife chained to extort money from her family. She noted that the moment the rabbinical court permitted publication of his photograph on social media, intensive negotiations came to a successful conclusion within just a few days.

Despite the fact that this method had been in use in the United States, as well as in Israel, it was this case that brought it into public debate in Israel.

Reservations: A Dangerous Tool in the Hands of the Laity

R. David Stav, the chief rabbi of Shoham and chairman of the Tzohar rabbinical organization, is quite hesitant to accept the conclusion of the court. Rashi and Rosenberg summarize the core of his hesitation, which we noted above: social-media shaming may make weaponizing information possible again, but only by granting the power to the laity, and thus removing most of the restraint the rabbinical courts may have held:

> Social media reconstitutes the effectiveness of rabbinical courts' social punishment, but in doing so grants access to such a strong tool to individuals who may not be bound by the seriousness of a rabbinic court, as well as to religious court judges who might be too hasty.

While R. Stav says he would act if a court were to issue a formal ruling, he outlines the specific concerns that must be taken into account first:

1. Embarrassing people publicly is a grave sin. Thus, any court that decides to utilize such a dangerous tool must justify that decision fully.
2. Due to this, R. Stav thinks that it might even be better for the court to utilize its power to imprison the husband. This method avoids embarrassment (and, I would assume, remains fully in the hands of the court to reverse if and when the husband relents).

3. Setting a precedent of legitimating social-media shaming may be dangerous, as it may be used by other courts when not legitimate, or by individuals without rabbinic sanction.

As mentioned above, R. Stav does not forbid it; he just expresses his concerns. As he puts it, "I warn against releasing the brakes suddenly, and from here if someone does something we do not like, it is not a reason to embarrass him in public."

R. Chaim Navon puts the concern more succinctly:

> Once, when communities were communities, this is what excommunication looked like: effective social ostracism. Rabbinical courts made measured use of it against various scoundrels. The weakening of the communities alongside social mobility decreased the effectiveness of this tool. For these reasons, someone ostracized or excommunicated simply showed contempt for the rabbinical court, or at the most moved somewhere else and started over again. Social media in fact have restored the effectiveness of excommunication, and have returned it to what it was meant to be.

Rashi and Rosenberg go on to explain:

> However, exactly for this reason, R. Navon stipulates the border between shaming sponsored by the rabbinical court and the personal shaming of Internet surfers, which he considers "*lynchtranet* of someone just because I don't like him, or I suspect him, or I don't like his opinions, or he said something bad – that is a disgrace. Something completely different is to cooperate with a ruling of the rabbinical court, which checked out matters scrupulously, before it determined on such a step."

The Positive

Implicit in the arguments of R. Stav and R. Navon is that there is a fundamental difference between the courts or leadership and the laity in terms of their responsibility to achieve justice. Thus, as the classic models of social shaming were in the hands of the leaders, and social-media shaming is not, they are hesitant to use these modern equivalents, despite their effectiveness.

However, R. Asher Weiss argues that there are many obligations which primarily devolve on specific groups of leaders (political, judicial, or religious), but secondarily devolve on all people. Among those, he counts the commandment to ensure the execution of justice.

He bases this on a comment of Rashi. In the middle of discussion of the parameters of "*Uviarta hara mikirbekha*," "And you shall get rid of evil from your midst" (Deut. 17:7, Ḥullin 138b–139a), a verse used to describe the goals of the court, Rashi (139a, s.v. *uviarta*) extends this beyond the court. Specifically, he writes that this same obligation mandates that anyone who finds someone liable for the death penalty must bring him to court to face justice. Thus, R. Weiss argues, while the obligation to execute justice is primarily focused on the courts, the average person also has a mitzva to be involved.

Though he does not invoke the above argument explicitly, R. Yuval Cherlow, an Israeli *rosh yeshiva*, seems to take an approach like this to explain his more positive approach to the ruling of the *beit din* and the acceptability of involving the laity in the process of shaming as a tool to rectify an injustice. While R. Weiss makes this argument at a fundamental level, R. Cherlow focuses on the pragmatic aspect and the way social media has made this a practical necessity. As Rosenberg and Rashi write:

> In his opinion, the ethical decision to use social media to write or share an embarrassing post is given to each person, and not just to religious institutions. R. Cherlow emphasizes that in the age of social media the border between the individual and social institutions has been blurred, and sometimes the power of the individual to correct social wrongs is greater than that of traditional institutions, which accordingly obliges the individual to be part in this objective of fixing the injustice, and that it is the duty of the rabbis to lay down Jewish ethical rules and make them available to everyone.

Additionally, he focuses on the *Pitḥei Teshuva*'s framing of the issue: not just the potential prohibitions involved, but the dangers in not acting and the potential mitzvot one will be derelict in fulfilling.

> According to R. Cherlow, the starting point for Jewish ethics concerning shaming via social media is not what is "permitted," but rather what is "obligatory": Jewish ethics holds that the concept of "the public's right to know" is a distorted one. The public does not have a right to know everything about people's private lives. Jewish ethics does recognize "the public's right to know," namely, those things that the public must know – it is an obligation to publicize them. It is not always easy to differentiate between the two, yet it is important that this be a guiding light for the one publicizing.

Rav Cherlow does not deny the potential dangers involved, and thus warns anyone using these tools to be careful, as public humiliation can literally cause danger to human life, as we will explore below. Whether as formal halakhic rules based on an expanded notion of *to'elet* (a position we alluded to previously), or as good advice, he presents a version of the *Ḥafetz Ḥayim*'s conditions for *to'elet* that shed light on the concerns one must take into account when using these dangerous tools:

- **Truth**: The shaming writer must write the truth, the whole relevant truth, and nothing but the relevant truth. It is forbidden for a person to write what that individual does not have direct knowledge of (one may write, for example, "I assume"), and one must avoid manipulation and must distinguish between facts and commentary. This halakhic principle is based on the Torah prescription, "Keep your distance from a false matter" (Ex. 23:7). This is the only thing from which the Torah explicitly commands us to distance ourselves.
- **Necessity**: If there are other ways to solve the problem with equal effectiveness, one must take that path and not defame in public. On the other hand, if there is a real necessity to publicize, then

one is forbidden to remain silent, as the Torah has commanded us, "*Lo taamod al dam re'ekha*" and "*Uviarta hara mikirbekha.*"

- **Proportionality**: The fact that it is permitted, and perhaps even an obligation, to publicize matters does not relieve the publicizer of doing so only in the required proportion. Facts which are not necessary (even if they are true), and which may harm someone who does not deserve to be harmed, must not be publicized.
- **Caution**: One must be cautious about causing greater harm by publicization and causing much greater harm to the wrongdoer than is due.

Rav Cherlow adds another point that he says is not a halakhic, but rather an ethical, condition, since alongside the explicit publicization of issues, it is right and proper to leave open the opportunity for the person being shamed to correct the wrong.

While R. Cherlow uses the basic structure of the *Ḥafetz Ḥayim,* his language points in the direction of the *Pitḥei Teshuva.* Rashi and Rosenberg note that he focuses not on permitted versus forbidden, but on forbidden versus obligatory. R. Cherlow's summary of his position is as follows:

> On the one hand, without dissemination of the required information a tool in this fight has been lost, but, on the other hand, there are many opportunities for manipulation and using the reader's good intentions for base purposes. Accordingly, it is worth using this tool as seldom as possible....
>
> And even so, according to the questions in the Babylonian Talmud concerning slander, several principles can be stipulated for sharing the dissemination of shaming.
>
> Firstly, the reader of shaming must internalize that what he reads is not a fact but a story or narrative of someone who is writing him something, of which it is reasonable to assume that part is correct and part unclear.
>
> Secondly, the shaming reader must make an effort to hear the position of the other party, the wrongdoer, based on

> the injunction to rabbinical court judges, "Hear out your fellows and judge them righteously." Any reading of shaming-type publications is a quasi-judgmental exercise, and requires making an effort to hear what can be known from both sides.
>
> Thirdly, the shaming reader must assess the necessity of disseminating these matters. If the things you pass on are not helpful, it is prohibited to convey them; if what you publicized is necessary to deal with wrongdoing, as it appears as far as possible, you are obliged to pass it on, stating: "Be advised that I am conveying information that I do not know to be correct, but it is important to pass it on, decide for yourself" or similar.

This basic analysis supports some of our central theses in the past several sections: namely, that the more expansive approaches to when publicizing negative information can or must be used stem from those who follow the *Pitḥei Teshuva.* They frame the question not as forbidden *lashon hara* versus permitted *lashon hara*; rather, they see positive obligations pushing one to publicize as strongly as the prohibitions of *lashon hara* push one to be silent. However, as we noted, practically, even such *posekim* will find inspiration in the limitations of the *Ḥafetz Ḥayim,* as they are helpful to navigate and balance the complex halakhic issues involved in these kinds of questions.

There Is No Escape

We noted that R. Michoel Zylberman explains that the classic *harḥakot* of Rabbenu Tam were not considered coercive from the vantage point of halakha. This was because the husband could always leave the community, and thus his choice to remain and grant the *get* was considered to be of his own volition. All the rabbis discussed here assume that the modern equivalents would not be more problematic at this level. R. Zylberman notes, however, that one could make an argument that they would, though he does not actually endorse this position:

> Arguably, this reason may apply in fewer situations in our more mobile, contemporary society with enhanced communication abilities.

In fact, ORA, the Organization for the Resolution of Agunot, claims that their use of social media is intended to prevent the escape of the husband:

> We want their names and faces to be known throughout the United States and worldwide, so they can't escape or hide in another community, that his back will be against the wall.... We aim to make them so famous, they can't slink away, change their names and continue their abuses toward their families.[11]

Still, the vast majority of *posekim* have not taken the view that this invalidates *gittin.*

Conclusion

The analysis of the benefits and dangers of using social-media shaming to accomplish important goals sheds light on the unique ways in which social media forces us to rethink how we apply *to'elet* and related categories. Additionally, as we have seen in other areas, social media affects the ways in which the laity relates to rabbinic authorities, changing their relationship. The fact that social media has recreated the ability to forge global communities not run by traditional rabbinic authorities affects the exact way in which classic halakhic mechanisms may be applied.[12]

---

11. Quote taken from Machtinger below.
12. For a full analysis of the ways in which these mechanisms have actually played out in recent cases, see: *A Socio-Legal Investigation of 'Get' Jewish Divorce Refusal in New York and Toronto: Agunot Unstitching the Ties that Bind,* by Yael C. B. Machtinger, available at: https://yorkspace.library.yorku.ca/xmlui/bitstream/handle/10315/34525/Machtinger_Yael_CB_2017_PhD.pdf?sequence=2&isAllowed=y.

Chapter 25

The Dangers of the Shame Storm: Public Humiliation in Halakha

The Destructive Power of Social Media: Several Cautionary Tales

In the previous chapter, we have explored the principles that justify or mandate weaponizing information to solve a social or religious problem. However, while these exceptional cases require more extensive analysis than the standard ones, this does not change the fact that in most cases, sharing negative information about people is prohibited and constitutes a host of biblical violations, whether they be classified as *lashon hara* or more generic prohibitions such as *onaat devarim* (the prohibition against hurting people with words).

Additionally, *Ḥazal* have particularly harsh things to say about people who embarrass others publicly. In any case where sharing such information on social media is illegitimate, one can only imagine how egregious *Ḥazal* would have considered this sin. This is true even in cases in which the information being shared is true, as it is still *lashon hara*. Additionally, as R. Daniel Feldman points out and we cited, even when a particular fact is technically true, that does not mean that the picture it will cause people to paint is an accurate portrayal of the person's entire personality. This problem is acutely dangerous on social media.

Recently, several articles have been written which focus on these issues. They have commented on how social media has created a culture that encourages shaming people for indiscretions, real or imagined, often out of proportion to the gravity of the crime – and the consequences are grave. For example, David French recently wrote about one case of social shaming:

> When you think of the sheer vindictiveness of what happened to Oklahoma quarterback Kyler Murray, it takes your breath away. On the very night of his greatest career triumph, a reporter dug up his old tweets (composed when he was a young teenager), reported on the most offensive insults, and immediately and irrevocably transformed his online legacy. Now he's not just "Kyler Murray, gifted quarterback and humble Heisman winner," but also the man who was forced to apologize for his alleged homophobia. And for what purpose? Which cause did the reporter advance? Where was the cultural gain in Murray's pain?
>
> And he's but the latest victim of a malicious online world that seeks to destroy people in the moment of their triumph. It's happened to athletes, to entertainers, and even to "regular" folks who enjoy the slightest bit of fame or acclaim in the public eye. It's almost a joke at this point – when are we going to find out that this person who did this wonderful thing is actually terrible on Facebook or dreadful on Twitter?
>
> The incidents happen so fast, and the firings are so quick, that they start to blur together. Can you remember November's victims? October's? Who lost their jobs this summer? Who was forced to apologize this spring?

> *Well, if you can't remember, I can assure you that the victims do, and the experience transforms their lives.* (Emphasis mine)[1]

As R. Feldman notes, even when the information is true, the image that individual facts project to the world, especially through social media, is unfair. Even more so, the "guilty" party may have changed. However, the nature of social-media shaming is that it does not take this into account. It is unforgiving.

Furthermore, the problems French outlines reflect the same sentiments that the *Ḥafetz Ḥayim* presents in several of his conditions for *to'elet*: specifically, the consequences of the shaming are out of proportion to the "crime," the "crime" and its gravity seem to have been exaggerated, there is no justifiable reason for publicizing the indiscretion – and even if there were, I would add, no attempt was made to achieve that goal without the *lashon hara.*

French continues to capture another concern of the *Ḥafetz Ḥayim.* The *Ḥafetz Ḥayim* argues that one should first rebuke the sinner to see if he or she will change his or her ways. As French notes, in many cases public shaming happens even after the person has repented, which from a halakhic perspective makes the shaming superfluous, meanspirited, and forbidden:

> Take any given controversy, and you'll usually find that the person at the center isn't proud of what they did. They wish they hadn't done it. At some level, the person at the center of the shame storm is also ashamed of themselves.
>
> But then, in this terrible new world, *you can't ever shake the wrong thing you did.* Never. It clings to you. It defines you. It becomes, to some people, the entirety of who you are.

1. https://www.nationalreview.com/2018/12/kyler-murray-helen-andrews-shame-mob-america-intolerance/amp/?__twitter_impression=true&fbclid=IwAR2CuoqEHfGs5xXuv3GR8JEe9-yCsFNz1bofgFEqdKMvOw8_NIALG3mHQdg.

French further notes the possibility that the fury and intolerance present in the culture created by smartphones and easy access to social media may have contributed to the increase in teen depression and suicide, a possibility raised by Jean M. Twenge in her provocatively titled "Have Smartphones Destroyed a Generation?"[2]

Helen Andrews recently wrote about her own experiences in an aptly named article, "Shame Storm."[3] She describes the beginning of her ordeal as follows:

> In October 2010, I appeared on a panel to promote a book of essays by young conservatives, *Proud to Be Right: Voices of the Next Conservative Generation*. The moderator was Jonah Goldberg. One of the other panelists was my ex-boyfriend Todd Seavey. During the Q&A, Todd launched into a rant about my personal failings. He accused me of opposing Obamacare on the grounds that it would diminish human suffering, which allegedly I preferred to increase; of wanting to repeal laws against fistfights for the same reason; of being a sadistic and scheming heartbreaker in my personal life; and of generally living according to a "disturbing" and "brutal" set of values. For three minutes and forty-five seconds, which, unfortunately for me, were captured on film for broadcast two weeks later on C-SPAN2, he made an impassioned case that I was a sociopath.

In her piece, Andrews admits that she was less than an ideal girlfriend to Todd. However, his accusations were exaggerated and made from a place of pain. As the *Ḥafetz Ḥayim* notes, *lashon hara leto'elet* should be shared out of a sense of responsibility, not vindictiveness, which was clearly the case here. Andrews then discusses the repercussions of this video, which she describes as a "shame storm":

2. https://www.theatlantic.com/magazine/archive/2017/09/has-the-smartphone-destroyed-a-generation/534198/. See, more extensively, her *iGen: Why Today's Super-Connected Kids Are Growing Up Less Rebellious, More Tolerant, Less Happy – and Completely Unprepared for Adulthood – and What That Means for the Rest of Us* (Simon and Schuster, 2017).
3. https://www.firstthings.com/article/2019/01/shame-storm.

> I braced myself for the broadcast. Maybe no one would notice? Within minutes, the offending clip had been posted on YouTube, where it got half a million hits in the first forty-eight hours. It made the evening news on Washington's Fox affiliate. Greg Gutfeld did a segment about it on *Red Eye*. It was written up in Gawker, the *Washington Post*, Talking Points Memo, and a hundred lesser sites, and then written up again when Todd expanded his remarks about me into a series of blog posts on his personal website.

Andrews writes that the follow-up was so bad that she accepted an offer from her new boyfriend, now husband, to move to Australia. However, even then, as we mentioned above, that was insufficient:

> Moving to the other side of the world did not diminish the video's place in my life as much as I thought it would. It was still the first result when you Googled my name, which presumably is one reason I couldn't find a job for the first eighteen months. Eventually, I found a position at a think tank. When I released my first report, an Australian MP tweeted a link to the video and asked why anyone should care about this nutcase's opinions on regulation. Even after I got married and took my husband's last name, the video still popped up on social media when I did a TV appearance or had an op-ed in the paper. In 2017, when I moved back to Washington, D.C., and started meeting some of the younger writers in town, it took them less than a week to find the clip and ask me about it. Most of them had been in high school when it happened.

Andrews adds one more point that fits with many of the values we have explored in previous sections. Deciding what is *to'elet* is difficult. This is especially hard on social media:

> The more online shame cycles you observe, the more obvious the pattern becomes: Everyone comes up with a principled-sounding pretext that serves as a barrier against admitting to themselves that, in fact, all they have really done is joined a mob. Once that barrier is erected, all rules of decency go out the window, but the

> pretext is almost always a lie. Matthew Yglesias once claimed that the reason he mocked David Brooks for his divorce was because Brooks had written columns about the social value of marriage, but I do not believe him. He did it because it's fun to humiliate your political opponents.

Toward the end of her article, Andrews makes a similar point to that of R. Stav and R. Navon: the dangers inherent in using social-media or internet shaming do not make it illegitimate. It just means that this technique should be used as rarely as possible, especially as it is seldom productive, and it remains in the public sphere forever:

> The solution, then, is not to try to make shame storms well targeted, but to make it so they happen as infrequently as possible. Editors should refuse to run stories that have no value except humiliation, and readers should refuse to click on them. It is, after all, the moral equivalent of contributing your rock to a public stoning. We should all develop a robust sense of what is and is not any of our business. Shame can be useful – and even necessary – but it is toxic unless a relationship exists between two people first. A Twitter mob is no more a basis for salutary shaming than an actual mob is for reasoned discussion. That would be true even if the shaming's relics were not preserved forever by Google, making any kind of rehabilitation impossible.

The Gravity of Public Humiliation in Halakha

Thus, we must take into consideration that public humiliation, especially in our world connected by the internet and all forms of social media, can destroy lives and, in some cases, literally lead to suicide. This may help us understand some of the sentiments expressed by *Ḥazal* which equate embarrassing people publicly with murdering them. The central presentation of this law is part of a broader discussion in Bava Metzia about the prohibition of hurting people using words, *onaat devarim*. The specific prohibition to embarrass people is derived from Leviticus 19:17:

> You shall not hate your kinsfolk in your heart. Reprove your kinsman but incur no guilt because of him.

Rashi (ibid.) summarizes the interpretation by *Ḥazal* in several places (*Sifra, Kedoshim* 4:8; Arakhin 16b) that even though offering rebuke is a mitzva, this does not, in most cases, legitimate doing so publicly in a way that embarrasses the sinner:

> Through rebuking him, you shall not expose him to shame (lit., make his face grow pale) in public, in which case you will bear sin on account of him.

In *Pirkei Avot* (3:11), we learn that if one does violate this prohibition, despite many merits that the rebuker may have, he or she loses his or her share in the World to Come!

> Rabbi Elazar of Modi'in says: One who profanes the *Kodashim* (sacred material); one who desecrates the holidays; one who whitens (embarrasses) the face of another in public; one who nullifies the covenant of Avraham our father, peace be upon him; one who reveals meanings in the Torah that run contrary to the law – even though he has Torah knowledge and good deeds, he has no share in the World to Come.

The Talmud (Bava Metzia 58b; Sota 10b) outlines how far one must go to avoid the sin of embarrassing others. The framing for the Talmud's comments is the story of Yehuda and Tamar (Gen. 38). Tamar marries Yehuda's oldest son, Er. However, Er is evil and God kills him. In an act of proto-*yibum* (levirate marriage), Yehuda's second son, Onan, marries Tamar to have children to perpetuate the legacy of his brother Er. Onan, however, has no interest in having children who would be the spiritual heirs of Er, so he refuses to consummate his relationship with Tamar, insisting that all sexual relations end with coitus interruptus to prevent her from becoming pregnant. For this sin, God kills him as well. Without understanding the background, Yehuda concludes that it is Tamar's fault that his sons have died. Thus, he refuses to let her marry his third son,

Shela. However, he does not tell her this explicitly. Rather, he stalls and tells Tamar to wait at her father's home until Shela will be old enough to marry her and carry on the legacy of his brothers.

After a time, Tamar realizes that Yehuda is merely stalling. Desiring to carry on the legacy of her husband(s), Tamar disguises herself as a prostitute and waits by the road until Yehuda comes and propositions her. Yehuda does not have the means to provide payment. Thus, Tamar, demands that he leave collateral: his seal, cord, and staff. Yehuda later attempts to pay through a messenger. However, the "prostitute" has disappeared.

Months later, people realize that Tamar is pregnant. Not knowing that she is pregnant from Yehuda, which would be legitimate in the pre-Sinaitic context of levirate marriage, he assumes that she has slept with someone not from the family of Yehuda, which would be a kind of adultery, as she is destined to marry Shela. Yehuda, as leader of the family, sentences her to death. Rather than tell the truth publicly, she sends a message to Yehuda which elicits his admission that she is correct:

> As she was being brought out, she sent to her father-in-law, saying: "By the man whose these are, am I with child." And she added, "Examine these: whose seal and cord and staff are these?"
>
> Yehuda recognized them, and said, "She is more in the right than I, inasmuch as I did not give her to my son Shela." (Gen. 38:25–26)

The question that bothers the Talmud is the following: Why doesn't Tamar simply tell the truth? Her life is on the line. By putting the ball in Yehuda's court, she is risking that he may attempt to hide the truth and kill her, burying the evidence of his sin with her. With this background, we can understand the Talmud's striking conclusion:

> The verse concerning Tamar then states: **"She sent to her father-in-law, saying: By the man whose these are, am I with child"** (Gen. 38:25). The Gemara comments: **And let her say to him** explicitly that she was impregnated by him. **Rav Zutra bar Tuviyya says** that **Rav says, and some say Rav Ḥana bar**

> **Bizna says** that **Rabbi Shimon Ḥasida says, and some say** that **Rabbi Yoḥanan says in the name of Rabbi Shimon ben Yoḥai: It is more amenable for a person to throw himself into a fiery furnace** if faced with the choice of publicly embarrassing another or remaining silent even if it leads to being burned, **and not humiliate another in public. From where do we** derive this? **From Tamar,** as she was prepared to be burned if Judah did not confess, rather than humiliate him in public. (Sota 10b)

The *Midrash Tanḥuma* (*Parashat Vayigash*) expresses similar sentiments, arguing that Yosef refrains from revealing his identity to his brothers while the guards are present, though being alone with his brothers puts him in danger, in order to prevent his brothers from being humiliated.

Is this to be taken literally? A simple understanding of this passage would imply that the prohibition to embarrass others publicly is a cardinal sin. However, this would violate the basic rule established in several places in the Talmud, according to which there are only three cardinal sins:

> **Rabbi Yoḥanan says in the name of Rabbi Shimon ben Yehotzadak:** The Sages who discussed this issue **counted** the votes of those assembled **and concluded in the upper story of the house of Nitza in** the city of **Lod:** With regard to **all** other **transgressions in the Torah, if a person is told: Transgress** this prohibition **and you will not be killed, he may transgress** that prohibition **and not be killed,** because the preserving of his own life overrides all of the Torah's prohibitions. This is the *halakha* concerning all prohibitions **except for** those of **idol worship, forbidden sexual relations, and bloodshed.** (Sanhedrin 74a)

Despite this, several Rishonim accept the simple understanding of the Gemara. Tosafot, for example, write that this is a cardinal sin; however, as the prohibition is not explicit in the Torah, it is not counted in the list of three cardinal sins:

> It seems that the reason it is not mentioned with the three things for which one gives up his life, idol worship, forbidden sexual relations, and bloodshed, is because embarrassing others is not explicit in the Torah, and it only mentions explicit sins. (Tosafot Sota 10b)

This is surprising, as one would have assumed that non-explicit sins are less, rather than more, severe!

Rabbenu Yona (*Shaarei Teshuva 3:141*) argues differently, reasoning that embarrassing people, which causes the blood to drain from their faces, is a subset of bloodshed; hence, it is indeed among the "big three."[4]

As surprising as this is, no less an authority than R. Shlomo Zalman Auerbach (*Responsa Minḥat Shlomo* 1:7) accepts this position as the majority position in Rishonim and thus binding halakha. He even has lengthy discussions on why we don't apply the rules of *rodef*, a pursuer, to one attempting to embarrass someone else; if one sees a would-be murderer chasing a victim, one is obligated to intervene, even if that requires killing the pursuer. R. Shlomo Zalman thus raises the possibility that one could kill someone to prevent the embarrassment of the "victim." He similarly discusses whether one could violate Shabbat, or other prohibitions, to prevent such humiliation.

R. Shlomo Zalman claims that the only outlier among the Rishonim who does not accept that embarrassing others publicly is a cardinal sin is the Meiri (Berakhot 43b, Sota 10b) who understands this passage as mere rhetoric. R. Yehuda Herzl Henkin (*Responsa Benei Vanim* 1:41), however, notes that in fact the majority position in Rishonim and Aḥaronim is that humiliating others is not a cardinal sin and rules accordingly.[5]

However, the very fact that such a conclusion could have been reached points to the strength of the rhetoric that *Ḥazal* use. Rivash (*Responsa* 171), while explaining why many of the sins that *Ḥazal* equate with cardinal sins are not in fact on that level, clarifies why *Ḥazal* use such harsh rhetoric:

---

4. *Shulḥan Arukh, YD* 157:1, records the position of the Ran that even the subsidiary prohibitions of the three cardinal sins carry the weight of the primary sins.
5. More positions on each side of this debate can be found in the responsum of R. Henkin cited above, and in R. Daniel Feldman's *The Right and the Good* (Yashar Books, 2005), ch. 1.

> They do not say regarding it that one should die rather than violate, as by the three sins. This never entered anyone's mind, and no person thought it. Rather, it is the ways of Sages to exaggerate the magnitude of sins so people will refrain from stumbling in them.

In other words, even if we rule like R. Henkin, the strength of the rhetoric indicates that at some level, public humiliation can feel as bad as murder. As we noted, in the world of social media, this is even truer, and in some cases, actually leads to suicide, literally introducing a level of *pikuaḥ nefesh.*

An Option to Sacrifice One's Life?

As we noted, the Talmud seems to entertain the position that humiliating others is a cardinal sin. Whether this is indeed the Talmud's intent is a dispute among the Rishonim and the Aḥaronim, and even among modern authorities. There is, however, a middle position worth exploring.

R. Aryeh Klapper suggests the following: Considering how some cases of humiliation may indeed be life-shattering, perhaps the Talmud's intent is that one has the *option* to sacrifice his or her life rather than destroy the life of another. This does not mean that all cases rise to that level, but perhaps the Talmud is open to some cases fitting that bill and wants people to be able to choose to sacrifice themselves to protect potential victims.

Social media and the internet in general have created an atmosphere in which a "shame storm" may dog people for years, preventing them from getting jobs or forging healthy relationships, as well as creating a host of other problems. In such a world, a perspective like this has a certain appeal and may be defended on the basis of several positions expressed by Rishonim, Aḥaronim, and *posekim.*

Obligation or Permission

In general, there is a dispute between the Rishonim as to whether the "big three" are the only sins one for which one is *obligated* to sacrifice his or her life, or the only sins for which one is *permitted* to sacrifice his or her life. According to the latter position, barring cases of *she'at hashemad,* a period of persecution when Judaism as a religion is under attack (at which time the rules are different regardless), one is obligated to live rather than sacrifice his or her life in order to refrain from violating the majority of mitzvot.

The latter position is taken by the Rambam, who forcefully writes as follows:

> It is mandatory upon the whole house of Israel to sanctify this Great Name, for it is said: "And I shall be sanctified among the children of Israel" (Lev. 22.32). They are also charged not to blaspheme Him, for it is said: "And ye shall not profane My holy Name" (ibid.).
>
> How are these commandments to be observed? If an idolater will force an Israelite to transgress one of the commandments of the Torah and threaten him with death for disobedience, it is mandatory that he transgress the commandment and be not put to death, for it is said concerning the commandments: "That which a man may do and live by it" (ibid. 18.5) – "live by it, but not die for it." Thus, if he chose death and did not transgress, his blood be upon his own head.
>
> Whereat are these words directed? Concerning all other commandments, save idolatry, adultery and bloodshed. For respecting these three commandments, if one will say to him: "Transgress one of the three, or die," he shall die, and not transgress. (Rambam, *Hilkhot Yesodei HaTorah* 5:1–2, Glazer translation)

The Rambam rules that one who sacrifices his life in any case other than those mandated by the Torah is essentially committing suicide. A simple reading of the Rambam implies that *not sacrificing* one's life for the mitzvot that are not cardinal sins is a more primary fulfillment of sanctifying God's name than martyring oneself for the "big three"![6]

Tosafot (Avoda Zara 27b, s.v. *yakhol*), however, rule that one is entitled to sacrifice one's life for the other sins; one is simply not obligated to.

---

6. See my article, *"BeInyan Yaavor VeAl Yeihareig"* (*Beit Yitzḥak*, vol. 41), where I develop this position. See, however, the other explanations of the Rambam cited there.

R. Daniel Feldman[7] suggests that it is this position that leads Tosafot to understand that humiliating others is a cardinal sin, as one always has the option to sacrifice his life rather than violate a sin. Thus, if the Talmud singles out a specific sin, it must be because that sin carries with it an obligation to give up one's life.

R. Yehuda Herzl Henkin (*Responsa Benei Vanim* 1:41), however, raises a different possibility. Perhaps Tosafot hold that there are three categories:

1. The three cardinal sins, for which one must sacrifice his or her life.
2. The majority of mitzvot, for which one is entitled, but not obligated, to sacrifice his or her life.
3. Mitzvot for which one is encouraged, though not obligated, to sacrifice his or her life.

Perhaps Tosafot relegate the sin of public humiliation to the third category. One could suggest, as R. Klapper does, that this would only be true in particularly egregious cases.

The *Penei Yehoshua* (Bava Metzia 59a) suggests a similar formulation within the perspective of the Rambam: even if one thinks, like the Rambam, that for most mitzvot, one either is obligated or forbidden to martyr oneself for its fulfillment, perhaps the prohibition of humiliating others is severe enough that one is allowed to give up one's life, and if one does, it is not considered suicide.

The intent of the above analysis is not to offer practical halakhic guidance. Most *posekim*, R. Shlomo Zalman Auerbach notwithstanding, fully reject the position that this sin of publicly humiliating others requires or permits martyrdom more than any other non-cardinal sin (see the writings of R. Henkin and R. Feldman for fuller lists). Rather, this discussion is meant to highlight the severity with which halakhic authorities view public humiliation, understanding, therefore, how critical it is to avoid using the tools of social media which exacerbate the issue of causing such harm.

---

7. *The Right and the Good*, 5.

Why Is Public Humiliation like Murder?[8]

As we have seen, the Talmud compares humiliation to murder. What is it, however, that lends it this quality? The Talmud offers a physiological explanation: it causes the blood to drain from one's face – hence the talmudic term for humiliation is *halbanat panim,* the whitening of the face.

However, the *Midrash Shmuel* quotes R. Menachem of the House of Meir, describing a state which, as R. Daniel Feldman puts it, "will be familiar to anyone who has ever been truly embarrassed."[9] The *Midrash Shmuel* states:

> One who is humiliated, his face first turns red, and then turns white, because due to the magnitude of the shame, his soul "flies away," as if it wanted to leave the body…once the blood returns to its source, the face turns white, like someone who had died…. (*Midrash Shmuel* on Avot 3:15, translation from Feldman)

In other words, true, deep shame and embarrassment make someone want to die. As we noted previously, social-media shaming has been linked to increased rates of suicide, further deepening this link in a terrifying way.

Losing One's Share in the World to Come

In a different Aggadic passage that we have already mentioned, the Gemara suggests that this sin erases one's share in the World to Come, even more so than cardinal sins such as adultery. The context for this is King David's being shamed by others in the aftermath of the incident with Batsheva:

> **David said before the Holy One, Blessed be He: Master of the Universe, it is revealed and known before You that if** my tormenters **were to tear my flesh, my blood** [*dami*] **would not flow to the ground,** due to excessive fasting.
>
> **And moreover,** they torment me to the extent that **even at the time** when **they are engaged** in the public study of the

---

8. This discussion is paraphrased from R. Daniel Feldman, cited above.

9. Ibid., 6.

> *halakhot* **of leprous sores and tents** in which there is a corpse, i.e., halakhic matters that have no connection to my sin, **they say to me: David, one who engages in intercourse with a married woman, his death** is effected **with what** form of execution? **And I say to them: One who engages in intercourse with a married woman** before witnesses and with forewarning, **his death is by strangulation, but he** still **has a share in the World-to-Come. But one who humiliates another in public has no share in the World-to-Come.** The transgression of you, who humiliate me, is more severe than my transgression. (Bava Metzia 59a)

Rabbenu Yona (*Shaarei Teshuva* 3:141), who believes that humiliating others is a subset of murder and is also a cardinal sin, understands the rationale simply. This is a case of murder in which the sinner will not realize the gravity of his sin. Thus, he will remain an unrepentant murderer.

The Rambam, however, argues that shaming others, when unjustified, is indicative of the lowest of characters:

> And they have already mentioned things besides these, that if one does them, he has no share in the world to come: they said (Bava Metzia 59b), one who whitens the face of his fellow in public and one calls his fellow by his nickname and (Yerushalmi Hagiga 2:1) one who derives honor from his friend's disgrace. Since one would not do from these acts – and even though one might think them to be light sins – except for one with an inferior spirit that does not have wholeness and is not fitting for the world to come. (Rambam, *Commentary on the Mishna*, Sanhedrin 10:1, Sefaria translation)

While Rambam himself seems to limit this to habitual violators (see *Responsa Iggerot Moshe* 5:20:14), one could argue the same even for a single violation. To stoop to such a level, without taking into account the destruction it may cause for the lives of others, is representative of callousness.

R. Feldman notes from the *Midrash Eliyahu* that it may be that this stringency is due to the staying power of humiliation: "Physical death occurs once and is over with, while the emotional pain lasts and reverberates" (Feldman, 17). As we saw from the anecdotes we cited previously, in the digital age, this insight is particularly poignant.

The *Penei Yehoshua* (Bava Metzia 58b) offers another possibility in the name of the *Tosefot Yom Tov,* citing *Midrash Shmuel.* Humiliation strips away a person's sense of dignity. As human beings are created in the image of God, embarrassing others shows that one has no concern for the inherent godliness in all people. R. Shammai Kehat Gross takes this position as well (*Responsa Shevet HaKehati* 1:361).

Not Only Verbal

It should be noted that the prohibition is violated whether or not words are used. R. Eliezer of Metz (*Yere'im* 180 [51 in old printings]) argues that one can violate *onaat devarim,* hurting people with words, even by "displaying a displeasing countenance" (Feldman, 20). The *Sefer Ḥasidim* (972) goes so far as to argue that a greater scholar should not attend the lecture of a lesser scholar, as it will intimidate him. As R. Feldman summarizes the consensus of the *posekim,* "All humiliation is subsumed under the umbrella of verbal oppression, as it inflicts emotional pain." Thus, it would not matter whether one humiliates using words or by publicizing an embarrassing photo or meme; any such act would cause one to violate the prohibition.

We noted previously that the *posekim* generally assume that the same is true for *lashon hara*: one violates the prohibition regardless of how the information is transmitted.

In Public

Is the prohibition only violated in public? If so, what qualifies as "in public"?

Several *posekim* assume that the prohibition is equally grave whether the humiliation occurs in front of a crowd or in private. For example, R. Henkin notes that in several manuscripts of the *Tur* (*ḤM* 420) and Rambam (*Hilkhot Ḥovel UMazik* 3:7), the phrase is not, as in our Talmud, "*hamalbin penei ḥavero barabim,*" but rather "*hamalbin penei ḥavero bidvarim*" – not "one who humiliates his fellow in public," but rather "one who humiliates his fellow with words."

R. Henkin prefers the latter variant. However, he notes that even were one to reject this version, the legal conclusion would be the same.

He assumes that the Gemara only discusses public humiliation, as it is being in the presence of others that usually generates the embarrassment. In private, it is more difficult to embarrass others.

He further notes that even the classic passage with which we began, discussing the actions of Tamar, seems to prove this. Tamar sends her letter to Yehuda privately, which means she could have revealed that he is the father directly without shaming him. The fact that she risks her life rather than embarrass him privately (and even in that case, certain Rishonim suggest that this is a cardinal sin) proves that the prohibition is equally binding whether in public or in private. He rejects the possibility that the letter she writes is being read publicly, as there is no indication that this is the case.

The *Peri Megadim* (*OḤ Eshel Avraham* 156) rules similarly. However, he does think that the sin is worse if an audience is present, and he notes that both points emerge from the rulings of the Rambam. In his introduction to *Hilkhot De'ot,* the Rambam formulates the prohibition *shelo lehalbin panim,* not to embarrass. He elaborates: "From this we learn that it is forbidden to put an Israelite to shame, needless to say publicly" (6:8). This position is also taken by the *Kol Bo* (67), *Ḥafetz Ḥayim* (*Ḥovat HaShemira* 14), and many others (see Feldman, 18–19).

Others, such as the *Semak* (126), do require an audience – but an audience of how many? While *rabim* often refers to ten people, most *posekim* assume that is not the intention here. Rather, drawing on the extensive discussions among the *posekim* that we have seen about the power of three people to ensure that something becomes well (or even universally) known, they assume that this may be the number; any embarrassment that will become known causes enough harm to the victim as to violate this prohibition. R. Feldman notes that this is the position of the *Peri Megadim* in *Matan Sekharan shel Mitzvot;* of the *Binyan Tziyon;* of R. Efrayim Greenblatt (*Responsa Rivevot Efrayim* 6:453:2); and others. R. Binyamin Zilber (*Responsa Az Nidberu* 8:63) argues that this total includes both the speaker and the victim, so only a single witness makes the act public.

R. Feldman (p. 19) notes that:

> Several authorities suggest an intriguing possibility. It is conceivable that the prohibition exists in full force, regardless of the

> presence or absence of an audience. However, in order to incur the condemnation discussed in the Talmud, such as forfeiting one's portion in the world to come as well as the exhortation toward martyrdom, the transgression must be committed in public.[10]

Ostensibly, social media shaming can transform any humiliation into a public one, with all the attendant implications. The uniqueness of social media, and the internet generally, is that even in the privacy of one's home, one can destroy reputations with a tweet, a Facebook or Instagram post, or as in Helen Andrews's case, a diatribe on YouTube.

Cyberbullying

As noted above, many *posekim* assume that one violates all of these prohibitions whether or not an audience is present. However, even in a case when no humiliation is caused, one does violate the more general prohibition of *onaat devarim,* literally oppression with words. While verbalization is implied, the *posekim* assume that one violates *onaat devarim* using any means that can hurt others. The Talmud describes this prohibition as follows:

> **MISHNA: Just as** there is a prohibition against **exploitation** [*ona'a*] **in buying and selling, so is there *ona'a* in statements,** i.e., verbal mistreatment. The mishna proceeds to cite examples of verbal mistreatment. **One may not say to** a seller: **For how much** are you selling **this item, if he does not wish to purchase** it. He thereby upsets the seller when the deal fails to materialize. The mishna lists other examples: **If one is a penitent,** another **may not say to him: Remember your earlier deeds. If one is the child of converts,** another **may not say to him: Remember the deeds of your ancestors, as it is stated: "And a convert shall you neither mistreat, nor shall you oppress him"** (Exodus 22:20).

10. See *Responsa Shevet HaKehati* 1:361 and other sources in n. 106.

> **GEMARA: ...How so? If one is a penitent,** another **may not say to him: Remember your earlier deeds. If one is the child of converts,** another **may not say to him: Remember the deed of your ancestors. If one is a convert and** he **came to study Torah,** one **may not say to him:** Does the **mouth that ate unslaughtered carcasses and animals that had wounds that would have caused them to die within twelve months [*tereifot*],** and **repugnant creatures, and creeping animals, come to study Torah that was stated from the mouth of the Almighty?**
>
> **If torments are afflicting** a person, **if illnesses are afflicting him, or if he is burying his children,** one **may not speak to him in the manner that** the **friends of Job spoke to him: "Is not your fear of God your confidence, and your hope the integrity of your ways? Remember, I beseech you, whoever perished, being innocent?"** (Job 4:6–7). Certainly you sinned, as otherwise you would not have suffered misfortune. (Bava Metzia 58b)

The Gemara outlines many cases: reminding people of their past sinful ways, failing to show sympathy when comforting one who is in pain, and others. The Gemara even includes certain cases of window-shopping, in which one pretends to be interested in buying and wastes the store-owner's time with no intention to buy. (The implications for those who waste the time of sales representatives while planning to buy the item online should be obvious.[11])

The Gemara notes that often it is not clear whether the harm is intended, allowing people to get away with their crimes. To forestall this, the Gemara notes:

> Verbal mistreatment is not typically obvious, and it is difficult to ascertain the intent of the offender, **as the matter is given to the heart** of each individual, as only he knows what his intention

11. For more, see: https://www.yutorah.org/sidebar/lecture.cfm/870328/rabbi-jonathan-ziring/onaat-devarim/.

> was when he spoke. **And with regard to any matter given to the heart, it is stated: "And you shall fear your God"** (Lev. 25:17), as God is privy to the intent of the heart. (Ibid.)

The Gemara further notes that as verbal oppression causes emotional pain which affects one's self, rather than one's money, and can never be repaid, it is in many respects worse than monetary oppression.

It should be obvious, therefore, that even in cases where humiliation does not occur, cyberbullying of all sorts would be forbidden under the category of *onaat devarim*. Below is an extensive description of cyberbullying by the US government's website[12] designed to prevent it:

> Cyberbullying is bullying that takes place over digital devices like cell phones, computers, and tablets. Cyberbullying can occur through SMS, Text, and apps, or online in social media, forums, or gaming where people can view, participate in, or share content. Cyberbullying includes sending, posting, or sharing negative, harmful, false, or mean content about someone else. It can include sharing personal or private information about someone else causing embarrassment or humiliation. Some cyberbullying crosses the line into unlawful or criminal behavior.
>
> The most common places where cyberbullying occurs are:
>
> - Social Media, such as Facebook, Instagram, Snapchat, and Twitter
> - SMS (Short Message Service) also known as Text Message sent through devices
> - Instant Message (via devices, email provider services, apps, and social media messaging features)
> - Email

As we have discussed, the reach and durability of information on the internet mean that the sin involved is worse when committed over social media and the like, as noted by the government.

12. Available at: https://www.stopbullying.gov/cyberbullying/what-is-it/index.html.

Special Concerns

With the prevalence of social media and digital forums, comments, photos, posts, and content shared by individuals can often be viewed by strangers as well as acquaintances. The content an individual shares online – both their personal content as well as any negative, mean, or hurtful content – creates a kind of permanent public record of their views, activities, and behavior. This public record can be thought of as an online reputation, which may be accessible to schools, employers, colleges, clubs, and others who may be researching an individual now or in the future. Cyberbullying can harm the online reputations of everyone involved – not just the person being bullied, but those doing the bullying or participating in it. Cyberbullying involves unique concerns in that it can be:

Persistent – Digital devices offer an ability to immediately and continuously communicate 24 hours a day, so it can be difficult for children experiencing cyberbullying to find relief.

Permanent – Most information communicated electronically is permanent and public, if not reported and removed. A negative online reputation, including for those who bully, can impact college admissions, employment, and other areas of life.

Hard to Notice – Because teachers and parents may not overhear or see cyberbullying taking place, it is harder to recognize.

Conclusion

While the nature of the prohibitions of *onaat devarim* and public humiliation may not fundamentally change in the era of social media, the scope of the damage it can cause and the ease with which these crimes can be committed make it more important than ever to understand the gravity of the sin that misuse of these tools may entail. However, as we have seen in the case of *agunot,* that same power opens up opportunities. The challenge of the digital age is to be sensitive to the unique situation, embracing the potential benefits while being aware of the pain that can be caused when these tools are misused. We now move to the case of fake news, which combines many of these topics.

Chapter 26

Fake News

Introduction

Much of the recent discussion about the dangers of social media has focused on the question of "fake news." Especially considering the impact of misinformation in American and British elections, as well as false information that was shared about Covid-19, many have called for more active involvement by internet companies to control fake news. Facebook's community standards indeed officially state that they want to promote:

> Authenticity: We want to make sure the content people are seeing on Facebook is authentic. We believe that authenticity creates a better environment for sharing, and that's why we don't want people using Facebook to misrepresent who they are or what they're doing.[1]

Cass Sunstein recently published a book focusing on the legal and moral issues surrounding this problem, entitled *Liars: Falsehoods and Free Speech in an Age of Deception* (Oxford University Press, 2021).[2]

---

1. https://www.facebook.com/communitystandards/.
2. For a recent halakhic take, see: https://www.baishavaad.org/hosting-postings-is-facebook-responsible-for-its-content/.

Sunstein explains why these problems are exacerbated by recent technology.

> These issues are always important, but in the modern era, they have new urgency. One reason, of course, is the rise of modern technologies, which allow falsehoods to be spread in an instant. If you want to circulate a lie about safety or health, or about a prominent person, you can do that with ease. If you want to sell a product by lying about it, you can try, starting today.... But the damage done by false statements goes beyond reputational injury. A foreign government might run falsehoods on social media in order to swing public opinion, to intensify social antagonisms, to promise a cause, or to weaken an adversary.

He further notes that the technology that enables pernicious lies is only getting more powerful. "Deepfakes make it very difficult or even impossible to distinguish between a false depiction of events and the real thing."

Based on this danger, Sunstein goes on to "argue that officials should have the authority to regulate (some) false statements, deepfakes, and doctored videos. Even more clearly, television networks, newspapers, magazines, Facebook, Twitter, YouTube, and other social media platforms should be doing more than they are now doing to control the spread of falsehoods." Many share this belief, though the exact strategies, both legal and self-imposed, are subject to much dispute. We will explore the halakhic reasons for opposing fake news, which will hopefully contribute to the conversation.

It is worth noting, however, that the claim that a lie is halakhically or morally wrong does not necessarily imply that we would advocate that a secular government deem such lies illegal. As Sunstein approvingly cites from Nicholas Hatzis:

> The fact that lying is morally wrong is not a sufficient condition for making it a legal wrong too. We wouldn't think that the government is justified in punishing every moral wrong, nor would we find the prospect of living under such a regime attractive.

> Something more is required before our moral failures can legitimately become the business of the state.[3]

Our goal is to outline a halakhic perspective which will inform how we act, whether or not it will or should be enshrined in secular law.

What Is Fake News?

For a colloquial understanding of fake news, let us turn to Wikipedia:

> Fake news or junk news or pseudo-news is a type of yellow journalism or propaganda that consists of deliberate disinformation or hoaxes spread via traditional print and broadcast news media or online social media...
>
> Fake news is written and published usually with the intent to mislead in order to damage an agency, entity, or person, and/or gain financially or politically, often using sensationalist, dishonest, or outright fabricated headlines to increase readership. Similarly, clickbait stories and headlines earn advertising revenue from this activity.
>
> The relevance of fake news has increased in post-truth politics. For media outlets, the ability to attract viewers to their websites is necessary to generate online advertising revenue. Publishing a story with false content that attracts users benefits advertisers and improves ratings. Easy access to online advertisement revenue, increased political polarization, and the popularity of social media, primarily the Facebook News Feed, have all been implicated in the spread of fake news, which competes with legitimate news stories. Hostile government actors have also been implicated in generating and propagating fake news, particularly during elections.
>
> Fake news undermines serious media coverage and makes it more difficult for journalists to cover significant news stories. An analysis by BuzzFeed found that the top 20 fake

3. Nicholas Hatzis, "Lying, Speech and Impersonal Harm," *Law and Philosophy* (2019), p. 519. Available at: https://doi.org/10.1007/s10982-018-9338-4.

news stories about the 2016 U.S. presidential election received more engagement on Facebook than the top 20 election stories from 19 major media outlets. Anonymously hosted fake news websites lacking known publishers have also been criticized, because they make it difficult to prosecute sources of fake news for libel.

The term is also at times used to cast doubt upon legitimate news from an opposing political standpoint, a tactic known as the lying press. During and after his presidential campaign and election, Donald Trump popularized the term fake news in this sense when he used it to describe the negative press coverage of himself. In part as a result of Trump's use of the term, the term has come under increasing criticism, and in October 2018 the British government decided that it will no longer use the term because it is "a poorly-defined and misleading term that conflates a variety of false information, from genuine error through to foreign interference in democratic processes."

Confirmation bias and social media algorithms like those used on Facebook and Twitter further advance the spread of fake news. Modern impact is felt for example in vaccine hesitancy.

There are two central issues that we will discuss:

1. The obligation to tell the truth and the prohibition to lie
2. *Hotzaat shem ra,* false *lashon hara* and libel

We dealt with a third potential issue, the obligation to judge favorably, earlier but we will make a few brief comments about it here as well.

Falsehood[4]

Judaism places a high value on truth, with Rabbi Ḥanina even referring to it as the "seal of God" (Shabbat 55a). The Torah warns against

4. Much of this section is based on R. Daniel Feldman's *The Right and the Good,* ch. 5: "More than the Best Policy: Honest."

falsehood in a unique manner, "Distance yourself from a false matter (*devar sheker*)" (Ex. 23:7).

[The Torah does warn "You shall not steal; you shall not lie; you shall not be false (*teshakkeru*) to one another" (Lev. 19:11), though the Talmud contends that this verse refers to the prohibition of speaking dishonestly in monetary matters. R. Shneur Zalman Dov Anusishky, in his *Responsa Matzav HaYosher* 6, argues that the simple meaning of the verse still holds legal weight. However, we will follow the view of the majority, focusing on the previously mentioned verse.]

On the one hand, one could take this language to indicate that this prohibition is particularly egregious or otherwise dangerous. The *HaKetav VeHaKabbala* argues that there is no sin that is more common; thus, it requires extra warning. The Seforno understands this verse as demanding a higher level of sensitivity – not only forbidding lying, but insisting that people not speak in ways which will teach others how to lie (as judges are warned in Avot 1:9). The *Orḥot Tzaddikim* (*Shaar HaEmet*) argues that this verse indicates that one must take care not to lie even inadvertently. R. Zalman Sorotzkin (*Oznayim LaTorah* on this verse) argues that the notion of keeping distance from falsehoods means that even in cases in which it is halakhically permitted to lie, one should try to avoid that situation. The *Sefat Emet* (*Sefat Emet al HaTorah, Shofetim* 5639) argues that this indicates that this sin is particularly severe. The *Sefer HaḤinnukh* (Mitzva 74) states that this language indicates how revolting falsehood is:

> The root of this commandment is well known, as falsehood is abominable and vile in the eyes of all. There is nothing more disgusting than it, and malediction and curse are in the house of its lovers. [This is] because God, may He be blessed, is a truthful God, and everything that is with Him is true. And blessing is only found and resting upon those that make themselves similar to Him in their deeds: to be truthful, like He is truthful; to be merciful, like He is merciful; and to be purveyors of kindness, like He is of great kindness. But [regarding] anyone whose deeds are the opposite of His good traits and are masters of falsehood – which is exactly the opposite of

His traits – the opposite of His traits will similarly always rest upon them. And the opposite of the trait of blessing which is with Him is malediction and curse; and the opposite of joy and peace and enjoyment which are with Him is worry, strife and pain. (Translation from Sefaria)

On the other hand, the lack of a clear statement, "Do not lie," may indicate that this prohibition is not a sweeping one. Indeed, the classic talmudic texts focus on the prohibition of lying in court settings, and this is noted by many of the commentaries on the verse. However, in that context, it is also clear that the prohibition entails more than simply refraining from telling an untruth; it requires maintaining a high standard of ethics in the courtroom. The passage in the Talmud continues over several pages, but let us take a few emblematic cases:

> **From where** is it derived that **a judge who knows that another** judge **is a robber** and is disqualified from serving as a judge; **and likewise, a witness who knows that another** witness **is a robber** and is disqualified from serving as a witness; **from where** is it derived **that he should not join him** in judgment or testimony? It is derived as **the verse states: "Distance yourself from a false matter."**
>
> **From where** is it derived that in a case where **a judge who knows** that the witnesses testifying before him are lying even though he is unable to prove it through their cross-examination and **with regard to the verdict** the result will be **that it is fraudulent, that he should not say: Since the witnesses are testifying** and I cannot prove their deceit, **I will decide** the case based on their testimony, **and let the chain** [*kolar*] of culpability for the miscarriage of justice **be** placed **around the neck of the** false **witnesses?** It is derived as **the verse states: "Distance yourself from a false matter."**
>
> The Gemara provides **a mnemonic** for additional *halakhot* derived from the verse: "Distance yourself from a false matter." **Three** relating to **a student; and three** relating to **creditors**; and three relating to a judge: **Rags, hears, and explain.**

From these cases, we see that the warning against falsehood includes cases in which the legal process is tainted, even when there is no guarantee that the result will be false. Additionally, it forbids one from hiding behind procedural truth – requiring one to seek the actual truth, even when one could not formally be blamed for a false outcome.

The Gemara continues to stress that truth requires people to set aside normal obligations of respect, seeking truth even when it demands asserting oneself over his teacher, and even prohibits one from trusting authority when the law forbids it:

> **From where** is it derived with regard to **a student who is sitting before his teacher and sees** a claim that provides **advantage for a poor** person **and disadvantage for a wealthy** person **that he shall not remain silent?** It is derived as **the verse states: "Distance yourself from a false matter."**
>
> **From where** is it derived with regard to **a student who sees his teacher who is erring in judgment that he shall not say: I will wait for** my teacher **until he concludes** the trial **and** then **I will contradict him and construct** a ruling **of my own so that the verdict will be attributed to my name?** It is derived as **the verse states: "Distance yourself from a false matter."**
>
> **From where** is it derived with regard to **a student whose teacher said to him: You know concerning me that** even **if** one were to **give me one hundred** times **one hundred dinars, I would not fabricate** a claim. Now, **I have one hundred dinars in the possession of so-and-so,** to whom I lent money, **but I have only one witness** of the two required to testify **about** the loan and enable me to collect payment; **from where** is it derived **that** the student **shall not join with** the other witness and testify? It is derived **as the verse states: "Distance yourself from a false matter"** (Ex. 23:7).
>
> The Gemara asks: Is it from the verse **"Distance yourself from a false matter" that this** matter **is derived? But** isn't **he certainly lying** in that case, **and** this is already stated, as **the**

> **Merciful One states: "You shall not bear false witness against your neighbor"** (Ex. 20:13)? **Rather,** the reference is to a case **where** the teacher **said to him:** It is **certain** that **I have one witness, and you come** and **stand there** beside him **and do not say anything, as** in that manner **you do not express a lie from your mouth.** Your silent presence will create the impression that I have two witnesses and lead the debtor to admit his debt. **Even so,** it is **prohibited** to do this, **due to that** which **is stated: "Distance yourself from a false matter."**

Finally, the command demands that the courts create an atmosphere that encourages truth-telling – by not allowing litigants to speak without the corrective presence of the opposing party:

> **From where** is it derived **that a judge should not hear the statement of** one **litigant before the other litigant comes** to court? It is derived **as the verse states: "Distance yourself from a false matter."**
>
> **From where** is it derived that **a litigant shall not explain** the rationale behind **his statements to the judge before the other litigant comes** to court? It is derived as **the verse states: "Distance yourself from a false matter." Rav Kahana teaches** that this halakha is derived **from** that which is written: **"You shall not accept** [*lo tissa*] a false report" (Ex. 23:1), which he interprets as though it is written: **You shall not cause** others [*lo tassi*] to accept a false report. (Shevuot 30b–31a)

Other texts do accept this verse as presenting a general obligation to be honest, and if the standard is high outside the court as it is within, as the sampling of laws above indicates, then the demands for honesty would be quite high indeed.

Take, for example, the following passage:

> One recites praise of **the bride as she is,** emphasizing her good qualities. **And Beit Hillel say:** One recites: **A fair and attractive bride. Beit Shammai said to Beit Hillel:** In a case **where** the

> bride **was lame or blind,** does **one say** with regard **to her: A fair and attractive bride? But the Torah states: "Distance yourself from a false matter"** (Ex. 23:7). (Ketubot 17a)

While the Talmud goes on to explain why Beit Hillel permit lying in this case, it is clear that under normal circumstances, they would agree that lying is prohibited. Based on this, many *posekim* assume that the prohibition applies even outside the context of a courtroom.[5]

The *Ḥafetz Ḥayim* (*Petiḥa* 11) takes this as obvious. He further argues that from the discussion in the courtroom we can extrapolate that even outside the court, it is even forbidden to say anything that *seems to be false, and obviously anything that has any falsehood mixed in.*

Some argue that it takes the form of a positive commandment rather than a prohibition.[6] Others agree, though they quote a verse in Psalms that "he who deals deceitfully shall not live in my house; he who speaks untruth (*dover shekarim*) shall not stand before my eyes" (Ps. 101:7, JPS).[7] The use of this verse, however, may indicate that the prohibition outside of court may be less strict.

It should be noted that the vast majority of *posekim* assume that the prohibition applies equally whether one lies verbally or in writing.[8] *Sefer Ḥasidim* (47 and 1058) adds that even nodding in such a way that a false impression is created causes one to violate this prohibition. Admittedly, there are dissenters (see, for example, the Ḥida in his *Brit Olam* on *Sefer Ḥasidim*), but we will assume for our purposes that this is the case. The same is the case for *lashon hara.* As cited above, R. Asher Weiss (*Minḥat Asher,* Lev. 41) notes that in that context, considering that central to that prohibition is the damage that can be caused, writing is obviously equivalent to speaking as it can also cause damage. Even if the problem is more about the personal ethics of the person speaking, writing seems to be an equally problematic act.

---

5. See, for example, *Yad HaKetana, De'ot,* ch. 10.
6. See, for example, *Semag, Aseh* 107; *Semak* 227; and sources quoted by Feldman, 64–65.
7. See *Oraḥ Meisharim,* 67.
8. See Feldman, 69–70, especially note 44.

When the Victim Is Not Present

R. Efrem Goldberg notes that the laws of falsehood in the courtroom setting provide particular insight into the world of social media. The *Sefer HaḤinnukh* explains that the reason the court cannot listen to the claims of one litigant without the other present is not (only?) so that the judges will not be biased, but rather because "people will speak idle words when not in front of their adversary." In other words, the litigants will feel freer to lie about their opponent if they don't need to look into their eyes as they dissemble. As R. Goldberg notes, the anonymity of the internet makes it easier to lie; even if one is identifiable, the somewhat impersonal nature of social media makes it easier to lie, knowing that one will not have to look the victim in the eyes.[9] We noted this insight earlier, as we addressed the view of Rabbenu Yona, who argues that negative information which it is necessary to publicize must be disseminated without anonymity; otherwise, people will doubt the veracity of the information, knowing that anonymity helps lower people's inhibitions.

Damaging Lies, or All Lies?

The *Yere'im* (235) seems to limit the prohibition to lies that harm others. However, the majority of *posekim*, as noted by R. Feldman, argue that the prohibition to lie holds even when no damage will be caused. (The question of when it is permitted to lie for the sake of peace or other valid reasons is beyond the scope of this discussion; see Yevamot 65b, Ketubot 17a, and Bava Metzia 23b.) The *To'afot Re'em* (commentary on *Yere'im* 235:1), however, argues that even the *Yere'im* would concede that lying which causes no harm would constitute a rabbinic violation. This, however, is challenged by R. Yerucham Fischel Perlow (commentary on the *Sefer HaMitzvot* of R. Saadia Gaon, *Aseh* 222), who suggests that according to this position, it would be permitted to lie when no harm is caused, and no prohibition, biblical or rabbinic, would be violated.

Sunstein notes that in secular ethical thought, the claim that lies are wrong because they cause damage is often derived from the theory of utilitarianism. However, it is worth noting that the damage must be

9. https://www.yutorah.org/lectures/lecture.cfm/873480/rabbi-efrem-goldberg/fake-news-and-absent-presence-the-dangers-of-technology/.

understood more broadly than simply whether or not a person is directly hurt from the lie. Sunstein writes as follows:

> [T]he Benthamite tradition focuses on the destructive consequences of lies. When people lie, they destroy trust. And when trust is destroyed, it becomes difficult or perhaps impossible for people to create cooperative or productive relationships.
>
> As philosopher Sissela Bok has written, "A society, then, whose members were unable to distinguish truthful messages from deceptive ones, would collapse." For example, "A warning that a well was poisoned or a plea for help in an accident would come to be ignored unless independent confirmation could be found."
>
> Even seemingly small lies, within the family or the workplace, can be far more corrosive than they might seem. They undermine subsequent interactions, giving rise to a pervasive and soul-crushing question: Can I trust what is being said now?
>
> If that question is constantly being asked, institutions become unable to function well. They may not be able to function at all. As Augustine said, "When regard for truth has been broken down or even slightly weakened, all things will remain doubtful." Augustine also said, "To use speech, then, for the purpose of deception, and not for its appointed end, is a sin."[10]

Thus, it is possible to argue that even according to those who believe lies are problematic because of the damage they cause, a broader understanding of damage may include cases in which the harm is not immediately evident.

However, on the other hand, these broader understandings of harm may not be sufficient to render a lie forbidden according to this

10. https://au.sports.yahoo.com/why-presidential-lies-even-worse-170036080.html. Versions of this are presented in ch. 3 of *Liars.*

standard. From a secular perspective, Nicholas Hatzis critiques a version of the more expansive view:

> [T]he fabric of trust is much more resilient than Shiffrin thinks. Despite the fact that we come in contact with falsehood, both as originators and recipients of it, on a daily basis, we don't despair of engaging in meaningful relations in our personal, social and professional lives, nor do we think that speech has lost its role as a means for expressing genuine mental content. Without closing our eyes to our and others' moral imperfections, so sensitively described by Shiffrin, we still find it possible to establish authentic connections. We learn to recognise indications of sincerity and build our own emotional and mental capacity to be sincere, and we develop our moral agency and a sense for morality's requirements. It is possible that when we find ourselves on the receiving end of insincerity, when our trust is betrayed and we realise that the other person has deliberately misled us, we feel that the possibility itself of sincere communication has been shattered to pieces. But if we are fortunate enough to have experienced sincerity in other relations, the pain and anxiety caused by particular instances of lying are mitigated and we are gradually able to regain our trust to speech as a medium for authenticity. Moreover, unless we are entirely blind to our faults, we are able to recall our own lying and see ourselves not as the perpetual victims of false speech but also as the occasional perpetrators. A realisation that the same person can be, at different times, both a sincere speaker and a liar can also help us accept that testimony, as a medium, can convey both truth and falsehood, without the latter spoiling the former.[11]

Thus, it may be that a model of this sort, ethically and halakhically, might necessitate a more direct understanding of harm.

---

11. Hatzis, *Lying Speech.*

Sunstein develops a model for thinking about the severity of lies, the latter three factors relating to the question of harm.[12] He argues that one must examine:

1. State of mind (lying, reckless, negligent, reasonable but mistaken)
2. Magnitude of harm (grave, moderate, minor)
3. Likelihood of harm (certain, probable, improbable)
4. Timing of harm (imminent, near future, reasonably soon)

The more severe, likely, and immediate the harm, the more obviously problematic the lie. The less, the easier it will be to justify the lie, or at least not put in effort to ensure that it is not spread (which we will discuss in a later chapter).

This model further supports the exceptions, briefly noted above, for when lying is permitted. Lying for the sake of peace, from this perspective, is legitimate because it avoids, rather than causes harm.

Why Is Lying Prohibited?

Many halakhic authorities note that there are two trends among *posekim* in terms of the rationales they offer for this prohibition. Some argue that the central issue is the problem of virtue: the Torah wants us to be honest. Alternatively, it is simply wrong to lie, considering the metaphysical value of truth as seen by statements of truth being identified with godliness. Others, the extreme example being that of the *Yere'im* cited above, focus on the problem of damage. As R. Feldman notes, a potential difference that may emerge is whether or not later telling the truth fixes the problem. While it may help reverse the damage, it cannot change the fact that one has spoken an untruth (see Feldman, 67; and *Responsa Shevet HaKehati* 3:299). However, in the age of the internet it may simply be impossible to fix the problem.[13]

From a secular perspective, Sunstein summarizes an alternative rationale to that of utilitarianism as being

12. Ch. 2, "Framework."

13. See Sunstein, ch. 6, "Falsehoods Fly," in *Liars*.

> rooted in the work of Immanuel Kant, the 18th-century German philosopher who emphasized the importance of treating people as ends rather than mere means.... Kant wrote, "By a lie a man throws away and, as it were, annihilates his dignity as a man." The Kantian tradition sees lying as a form of disrespect. As Harvard philosopher Christine Korsgaard puts it, "Lying is wrong because it violates the autonomy of the person to whom you lie."
>
> For Kantians, a lie denies the agency of its victims, making it akin to an act of violence. It counts as one of the roots of human evil.
>
> Liars treat others as mere means – as instruments for their own use. By resorting to deception, liars undermine people's ability to make their own decisions. That is degrading, a form of contempt. Liars refuse to recognize the dignity of their victims.[14]

Whether or not one adopts the specific Kantian claims, it is important to note that even in secular philosophy there are theories that see the problems in lies as fundamental, regardless of what harm they cause. Thus, the two approaches divide on whether lying is fundamentally problematic, or only when it causes damage.

The Value of Truth

From all the above, it seems clear that even if fake news is not created in order to cause damage, it remains problematic to write and disseminate such stories, even if less problematic than when it does. Furthermore, creating a culture in which truth is devalued by cavalierly accusing all who say things that are contrary to one's own interests as propagating fake news violates the sanctity of the truth and undermines the very seal of God. The extent to which social media has enabled this is objectively negative, whether or not one concludes that it is the responsibility of Facebook or any other company to stop its platform from being used for these purposes. A situation in which falsehood is tolerated and truth left unrecognized is objectively a travesty.

14. Ibid.

R. Goldberg notes that it is the value of truth that leads the *Sefer HaḤinnukh* to write that it is not only the speaker who must avoid falsehood; the audience must eschew untruths too. This is the "distancing" that the verse demands:

> And from the side of distancing, it warned us not to bend our ears at all to anything that is considered falsehood – and even if we do not know with certainly that it is a false matter. And [this is] similar to what they, may their memory be blessed, said (Ḥullin 44b), "Distance yourself from what is ugly, and from what is similar to it."

The Gemara states that the society of liars is among those who will never merit to see the Divine Presence (Sota 42a). From that perspective, the culture of fake news, whatever other violations it may entail, definitely runs counter to some of the most deeply held Torah values.

In addition to the problem in the falsehood itself, there are several other related prohibitions that are relevant.

Lashon HaRa

Sometimes fake news may consist of information that is technically true. However, focusing on and sharing the information disproportionally, presenting it as if this detail tells the whole story, may also be "fake," even if technically true. We developed this idea in our discussions of *lashon hara,* noting R. Daniel Feldman's arguments that due to psychological heuristics such as the "halo" and "devil" effect and other forms of confirmation bias, even true information can be essentially false, if the picture it paints is unfair. Harping on the minor indiscretions of an opponent to promote an agenda and divert criticism away from those within one's ideological camp seems to run afoul of this.

Even information which it might be necessary to share under the broad category of *to'elet* and related principles is often presented in problematic ways. As we have discussed, the *Ḥafetz Ḥayim* requires that the information be verified independently and be shared without exaggeration, for constructive rather than personal reasons (i.e., not as part of a vendetta or agenda), only when the goal could not have been achieved through other means, and without anonymity. Many instances of fake news violate many, if not all, of the above conditions. Fake news tends to be shared specifically to support an agenda and vilify an opponent, is often conspiratorial and sensationalist, and is shared due to animosity, rather than any sense of righting a wrong. While sometimes the information is shared under people's actual names, it is often shared under false online personas. Whichever framing one accepts to define the parameters of when negative information may be shared, fake news does not seem to pass the test.

Hotzaat Shem Ra

An even more egregious problem, however, is when the libelous information is indeed false. This category is referred to by the Rambam and the *Ḥafetz Ḥayim* as *hotzaat shem ra* (though as noted previously, the taxonomy for the various prohibitions which fall under *lashon hara* is debated). This phrase first emerges from the Torah's discussion of a husband who falsely accuses his new wife of not being a virgin:

> A man marries a woman and cohabits with her. Then he takes an aversion to her and makes up charges against her and defames her, saying, "I married this woman; but when I approached her, I found that she was not a virgin." In such a case, the girl's father and mother shall produce the evidence of the girl's virginity before the elders of the town at the gate. And the girl's father shall say to the elders, "I gave this man my daughter to wife, but he has taken an aversion to her; so he has made up charges, saying, 'I did not find your daughter a virgin.' But here is the evidence of my daughter's virginity!" And they shall spread out the cloth before the elders of the town. The elders of that town shall then take the man and flog him, and they shall fine him a hundred [shekels of] silver and give it to the girl's father; for the man has defamed (*ki hotzi shem ra*) a virgin in Israel. Moreover, she shall remain his wife; he shall never have the right to divorce her. (Deut. 22:13–19, JPS translation)

While the technical punishments discussed in this passage refer to only the specific case of a husband's slander of his bride, the Rambam's definition follows from this case.

The Yerushalmi (Bava Kama 8:7) propounds that the sin of falsely speaking negatively about others (assuming again the Rambam's definition of *hotzaat shem ra,* rather than following those who maintain that *hotzaat shem ra* includes even true gossip) is *sui generis*: one can never gain forgiveness. The *Penei Moshe* (s.v. *ein lo meḥila olamit*) understands this to mean that the victim need not forgive the perpetrator. While the Bavli (Yoma 87b) rules that generally one need only ask for forgiveness three times, after which the victim must forgive the sinner (with the exception of one's teacher who can withhold forgiveness), this does not apply to *hotzaat shem ra.* The Rema (*OḤ* 606:1) cites this. The *Taz* (ad loc. 3) cites the view of the *Mordekhai* (Yoma 723) that this means that the victim need not forgive the perpetrator, and withholding this forgiveness is not considered cruel, though normally failing to forgive does qualify as undue cruelty. However, he assumes that if one chooses to forgive the crime, it is forgiven. (See also *Peri Ḥadash* 1.)

However, the *Magen Avraham* (5), *Mishna Berura* (11), *Baḥ, Eliya Rabba* (5), and *Shulḥan Arukh HaRav* (4) cite the *Yam shel Shlomo* (Bava Kama 8:3) to argue that it is a *middat ḥasidut,* a pious activity, to forgive the sin. The *Terumat HaDeshen* (*Pesakim* 212) argues that the reason for this halakha is that once the libelous information has reached an audience, even if one repents, the audience may never hear the retraction. The damage is therefore permanent. The apology is thus insufficient to reverse the sin, allowing the victim to withhold forgiveness.

The *Levush* (*OḤ* 606:1) expands on this. Noting, as we have explored, that humiliation is akin to murder, he contends that as the lasting damage will potentially cause the embarrassment to continue, one cannot be blamed for not forgiving his or her daily murder! Thus, he argues that the victim need not forgive the crime and may hold a grudge, though that is normally prohibited as well. He does suggest that the perpetrator must do everything in his or her power to get the victim to forgive him or her – getting help from a thousand friends if necessary – but he acknowledges that even then, the victim may rightfully withhold forgiveness.

The *Arukh HaShulḥan* (ad loc. 2) notes that the victim need not forgive the one who committed *hotzaat shem ra,* but it is nevertheless pious to do so. Still, he suggests a caveat. Building on the talmudic dictum, "Your friend has a friend, and your friend's friend has a friend" (Arakhin 16a), all things said publicly (in front of three) may be assumed to spread; this provides an out. If, after spreading libel, one *publicizes* an apology and a retraction, one *may assume* that the correction will reach the original audience. If so, the victim must forgive the sinner.

However, the majority of *posekim* seem to reject this, acknowledging that it is nearly impossible for the retraction to reach the same number of people as the original gossip. Gossip is juicier than retractions. It is for this reason that mistakes that are made on the first page of a newspaper receive corrections and retractions on page six. It is also why unsubstantiated or disproven rumors live on for years, as anyone who pays attention to political campaigns knows too well. In fact, this is one of the central dangers of fake news. Cass Sunstein provides several examples of this and summarizes the findings: "Corrections of false impressions can actually strengthen those very impressions."[15] Those already inclined against a political figure, for example, after hearing that a negative rumor about that figure was false will often double down on their acceptance of that rumor, while those inclined toward the political figure will accept the correction, if they ever believed the negative information to begin with.

The scourge of fake news has become noteworthy specifically in the context of social media, with politicians and ethicists challenging companies like Facebook to prevent their platforms from being used for the dissemination of fake news; it is clear that the problems which may have always existed have now been exacerbated. As we discussed earlier, the unique staying power and reach that shaming has in the age of social media have made *Ḥazal*'s warnings all the more pertinent. The same can be said of *hotzaat shem ra,* which combines the problems of *lashon hara, sheker,* and public humiliation, as noted by the *Levush* above. As bad as public shaming is when there is truth to the accusations, it is worse when the content is vicious lies.

R. Daniel Feldman (*False Facts and True Rumors,* 194–195) notes that these central insights of *Ḥazal* are captured well by Daniel Solove in *The Future of Reputation:*

15. *On Rumors.*

> In the past, oral gossip could tarnish a reputation, but it would fade from memories over time. People could move elsewhere and start anew. The printed word, however, was different. As Judge Benjamin Cardozo wrote in 1931: "What gives the sting to writing is its permanence in form. The spoken word dissolves, but the written one abides and perpetuates the scandal." In the past, people could even escape printed words because most publications would get buried away in the dusty corners of libraries. The information would be hard to retrieve, and a sleuth would have to devote a lot of time to dig it up. The Internet, however, makes gossip a permanent reputational stain, one that never fades. It is available around the world, and with Google it can be readily found in less than a second.

In the past, rumors and falsehoods would readily spread around a small village, but the internet lacks the village's corrective of familiarity. In the village, people had a long history together and knew the whole story about an individual. However, now someone reading an online report about some faraway stranger rarely knows the whole story; the reader has only fragments of information, and when little is invested in a personal relationship, even information that is incomplete and of dubious veracity may be enough to precipitate ridicule, shunning, and reproach.

However, Solove, citing Judge Richard Posner, also suggests that there is truth to the *Arukh HaShulḥan*'s perspective:

> The rapid information-spreading power of the Internet can be a virtue too. Judge Richard Posner points out: "The blogosphere as a whole has a better error-correction machinery than the conventional media do. The rapidity with which vast masses of information are pooled and sifted leaves the conventional media in the dust. Not only are there millions of blogs, and thousands of bloggers who specialize, but, what is more, readers post comments that augment the blogs, and the information in those comments, as in the blogs themselves, zips around blogland at the speed of electronic transmission." Posner is

> certainly right – information does speed around the Internet at a breakneck pace. Errors can get corrected quickly. The best thing to do when faced with a malicious rumor is to spread correct information as rapidly as possible.[16]

Furthermore, as R. Feldman and Solove write, this only refers to fact-checking. When the information is technically true, but unwarranted (either it is unnecessary halakhically or it is exaggerated and thus false from a halakhic, if not technical, perspective), this qualification will not provide any solace:

> This works well when we clearly know the truth about something or someone. But what about when we don't? And what happens when facts are posted online that while true, are also of a private nature? With false information, the record can eventually be set straight. But with true information, there's no way to put the secret back in the bag.[17]

R. Feldman (198–199) goes on to note that social media has further encouraged the already negative potential of this kind of information to create dangerous group polarization. Furthermore, as we have discussed, many *posekim* assume that data shared anonymously is more problematic halakhically, as it is easier to share information without concern for consequences or veracity. In general discourse, this problem is referred to as the "online disinhibition effect." Being invisible allows people to engage in activity they would generally relate to as immoral.

[It must be noted that I make no claim as to whether the Yerushalmi follows the Rambam's taxonomy. It is possible that, according to the Yerushalmi, *lashon hara* has a unique status, for some of the reasons discussed above, such as the inability to undo the damage that has been done. While this would expand the cases to which this stringency is applied, it would in no way mitigate the severity of libelous

16. Daniel Solove, *The Future of Reputation: Gossip, Rumor, and Privacy on the Internet* (Caravan Books, 2007), 34, 37.
17. Ibid., 37–38.

gossip. In fact, if all the above stringencies apply even to true information, a fortiori we can derive how terrible and unforgivable it would be to spread lies about others.]

Brief Note On *Hotzaat Shem Ra* About the Dead

It is worth noting that the *Mordekhai* and many of the commentaries cited above discuss a *ḥerem* that was instituted against those who committed *hotzaat shem ra* against the dead, despite the fact that the Talmud (Berakhot 19a) states that speaking about the dead is like speaking about a rock – i.e., it is meaningless. While fascinating, we will not discuss that extensively here.

Let us note, however, that in order to define the parameters of this decree, it is important to know whether the *Mordekhai*, as noted in our discussion of the Yerushalmi, understands *hotzaat shem ra* as being limited to false information or not. If, like other Ashkenazic Rishonim, such as Rashi and *Sefer Ḥasidim* (cited in the above chapters on *lashon hara*), he understands the phrase to mean true gossip, then it would be forbidden to speak negatively about the dead even when the information is true. If, however, he accepts the Rambam's taxonomy, it would be permitted to share true gossip about the dead. My tendency is to accept the stricter read, as it is more likely that the *Mordekhai* would have been influenced by the definitions prevalent in Ashkenaz than those of the Rambam. Even if he was not, it is possible that in this passage he is not being overly precise in his terminology.

However, two recent writers, Professor Nahum Rakover[18] and R. Dr. Zev Eleff,[19] accepting the definitions of Rambam, deduce that the *ḥerem* was limited to false information but indeed permitted true gossip. These two positions are the subject of discussion in a responsum by R. Binyamin Zilber (*Responsa Az Nidberu* 14:68), with the questioner suggesting the lenient position and R. Zilber accepting the stricter view I advanced above.

18. *Al Lashon HaRa VeAl Anisha Aleha BaMishpat HaIvri, Sinai* 22, reprinted here: http://www.daat.ac.il/daat/kitveyet/sinay/allashon1-4.htm.
19. *Beit Yitzḥak* 42 (Yeshiva University, 2011).

Accepting the Information[20]

Central to the issue of fake news is not just those who speak and write it, but those who accept it. In halakha, it is prohibited to accept *lashon hara*:

> **And Rav Sheshet** further **said, citing Rabbi Elazar ben Azarya: Anyone who speaks slander, and anyone who accepts** and believes the **slander** he hears, **and anyone who testifies falsely about another, it is fitting to throw him to the dogs, as it is stated:** "And you shall not eat any flesh that is torn of beasts in the field, **you shall cast it to the dogs**" (Ex. 22:30), **and afterward it is written: "You shall not utter [*tissa*] a false report;** put not your hand with the wicked to be an unrighteous witness" (Ex. 23:1). Uttering rumors is here equated to delivering false testimony. Furthermore, **read into** the verse as though it stated: **Do not cause** a false report **to be accepted [*tasi*]**, i.e., do not lead others to accept your false reports. (Pesaḥim 118a)

The Rambam (*Hilkhot Sanhedrin* 21:7) seems to accept this as a biblical prohibition. Rabbenu Yona writes that the prohibition is to "establish in your mind that the information is true and to look down on the one whom it was said about" (*Shaarei Teshuva* 3:213). R. Josh Flug summarizes an alternative formulation by R. Moshe Sternbuch (*Responsa Teshuvot VeHanhagot* 1:555):

> We are not angels and when we hear something and it sounds like it is true, human nature is to accept it as truth. Therefore, he suggests that the prohibition is to change one's perspective on a person based on what one heard.

Sunstein argues that this is one of the greatest dangers of fake news.

> "[T]ruth bias": people tend to think that what they hear is truthful, even if they have excellent reason not to believe what they

20. I draw here on R. Feldman's work, as well as a *shiur* on rabbanan.org by R. Josh Flug.

> hear. If people are provided with information that has clearly been discredited, they might nonetheless rely on that information in forming their judgments. Similarly, people are more likely to misremember, as true, a statement that they have been explicitly told is false than to misremember, as false, a statement that they have been explicitly told is true.[21]

The exact parameters of when one is allowed to accept *lashon hara* hangs on the Gemara's debate about whether or not King David accepted a false report.

In II Samuel (chs. 9, 16, 19) we are told about David's attempt to protect the family of Yehonatan, the son of Shaul, who had been his loyal friend. David learns that Yehonatan has a crippled son, Mefivoshet, and grants him the estate of Shaul and provides for him from his own estate. During the rebellion of David's son Avshalom, Tziva, a servant of Mefivoshet, lies to David and tells him that Mefivoshet supports the rebellion and hopes that David will lose the monarchy. As punishment, David promises to confiscate the property of Mefivoshet and grant it to Tziva. Mefivoshet eventually clarifies that this is a lie, and offers to split the estate, though Mefivoshet tells David he does not care and professes his loyalty to David.

Rav claims that David violates a prohibition for accepting the slanderous report by Tziva.

Shmuel, on the other hand, argues that David is justified in accepting the report, though it turned out to be mistaken. David sees Mefivoshet in a state of mourning when David returns from fleeing Avshalom, and he thinks that Mefivoshet is mourning because David has *returned,* when in fact he has been mourning because David has been chased away, and he has not yet finished his mourning when David returns. His loyalty is bolstered by his rejection of the estate. Thus, Shmuel argues that fundamentally, David is justified in accepting the report because it seems that Mefivoshet is indeed upset about David's success, though it turns out the opposite is the case.

---

21. Sunstein, ch. 6, "Falsehoods Fly."

The *Semag* (*Lo Taaseh* 10) rules in accordance with Shmuel, arguing that it is permitted to accept *lashon hara* when one sees reason to believe it is true.

The irony of this is that this story proves that even when one can justify believing a story, one should be wary because it could be that the story is more complicated. This supports the claim of the *Ḥafetz Ḥayim* (*Hilkhot Lashon HaRa, Be'er Mayim Ḥayim* 7:26) that one must have many reasons to believe the information before accepting it.

This should serve as a warning when it comes to news in the age of social media; much care must be taken to ascertain the veracity of information before accepting it. Even when it may be justified to accept it, there may still be reason to take extra care before coming to conclusions.

Sunstein ends the body of his book *On Rumors* with a call for people to choose a future in which we carefully accept the information that is spread:

> [I]n the domain of rumor transmission, culture and social norms probably matter even more. Everything depends on what propagators do and on how they are received. We could imagine a future in which propagators –whether self-interested, altruistic, or malicious – are rewarded, directly or indirectly, for spreading false rumors and for showing no concern for the question of truth; in which cascade effects and polarization ensure that countless people believe those falsehoods; and in which biased assimilation ensures that many baseless beliefs are impervious to change. In such a future, people's beliefs are a product of social networks working as echo chambers in which rumors spread like wildfire. In such a future, people are especially likely to believe claims that originate, or at least appear to originate, within their particular group and that fit with their own wishes, fears, and inclinations. In such a world, people are entirely willing to accept rumors that cast others in a terrible light, especially when those others are, or are easily seen as, adversaries. By contrast, we could also imagine a future in which those who spread false rumors are categorized as such and marginalized; in which cascade effects are blocked by individuals or groups who think independently; in which group

polarization is contained by a broad social awareness of that very phenomenon; and in which people, humble and aware of their own fallibility, are more open to the truth. In such a future, people would be fully alert to the fact that for both the most and the least powerful, false rumors threaten to be part of the stuff of daily life. Of course they listen to rumors, but they view them with a degree of distance and scrutiny, seeing their appearance on the Internet as akin to their appearance in tabloid magazines. In such a future, people approach rumors skeptically even when they provide comfort and fit with their own biases and predilections. The choice between these futures is our own.

Judging Favorably

As R. Flug notes, conceptually, the prohibition of accepting *lashon hara* is related to the obligation to judge favorably, which we discussed above. The *Ḥafetz Ḥayim* (*Hilkhot Lashon HaRa* 6:7–8) states, however, that there is a difference. For example, someone can present a story as positive, while the listener will take it negatively, thus failing to judge favorably though no *lashon hara* has been spoken. On the other hand, while there are cases that lean toward a negative interpretation regarding which one need not judge favorably, the prohibition of accepting *lashon hara* demands higher standards. For the unique ways in which social media has shaped how and when one must judge favorably, see our earlier discussions.

Applications

From all we have seen, it seems that halakha gives us good reason to be alarmed at the culture of fake news, which challenges the values of truth, entailing violations of *lashon hara* and *hotzaat shem ra* and a failure to judge favorably. As the prohibitions of accepting *lashon hara* indicate, there is not only an obligation upon those sharing the information to use discretion; the moral and halakhic onus lies equally on the shoulders of the consumers of that media to be discerning. We may hope that this will lead to a more civil culture which values truth and avoids needless gossip and libel.

While social media companies have begun to combat falsehoods, one can wonder whether more is needed. As Cass Sunstein argues, it may be that more is demanded than the current standard set by Facebook:

> Reducing the spread of false news on Facebook is a responsibility that we take seriously. We also recognize that this is a challenging and sensitive issue. We want to help people stay informed without stifling productive public discourse. There is also a fine line between false news and satire or opinion.
>
> For these reasons, we do not remove false news from Facebook but we significantly reduce its distribution by showing it lower in News Feed.[22]

Reducing visibility may be a fair compromise between protecting truth and free speech, but if the latter is particularly pernicious, it may not be enough. On the other hand, as we have noted, the halakhic perspective cannot be directly mapped onto the secular scene for several reasons:

1. We are dealing with secular law rather than religious norms.
2. We are dealing with companies that may not have the same halakhic concerns as people.
3. We are often dealing with non-Jews or those not committed to halakha.
4. Practically, demanding active removal of problematic material might lead to other problems, such as selective removal, biased application of rules, and the like, which might militate practically toward a more hands-off approach. This does not negate the problem of fake news, but it does suggest that sometimes the "solution" may be worse than the problem.
5. This relates to another point, which is that being too active in removing falsehoods might "chill truth," meaning dissuade people from speaking the truth for fear of being called out as a liar. (Sunstein raises this as a reason for limiting legal consequences for not removing fake news.)

---

22. Community Standards, https://transparency.fb.com/policies/community-standards/false-news/, cited by Sunstein, *Liars*, ch. 4.

Nevertheless, in general, halakhic values would dictate that we should take whatever measures can practically be taken without running these risks. To take some suggestions from Sunstein, some of which are already being used by several internet companies:

1. Warnings and disclosures could be used to inform people that what has been said is not true.
2. A general right to command correction or retraction after a clear demonstration that a statement is both false and damaging. (In halakha, we might not demand the latter.)
3. Downgrade defamatory statements where they cannot be removed due to legal reasons.[23]

Sunstein further notes that this would be true of lies that hurt people in general, such as medical misinformation about Covid-19.[24]

While the right balance has yet to be worked out, the attempt to make the internet a more honest place is surely to be encouraged. Sunstein ends his book as follows:

> Private institutions, including television networks, magazines, newspapers, and social media providers, should be acting more aggressively to control defamation and other falsehoods and lies. They should be doing more than they are now doing to prevent the spread of misinformation involving health and safety and of doctored videos. They should reduce the coming spread of deepfakes. These are specific conclusions, but they bear on some of the largest and most general questions in all of politics and law, and indeed in daily life itself. Hannah Arendt put it this way: "What is at stake here is this common and factual reality itself, and this is indeed a political problem of the first order." The principle of freedom of speech should not be taken to forbid efforts to protect reality.

Without taking a stand on the US legal issues, it is hard to argue that halakha would not agree with this call.

---

23. Based on ch. 7, "Your Good Name."
24. Ch. 8, "Harm."

Section 5

Mediated Experience, *Minyan*, and Mitzvot

Chapter 27

The Virtual *Minyan*

The question of whether mitzvot can be performed through mediated experience, ranging from microphones to videoconference, has been much discussed as these technologies developed. These issues took on a more urgent tone during the Covid-19 lockdowns when people could not attend *minyan*, could not attend synagogue for the reading of the Megilla, and generally, in-person religious activities were limited. While a full analysis of these issues requires its own book, a survey of the central arguments, and what they reflect about the nature of community and experience, is necessary. In general, the question of how halakha views mediated experience is critical in order to understand how halakhic practice will look in the coming years.

Minyan

The Mishna rules that communal prayer, the reading of the Torah, and several other ritual acts require a quorum of ten men. The Talmud (Megilla 23b) offers several sources for this:

> **From where are these matters,** i.e., that ten people are needed in each of these cases, derived? **Rabbi Ḥiyya bar Abba said that Rabbi Yoḥanan said:** It is **as the verse states: "And I shall be hallowed among the children of Israel"** (Lev. 22:32), which indicates that **any expression of sanctity may not be** recited in a quorum of **fewer than ten** men.
>
> The Gemara asks: **From where** in the verse may this **be inferred?** The Gemara responds that it must be understood **as Rabbi Ḥiyya taught: It is inferred** by means of a verbal analogy [*gezera shava*] between the words **"among," "among." Here, it is written: "And I shall be hallowed among the children of Israel," and there,** with regard to Korah's congregation, **it is written "Separate yourselves from among this congregation"** (Num. 16:21). Just as with regard to Korah the reference is to ten men, so too, the name of God is to be hallowed in a quorum of ten men.
>
> The connotation of ten associated with the word "among" in the portion of Korah is, in turn, **inferred** by means of another verbal analogy between the word **"congregation"** written there and the word **"congregation"** written in reference to the ten spies who slandered Eretz Yisrael, **as it is written there: "How long shall I bear with this evil congregation?"** (Num. 14:27). Consequently, **just as there,** in the case of the spies, it was a congregation of **ten** people, as there were twelve spies altogether, and Joshua and Caleb were not included in the evil congregation, **so too, here,** in the case of Korah, the reference is to a congregation of **ten** people. The first several items mentioned in the mishna are expressions of sanctity, and they consequently require a quorum of ten.

As the Talmud in Berakhot (6a) establishes, it is in a group of ten that the Divine spirit comes to rest:

> **And from where** is it derived that **ten people who pray, the Divine Presence is with them? As it is stated: "God stands in**

> **the congregation of God,"** and the minimum number of people that constitute a congregation is a quorum of ten.[1]

The Mishna (Avot 3:6) asserts that the same is true of ten who study Torah together, though the Mishna elaborates that smaller groups may be worthy of some Divine Presence as well. The simplest understanding, as accepted by many authorities, is that this is the reason for the value of praying with a *minyan*.[2] R. Moshe Feinstein, however, pushes back on this, noting that the Talmud states that God's presence is found in the synagogue, and thus does not seem to be dependent specifically on the presence of a quorum. Thus, he finds the value of praying with a quorum in a passage from several pages later in the Talmud:

> Rav Naḥman saw that Rabbi Yitzḥak was struggling to find a way for him to engage in communal prayer. **He asked: What is** the reason for **all this** fuss? Rabbi Yitzḥak **said to him: As Rabbi Yoḥanan said in the name of Rabbi Shimon ben Yoḥai: What is** the meaning of **that which is written: "But as for me, let my prayer be unto You, Lord, in a time of favor;** O God, in the abundance of Your mercy, answer me with the truth of Your salvation" (Ps. 69:14)? It appears that the individual is praying that his prayers will coincide with a special time of Divine favor. **When is a time of favor?** It is **at the time when the congregation is praying.** It is beneficial to pray together with the congregation, for God does not fail to respond to the entreaties of the congregation. **Rabbi Yosei, son of Rabbi Ḥanina, said that** the unique quality of communal prayer is derived **from here: "Thus said the Lord, in a time of acceptance I have answered you and on a day of salvation I have aided you"** (Is. 49:8). **Rabbi Aḥa, son of Rabbi Ḥanina, said** that it is derived **from here: "Behold, God is mighty, He despises no one"** (Job 36:5). He adopts an alternative reading of the verse: "Behold, God

1. See, however, *Pnei Yehoshua*, s.v. *amar ravin*, for a different explanation of this passage.
2. This seems to be the position of *Arukh HaShulḥan*, *OḤ* 55:20, and was the starting point of R. Yitzchak Mordechai HaKohen Rubin in his discussion about forming a *minyan* during Covid-19 lockdowns, and central to the argument of R. Tzvi Reisman.

> will not despise" the prayer of "the mighty," i.e., the community. **And it is written: "He has redeemed my soul in peace so that none came upon me; for there were many with me.** God shall hear and answer them..." (Ps. 55:19–20). This verse teaches that the prayer was answered because there were many with me when it was offered. (Berakhot 7b–8a)

Rather than contend that it is God's presence that makes the communal prayer accepted, R. Feinstein argues that this is a distinct value, though he does not explain why communal prayer has this power.[3] *Peri Ḥadash* (*OḤ* 90:9) cites this passage for the ruling that one should always try to pray with a *minyan*. *Olat Tamid* (*OḤ* 90:9) similarly grounds the value of a *minyan* in this passage, specifically noting the following line in the Talmud:

> **That** last proof **was also taught** in a *baraita*. **Rabbi Natan says: From where do we know that the Holy One, Blessed be He, does not despise the prayer of the masses? As it is stated: "Behold, God does not despise the mighty," and it is written: "He has redeemed my soul in peace so that none came upon me;** for there were many with me." (Berakhot 8a)

R. Avraham Gombiner (*Magen Avraham, OḤ* 90:15) seems to ground it in a more universal principle of *berov am hadrat melekh,* "A numerous people is the glory of a king" (Prov. 14:28; see, for example, Rosh HaShana 32b).[4]

What are the parameters for forming this quorum?

The question of virtual/remote *minyanim* was raised in earnest during the lockdowns due to Covid-19.[5] The consensus of halakhic authorities, as

3. R. Feinstein reiterates this point in the following responsa.
4. These need not be exclusive, as *Ba'er Heitev* (90:11) and *Mishna Berura* (90:28), for example, cite both *Magen Avraham* and *Olat Tamid*. See further discussion in *Peri Megadim* and *Levushei Serad*.
5. For an older discussion: https://web.archive.org/web/20140626215338/http:/jewishlinkbc.com/index.php?option=com_content&view=article&id=2867:congregation-bnai-yeshurun-hosts-first-ever-internet-minyan&catid=150:news&Itemid=562.

far as this author can tell, rejects the possibility of constituting a *minyan* without the physical presence of ten men in a shared space to create the quorum. For all its benefits, communication technology cannot provide that. One modern author puts the issue succinctly:

> When a quorum of ten are in one place – the *Shechina* dwells amongst them. Therefore, even an iron curtain would not block any who wish to join them from connecting with *HaKadosh Baruch Hu* on this higher level. Certainly, one cannot be counted towards a *Minyan* if he is not in the same location as the other. However, can he listen to a minyan using Skype and answer *Amen*?[6]

R. Dovid Lichtenstein writes similarly, noting that it should be obvious, despite recent attempts to argue otherwise.[7] However, it is not entirely clear why this conclusion, while widely accepted and eminently plausible, has not been challenged. Furthermore, the exact definition of joint presence is much debated. To understand this, we must present the arguments that exist, and note those that have not been made.

The basis for this is as follows. In the context of the definition of a "house" for the purposes of eating the *korban Pesaḥ*, the Talmud states:

> **Rav Yehuda said** that **Rav said: And** the *halakha* is **similar with regard to prayer,** in that one who is standing outside the doorway cannot be included together with those praying inside. The Gemara notes that Rav **disagrees with Rabbi Yehoshua ben Levi, as Rabbi Yehoshua ben Levi said: Even a barrier of iron does not separate between the Jewish people and their Father in Heaven.** Barriers are irrelevant with regard to prayer. (Pesaḥim 85b)

On the one hand, the Talmud insists that the members of a *minyan* occupy the same space. Indeed, in another passage (Eiruvin 92a), the Gemara details what is considered "standing in the same courtyard"

6. Available at: https://theshc.org/skype-minyan/.
7. See Lichtenstein, supra n. 5.

when two lots of different sizes open into each other, analyzing where the different groups, as well as the leader, are standing, assuming that when a larger courtyard opens into a smaller, the quorum can consist of nine/majority (see below) in the larger space with the remainder in the smaller, but not vice versa. On the other hand, the Talmud records the position of Rabbi Yehoshua ben Levi (also cited in the context of the Priestly Blessing [Sota 38b]) that nothing can separate between the Jewish people and God, implying that the members of the *minyan* can be separated. Rashi (Pesaḥim ad loc., s.v. *vekhen litefilla*) seems to understand this dispute as to whether people standing on two sides of a wall can join to form a *minyan*. Ramban (ibid.) limits even this to a very specific case where the people are standing by the threshold of the open door, but assumes that even Rashi rejects any understanding that people in two houses can join for a *minyan*. *Tosafot Rid* (s.v. *min haagaf*) understands this passage like Rashi, but takes the discussion in Eiruvin as evidence that the possibility of people in different spaces joining for a *minyan* is unequivocally rejected.

Many other Rishonim, however, reject that anyone ever entertained the possibility that people in different spaces can create a quorum. Tosafot (s.v. *vekhen litefilla*, Eiruvin 92b, s.v. *tisha*), for example, argue that all positions agree that people in different spaces cannot join for a *minyan*. Rabbi Yehoshua ben Levi argues that when there is a *minyan* in a space, those behind the synagogue can *respond*, and Rav Yehuda citing Rav rejects even this. As noted above, even those who accept that a theoretical position existed in the Talmud that a quorum can be created by groups in different spaces may not entertain the possibility that this was accepted as practical law. The authorities divide on whether such people are considered to be fully praying with the *minyan* or are merely permitted to respond. *Ḥayei Adam* (30:1, based on Radbaz 2:650, followed by *Mishna Berura* 55:58) rules that it is merely a permission to respond. *Mishna Berura* (55:52) therefore rules it is best to fully join the *minyan*.[8] *Arukh HaShulḥan* (55:23) argues, on the other hand, that once a *minyan* is constituted, all those who join in are fully part of the *minyan*, a position also found in *Shaarei Teshuva* (55:14) and *Ḥazon Ish* (cited

8. See also R. Shlomo Zalman Auerbach, *Halikhot Shlomo, Tefilla* 5, n. 18.

in *Orḥot Rabbenu*, vol. 3, 208). R. Menachem Wieder (*Minḥat Tzvi* 21) argues that this depends on the following: If the purpose of a *minyan* is to ensure that the Divine Presence is present, once the group has been created, that goal is achieved and anyone can join the *minyan*. If, however, the purpose is to create a community, and the standards are lower for responding to *devarim shebikedusha* than they are for creating communal prayer (similar to R. Feinstein above), then this is not achieved with this arrangement.

(It is worth noting that Tosafot Sota 38b–39a, s.v. *meḥitza*, seems to be even more limiting, arguing that the leniency of R. Yehoshua ben Levi is limited to the case of the Priestly Blessing.)

Furthermore, there it is not clear whether the above leniencies, to the extent that they exist, include cases where the two groups are actually in separate domains. For example, the Yerushalmi (Berakhot 7:5) in the context of *Birkat HaMazon* (see below) assumes that sight can in certain cases join groups in two houses. Ramban (Pesaḥim 85b) argues that in the Bavli such a possibility is wholly rejected. The only possibility of joining is within a single domain, or perhaps from one domain to a non-domain, but not between separate houses. Others believe that two houses can only join in the case of *Birkat HaMazon* if the two groups started the meal with the plan to eat and recite *Birkat HaMazon* as one, thus limiting this possibility to *Birkat HaMazon*. *Arukh HaShulḥan* (55:20) specifically limits the case to where one group is in the synagogue and the others are behind the synagogue, meaning not in a separate house. If they are, then the leniencies do not apply. According to these sources, it is clear that *minyan* requires joint presence of the members of the quorum.

The main authority who raises the possibility that there is a way for people in different domains to create a *minyan* is Rashba (*Responsa Rashba* 1:96). He was asked why the *ḥazan*, prayer leader, is considered part of the *minyan* when he stands on a platform elevated more than ten *tefaḥim* from the rest of the synagogue. He offers two arguments. First, he suggests that as it is used as part of the synagogue, it is considered part of it. Second, he argues that *efshar lomar*, it is possible to contend, that as the *ḥazan* and community *ro'in elu et elu*, see each other, that is sufficient to join them. This is based on a law in the context of *Birkat HaMazon*, Grace After Meals:

> The mishna states a *halakha* with regard to two groups joining together: **Two groups that were eating in one house, when some** members of each group **can see each other, they may combine to** form a ***zimmun*****. And if not, these recite a *zimmun* for themselves and those recite a *zimmun* for themselves.** (Berakhot 50a)

As Rashba understands it, in this context, the Talmud allows the formation of a *zimmun,* the three-person quorum needed to recite *Birkat HaMazon* together, if members of the various groups can see each other (a requirement that can be waived if there is a waiter who serves the two groups; see 50b). *Arukh HaShulḥan* (*OḤ* 55:20) suggests that even according to this position, only one of the ten can be located outside the central space, but not more. (Similar qualifications emerge in the passage in Eiruvin, though Tosafot and Rashba ad loc. assume that the issue is avoiding an equal split of five and five, but if the majority is in the larger space, the quorum can be formed.)

Many, however, reject this possibility for one of two reasons. As Ramban (Pesaḥim, ibid.) notes, *Birkat HaMazon* has lower requirements, as the group in question already chose to join together to eat, creating a presumption that they are part of the same group that is not true in the case of *minyan*. Thus, even if sight is sufficient to create a *zimmun,* it may not be enough for a *minyan*. Furthermore, many authorities assume that the case is not the *creation of a zimmun, but rather the joining together of two groups that already constitute independent groups of three* (see *Imrei Noam* of Gra on Berakhot 50a and *Biur Halakha* 195:1). R. Shimon ben Tzemach Duran (*Responsa Rashbash* 37) elaborates. He notes that in the case of *zimmun,* the question is not the creation of a group, but the ability of one person to recite *Birkat HaMazon* on behalf of the group (the original way of having a *zimmun,* though not usually practiced anymore). Furthermore, once the people in question ate together, they are obligated to recite *Birkat HaMazon* as a group, thus the group already exists, making the standards for joining them lower. Furthermore, as he rules that the case is where the issue is two separate groups who are already obligated in *zimmun,* the issue is truly just combination rather than creation. In the case of a *minyan,* the issue is the creation of the community. For this, physical presence of ten people in a shared space is necessary.

As R. Menachem Wieder (*Minḥat Tzvi* 19) discusses at length, many line up to take these two formulations, some who do not allow sight to join together multiple groups of three to create a *minyan* for *Birkat HaMazon,* the position of Rashbash himself.[9] Others allow the *minyan* for *Birkat HaMazon* to be created from two groups of five joined by sight, and assume the nature of *minyan* to be different in the context of *tefilla* and *Birkat HaMazon* (see, for example, Meiri's comments in Berakhot; *Taz, OḤ* 195:1).

During the coronavirus pandemic and its lockdowns, the issue of "porch *minyanim,*" where people stood in their own property and joined others to pray, was much discussed. The position of *Shulḥan Arukh* on the above issue is not entirely clear. In the case of *Birkat HaMazon* (*OḤ* 195), it is clear that sight is sufficient to join two groups. However, in the case of *minyan,* he cites the limitations from Eiruvin that require the two groups to be in the exact same space (*OḤ* 55:13). However, he then refers to a case in which those behind a synagogue can join the *minyan* if there is a window (ibid., 14). Some (*Peri Ḥadash, OḤ* 55:12 and *Peri Megadim, Mishbetzot Zahav* 55:12) rule accordingly like Rashba, allowing groups to join for a *minyan* based on sight.

Many commentaries, however, rule against this understanding. Some (*Erekh Leḥem* ad loc.) suggest that it refers only to a case where the person physically sticks his head into the synagogue or stands on the threshold, thus only slightly expanding the definition of "being in the same place." Regardless of the exact argument made, many assume that sight remains sufficient only in the context of *Birkat HaMazon.*

There seems to be a contradiction (as noted by R. Hershel Schachter in his responsum on porch *minyanim*) as to the position of the *Mishna Berura.* In *OḤ* 195:1, he rules in accordance with Rashbash against Rashba, arguing that sight is not sufficient for the purposes of *minyan.* In *OḤ* 55:13, he seems to accept Rashba, at least in cases of great need.

Practically, some halakhic authorities (R. Schachter, R. Yitzchak Yosef) completely rejected the possibility of porch *minyanim,* even in cases where there was no alternative. Others, such as R. Asher Weiss,

9. See, however, Wieder, who takes up the question of whether this would be the case even if the ten people originally started their meal together.

ruled that one could rely on it, even arguing that Rashba's "it is possible to say" was not an expression of doubt but a clear ruling, though he still does not endorse relying on this under normal circumstances. *Arukh HaShulḥan* (55:20, cited in *Heviani Ḥadarav, Hilkhot Tefilla* 6, n. 28) assumes that this means seeing only the face of those joining.[10] There are further disputes as to whether sight per se is needed or hearing suffices, whether sight through glass is enough, and what the status is at night when practically, one's vision is limited. Some were hesitant to allow reliance on sight alone, and thus permitted it only in dire circumstances and demanded finding ways to limit blessings in vain, such as suggesting that the *ḥazan* have in mind that his repetition of the *Amida* be considered an optional additional prayer in case the "porch *minyan*" was not valid. (See the responsum of R. Moshe Sternbuch, and slightly stricter, that of R. Yitzchak Mordechai HaKohen Rubin.)

Many of the above authorities raised more technical issues, such as whether the group for a *minyan* could join when separated by different domains, or whether a *minyan* could be held when there was excrement or similar things between the groups that forbid the recitation of prayer. They also raised questions as to whether these caused problems for communication technology. However, the details are beyond the parameters of our discussion.

Similar debates were raised in other cases of quarantine. For example, R. Chaim Yosef David Azulai (Ḥida, *Maḥazik Berakha, OḤ* 55:11) discusses a case of quarantine in Italy, in which guards would not allow people in two adjacent houses to mix. Ḥida ruled that people from two houses who could see each other could join based on Rashba. However, his colleague R. Yosef Chazan (*Responsa Ḥikrei Lev, OḤ* 1:28) rejects this even in cases of dire need.

Despite all the voices who accepted sight for the purpose of creating porch *minyanim* and the like, none ruled that a *minyan* could be created through Zoom or other virtual means. Why not?

1. It is possible that they reject virtual sight as sight. However, as we will see, many accept that sound transmitted across such media is

10. See the summary of these issues in *Heviani Ḥadarav, Hilkhot Tefilla*, 18–27.

considered direct sound, and in certain cases, sight as well. Thus, this must be explored.

2. It is possible that the Rashba does not mean that sight itself is the issue, but rather that sight is the mechanism through which people in close proximity can become part of the same place, and being in the same place is the real standard.

The latter possibility seems most likely to this author, and is taken as the obvious interpretation by R. Menachem Wieder (*Minḥat Tzvi* 19), as well as R. Shammai Ofer Hyman (*Tzohar*, vol. 7, 278–282). The latter argues that on theological grounds, if the purpose of creating a *minyan* is for the Divine Presence to dwell among the people, there must be a place where the group and the Divine Presence are situated, so to speak. However, R. Yosef Tzvi Rimon argues that while this may be true for many authorities, such as Ramban who rules that the Bavli always rejected joining two separate houses and only entertains joining groups that are located within a single house in which the people are within sight of each other, he believes that the Rashba requires sight alone. Nevertheless, he never raises the possibility of creating a full virtual *minyan*.[11] To understand this, we must turn to the question of whether virtual sight is equivalent to actual sight.

11. It is worth noting that even in the Conservative community, the majority position utterly rejected the creation of Zoom *minyanim*, though a minority voice extended the position of Rashba to allow such *minyanim* under dire circumstances. https://www.rabbinicalassembly.org/story/cjls-guidance-remote-minyanim-time-covid-19.

Chapter 28

The Webcam in Halakha: Mitzvot

Introduction

In recent years, there have been a series of articles analyzing various areas of halakha and the potential to utilize webcams to fulfill mitzvot or achieve other halakhic goals. R. Dovid Lichtenstein recently published a brief survey of many of these issues, including whether a webcam can be used to solve *yiḥud* (seclusion between men and women) or to provide supervision for *ḥalav Yisrael,* as well as a series of other issues,[1] as did R. Tzvi Reisman.[2] We will not analyze every detail, and we will draw heavily on recent sources to survey the issues succinctly. The goal will be to outline enough of the issues so as to highlight points we have made throughout this book.

Fulfilling Mitzvot

A principle found throughout halakha is that people may fulfill certain mitzvot by listening to the performance of others, such as by hearing

1. *Headlines: Halachic Debates of Current Events,* ch. 30, "The Webcam in Halacha" (OU Press, 2014).
2. See *Ratz KaTzvi,* vol. 3, *Kiyum Mitzvot VeDinei Torah Al Yedei Matzlemat Video.*

the shofar blown, Kiddush recited, the Megilla read, etc. May one fulfill one of these mitzvot by listening to its performance indirectly, though a microphone, telephone, webcam, or even a recording?

The modern *posekim* debate this. Some feel strongly that one may not use any of the above, assuming that mitzvot require hearing the sounds directly. This is the position of R. Shlomo Zalman Auerbach (*Responsa Minḥat Shlomo* 1:9), based on the following ruling of the Gemara that one cannot fulfill the mitzva of hearing the shofar through hearing an echo.

> If **one sounds** a *shofar* **into a pit, or into a cistern, or into** a large **jug, if he** clearly **heard the sound of the *shofar*, he has fulfilled** his obligation; **but if he heard the sound of an echo, he has not fulfilled** his obligation. (Rosh HaShana 27b)

R. Auerbach argues that one must hear the actual sound of the one performing the mitzva on behalf of others. Scientifically speaking, a microphone produces a sound that is similar to the original voice, but it does not actually amplify the original sound. Thus, even a microphone, and certainly any other mode of electronic communication, cannot be used to discharge someone else's obligation to hear the performance of a mitzva.

However, other *posekim* argue that it is not relevant whether one physically hears the original sound, as what is important is the experience. Does one perceive oneself as hearing the original sound? The *Ḥazon Ish* (cited by R. Auerbach) argues that one does, as the sound is heard through the microphone almost immediately after it is made. R. Moshe Feinstein (*Responsa Iggerot Moshe, OḤ* 2:108, 4:126) goes further, noting that one never really "hears someone's voice" but rather the vibrations in the air caused when someone talks. Thus, sounds conveyed through microphones are basically as direct. However, he is hesitant to allow this under normal circumstances, as he is not wholly convinced by the argument. Thus, he does not allow using it to discharge biblical obligations.

R. Chaim Jachter assumes that the majority of *posekim* follow R. Auerbach:

> In particular, most mid- and late-twentieth-century authorities, who benefited from a greater understanding than their predecessors of how microphones operate, reject the use of microphones for the performance of mitzvot, with the possible exception of Torah reading. They argue that one hears an electronically reproduced sound over these devices, whereas the Halakha requires one to hear the actual sound of a shofar, or voice of the reader. They note that this reproduction is substantially inferior to hearing an echo since it lacks any trace of the original sound, whereas echoes come from the original sound waves. According to R. Shlomo Zalman, blowing the shofar over a sound-system is analogous to pressing a button on a computer that produces the sound of a shofar.[3]

However, there are significant modern *posekim* who continue to rule in accordance with R. Feinstein, or at least to entertain his view as viable, and it seems that they are at least as numerous those who oppose his position. For example, R. Asher Weiss, while conceding that what one hears from a microphone or telephone is not the original voice, argues that halakha is concerned with perception and experience, and one feels as if one is hearing the voice directly. When necessary, many *posekim* allow fulfilling mitzvot using microphones, loudspeakers, or telephones. (See *Responsa Tzitz Eliezer* 8:11 concerning reading Megilla in hospitals over the sound system, and *Responsa Iggerot Moshe, OḤ* 4:91 about Havdala.)

The *posekim* who allow fulfilling mitzvot even over the telephone would allow audio mitzvot over a webcam as well. However, it is worth wondering whether a position could be constructed which allows fulfilling mitzvot over a webcam but not a telephone, in the spirit of those *posekim* who feel that the critical issue is the experience of direct hearing, rather than the scientific question of what sounds one hears. Before we discuss that, we turn to a less demanding halakhic issue.

Responding *Amen*

Even *posekim* who reject fulfilling mitzvot over a microphone accept that one may respond *amen* to a *berakha* heard in this manner, based on the

3. *Gray Matter*, vol. 2 (Yashar Books, 2006), 239. See there for other positions.

Gemara's description of the procedure in the synagogue of Alexandria (Sukka 51b):

> **It is taught** in a *baraita* that **Rabbi Yehuda says: One who did not see the great synagogue [*deyofloston*] of Alexandria of Egypt never saw the glory of Israel. They said** that its structure **was like a large basilica [*basileki*],** with **a colonnade within a colonnade. At times there were six hundred thousand** men **and** another **six hundred thousand** men **in it, twice the number of those who left Egypt. In it there were seventy-one golden chairs [*katedraot*], corresponding to the seventy-one** members **of the Great Sanhedrin, each of which** consisted of **no less than twenty-one thousand talents of gold. And** there was **a wooden platform at the center. The sexton of the synagogue** would **stand on it, with the scarves in his hand. And** because the synagogue was so large and the people could not hear the communal prayer, **when** the prayer leader **reached** the conclusion of a blessing requiring the people **to answer amen,** the sexton **waved the scarf and all the people** would **answer amen.**

R. Jachter summarizes the conclusions derived by *posekim* from this gemara:

> Rashi (Berachot 47a s.v. *Yetomah*) and *Tosafot* (Sukkah 52a s.v. *Vekeivan* and Berachot 47a s.v. *Amen*) both ask, why could the Alexandrians answer "*amen*" on the basis of a banner if the Gemara (Berachot 47a) forbids answering "*amen*" without hearing the actual *berachah*? The Gemara refers to such a reply as an *amen yetomah*, "an orphaned *amen*." Rashi and *Tosafot* (in Berachot) explain that the people in Alexandria knew which *berachah* was being recited, despite the fact that they did not hear it, whereas the problem of an *amen yetomah* exists only when one lacks any knowledge of what the leader has uttered. Elsewhere (Sukkah 52a), *Tosafot* cite Rabbeinu Nissim Gaon, who suggests a different approach. He claims that the prohibition against reciting an *amen yetomah* applies only when answering "*amen*" to a

> *berachah* that one is obligated to recite and he wishes to fulfill his obligation by answering "*amen*," such as the *berachot* before blowing the *shofar* or reading the Megillah. On the other hand, he suggests that the Alexandrians relied on the flag system for responding only to those *berachot* that they were not obligated to recite.
>
> The Shulchan Aruch (Orach Chaim 124:8) rules that the problem of an *amen yetomah* applies only to those *berachot* that one is obligated to recite, while the Rama and Ashkenazic *Acharonim* rule that the problem exists in other cases, too. Accordingly, the Rama prohibits responding "*amen*" to any *berachah*, even when one is not obligated in it, if one does not know precisely which *berachah* is being recited.
>
> Accordingly, R. Shlomo Zalman rules that if one hears via a microphone a *berachah* that he is not obligated to recite, he may answer "*amen*." This situation commonly arises at weddings, where members of the audience hear the *berachot* only over loudspeakers. The bride and groom, who must hear these *berachot*, do hear the actual sound, as they stand right next to those who recite the blessings.[1]

The distinction made by R. Auerbach highlights a point that we have seen in the past: information-based halakhot may shift due to innovations in communication technology. As understood by the Rishonim, at least the response of *Amen* to non-obligatory blessings is about the knowledge that those blessings have been said. On the other hand, fulfilling mitzvot requires actual experience, and here the *posekim* divide on whether these indirect means are sufficient. R. Ovadia Yosef (*Responsa Yeḥaveh Daat* 2:68) formulates a position similar to R. Auerbach, who makes the distinction essentially in this way, allowing responding *Amen* to *Seliḥot* heard over the radio, but forbidding fulfilling mitzvot in that way.

This distinction also explains why even *posekim* who allow fulfilling mitzvot over the telephone do not allow one to use a recording.

4. Ibid., 240–241.

This, for example, is the position of R. Natan Schlissel, a student of the *Minḥat Elazar.*[5]

Sight

Most of these sources relate to mediated audio experience. However, for some mitzvot (and possibly, as we saw above, *minyan*) the issue may be *sight,* rather than hearing.

Background from Testimony

There are several key talmudic sources that deal with the question of whether one can fulfill mitzvot through indirect means. The first is the following passage (Rosh HaShana 24a) concerning testimony for the sanctification of the new moon:

> **The Sages taught** in another *baraita* that if the witnesses say: We did not actually see the moon, but **we saw it** reflected **in the water,** or **we saw it** reflected **in** a glass **lantern,** or **we saw it through** thin **clouds, they** may **not testify about it,** as only a direct sighting of the moon is acceptable.

As we discussed in our chapter on the video-teleconferenced *get,* this may be understood either as a technical or fundamental problem. We might derive from here that in principle, testimony does not require direct sight, but reflections are not reliable enough to ascertain facts for testimony. Alternatively, we might understand that testimony requires direct exposure, and seeing a reflection is therefore insufficient. As R. Lichtenstein notes, both Rabbenu Ḥananel and the *Mefareish* on the Rambam (*Hilkhot Kiddush HaḤodesh* 2:5) argue that the issue is merely one of verification. Based on this, we might argue that an indirect sight that is perfectly clear, such as a reflection, might be sufficient for testimony, a position entertained by the *Birkei Yosef* (*ḤM* 35:11). R. Lichtenstein notes that the above presentation is helpful in understanding the dispute between the *posekim* concerning fulfilling mitzvot

5. Printed in *Yerushat HaPeleita* 5766, ch. 10, 28.

over microphone and telephone – and correspondingly, the webcam. However, it may also be distinct.

These sources were raised for many kinds of mediated experiences. At one level, several sources wondered whether mitzvot that require sight can be performed by those wearing glasses. R. Yaakov Hagiz (*Responsa Halakhot Ketanot* 1:99) argued that one wearing glasses can fulfill the mitzva of reading the Torah. The basis for his argument was the following passage in the Talmud:

> **Rava said: Opposite feces** covered only **by** a **lantern**-like covering, which is transparent, **it is permitted to recite *Shema*.** But **opposite nakedness** covered only **by** a **lantern**-like covering, **it is prohibited to recite *Shema*. Opposite feces in a lantern, it is permitted to recite *Shema*** because with regard to **feces,** the ability to recite *Shema* **is contingent upon covering,** as it is said: "And cover your excrement" (Deut. 23:14), **and** although it is visible, **it is covered.** On the other hand, **opposite nakedness** covered only **by** a **lantern**-like covering, **it is prohibited to recite *Shema*; the Torah said: "And no indecent thing shall be seen in you"** (Deut. 23:15), **and** here **it is seen.** (Berakhot 25b)

The law is that one may not recite *Shema* in the presence of *erva,* nakedness. In this case, even when the nakedness is separated by glass, reciting *Shema* is prohibited. From here, R. Hagiz derives that sight mediated through glass is still sight. Elsewhere (1:274), in the context of whether one is obligated to stand for Torah scholars when seeing them through glass, R. Hagiz write emphatically that this sight is fully considered sight. *Tiferet Yisrael* (Nega'im 2:4, Boaz) derives from R. Hagiz that in general, sight through glasses is considered sight. This seems to be the dominant position, as recorded by *Shevut Yaakov* (1:126) and documented extensively by R. Ovadia Yosef (*Responsa Yeḥaveh Daat* 4:18). *Shevut Yaakov* clarifies that it is even true for those who would not be able to see without glasses. However, R. Shlomo Kluger rejects this, forbidding one who needs glasses from slaughtering an animal.

Magen Avraham (*OḤ* 426:1) seems to permit reciting *Kiddush Levana* through a window or other clear glass, which follows this tradition. He further permits reciting Havdala when the flame is seen though glass (298:20). R. Ovadia Yosef (*Yabia Omer* 1:17), however, notes that many require sight of uncovered fire specifically for this blessing. He contends that this is because fire always existed in potential, and after the Sabbath, Adam "revealed" fire for the first time, which we commemorate during Havdala. To reenact the revelation of fire that was always present in potential, we need to see the fire directly. This analysis highlights that what may be considered direct experience in some contexts may be considered mediated in other contexts.

Ba'er Heitev (*OḤ* 426:1) cites R. Shmuel Abohav (*Responsa Devar Shmuel* 242) as forbidding reciting *Kiddush Levana* through a glass lens (it is not clear exactly what he is referring to). Upon reading the reference in *Ba'er Heitev*, one might think that fundamentally, such mediated sight is not halakhically considered sight, thus being insufficient for this blessing. However, in the original responsum, as noted by *Shaarei Teshuva* (*OḤ* 426:1) as well, R. Abohav seems to be worried about verification that the moon is indeed visible. Thus, if a person who is present confirms the visibility of the moon without seeing through glass, R. Abohav permits reciting the blessing. (It is also unclear to what extent sight is necessary for this blessing, as the commentaries are divided on whether a blind person may recite the blessing, arguing that it is a blessing on the natural phenomenon of the new moon rather than on seeing the moon at that time.)

Many, however, distinguish between mediated sight that does not magnify or distort, and mediated sight that does. They distinguish between cases in which something is seen directly, through glass, which is considered sight, and cases in which something is seen through a mirror or something that distorts the image.[6]

R. J. David Bleich provides an explanation for this and extends the analysis for future technologies:

> Eyeglasses correct a distortion caused by a malfunction of the eye and thereby restore normal vision to the wearer; magnification by means of a telescope or other instrument results in a visual

6. See, for example, *Responsa Devar Shmuel* 242, *Shevut Yaakov* 1:126.

> phenomenon not perceived under normal conditions. Eyeglasses are designed to restore normal visual capacity; magnification gives rise to a visual perception quite different from the "normal."
>
> The distinction becomes even sharper if one is mindful of the fact that optical perception is a neural phenomenon that takes place in the brain; the eye is simply a medium that transports visual stimuli. "Sight" is what occurs when those stimuli affect optical receptors. Corrective lenses allow the compromised eye to do what a natural eye is capable of doing. Pushed to the extreme, this analysis would lead to a conclusion that, if medical technology succeeds in perfecting such a device, use of a functional prosthetic eye would result in "sight" cognized as such by Halakhah. In contradistinction, magnification distorts light waves so that the stimuli operating upon the optical center in the brain are not generated solely by the object perceived but are distorted by the interposed prism.[7]

Some distinguish between contexts. For example, R. Ovadia Yosef in several responsa (*Yabia Omer, OḤ* 1:7, 6:12, *Yeḥaveh Daat* 4:7) assumes that whenever the issue in question is one of *erva,* nakedness, and other sexual exposures, mediated sight is equivalent to sight. The basis of his argument is that the prohibition against seeing *erva* is one due to the improper thoughts that it causes. Thus, if images can similarly cause such thoughts, then mediated sight in this context must be equivalent to sight. Furthermore, as *Shema* and prayer (namely the *Amida*) cannot be recited in the presence of *erva,* he forbids reciting *Shema* in the presence of a television when a show is playing in which parts of the body that qualify as *erva* are exposed. See also R. Yitzchak Weiss (*Responsa Minḥat Yitzḥak* 2:84, *Responsa Karnei Re'em* 217).

However, while it is obviously forbidden to view such images, that does not entail R. Yosef's conclusion. The Talmud (Sanhedrin 39b) cites a case of Jezebel and Ahab and states that they had images of prostitutes painted on their chariot to provoke him sexually, thus recognizing the power

7. "Survey of Recent Halakhic Periodical Literature: Video Surveillance," *Tradition* 45:2.

of sexual images. The Talmud forbids so much as watching animals copulate as it may incite sexual thoughts and potentially lead to seminal emissions (Avoda Zara 20a–b). It further forbids looking at the clothing of a woman one knows even when the clothing is not on her, hanging in a closet or the like (ibid.). Nevertheless, there is a distinction between forbidding such images because they provoke sexual thoughts and defining them as *erva,* ruling that the mediated sight in these cases is considered sight.

Many authorities, therefore, while they agree that it is forbidden to view these images, specifically do not qualify this sight as sight. Thus, they permit reciting *Shema* in their presence. See, for example, *Responsa Naḥalat Binyamin* 26 and *Responsa Divrei Yosef* 2:23. More recently, Rabbis David and Avraham Stav embrace this position in their discussion of what programs can be viewed on television. There are several who contend that it may violate the prohibition of *venishmarta mikol davar ra,* which includes avoiding seeing or thinking about things that will lead to seminal emissions, but not the prohibition violated by seeing sexual images. R. Yehoshua Zilber argues that these images are not a violation of *lo taturu aḥarei levavekhem* (literally, "Do not stray after your eyes"), which is a visual-based prohibition, and the other prohibitions of provoking sexual thoughts which are not essentially visual in nature (see *Responsa Az Nidberu* 10:35 and 11:51). Many distinctions are raised as to how to flesh out these rules with regard to images on television and in pictures, paintings, and other media (see *Gan Na'ul,* ch. 13 throughout).

Other Topics

The issue of the webcam in halakha is raised in many contexts. For example, some suggest that it can prevent men and women who are secluded from violating *yiḥud,* the prohibition for them to be alone. Others raise the issue of whether seeing through a webcam can be considered seeing for the purpose of defining milk as *ḥalav Yisrael,* milk that was milked by a Jew or in the presence of a Jew. The same responsum of *Shevut Yaakov* deals with the question of *ḥalitza,* the "divorce" from *yibum,* levirate marriage, that must be witnessed. These cases and others are raised by Rabbis Lichtenstein, Reisman, and Bleich above. In each case, the *posekim* deal both with the question of what qualifies as sight and what standards are demanded by the particular law in question.

Returning to *Minyanim*

Thus, we have seen some who in some circumstances do consider seeing through a webcam as seeing. If one accepts the position that even according to Rashba, sight is only helpful if there is also physical proximity, as the central issue is joint presence, then these sources do not relate to *minyan*. However, if one accepts a radical read of Rashba, such as that presented by R. Rimon, in theory one could construct a position that would allow the creation of a Zoom *minyan*, at least with all members having their cameras on and looking at each other. However, as we noted, no authority accepted such a position. The reasons for this are many.

1. Many *posekim* do not accept the Rashba and require joint physical presence.
2. Many understand Rashba to also require presence.

   Both of these understandings may be based on the notion that the standard is higher for *minyan,* either to create the presence of the community, or that of God, depending on what the purpose of *minyan* is, as discussed above.

3. One does not accept the position that mediated sound or sight is sufficient for the fulfillment of mitzvot.
4. One accepts sound but not sight, as the standards may be different.

It is worth noting that *posekim* may not want to stretch to justify such *minyanim* as they could destroy the communities that can only be created by the physical presence of the synagogue.[8] All of these positions highlight the extent to which changes in communication technology force us to define community and experience as they manifest in different areas of life and halakha. As noted, the unique demands of *minyan* combine such that no authority felt that a virtual *minyan* would be considered a *minyan*.

8. These issues are discussed at length by my long-time *ḥavruta*, R. Dr. Shlomo Zuckier, in an unpublished paper, "*Da Lifnei Mi Ata Omed*: Recent Approaches to Virtual Presence in Jewish Ritual."

It is worth noting that R. Benny Lau recorded that in his discussion with R. Eliezer Melamed, he entertained using Zoom *minyanim* only for the Mourner's *Kaddish,* as the standards for *minyan* may be lower and there is no risk of a blessing in vain. However, this position was neither fleshed out, nor accepted by most authorities.[9]

Praying at the Same Time as the *Minyan*

However, we have seen that a certain kind of community can be created through identification rather than geography. Is there a parallel for *minyanim*? It seems that the closest parallel is the question of whether there is value to praying at the same time as the community when one cannot make it to synagogue.

The presence of a *minyan* causes God to "dwell in the community" (Berakhot 6a). The Gemara goes on to argue that God is more likely to accept the prayers of the community than those of the individual. In that context, the Gemara introduces a story which indicates that one may tap into these benefits, at least partially, by praying at the same time as the community, even without attending the synagogue:

> **Rabbi Yitzḥak said to Rav Naḥman: Why did the Master not come to the synagogue to pray?** Rav Naḥman **said to him: I was** weak and **unable** to come. Rabbi Yitzḥak **said to him: Let the Master gather ten** individuals, a prayer quorum, at your home **and pray.** Rav Naḥman **said to him: It is difficult for me** to impose upon the members of the community to come to my home to pray with me (*Sefer Mitzvot Gadol*). Rabbi Yitzḥak suggested another option: **The Master should tell the congregation** to send a **messenger when the congregation is praying to come and inform the Master** so you may pray at the same time.
>
> Rav Naḥman saw that Rabbi Yitzḥak was struggling to find a way for him to engage in communal prayer. **He asked: What is** the reason for **all this** fuss? Rabbi Yitzḥak **said to him: As Rabbi Yoḥanan said in the name of Rabbi Shimon ben Yoḥai:**

9. https://tinyurl.com/2p9fptyu.

> **What is** the meaning of **that which is written: "But as for me, let my prayer be unto You, Lord, in a time of favor;** O God, in the abundance of Your mercy, answer me with the truth of Your salvation" (Ps. 69:14)? It appears that the individual is praying that his prayers will coincide with a special time of Divine favor. **When is a time of favor?** It is **at the time when the congregation is praying.** It is beneficial to pray together with the congregation, for God does not fail to respond to the entreaties of the congregation.
>
> **Rabbi Yosei, son of Rabbi Ḥanina, said that** the unique quality of communal prayer is derived **from here: "Thus said the Lord, in a time of acceptance I have answered you and on a day of salvation I have aided you"** (Is. 49:8).
>
> **Rabbi Aḥa, son of Rabbi Ḥanina, said** that it is derived **from here: "Behold, God is mighty, He despises no one"** (Job 36:5). He adopts an alternative reading of the verse: "Behold, God will not despise" the prayer of "the mighty," i.e., the community. **And it is written: "He has redeemed my soul in peace so that none came upon me; for there were many with me.** God shall hear and answer them..." (Ps. 55:19–20). This verse teaches that the prayer was answered because there were many with me when it was offered. (Berakhot 7b–8a)

Rabbenu Tam (Avoda Zara 4b, s.v. *keivan*) argues that the benefit is not as great as attending the synagogue. Thus, he argues, one's prayers are not rejected if one prays at the same time as the community, but they will not be as easily accepted by God as they would were one to pray with the community.

However, a recent article by R. Daniel Mann notes how complicated this notion may get when, in a community, there is not a single geographically defined *minyan* with which one identifies. He notes that in a world with a single *minyan* in town, it is easy to define one's community; this gets harder when even a single geographic community has many *minyanim,* not to mention different spheres of identification. R. Mann encourages thinking about this halakha from the perspective of identification, focusing on the *minyan* one normally attends.

We reproduce the question posed to R. Mann and the relevant part of his answer:

> ***Question***: The Shulchan Aruch (Orach Chayim 90:9) rules that one who cannot make it to a *minyan* should try to *daven* at the same time as a *minyan*. Given the multiple *minyanim* we find in one town, how does one fulfill that obligation today?
>
> ***Answer***: ... Let us now address your question. The closest source we have found in the *Rishonim* is in the Semag (*Aseh* 19, p. 102a, cited by the Rama, OC 90:9), who says that if there is no local *minyan*, one should follow the time that "communities of Israel" *daven*. This implies that, ideally, one follows the local *minyan* but that there could be some type of official average time. We do not know the extent to which there was a uniform time in his days, but we cannot identify such a time nowadays. (There is a general preference for *vatikin*, but if the Semag had that time in mind, he would have said it.)
>
> The Mishna Berura (90:31) seems to say that in places where there are many *minyanim*, all times are good. However, he and his source, the Chayei Adam (16:3), is talking about refraining from *davening* before the right time, and says that it does not apply when there are many *minyanim*. One can still ask whether there is something to do if one specifically wants to avail himself of the positive element. Ishei Yisrael (8:32) seems to say that all times are good. Avnei Yashfe says in the "name" of an unnamed *gadol* that in such a case there is no preference (sounding like nothing is particularly good). However, we prefer the following compromise approach. R. S. Z. Auerbach is quoted as saying that the *gemara* implies that this matter requires one to focus on a specific *minyan* (Ishei Yisrael, op. cit.). While it is not clear to us where R. Auerbach saw this in the *gemara*, it leads in the logical direction of his disciple, R. Neuwirth (cited ibid.). If one usually *davens* with a specific *minyan* but cannot make it on a certain day, he gets the positive element of *davening* when he *davens* at the same time as they do even if there are many other *minyanim* in town. (This makes particular sense if this matter depends

> more on psychology than on mysticism.) R. Neuwirth brings an interesting precedent from the Sha'ar Hatziyun (551:56) that if one is eating *fleishig* at *seuda shlishit* during the Nine Days, he should stop when his regular *shul* has *davened Ma'ariv*. If one is not connected to a specific *minyan* and there are many *minyanim* in town, then there is apparently neither anything positive nor any requirement to try to correspond to some random *minyan*.[10]

R. Mann's piece is a wonderful attempt to analyze the ways in which we create and identify communities in the modern period, an issue that has come up regarding many of the halakhic issues we have analyzed in this book.

The recent internet *minyanim* which allow people to pray at the same time as a particular community, even if not their own, reflect the ways in which communication technology has allowed us to "identify" with communities other than our geographic ones. While not everyone accepts its validity, R. Hershel Schachter is quoted as allowing those who cannot reach the synagogue to respond *amen* to such *minyanim* and generally take advantage of this opportunity.[11] During the Covid-19 lockdowns, many *posekim* suggested ways of utilizing this mechanism to create some semblance of communal prayer.

Conclusion

While there are many more angles to be explored concerning the fulfillment of mitzvot through various modes of digital communication, the positions taken by *posekim* shed light on the ways in which these tools affect our experience, expand our notions of community, or remind us of the limits to which those definitions can be expanded. And in some cases, all will agree that nothing can replace physical presence, connection, and community.

---

10. Available at Eretz Hemdah: https://eretzhemdah.org/newsletterArticle.asp?lang=en&pageid=4&cat=7&newsletter=958&article=3669.
11. See supra, n. 6.

The fonts used in this book are from the Arno family

Maggid Books
The best of contemporary Jewish thought from
Koren Publishers Jerusalem Ltd.